The Aliens Ar

The Aliens Are Here

Extraterrestrial Visitors
in American Cinema
and Television

FRASER A. SHERMAN

McFarland & Company, Inc., Publishers
Jefferson, North Carolina

LIBRARY OF CONGRESS CATALOGUING-IN-PUBLICATION DATA

Names: Sherman, Fraser A., author.
Title: The aliens are here : extraterrestrial visitors
in American cinema and television / Fraser A. Sherman.
Description: Jefferson, North Carolina : McFarland & Company, Inc., Publishers, 2022
| Includes bibliographical references and index.
Identifiers: LCCN 2022037254 | ISBN 9781476685045 (paperback : acid free paper) ∞
ISBN 9781476647623 (ebook)
Subjects: LCSH: Extraterrestrial beings in motion pictures. | Extraterrestrial
beings on television. | Science fiction films—United States—History and criticism.
| Science fiction television programs—United States—History and criticism. |
BISAC: PERFORMING ARTS / Film / Genres / Science Fiction & Fantasy |
PERFORMING ARTS / Television / Genres / Science Fiction, Fantasy & Horror
Classification: LCC PN1995.9.E974 S54 2022 | DDC 791.43/675—dc23/eng/20220921
LC record available at https://lccn.loc.gov/2022037254

BRITISH LIBRARY CATALOGUING DATA ARE AVAILABLE

ISBN (print) 978-1-4766-8504-5
ISBN (ebook) 978-1-4766-4762-3

Front cover: Scene from *The Day the Earth Stood Still*,
2008 (20th Century Fox/Photofest)

Printed in the United States of America

*McFarland & Company, Inc., Publishers
Box 611, Jefferson, North Carolina 28640
www.mcfarlandpub.com*

To LeAnn, always and forever.

To Dad, my siblings Craig and Tracy, my niece Paige,
and to Dori and Cindy who are sisters in all but blood.

To Trixie, Dudley, Wisp and Snowdrop,
even though you'll never read this.

Acknowledgments

Once again, my friend Ross Bagby's expertise with this kind of movie, and most particularly with *The X-Files*, made this book much better than it would have been without him.

While I owe all the authors in my bibliography, the late Bill Warren's *Keep Watching the Skies!* was extremely helpful when writing about movies of the 1950s and early 1960s.

Members of the Durham Science Fiction Writers Group beta-read several chapters and their feedback was invaluable. Thanks to all y'all.

And thanks to my editor, Dré Person, for answering my various questions about the process.

Table of Contents

Introduction

"Watch the skies, everywhere. Keep looking—keep watching the skies."
—*The Thing from Another World*

They're immigrants, invaders and refugees, conquerors, lovers and heroes. Cute creatures that want our candy. Monsters that want to eat our flesh. Rapists who want to impregnate human women. Stern uncles who want to save us from destroying ourselves. They come here by accident. They come here by design. We go out into space and bring them back with us. They're aliens. Extraterrestrials. Spacemen. Little green men. EBEs. The Greys. The Reptilians. ETs. Men from Mars.

The first sign they've arrived is often a meteor streaking across the sky, landing just a few miles from the protagonists. To the audience, it's obvious the meteor isn't a meteor, so we wait expectantly for the cast to realize the truth. In other films it's an impossible blip on the radar screen or a news report about flying saucers. If the aliens land somewhere isolated—a polar research station, a small California town—the humans may be on their own, with no one they can contact for help. If a UFO hovers over Washington or other big cities it's a national crisis, possibly beginning a war of the worlds.

Millions of people have been fascinated by the possibility that we are not alone in the universe and our neighbors from other worlds might someday come here—or already have. Novels, short stories, comic books and occasionally plays have told stories about aliens visiting us. Movies and television are part of this tradition, and they form the subject of this book: screen stories of visitors from other worlds, how the aliens react to us and how we react to them.

Alien Visitors in Fiction: A Brief History

The first story to have a visitor from outer space come down to Earth was Voltaire's *Micromegas*, from 1752. The eponymous ET is a 120,000-foot-tall giant coming from a planet vastly larger than Earth (far from the last time a giant from a giant world would appear in a science fiction story). Initially unable to believe Earth has sentient life—surely those little creatures can't have intelligence?—Micromegas learns his error, but still chuckles at humans' presumption they're the center of the universe. Many future visitors would find us equally amusing.

Things really began to get going in the second half of the 19th century. *An Inhabitant of the Planet Mars* (1865) by Henri de Parville has a Martian mummy uncovered inside a meteorite. In *Letters from the Planets* a clergyman becomes fiction's first alien abductee, then gets a tour of the solar system. C.C. Dail's *Wilmoth the Wanderer* has a

Saturnian visit Earth in prehistory, where, by selective breeding he creates Homo sapiens and rules over them. That's another idea that would crop up in later genre works. *On Two Planets* (1897) by Kurd Lasswitz has regular space traffic from Mars to Earth, with a permanent Martian base at the North Pole.[1]

All those books, and others like them, have faded into obscurity. The one everyone knows, if only by reputation, is H.G. Wells' *War of the Worlds*. Wells' 1897 book showed aliens invading and colonizing our planet the way Europe colonized and butchered much of the rest of the world. Although Wells drew on the "future war" genre of the era—stories about the next big war—his novel simultaneously created the alien invasion story. Many science fiction writers would follow the trail Wells blazed. *War of the Worlds* would also spawn a legendary radio broadcast, multiple film adaptations (it's now public domain, so no rights issues) and a TV series.

The movies took much longer to embrace extraterrestrial visitors than print fiction. Some aliens appeared in silent films, but they were more fantasy than science fiction. *When the Man in the Moon Seeks a Wife* (1908) has the first of many aliens arriving on Earth to mate, but he does so in a hot air balloon. *A Message from Mars* (1913) treats the Martian more like a fallen angel. Exiled from his planet, he redeems himself by forcing Earth's most selfish man to reform. *Algol* (1920) is the flip side, a demonic alien who shows an inventor how to generate cheap, limitless power, then twists this gift into a nightmare for the world.

Things might have been different if Cecil B. DeMille's plans for a silent *War of the Worlds* had come to pass, but the movie never got made. Instead we had to wait until the 1940s for more alien visitors. The decade gave us cartoons and two film serials about that exciting new comic-book character Superman. We also met the first alien invader in the 1945 serial *The Purple Monster Strikes*. We also had the first flying saucer sighting in 1947, launching an American obsession that inspired multiple films, starting with 1950's *The Flying Saucer*.

In the 1950s, science fiction movies bloomed. The public's interest in flying saucers didn't hurt the genre. Neither did the success of *Destination Moon* in 1950, the first serious science fiction film about travel in space. Satisfied there was an audience, studios began making A-list alien visitor films such as *War of the Worlds* alongside films that were decidedly not A-list, such as *Invasion of the Saucer Men*.

UFOs became less of an obsession in the 1960s, and fewer alien visitors arrived in the movies. TV, however, took up some of the slack. A Martian (Ray Walston) crashed on Earth and moved in with a young reporter (Bill Bixby) in the paranormal sitcom *My Favorite Martian*. In *The Invaders*, architect David Vincent (Roy Thinnes) discovered aliens infiltrating human society, laying the groundwork for conquest. Some episodes of *The Twilight Zone* and *The Outer Limits* also featured aliens on Earth.

In the decades since, alien visitors have appeared steadily on the big and small screen. The results range from smash hits such as *Independence Day*, *Superman* and *The X-Files* to flops such as *The Phoenix* and *Annihilator*. Aliens have appeared in comedies, war stories, monster yarns, conspiracy theories, allegories, musicals and stories of social or political commentary.

That sheer flexibility is part of the reason aliens keep appealing. Adding aliens can turn a film in another genre into science fiction, giving a twist to conventional genre formulas. Orphans fleeing a cruel caregiver is an old trope; in *Escape to Witch Mountain*, the orphans are aliens and the caregiver is a millionaire who wants to exploit their powers.

Alien visitors also make a great mirror for us to look at ourselves. When aliens attack, do we run or fight? Do we give peace a chance or go nuclear? Kneel to our alien overlords or join the resistance? Will we welcome the alien immigrant among us or shun them in loathing? *Alien Nation* looks at immigration and racism through an extraterrestrial lens. Mork of *Mork and Mindy* mocks our social conventions. *Invasion of the Body Snatchers'* pod people remind us that love matters, even when it hurts.

Another factor is that science fiction seems more plausible to many people than fantasy or supernatural horror. The alien-abduction thrillers *Dark Skies* and *The Fourth Kind* recycle multiple horror tropes but rationalizing the horror as the work of extraterrestrials can pull in people who'd turn up their nose at stories of supernatural horror. It's true there are many scientific and logical arguments against UFO abduction accounts being true, but they *feel* scientific. For the purposes of fiction, that's good enough.

Alien visitors also play to one of film's strengths, visual spectacle. Grotesque monsters. Flying saucers blasting Earth's great monuments or blowing up the White House. The sleek beauty of the sinister Martian flying vessels in the 1953 *War of the Worlds*. The dark, shadowy, frequently claustrophobic environment of *The X-Files*. Few movies match the complex ideas of the best science fiction—the science in most of these films is notoriously hand-wavy—but there's still something cool about seeing this stuff on screen. Not to mention the actors: lines that would sound trite on the page can delight on a talented actor's lips.

These productions draw from a variety of sources. Print science fiction has been adapted into movies and TV productions including *The Whispers*, *War of the Worlds* and *Invasion of the Body Snatchers*. Alien visitor stories also draw on previous film and TV productions, remaking them, imitating them or trying to top them. They also draw on sources outside the genre: *X-Files* creator Chris Carter's inspirations included the 1970s horror series *Night Stalker*. Roland Emmerich says he modeled *Independence Day* on disaster movies.

These films are also heavily influenced by real-world UFO beliefs and encounters. Steven Spielberg consulted with UFO researcher and astronomer J. Allen Hynek for *Close Encounters of the Third Kind*. Some directors believe in UFOs while others will say so for publicity. Mikel Conrad, the director of 1950's *The Flying Saucer*, publicized his film by claiming the saucer in the film was real and he'd seen it fly. That was a hoax.[2]

My first chapter will give a brief history of America's interest in unidentified flying objects, to provide context for the fiction. Each chapter after that focuses on a different topic in alien-visitor films: abductions, invasions, friendly aliens, genre mashups, gods from outer space and so forth. The chapters cover the common elements and themes in those subgenres, with a couple of productions spotlighted as examples and several films discussed at shorter length. Each chapter ends with capsule descriptions of other related films.

The book covers aliens on Earth as opposed to off-world encounters such as *Alien* or *Queen of Outer Space*. I've focused on American films and television as I don't have space to cover Japanese kaiju and other foreign material. The spotlight films are those I found the most informative and enjoyable to write about, not necessarily the most successful or respected. That I don't go into detail on *Close Encounters of the Third Kind* or *Arrival* isn't a commentary on their worth.

Given the astonishing array of cuts, director's cuts, special extended editions and deleted scenes, I can't guarantee that any version of the film you watch is the same one I caught. If you don't remember a scene I describe or my running time is shorter than your DVD, neither of us is delusional.

Now read on. Hopefully you'll find what follows an out-of-this-world experience.

ONE

They Came from Beyond

A Short History of the UFO Phenomenon

"I saw a flying saucer today."
"You mean one from—up there?"
—*Plan Nine from Outer Space*

Ever since the 1950s, alien visitor films have been intertwined with real-world UFO sightings and beliefs. Flying saucers hovering over our cities or landing to make first contact. Based-on-truth stories of alien abductions. Claims that the gods our ancestors worshipped were EBEs (extraterrestrial biological entities) descending from the stars.

Conversely, films and TV have influenced Ufology. Saucer sightings shot up after Klaatu arrived in one in *The Day the Earth Stood Still*. The Greys became the primary image of extraterrestrials after Steven Spielberg used them as the aliens of *Close Encounters of the Third Kind*. The TV miniseries *V*, with reptilian aliens disguised as humans, may have encouraged stories of Reptilian alien visitors hiding among us. Entire books have been written about Ufology and its relationship with UFO fiction; think of this chapter as a Cliff's Notes version.[1]

The history of humans witnessing wonder craft in the sky goes back long before flying saucers. There's the flying wheel in the Old Testament book of Ezekiel; a mysterious airship reported by multiple witnesses in the 1890s; the glowing lights or "foo fighters" the 415th Night Fighter Squadron saw traveling alongside their planes in World War II. In February 1942, reports of an unidentified object over Los Angeles led to the military raking the skies with anti-aircraft fire. Despite reports of enemy bombers, there was nothing there to hit.[2]

For skeptics that shows UFOs are the latest version of old folk beliefs and modern panics. Coming shortly after Pearl Harbor, it's hardly surprising Los Angelinos panicked about a possible threat. For believers, Ezekiel's wheel is a historical UFO encounter; the foo fighters could have been UFOs; and perhaps a spaceship hovered over LA in 1942.

One thing everyone can agree on is that in 1947, pilot Kenneth Arnold kickstarted the modern interest in UFOs. Arnold reported seeing a squadron of crescent shaped craft alongside his plane, leaping through the air like saucers skipped over water. That description transmuted as it spread into a report of "flying saucers." Other saucer sightings followed, and soon became an obsession for millions of Americans. Were they real? Even if some sightings could be explained away, did that discredit all of them? If they were real, where did they come from?

Arnold believed he'd seen secret military aircraft. That was the view of *The Flying Saucer* (1950), which assumed there was a single, super-fast craft built by an Earth

The Day the Earth Stood Still (1951) was the first movie to show us an extraterrestrial saucer in flight. It also gave us film's first iconic robot, captured on the poster.

inventor. The hero's mission is to find the inventor before Russian spies steal the saucer. The belief in an earthly source for UFOs never went away, but most believers favored an extraterrestrial origin.

The government was as curious about them as the general public. In 1947, Lt. General Nathan Twining told his superiors at the Pentagon that the "flying discs" were real and more maneuverable than any known aircraft. The military investigation began with Project Sign in 1948, later renaming it Project Grudge and, in 1952, Project Blue Book. Blue Book's final report said all but 701 sightings could be explained; none of them suggested UFOs were a threat or involved advanced technology, let alone aliens. A 2021 Pentagon report said that many sightings remain unexplained but took an agnostic stance on the possibility of alien involvement.[3]

The project's most significant legacy was Captain Edward Ruppelt coining "unidentified flying object" as a name for foo fighters, flying saucers and similar phenomena. "Flying saucer" had come to mean the same thing as "spaceship." Ruppelt hoped using a clinically descriptive term—they are literally flying objects we haven't identified—would avoid any presumptions about their origins. It didn't work: "UFO" soon came to be just another name for alien spacecraft. The Pentagon now prefers "unidentified aerial phenomena."[4]

A second legacy was that Blue Book scientific consultant J. Allen Hynek defined the three types of "close" encounters: sightings (first kind), physical evidence (second kind) and human/alien contact (third kind). This would later be immortalized in the title of Spielberg's *Close Encounters of the Third Kind*, on which Hynek served as consultant.[5]

America was fascinated by flying saucers throughout the 1950s. The craze spawned toys, comic-book stories, novelty songs and alleged nonfiction books (*They Knew Too Much About Flying Saucers, Flying Saucers Uncensored, Flying Saucers from Outer Space*) as well as influencing alien visitors movies. Even after humans entered left Earth in rockets and then space shuttles, the flying saucer remained the default image of alien spaceships. In the comedy *What Planet Are You From?* (2000) the aliens marvel that we humans are so primitive, we haven't figured out circular craft work better than rockets.

Along with the flying saucer image, the craze also gave us the words mothership (from George Adamski's *Flying Saucers Have Landed*) and men in black (from Gray Barker's 1956 book *They Knew Too Much About Flying Saucers*).[6]

America became less UFO-obsessed in the 1960s, but the decade contributed two new wrinkles to UFO beliefs. A couple named Betty and Barney Hill went public in 1966 with a story they'd been abducted and experimented on by aliens several years earlier. While they weren't the first account of alien abduction to gain public attention, their story had a permanent impact on UFO belief. By the end of the century, abduction by UFO—a close encounter of the fourth kind—had become a staple of ufology and alien-visitor fiction.

The second development was Erich von Daniken publishing *Chariots of the Gods* in 1968. The author won himself a permanent place in the history of pseudoscience with claims that mythology and religion were our ancestors' interpretation of visits by advanced extraterrestrials. What if Sodom and Gomorrah were wiped out by atomic bombs? Wouldn't it have taken advanced technology to build the pyramids? Were the Nazca carvings in Peru intended as ancient landing strips for saucers?

This is another idea that crops up in folklore: many large earthworks in England have been identified as supernatural in origin. It's also a trope in science fiction, such as

Nelson Bond reworking *Genesis* into 1942's "The Cunning of the Beast." Von Daniken presented the idea as fact and spread it way beyond the boundaries of science fiction fandom. Some films toss off the concept of "ancient astronauts" or "gods from outer space" in passing (*Hangar 18, The Fourth Kind*), while others make it integral to the story (*Stargate, The Eternals*). Chapter Nine has more details.

While UFO sightings and stories continued through the 1970s, the next major addition to the mythos was an alleged 1947 alien encounter that attracted fresh attention in the 1980s. In 1947, the Air Force announced that a plane based in Roswell, New Mexico had crashed into an unidentified aircraft. The next day they issued a correction: the aircraft had been a weather balloon. Nobody disputed that claim at the time. Even in 1975, in the alien-visitor film *Search for the Gods*, a character references Roswell as just one of many military bases their father served at. The location has no greater significance.

In the 1980s the conviction developed that the weather balloon story had covered up a real close encounter. It's become one of the widest-known UFO stories in both real life and fiction. The Roswell incident inspired the movie *Roswell* and the TV series *Roswell, Roswell New Mexico* and *Roswell Conspiracies: Aliens, Myths and Legends*. It's also used to ground alien-visitor stories in the real world. The alien in 2014's *Paul*, for instance, reveals he was flying the Roswell saucer; the Roswell crash is part of the *Independence Day* backstory; and in *The X-Files,* Deep Throat (Jerry Hardin) dismisses Roswell as a trivial incident compared to some of the UFO crashes he's seen. Dropping the name helps tie the story to our reality.

For some ufologists, Roswell is just one of many cases where the U.S. government hid the truth. The conspiracy and the "men in black" who enforce it have become part of alien visitor fiction as well as UFO lore. Or possibly the conspiracy is the opposite: UFO sightings are a smokescreen to cover up sightings of advanced experimental craft. Possibly alien-visitor films themselves are part of the conspiracy: author Robbie Graham concludes many filmmakers are secretly peddling government propaganda. They're conditioning us to accept aliens when the spacemen finally go public—*Paul* adopts this theory—or they're preparing us to fight instead of panicking.

Just as UFO sightings parallel older stories of strange visions in the sky, much of UFO lore and fiction overlaps with other beliefs. Alien abductions with hours of missing time resemble folktales about people taken by fairies. Fears of aliens subverting or manipulating us resemble political paranoia about Jews, Catholics, Nazis, Muslims and other supposed enemies of America. Stories of human/alien hybridization invoke old stories of changeling children and fears of "race mixing." Alien visitor films and TV shows also reflect these older beliefs and fears.

Despite the nightmarish alien-abduction accounts and stories of conspiracy, there are many positive accounts of close encounters too. Many UFO believers see meeting openly with aliens as a net gain for humanity, as does a lot of print science fiction. Reports of close encounters where aliens share cosmic wisdom also resemble encounters with angels and spirits.

Alien visitor films have mixed views on the merits of first contact. Will alien visitors come in peace or with ray-blasters blazing? Should we meet them with an open hand or a nuclear missile? Should we even try communicating with other worlds? In *Battleship*, one character complains contacting aliens would only invite them to attack and destroy us. The 2008 *Day the Earth Stood Still* makes the same argument and so have some real-world scientists. It's not just the risk of war: what if some scientist makes contact and tells lies, or offers promises he has no right to make?[7]

Can of Worms (1999) is a humorous example of this possibility. After teenage nerd Mike (Michael Shulman) experiences the worst day of his life, he sends a call out to the universe begging someone—anyone—to take him away. An alien talking dog (Malcolm McDowell) arrives to help him escape his oppressors. An alien lawyer shows up offering to sue the Earth. A PR flack offers to make Mike a galaxy-wide celebrity. And as Earth is advanced enough to open communication with the stars, it's no longer a legally protected planet. A crappy day at high school was a cakewalk by comparison to what Mike must deal with now.

Contact (1997), based on Carl Sagan's novel, assumes contact with other worlds is a good thing. Realizing there's intelligent life on Earth, the aliens arrange for us to make first contact (though they don't visit us here). The first meeting is friendly. That makes it an outlier in a genre where many films worry even going into space could cause a catastrophe. *The Andromeda Strain* (1971) is one of several movies wondering if satellites or spaceships could bring back something deadly from space. If we play it safe and stay on our own world, that's not an issue.

You'll see this pessimism, and some counterbalancing hope, in the chapters that follow.

Two

The Biggest Story That Could Ever Happen to Our World

Alien Invasion Films

"God is not an insurance agent."
—H.G. Wells, *War of the Worlds*

War movies have been popular for as long as movies have been around. Done well, the genre offers viewers patriotism, heroism, tragic but noble deaths and wall-to-wall epic excitement.

When it's a war against extraterrestrials, the dial on all that turns up to 11. As the trailer for *War of the Worlds* (1953) put it, an alien invasion is "the biggest story that could ever happen to our world, filling the screen with a mighty panorama of Earth-shaking fury!"

The first alien-invasion story, Robert Potter's 1892 *The Germ Growers*, involves shapeshifting ETs plotting to destroy humanity with biological warfare. It made little impact, leaving it to H.G. Wells' 1897 novel *War of the Worlds* to kick off the alien-invasion genre. A Martian army rockets itself across space to Earth, escaping their dying world for a planet with plenty of water and the potential for future growth. In addition to being an influential, ground-breaking SF story the novel was part of the 19th century's future war genre, established by George Chesney's 1871 tale *The Battle of Dorking*.[1]

Chesney wrote a gripping, realistic story of Germany's future victory over England that became a smash hit. Many authors followed in his wake, extrapolating how geopolitics, military policy and new technology such as iron-clad ships might play out in the next big war. Like Chesney, Wells' narrator looks back from long after the war to tell his story. Like Chesney, the narrator isn't a hero or central to the war effort. He's there to observe events and describe them for us, not to shape them.[2]

In other ways Wells departs from his future-war predecessors. There's little discussion of strategy, international relations and military technology. None of that's relevant when the foe is Martian invaders rather than French troops. The inspiration for *War of the Worlds* was when Wells' brother joked during a walk about what might happen if beings from another planet were suddenly to land and attack.

Wells took the ball and ran with it, writing a story about the brutality of colonial warfare from the viewpoint of the colonized. His narrator compares Britain's plight to that of Tasmania's aboriginal people, who were almost wiped out by English colonists. It also conveys the feeling of being a technologically inferior race targeted by superior weapons. The Martians attack with a laser-like heat ray and the Black Smoke, a form of poison gas. England has no defense against such weapons.

Wells, a religious nonbeliever, also mocks all belief that God will give our side victory. When a clergyman asks how God could tolerate such devastation, the narrator replies that "God is not an insurance agent." The novel emphasizes our victory was an evolutionary lucky stroke—the Martians have no resistance to the bacteria we live with—and not a triumph of good over evil.

War of the Worlds was a smash hit, and like many smash hits was immediately ripped off. Within a year, newspapers in New York and Boston had published their own unauthorized versions, changing the text for an American audience and setting the devastation in, respectively, New York and Boston. As science fiction developed as a genre, more alien invaders followed.

Where Wells' Martians want to wipe us out and colonize the planet, that's not always the case. Screen invaders have come to eat our flesh and steal our water (*V*), kidnap our women (*Mars Needs Women*), kidnap our men (*Devil Girl from Mars*), steal our brains (*Skyline*), steal our organs for transplants (*U.F.O.*), enslave us (*The Puppet Masters*) or simply make fun of us (*Martians Go Home*). Like Wells, almost all invaders have superior technology. Along with being able to cross the gulf from neighboring planets or distant star systems, they have force fields (*Earth vs. the Flying Saucers*), death rays (*Mars Attacks!*), mind-control technology (*It Conquered the World*) or robots (*Target Earth*).

Movies came much later to this subgenre than pulps, comics or radio. The first invader to hit the screen was Roy Barcroft's unnamed Martian in the 1945 Republic serial *The Purple Monster Strikes*. Layton (James Craven), a scientist investigating a meteor strike, discovers the meteor is a Martian space capsule. The Martian murders Layton and takes over his body. Layton has developed blueprints for a jet plane that can travel between Earth and Mars. The Martian plans to build the jet, fly back to Mars and then mass-produce the vessels for an invasion. Between his ruthlessness and his purple clothes—unrecognizable as it's a B&W production—he becomes known as the Purple Monster.

That the villain is an alien invader rather than an enemy spy doesn't affect the story much. The Purple Monster has little advanced technology and only one other Martian, named Marcia, shows up on Earth to help. It's unusual in that the Martians need Layton's plane—nobody calls it a rocket or a spaceship—rather than having their own spaceships. Arrival by meteor may reflect that Wells' Martians reached Earth the same way. Mistaking spaceships for meteors would be a standard set-up in future alien visitor films all the way from *It Came from Outer Space* (1953) to 2021's *A Quiet Place Part II*.

Given how common alien invaders were in the pulp magazines, why did it take so long for movies to get into the game? Partly just chance: before George Pal brought *War of the Worlds* to the screen, there'd been several unsuccessful attempts to adapt the novel, going back to the silent days. Beyond that, did World War II make a war against an alien world more thinkable? Or was the trigger the flying saucer craze that began in 1947, with the Purple Monster a random outlier?

The trigger might be as simple as box office success. *Destination Moon* (1950) proved a science fiction film could be profitable. Up to that point, science fiction wasn't held in high regard in the mainstream: it was kid stuff, ridiculous, badly written, never to be taken seriously. Outside of Universal horror films such as *Frankenstein*, science fiction films were almost all movie serials, a genre that, like the pulps was considered inferior, low-budget fare.

Destination Moon was a serious film about humanity making the first lunar landing. The director, George Pal, respected the genre and made several landmark science fiction films. Science fiction superstar Robert Heinlein cowrote the script. Even more importantly, the film made money. People continued deriding science fiction as unrealistic kid stuff, but Hollywood started taking it seriously.

Whatever the reason, the 1950s would see multiple films about aliens attacking Earth from space: *War of the Worlds, Target Earth, Earth vs. the Flying Saucers, Atomic Submarine* and more (invasion without armed force, as in *Village of the Damned* or *Invasion of the Body Snatchers*, will be covered in later chapters). The rate of invasion slowed down in following decades but picked up steam in the 1990s, with films including *Robin Cook's Invasion* (1997), *Independence Day* (1996) and the parodic *Mars Attacks!* (1996). In the 21st century, Earth has faced invasions in *Skyline* (2010), *Battleship* (2012) and *Falling Skies* (2011–15), not to mention multiple *War of the Worlds* adaptations.

Most invasion films have a straightforward storyline: aliens attack, humanity fights back, aliens lose. Typically, the protagonists are at the center of the fight—soldiers, scientists or someone with a key role to play. The crew of the *Atomic Submarine* (1960) investigate a series of mysterious disappearances around the North Pole and discover an alien vessel scouting Earth for an invasion. In *Rim of the World* (2019), four kids caught in the middle of an alien attack acquire information that may hold the key to stopping the invaders. Can they get it to someone who can use it?

Other films focus on the bystanders caught up in the carnage, without a heroic role to play. In *Target Earth* (1954), for instance, the protagonists are four people left behind in a citywide evacuation. When alien robots move in to kill stragglers there's no hope of fighting back. All the quartet can do is struggle to survive until the military finds a way to stop the war machines.

Another variation is to challenge the world with a single, super-powerful alien conqueror. In 1957's *Brain from Planet Arous*, Gor (Dale Tate) is a flying alien brain that takes over a human scientist (John Agar) as the first step to conquering both Earth and Arous. Unlike the Othered aliens described below, Gor isn't a typical Arousian but a criminal outcast. Vol (Tate again), an Arousian law-enforcer, shows up to help the scientist's fiancée (Joyce Meadows) take down Gor.

Even a film that follows the basic template faithfully can still be entertaining: it's the details of the war that matter, not the formula. Acts of heroism, love in the face of imminent death, heroic last stands, characters learning to stand and fight. Plus, of course, the visual spectacle, that "mighty panorama of Earth-shaking fury." Spaceships. Aliens. Explosions. Buildings and monuments shattering while people die in the rubble or in the glowing light of a death ray. This is where alien invasion films can top conventional war films. They offer bigger explosions and greater carnage than conventional weapons can deliver, and they can do it on American soil. The trailer for *Independence Day* grabbed audience attention by having an alien ship blow up the White House.

Although alien invasion films are war movies of a sort, they don't have much in common with the themes and tropes of mundane war films (for which, see Jeanine Basinger's classic book *The World War II Combat Film*). Some films, such as *Aliens in the Attic* (2009), don't involve the military, leaving it to civilians—kids in this case—to stave off the attack. In other films the military plays a role but can't accomplish anything. In the 1953 *War of the Worlds*, the military is completely ineffective. It usually takes science to pave the way for a military victory, such as figuring out how to destroy the robots in *Target Earth*. Only a few films, such as *Battle Los Angeles* (2011), show the military winning just by fighting harder.

These films are not hard science fiction. They don't devote much thought to what an alien invasion would plausibly look like or what kind of weapons and tactics aliens are likely to use. *Independence Day* has the invasion fleet take over Earth's satellite communications network to synchronize attacks on Earth's major cities. Given the ships are indestructible, they gain absolutely nothing by attacking together; it's not like we'd find unsynchronized attacks easier to fight off. However, it sets up a way for humanity to destroy their ships, as will be detailed later.

One way to defeat aliens armed with superior technology is to restrict the forces they can bring to bear. The invaders in several movies are an advance guard, not the full alien flotilla; destroy them and no more aliens will come. In *Battleship* (2012), the alien war vessel loses its communication array when it crashes into the ocean. The Navy not only has to destroy the ship, but it also has to stop them accessing Earth's communications grid to summon more of their kind. In *The Watch* (2012), Earth's fate likewise hinges on whether Ben Stiller can stop the aliens' murderous advance guard from phoning home.

In most alien invasion films, we win. In some, such as *Battle Los Angeles*, we win a big enough victory that even with the war ongoing, the audience can hope more triumphs will follow. In some films and television series we lose; the story is what happens after the aliens seize control. A story of occupation looks at how people react to power: do we oppose it? Submit to it? Protect other people from it? Will we be resistance, collaborators or just keep our heads down and hope it'll pass us by?

In *V* (1983), the alien Visitors appear to come in peace, then declare martial law. Some cops have no problems becoming enforcers for the new regime while other officers turn a blind eye to refugees and dissenters. *Falling Skies* focused on the armed resistance after aliens crush the world's government and take over. The ambitious but hopelessly muddled *Captive State* (2019) shows a world where our alien conquerors use tracking technology and drone strikes to eliminate anyone disloyal. Is there anyone willing to strike back?

Othering the Aliens

The future war stories of the 19th century took sides. The author's nation was proud and virtuous, even if its military forces weren't strong enough to win. The enemy nation was the very devil, ruthless and unprincipled. *War of the Worlds* didn't go that route. Wells portrayed the battle against the Martians as a Darwinian struggle for existence, not white hats vs. black hats. England's fate in the novel was no different from what England and other European nations had done to other, weaker peoples around the world. Nor were the Martians torturing humans for their science any crueler than human scientists who vivisected animals.

Few alien invasion films, including the adaptations of Wells' novel, take that view. It's a given that humans vs. aliens is a fight of good vs. evil and the invaders are the evil ones. In many films the invaders are completely Othered.

Othering paints a particular group of people such as Jews, Muslims or Asians as monsters or subhumans, undeserving of equal rights and the protection of the law. Future-war stories Othered the enemy. War movies have done the same, particularly when the enemy was nonwhite. World War II films portrayed Germans as a good race subjugated by an evil ideology; the Japanese, by contrast, were sadistic, subhuman fiends. Westerns often show the same Othered attitude toward Native Americans.

Those attitudes aren't as acceptable as they used to be—unless the Other is a fictitious alien species. A modern film showing the Japanese as sadistic monsters who deserve extinction would trigger backlash. Wiping out evil aliens doesn't generate the same outrage.

Alien invaders in these movies are ruthless, merciless and brutal. They don't follow human rules of war. Usually they don't demand our surrender, they just kill us. Comparing humans to vermin is a standard method of Othering; a movie describing Jews or Muslims that way would generate complaints. When President Whitmore (Bill Pullman) calls the aliens in *Independence Day* locusts, it doesn't generate the same objections. The invaders have already destroyed Los Angeles and Washington, D.C., in unprovoked attacks; what respect do they deserve?

Midway through *Independence Day*, Whitmore makes telepathic contact with an alien POW. The communication confirms they're totally evil and want to wipe us all out. There's no room for negotiation with genocidal fiends so we're the good guys no matter what we do to them. *Battleship* uses the same telepathic trick to establish this is war without mercy, freeing us up to annihilate the invaders.

Characters in invasion films who think peace is possible are idiots, and frequently end up dead idiots. A pastor waving a prayer book reaches out to the Martians in the 1953 *War of the Worlds*. The Martians burn him to ashes. A West Coast party welcomes the aliens in *Independence Day*, seconds before the aliens' Death Star–like weapon blows up the city. Most of the cast in Tim Burton's *Mars Attacks!* are convinced that "an advanced civilization is, by definition, not barbaric." The Martians are, of course, completely barbaric and sadistic.

Some films make a show of considering the alien side, but not seriously. In *Earth vs. The Flying Saucers* (1956) we learn the invaders' initial attack resulted from a misunderstanding—we weren't able to translate their message in time—but they were always planning to conquer us, so it doesn't make a difference. Carrington (Robert Cornthwaite) in *The Thing from Another World* (1951) suggests that an intelligent plant-being may not realize animal life can be intelligent. It's a valid point, except that the Thing is a murderous monster. It doesn't care whether we're intelligent.

It Came from Outer Space (1953) is an exception to the rule. It opens like an alien invasion, with monstrous extraterrestrials kidnapping and replacing humans in the town near their crashed ship. It turns out, though, that they're not evil. They crashed to Earth in their people's first trip off-world and want to keep humans away until they repair their ship and leave. In *Chicken Little* (2005) what appears to be an alien invasion by tentacled monsters is an extraterrestrial couple desperately seeking their missing child.

Another part of Othering is that the aliens can be judged entirely by their race. Human characters have different views and attitudes; Carrington sides with the Thing while Hendry (Kenneth Tobey) sees it as a deadly threat. Aliens are all stamped from the same cloth. The enemy force in *Battleship* are all murderous, as are the Kryptonian invaders in 2013's *Man of Steel.* A few films offer us one token decent alien but that doesn't erase the Othering. It's the same sleight-of-hand used in films such as *Little Tokyo USA* (1942) which shows us one patriotic Japanese-American amidst a community of traitorous immigrants.

There are exceptions. In the *Transformers* cartoons and films, even the evil Decepticons have a variety of personalities. The squad of tiny alien invaders battling kids in *Aliens in the Attic* argues much the way a team of human astronauts on another world might.

SPOTLIGHT

War of the Worlds *(1953)*

Paramount. 85 minutes. Premiere August 13, 1953.

CAST: Gene Barry (Clayton Forrester); Ann Robinson (Sylvia Van Buren); Les Tremayne (Major General Mann); Lewis Martin (Pastor Matthew Collins); Robert Cornthwaite (Dr. Pryor); Sandro Giglio (Dr. Bilderbeck); Bill Phipps (Wash Perry); Paul Birch (Alonzo Hogue); Jack Kruschen (Salvatore), Vernon Rich (Col. Heffner), Housely Stevenson, Jr., (Mann's aide), Paul Frees (radio announcer), Walter Sande (Sheriff Bogany), Alex Frazer (Dr. Hettinger), Ann Codee (Dr. DuPrey), Ivan Lebedeff (Dr. Gratzman), Henry Brandon (Cop), Sir Cedric Hardwicke (Narrator), Carolyn Jones (Blonde), Pierre Cressoy (Man), Nancy Hale (Young Wife), Virginia Hall (Girl), Charles Gemora (Martian), Robert Rockwell (Ranger), Alvy Moore (Zippy), Frank Kreig (Fiddler Hawkins), John Maxwell (Doctor), Ned Glass (well-dressed man), Russell Conway (Rev Bethany) Jameson Shade (Deacon), David McMahon (Minister), Gertrude Hoffman (Woman Newsvendor), John Mansfield (Man), Freeman Lusk (Secretary of Defense), Don Kohler (Staff Colonel), Sydney Mason (Fire Chief), Peter Adams (Lookout), Ted Hecht (Reporter), Herbert Lytton (Chief of Staff), Ralph Dumke (Buck Monahan), Edgar Barrier (Prof. McPherson), Wally Richard (Reporter) Morton C. Thompson (Cub Reporter), Ralph Montgomery (Red Cross Leader), Jerry James (2nd Reporter), Bud Wolfe (Civil Defense Official), Jimmie Dundee (2nd Official), Joel Marston (MP), Patricia Iannone (Little Girl), Bill Meader (PE Official), Al Ferguson (Police Chief), Eric Alden (Big Guy), Rudy Lee (Boy), Gus Taillon (Elderly Man), Ruth Barnell (Mother), Dorothy Vernon (Elderly Woman), George Pal (Bum), Frank Freeman, Jr. (Bum), Hugh Allan (Brigadier General), Stanley W. Orr, Charles J. Stewart (Captains), Freddie Zendar (Lieutenant) Jim Davies (CO), Dick Fortune (Marine Captain), Edward Wahrman (Cameraman), Martin Coulter (Marine Captain), Douglas Henderson (Marine Officer), Waldon Williams (Boy), Hazel Boyne (Woman Who Screams), Cora Shannon (Old Woman) Mike Mahoney (Young man) Anthony Warde (MP Driver), Rex Moore (Bum) Dave Sharpe (Looter), Dale Van Sickel (Looter), Fred Graham (Looter), Bob Morgan (Civil Defense Official), James Seay (Flying Wing Pilot)

CREDITS: Director: Byron Haskin Writer: Barré Lyndon, based on H.G. Wells novel; Producer: George Pal; Art Director: Albert Nozaki, Hal Pereira; Photography: George Barnes; Music: Leith Stevens; Associate Producer, Frank Freeman, Jr.

In H.G. Wells' novel, a meteor landing in rural England turns out to be a Martian space capsule. The Martians attack from inside it, using a heat ray to destroy everything and everyone they see. Physically weak, they assemble giant, three-legged war machines in which they leave the landing site. The tripods' heat rays and a toxic "black smoke" slaughter the British military, though soldiers occasionally manage to take down a tripod.

Civilians within range of tripod attacks either flee or die. England becomes a nation of displaced people, scavenging food and occasionally resorting to violence; while the narrator alludes to reports of cannibalism, the behavior we see is more civilized than the mob scenes in the 1953 and 2005 film adaptations. The narrator hunts desperately for his wife after they're separated, but he can do little besides run from the Martians and observe events. Even when a Martian landing vessel crashes near the abandoned house where he's hiding, he makes no attempt to confront them. What good would it do?

After fifteen days, Earthly bacteria kills the Martians; the Mars environment wiped out their native micro-organisms, leaving them with no immunity. With the threat over, the narrator and his wife reunite. By the time he pens his account, years after the invasion, England has rebuilt. The rest of the world, conscious the Martians would eventually have attacked them too, refrained from attacking England while it was vulnerable. The narrator takes this as a hopeful sign for the world's future.

The success and popularity of Wells' novel led to a 1925 screen treatment at Paramount, intended for director Cecil B. DeMille. Like later American films of the book, it's set in the U.S. The cast includes a pacifist secretary of defense who refuses to spend money on armaments; a scientist who's invented both a death ray and a reflector that rebounds such rays on the attacker; and a beautiful woman that both men are in love with. One of the Martians is hot for her too—their master plan includes mingling the races to create a hybrid human/Martian society. Fortunately, the inventor's reflector destroys the Martians with their own ray-weapons—no need for bacteria. Nobody's lamenting this one didn't get made.[3]

In the 1930s Alfred Hitchcock approached Wells about adapting the book, but Wells said Paramount held the rights. Directors Serge Eisenstein and Alexander Korda had their names attached to it at various points but to no effect. Instead, it fell to Orson Welles' *Mercury Theatre of the Air,* a low-rated but prestigious anthology series, to do the first dramatization. Working with Howard Koch, Welles developed the idea of adapting *War of the Worlds* as a fake news broadcast. The Martians land at Grover's Mill, New Jersey. A terrified radio reporter witnesses them emerge from the crater and start killing, then the broadcast suddenly goes dead. It's a standard trick now, but shocking at the time.[4]

Contrary to popular legend, historian A. Brad Schwartz says, the broadcast didn't send America into a panic. Audience members who thought it was a real news report called their friends or contacted the police, but few people evacuated or tried to commit suicide. Most of the people who believed it was real thought it was an account of a German military attack or a natural disaster, not Martians.

In 1953, as George Pal wrapped up work on Paramount's *When Worlds Collide*, he suggested tackling *War of the Worlds* as his next project. Ann Robinson, who played Sylvia in the film, said Paramount only agreed because DeMille insisted Pal would do a great job.[5]

The film opens with footage from World War I and World War II, while narrator Cedric Hardwicke reminds us that technology played a major part of both world wars. Now, though, we face something worse, not science in a world war but "the terrible weapons of super-science" in "a war—of the worlds!" Cue the credits.

When the credits stop, Hardwicke quotes from the opening of the novel to say that while humanity went about its daily business, Martians analyzed us with calculating, advanced minds. They were ready to leave their barren home and in all the Solar System, Earth was the world best suited to their survival.

What looks like a meteor arcs across the California sky, eventually crashing to Earth, a "real" event Hardwicke contrasts with the myth of flying saucers. Residents of the nearest town are tickled pink: the crater will be a natural tourist attraction, "better than a lion farm or a "snake pit," both of which were common regional attractions in the pre-theme park era. Local officials, however, want to know more about what just crashed to Earth. Conveniently, physicist Clayton Forrester (Gene Barry) is fishing in the area with some colleagues.

Forrester is a certified genius: astrophysicist, nuclear physicist, former employee at the Oak Ridge nuclear research lab (the facility processed uranium for the Manhattan Project) and "the man behind the new atomic engine." He's also a licensed pilot who flew his friends up to the fishing camp. After the officials contact him, Forrester heads for the crater while his friends make it back to LA without him.

Forrester is one of several scientists in 1950s films whose backstory involves atomic research. Carrington (Robert Cornthwaite) in *The Thing from Another World* was part of the Bikini nuclear test; Sorenson (Bruce Bennett) in *The Cosmic Man* worked on the Manhattan project. Nuclear science had much better press in the 1950s than it does today. The atomic bomb had ended World War II and remained America's ultimate defense against future threats. The decade optimistically anticipated peaceful uses for nuclear power such as electricity so cheap, it wouldn't be worth metering. Harnessing the power of the atom made a scientist both smart and patriotic.

At the meteor crater, Forrester meets Sylvia (Ann Robinson), who teaches library science in the local college. Ann tells the stranger how excited she is that Dr. Forrester, whose work was the subject of her master's thesis, will soon be in town. Forrester, who's a bit of a smug jerk, lets her ramble on about his awesomeness before he identifies himself.

Sylvia feels like a dry run for the female scientists and doctors who showed up in many 1950s SF movies, starting with 1954's *Them*. While she's following a more conventional female career track (teacher/librarian), she has a master's degree at a time when only a minority of Americans attended college. Like the later women scientists, she's a brain, though her intelligence doesn't play any role in the film. An older female scientist, Dr. DuPrey (Ann Codee), does appear later.

When Forrester's Geiger counter starts ticking, he warns everyone to back away from the meteor to avoid contamination. The radiation isn't mentioned again so perhaps it's just an excuse to empty the area in service of the plot. Forrester gets close enough to see the meteor is only slightly buried in its crater. He tells Sylvia that unless its hollow, its weight should have driven it much deeper. For him it's a puzzle; we viewers *know* that it's hollow.

With his research stalled, Forrester attends a square dance with Sylvia that night. Only three locals are still at the crash site when the meteor opens, projecting an ominous metal tentacle with a three-lobed electronic eye on its end. Spotting the eye, the men realize the meteor is a spaceship. After some discussion they rig up a white flag and approach the cylinder to talk—even aliens will respect a flag of truce, right? Wrong: a second tentacle with a red disc at the tip incinerates the men with a heat ray. It's one of the weaker special effects in the film. The human-shaped mounds of ash visible the next morning are much more chilling.

When the ray fires, the lights at the dance hall go out, as does the radio. Watches stop too, though we later see that cars work fine. When Forrester discovers a magnetic compass pointing to the meteor, he realizes the dance hall was hit by a magnetic wave.

Invaders in multiple later films would strike by using EMPs to fry our electronics but the effect here is inconsistent. A radio reporter makes a broadcast later, then all radio traffic shuts down, but the military's equipment other than radios works fine.

Forrester gets a lift to the meteor but the Martians disintegrate the car, almost killing him. Another meteor falls nearby. The military move in, setting up a perimeter to keep the aliens confined to the landing site. A reporter interviewing Forrester and other scientists provides some exposition about the Martians and we see people at parties, general stores and diners listening in. Major General Mann (Les Tremayne) arrives and tells Forrester other meteors have landed in Santiago, London, Naples, Fresno, Sacramento and Long Island; we learn later they've landed all around the world. Forrester assumes the landings are random; Mann says they're strategic. Nobody knows the strategy, however, because "once they begin to move, no more news comes out of that area."

The alien ships rise out of the capsule and attack. They are elegant and beautiful to behold, resembling metal manta rays with tentacles bearing the eye and the heat ray. Technically they're tripods, traveling on legs of magnetic energy rather than metal, but as the legs are only visible occasionally, they appear to fly. Forrester is in scientific awe.

Sylvia's Uncle Matthew (Lewis Martin), a minister, tells Mann he wants to approach the aliens in peace: "If they're more advanced than us, they should be nearer the Creator for that reason." When the general refuses, Matthew walks towards the Martians anyway, quoting scripture and waving a Bible. The Martians demonstrate their distance from the creator by annihilating him. They next turn their rays on Mann's makeshift military camp, disintegrating or burning everything and everyone. Forrester realizes the rays break down the bonds that hold matter together, which means no physical defense can stop them. He's no longer thrilled by the science, though—he's terrified.

The Army fights back but the ships generate forcefields that render them invulnerable. The Army retreats, while Forrester flies himself and Sylvia away from the front lines. He stays low above the surrounding forests to avoid Air Force planes, but when he has to avoid Martian ships as well, he crashes. He and Sylvia flee to an abandoned farmhouse, spending the night huddled together. Next morning, Sylvia cooks breakfast while the couple swap stories. Where he's an only child, she's one of nine kids. The tension of the invasion, she says, reminds her of when she got lost as a child; terrified, she ran to the only place she felt safe, her uncle's church.

Their idyll ends when another cylinder lands from space, smashing into the farmhouse. A Martian manta ship emerges and sends its eye probing into the building. The two humans hide, but a Martian creeps inside and taps Sylvia on the shoulder. She screams, then screams more at the sight of the alien, a grotesque figure with long, floppy arms and three-fingered hands (Wells' Martians were giant blobs). Forrester chops its hand off with the farmer's axe, sending it fleeing, then he lops off the electronic eye from its metal cable. He and Sylvia flee the farmhouse to get the prizes back to someone who can study them.

It's an effective scene but makes less sense than a similar scene in Wells. There, the Martians crash near the narrator's hiding place but don't emerge to explore. We're given no reason the Martian would risk itself by leaving the vessel; if they thought there was danger, why not just burn down the house?

The film then pauses to show us the big picture. Nations including India, England, France—the Eiffel Tower is in ruins—Bolivia, Turkey and China are battling their own invaders. There's no reference to the USSR though a military map in a later scene shows alien activity there. In a hat tip to Wells' birthplace, Hardwicke tells us England has been particularly hard hit, showing "the Martians appreciated the strategic significance of the British isles." The Martian magnetic waves have shut down radio everywhere, so the U.S. has to use high-altitude jets to communicate with the rest of the world. Everywhere the outcome of the war is the same. The Martians are invincible.

Forrester and Sylvia deliver the eye and the hand to a research laboratory. The lab hooks up the eye and we get a look at how they see us (distorted, with a green tint). The creature's blood shows they're anemic and physically weak compared to humans. Forrester suggests the key to victory is destroying them, not their war machines. In any other movie that would be followed by an insight how to do that. Here, science is as ineffective as military might, though Forrester's words do foreshadow the Martians' downfall.

Mann recaps what we've learned of their strategy: the Martian ships work in threes, marking off a triangle of territory and eliminating all opposition. To stop their advance on Los Angeles, the military intends to drop an atomic bomb more powerful than anything ever detonated before. As the U.S. detonated its first hydrogen bomb the previous year, this would imply a truly terrifying weapon. Forrester realizes that if the bomb fails, Mars will have conquered the world in six days. "The same number of days it took to create it," Sylvia says.

War of the Worlds is an anomaly in using nukes against the invaders; few movies of the 1950s did. Author Steffen Hentke suggests it's because there was little footage of nuclear explosions available at the time, and the ruins left by conventional bombing were more impressive than the blasted waste that nukes left behind. When later films went nuclear, it was usually a measure of desperation. In *Aliens vs. Predator: Requiem* (2007), for instance, the military nukes a small Colorado town because there's no other way to stop the alien Xenomorphs.

The bomb drops. A mushroom cloud engulfs the alien ships, but they emerge unscathed. The military orders Los Angelinos to evacuate and the city dissolves into panic, looting and carjacking. It's a reaction seen in multiple later films ranging from *Chicken Little* to *Day of the Triffids* (1962).

Forrester attempts to gather a truckload of scientific equipment and set up a makeshift lab out of town. Sylvia drives his colleagues to the same destination in a school bus. Carjackers jump Forrester and drag him from the truck, ignoring his pleas to let him at least unload the equipment. Forrester guesses correctly that the bus has been carjacked too, leaving Sylvia trapped in Los Angeles. Guessing where she'd feel safe, he runs between different houses of worship, searching through the praying crowds and finally finding her. They embrace just as a Martian ship flies over the street outside. The sound of its rays fills the building, the church roof begins to collapse ... then silence. When they look outside, the ship has crashed into a nearby building. The hatch opens showing a Martian limb as it twitches, then goes still. Humanity prayed for a miracle and its prayers were answered. Hardwicke's narration explains that it's victory due to bacteria, "the smallest thing God put on the Earth."

Pal's film is a pleasure to watch even today, but it must have been truly remarkable at the time. Nobody had ever shown a full-scale alien invasion on the screen before. Bill Warren, an expert on 1950s science fiction films, has spoken about how mind-blowing this vision of a world war was to him as a kid. And it is a *world* war, showing the international scope of what's happening. By contrast *Independence Day* only nods to the war outside the U.S. The visuals are amazing, and making Forrester an active participant in the war works better than Wells' disengaged observer would have.

Unlike most characters in 1950s science fiction films, Forrester has something of a character arc. When he first meets Sylvia, he barely acknowledges her as he studies the meteor site, though he does enjoy her flattering assessment. When it becomes obvious what they're facing, he's more intrigued by the science than alarmed by the threat. By the end of the film, he's scared for himself, his world and for the vanished Sylvia. Barry's better at conveying flippancy than fear but he's better here than usual.

A standard criticism of the film is that Clayton/Sylvia develops too fast to be meaningful. Scriptwriter Barré Lyndon originally planned to have the Forrester character, like Wells' narrator, hunting his missing wife. The studio insisted on a boy-meets-girl element. While it's cliched, the events are the kind of pressure cooker in which people can bond fast. Thousands of similarly hasty marriages happened during World War II, within living memory of the adults in the original audience.

If there's any weakness in *War of the Worlds*, it's the pointlessness of human heroism. It's inspiring to know how hard the world fought but hiding until the bacteria kill the Martians would have had the same effect. In Wells, the British do manage to down a couple of tripods. That might have been a better approach for the film.

The movie had a sequel of sorts, a 1988 syndicated TV series. In *War of the Worlds,* it turns out the dead Martians were only comatose. Reviving, they discover they can take over human bodies as protection against disease. They then launch a covert new war against humanity.

War of Worlds *(2005)*

Paramount Pictures; Dreamworks Pictures; Amblin Entertainment; Cruise/Wagner Productions. 116 minutes. Release date June 29, 2005.

CAST: Tom Cruise (Ray), Dakota Fanning (Rachel), Miranda Otto (Mary Ann), Justin Chatwin (Robbie), Tim Robbins (Harlan Ogilvy), Rick Gonzalez (Vincent), Yul Vâsquez (Julio), Kenny Venito (Manny), Lisa Ann Walter (Bartender), Ann Robinson (Grandmother), Gene Barry (Grandfather), David Alan Basche (Tim), Roz Abrams (Herself), Michael Brownlee (TV Reporter Osaka), Camillia Sanes (News Producer), Marlon Young (Cameraman), John Eddins (News Van Driver), Peter Gerety (Hatch Boss), David Harbour (Dock Worker), Miguel Antonio Ferrer (Brazilian Neighbor), January LaVoy (Neighbor's Wife), Stephen Geveon (Neighbor with Lawnmower), Julie White (Woman), Marianni Ebert (Hysterical Woman), Rafael Sardina (Mechanic's Assistant), Amy Ryan (Neighbor with Toddler), Ed Vassalo, Michael Arthur (Intersection Guys), Danny Hoch (Intersection Guy Cop), Man Studying Street (Sharrieff Pugh), Erika LaVonn, Christopher Evan Welch (Photographers), John Michael Bolger, Omar Jermaine (Men Holding Women), Robert Cicchini (Guy in Suit), Jim Hanna (Bus Driver), Onlookers (Tracy Howe, Adam Lazarre-White, Vito D'Ambrosio, Laura Zoe Quist, Ana Maria Quintana, Lorelei Llee), Narrator (Morgan Freeman)

CREDITS: Director: Steven Spielberg; Screenplay: Josh Friedman, David Koepp, based on the novel; Producers: Kathleen Kennedy, Colin Wilson; Executive Producer: Paula Wagner; Photography: Janusz Kaminski; Production Designer: Rick Carter; Editor: Michael Kahn; Costume Designer: Joanna Johnston; Music: John Williams; Senior Visual Effects Supervisor: Dennis Muren; Visual Effects Supervisor: Pablo Helman

In Steven Spielberg's post–9/11 take on Wells, protagonist Ray Ferrier (Tom Cruise) is an a-hole divorced father and Hoboken dockworker. His ex, Mary Ann (Miranda Otto), and her husband are heading to Boston for the weekend so Ray's taking custody of teenage Robbie (Justin Chatwin) and pre-teen Rachel (Dakota Fanning). Ray is a blue-collar divorced-dad stereotype: he shows up late to collect the kids, has no food in the house and an engine he's working on takes up the middle of his living room floor.

Ray's completely hopeless at connecting with his kids. He tells the same dad jokes over and over. He nags Robbie into playing baseball in the backyard, despite his son's obvious lack of interest. Ray tells Rachel to order food in so he doesn't have to go shopping but he's disgusted when she buys hummus. Robbie says at one point that Ray only cares about himself, which seems accurate.

Morgan Freeman provides the narration, once again warning us of those vast, unsympathetic intellects regarding our planet. TV news reports a series of lightning storms around the world, followed by power blackouts and earthquakes. When one of the lightning storms strikes Hoboken, power goes out, watches stop and cars go dead. Next come freak winds and a towering tripod rising from under the Earth. Ray's neighbors react with a mix of terror and excitement, recording events on their phones. Then it's all terror as the tripod disintegrates people left and right, sometimes leaving nothing but their clothes or their phones. This seems implausibly precise, but the visual effect is cool.

Terrified, Ray steals a car from a nearby garage—the mechanics just replaced the fried starter—and takes off with his kids. They make it to Ray's ex's house, but the couple are still up in Boston. By now Rachel's terrified, Robbie is furious that Ray's not doing more to comfort her and Ray's close to snapping. When he makes PB&J sandwiches for them, Robbie points out Rachel has peanut allergies; furious, Ray flings the sandwich at the window. When he has to assert his authority, the best he can do is tell Robbie "every time you guys don't listen to me—I'm telling your mother. I'm making a list."

As the tripods approach the neighborhood, Ray and the kids hide in the basement. That's fortunate, as a plane crashes into the house. Emerging, Ray discovers a couple of reporters scavenging food from the empty plane; presumably it crashed because the aliens disintegrated everyone inside. The reporters tell Ray about the National Guard fighting the tripods and losing, due to the aliens' force fields. One reporter plays a videotape in slow motion, showing the lightning is a transporter delivering the aliens to the buried tripods. Ray is horrified to realize the invasion is happening everywhere.

When the military pass through town, Ray refuses to let Robbie enlist. Robbie asks why his dad objects when he's never cared about his son before, but reluctantly joins Ray and Rachel driving north to Boston. When Ray stops the car because of refugees blocking the road ahead, a terrified man demands the keys at gunpoint. The Ferriers get out and join the long line of walkers heading for a ferry to take them north. They hear stories from their companions about how the war is going elsewhere, though neither we nor Ray can know if they're true.

After they reach the docks, a tripod appears to the south, panicking the crowd to storm the ferry. The captain raises the gangplank once the ship's capacity is maxed out; the Ferriers barely make it on board and a friend of Ray's is left on the docks with her baby. A few stragglers are caught on the ramp but Robbie helps them aboard.

A tripod rises out of the water and blasts the ship. Ray and his kids dive into the water and make it to the north shore, joining another column of refugees. Robbie tries again to join the National Guard, Ray refuses but then Ray spots a concerned couple taking Rachel away to safety. Ray rushes to reclaim her, leaving Robbie to his own devices.

Rachel and Ray eventually hole up in the home of Harlan (Tim Robbins), an ambulance driver who thinks "this is not a war, any more than it's a war between men and maggots. This is an extermination." Humanity, he says, is up against superior weapons and attackers who've been planning this for millennia. Harlan's not giving up, though. He's digging an underground bunker from which he'll be able to launch sneak attacks. The Japanese, he said, successfully destroyed a couple of tripods so Americans can certainly do the same.

Next morning, Ray discovers invasive red alien weeds are growing in the area; a later shot shows much of the surrounding territory now looks red. Back inside he sees Harlan promising to care for Rachel if anything happens to Ray, a creepy moment that almost provokes Ray to violence. Then a metal eye-tentacle snakes in, forcing everyone to hide. Ray convinces Harlan not to attack. Satisfied the building is empty, three-legged spidery aliens enter and fool around with Harlan's possession. This scene makes more sense than in the '53 film, as the aliens are clearly acting out of curiosity. Harlan still wants to attack but Ray restrains him until the aliens leave.

Harlan looks out the window at the tripod and sees it draining blood from human captives (the aliens also fed on human blood in Wells' novel). Freaking out, he begins digging a tunnel, making enough noise Ray fears he'll draw the invaders' attention. Ray gets Rachel out of the way, then kills Harlan. While he's doing this, Rachel wanders outside, freezing in terror when she confronts a tripod. Ray emerges from the house in time to see the tripod take her. Grabbing grenades from Harlan's ruck, Ray lets the war machine capture him, blows it up from within and escapes with his daughter.

Ray having finally stepped up as a father, the film moves fast to its conclusion. Ray and Rachel reach Boston without too much trouble. As they arrive in the city, a military unit tells Ray the machines are running haywire, but nobody knows why. A missile shot successfully downs a tripod, which disgorges gallons of stored human blood. A hatch pops open and a single alien arm flops limply into sight, just like the Pal film. The war is over.

Ray reaches Mary Ann and turns Rachel over to her while his former in-laws (Gene Barry, Anne Robinson) watch approvingly. For the first time in the film, Mary Ann looks at him with respect. So does Robbie when he shows up, alive; he and Ray embrace. Freeman's voice then tells explains what happened, adding that humanity's immunity to the bacteria that killed our enemies proves we remain masters of the world by right. No amoral Darwinian struggle here.

In the DVD special features, Spielberg and screenwriter David Koepp made a conscious choice to play things differently from George Pal and subsequent alien invasion films. They avoided the destruction of any landmarks and picked a protagonist who, like Wells' narrator, is just an average Joe. Ray has no insight into the big picture, no clue to what's happening in the war except what he hears from other people. Knocking out electronic communications leaves humans with the same limited communication methods as the 1800s. Ray's not a hero, not a key player, just someone who wants to stay alive and, eventually, to protect his children.

Going with tripods rather than flying ships harks back to Wells. The tripods lack the malevolent beauty of Pal's Martian ships, but they are impressively intimidating, moving smoothly but delivering death at the drop of the hat. Having the tripods emerge from underground rather than descend from the heavens was a less effective change. If the aliens planted the tripods on Earth millennia go, why wait until now to take over? Why not just arrive with the tripods? As in many alien invasion films, we never learn anything about the aliens' backstory or motives, we're just supposed to accept they have reasons.

Spielberg has said this movie stems from two roots—his unsatisfying relationship with his father and the horror of 9/11. Just as *E.T.* deals with a divorced, broken family (see Chapter Twelve), so does this film. While the father in *E.T.* is simply absent, Ray is a horrible parent. It's not that he finds the kids cramping his lifestyle—he doesn't seem to have a lifestyle, even when he's living by himself. He's miserable, with or without the kids; I get the feeling he may have been the same way even when married.

The 9/11 trauma comes out in scenes showing America, or at least the small part of it Ray crosses, in shock at being under attack. When the tripod attacks Ray's neighborhood, people he was talking to a moment before are suddenly dead without even a body to bury. That was also the case with 9/11—even 20 years later, more than 1,100 victims at the Twin Towers remain unidentified. The deaths are far more intense than in the Pal film and wherever Ray goes, he sees random devastation. In one scene as he and the kids are walking along, a train hurtles by on fire. In another, after the tripod has blasted the ferry, clothes suddenly rain down from the sky on Ray and Rachel.

Nine-eleven wasn't in my mind when I first saw *War of the Worlds* in 2005, though. By then American troops had occupied Iraq, overthrown its leader, Saddam Hussein, and were fighting a growing insurgency. I assumed that in Spielberg's *War*, we were the Iraqis. Following Wells, Spielberg was showing America what it felt like to have your country occupied by a military force vastly superior to your own. To have destruction constantly raining down from above, leaving the country in ruins and survivors in despair.

Even knowing Spielberg's intentions, the film still suggests Iraq to me rather than 9/11. While the terrorist attacks of September 11, 2001, were shocking, our reaction was more rage than despair and hopelessness. If the war on terror that followed was a fight between "men and maggots," Americans weren't the maggots.

Insurgency even seems to be a subtext in the film. Harlan talks about how the occupying nation in a war always loses. Robbie is writing a paper on the Algerian guerrilla war that drove out the French colonial occupiers. Screenwriter David Koepp compares Robbie's desire to enlist to Palestinian youths throwing rocks at Israeli soldiers—even if it's ineffective and possibly suicidal, Robbie's going to do *something*.

The Asylum, notorious for making direct-to-video "mockbusters" of current films, released *H.G. Wells' War of the Worlds* (2005) to coincide with the Spielberg film. C. Thomas Howell played George Herbert, an astrophysicist struggling to find his family amidst the chaos. The alien attack vehicles are insectoid tanks; the budget means we can't tell how invulnerable they are, as the opposition is limited to a handful of men with guns. A 2008 sequel, *War of the Worlds 2: The Next Wave* has the aliens—bizarrely identified as both Martians and time travelers—capturing humans to figure out how to develop immunity to Earth's bacteria. George eventually wipes them out with a super-potent flu bug. Neither film is worth seeing.

Independence Day *(1996)*

Centropolis, 20th Century–Fox. 145 minutes. Release date July 3, 1996.

CAST: Will Smith (Capt. Steven Hiller), Bill Pullman (Pres. Thomas J. Whitmore), Jeff Goldblum (David Levinson), Mary McDonnell (Marilyn Whitmore), Judd Hirsch (Julius Levinson), Robert Loggia (General William Grey), Randy Quaid (Russell Casse), Margaret Colin (Constance Spano), James Rebhorn (Albert Nimziki), Harvey Fierstein (Marty Gilbert),

Adam Baldwin (Major Mitchell), Dr. Brakish Okun (Brent Spiner), James Duval (Miguel), Vivica A. Fox (Jasmine Dubrow), Lisa Jakub (Alicia), Ross Bagley (Dylan), Mae Whitman (Patricia Whitmore), Bill Smitrovich (Captain Watson), Kiersten Warren (Tiffany), Harry Connick, Jr. (Capt. Jimmy Wilder), Guiseppe Andrews (Troy), John Storey (Dr. Isaacs), Frank Novak (Teddy), Devon Gummersall (Philip), Leland Orser (Techy), Mirron E. Willis, Ross Lacy (Aides), David Pressman (Whitmore's Aide), Vivian Palermo (Tech), Raphael Sbarge (Commander/Tech), Bobby Hosea, Dan Lauria (Commanding Officers), Steve Giannelli, Eric Paskel (Radar Techs), Carlos LaCamara (Radar Operator), John Bennett Perry, Troy Willis (Secret Servicemen), Tim Kelleher (Technician), Wayne Wilderson (Area 51 Technician), Jay Acavone (Area 51 Guard), James Wong, Thom Barry, Jana Marie Hupp (SETI Techs), Matt Pashkow (Second Officer), Robert Pine (Chief of Staff), Marisa Morell, Michael Winther, Dexter Warren, Paul LeClair (Coworkers), Capt. Michael "Chewy" Vacca (Lt. Peterson), David Chanel (Secret Service Agent), John Capodice (Marlo), Greg Collins (Military Aide), Derek Webster (Sky Crane Pilot), Mark Fite (Pilot), Eric Neal Newman (Pilot), Levani (Russian Pilot) Kristof Konrad (Russian Pilot), Kevin Sifuentes (Tank Commander), Elston Ridgle (Soldier),Randy Oglesby (Mechanic), Jack Moore (Mechanic), Barry Del Sherman (Street Preacher), Lyman Ward (Secret Service Guy), Anthony Crivello (Lincoln), Richard Speight, Jr. (Ed), Barbara Beck (Monica Soloway), Joe Fowler (Reporter), Andrew Warne (Reporter), Sharon Tay (Reporter), Peter Jozef Lucas (Russian Reporter), Yelena Danova (Russian Newscaster), Derek Kim (Korean Newscaster), Vanessa J. Wells (Newscaster), Jessika Cardinahl (German Video Newscaster), Gary W. Cruz (Video Newscaster), Ron Pitts (Video Newscaster), Wendy L. Walsh (Video Newscaster), Christine Devine (Video Newscaster), Mark Thompson (Video Newscaster), Ernie Anastos (Rex Black/NY Newscaster), Kevin Cooney (Atlantic Air CNC), Rance Howard (Chaplain), Nelson Mashita (Japanese Tech), Jeff Phillips (B-2 Pilot), Sayed Badreya (Arab Pilot), Adam Tomei (Sailor), John Bradley (Lucas), Kimberly Beck (Housewife), Thomas F. Duffy (Lieutenant), Andrew Keegan (Older Boy), Jon Matthews (Thomson), Jim Piddock (Reginald), Fred Barnes, Eleanor Clift, Jerry Dunphy, Jack Germond, Morton Kondracke, John McLaughlin, Barry Nolan, George Putnam (Themselves), Eric Michael Zee (Northridge Field Reporter), Pat Skipper (Redneck), Carlos Lara (Farmer Kid), Mike Monteleone (Butler), Lee Strauss (Elvis Fanatic), Lisa Star (woman on roof), Malcom Danare (Intellectual on Roof), Arthur Brooks (Trucker on Roof), Michael G. Moertl (Thief), James J. Joyce (Master CPO), Joyce Cohen (Kim Peters, reporter), Julie Moran (Entertainment Tonight Reporter), Robin Groth (Flagstaff News Anchor), Richard Pachorek (LAPD Helicopter Pilot)

CREDITS: Director: Roland Emmerich; Screenplay: Dean Devlin, Emmerich; Producer: Dean Devlin; Exec Producers: Roland Emmerich, Ute Emmerich, William Fay; Photography: Karl Walter Lindenlaub; Production Designers: Oliver Scholl, Patrick Tatopoulos; Editor: David Brenner; Music: David Arnold; Costume Designer: Joseph Porro; Associate Producer: Peter Winther

The first *War of the Worlds* came out right after the Korean War, when every adult in the audience would also have memories of World War II. The 2005 *War* came out during the occupation of Iraq and Afghanistan. *Independence Day* (1996), otherwise known as *ID4*, came out in the middle of a decade of peace.

By 1996, the Cold War had ended, the Berlin Wall was down, and the Soviet Union had collapsed under its own weight. There were no serious challenges to the United States' world dominance. There were wars—rolling back the occupation of Kuwait by Iraq, intervening in a genocidal Balkan conflict—but neither one threatened the United States. Nevertheless *ID4*, showing American cities devastated and landmarks demolished, took in $800 million at the box office, the best for any alien-invasion film.

The movie's opening scene, set on July 2, shows the Apollo 11 lunar landing site. We see an astronaut's footprints in closeup, then a huge shadow falls over the moon, setting dust trembling and swallowing the footprints, presumably due to the massive vessel's gravity well. Back on Earth a science lab picks up extraterrestrial radio signals and wonders why they're coming from the moon.

Where most invasion movies focus on a core character or a group of characters, *ID4* was written in the style of disaster movies, with an ensemble cast each dealing with their own issues and plot threads. The film jumps from scene to scene to introduce the key players. We start with President Thomas J. Whitmore (Bill Pullman), talking by phone with his wife Marilyn (Mary McDonnell), who's in Los Angeles for an interview. In the background, the PBS series *The McLaughlin Group* plays on TV with host John McLaughlin discussing how Whitmore's approval ratings have sunk to 40 percent. His guests agree the problem is that voters thought the former Gulf War fighter pilot would be a warrior in office; instead, he's a wimp.

Next, it's Julius and David Levinson (Judd Hirsch, Jeff Goldblum) playing chess. David, as we learn later, is a brilliant but unambitious computer engineer, an MIT graduate working as a tech troubleshooter for a cable company. He's a conscientious recycler and environmentalist who bicycles everywhere. Julius is a gruff old fart, a Jewish stereotype who chides his divorced son about not doing enough with his brains. When David returns to his job, his boss Marty (Harvey Fierstein) reports the company's satellite transmissions are all blocked. After studying the problem, David says it's as if the satellites were no longer there.

Sure enough, we see a family in California farm country watching *The Day the Earth Stood Still* on TV when the transmission goes out. The family patriarch is Russell Casse (Randy Quaid), a former Vietnam War pilot who's now a drunk making ends meet as a crop-duster. Not a good one, however: despite his son Miguel's (James Duval) efforts to stop him, Russell winds up spraying the wrong field. Casse blames his drinking on PTSD from an alien abduction.

When the alien ship becomes visible, Whitmore calls an emergency White House meeting. General Grey (Robert Loggia) warns against blasting it because of the damage if the pieces crash to Earth. Multiple smaller, but still huge, saucers leave the mother ship and fly into position over various Earth cities. Russian TV reports on panic in Moscow. Back in California, a reporter visits a diner and winds up hearing Casse's story of abduction. The locals, who've heard it before, snicker and mock.

Cut to the last of the key players, Marine combat pilot Capt. Hiller (Will Smith), waking up in bed with his girlfriend, Jasmine (Vivica A. Fox). Jasmine works as an exotic dancer to support her young son. Hiller plans to marry her—he hasn't proposed but he's bought the ring—even though that would be scandalous enough to kill his dream of piloting the space shuttle someday.

David discovers what's blocking transmissions are the alien ships using the satellites to signal each other. He also discovers they're counting down to a deadline—just like chess, the aliens are moving their pieces into position for a killer attack. David tries calling his ex-wife Connie (Margaret Colin) who's now Whitmore's press secretary. She won't put him through to her boss because David once punched out Whitmore, thinking he and Connie were having an affair. David, who doesn't drive, pressures his father into driving him to the White House. Julius does, though he insists David couldn't have discovered anything the government doesn't already know.

Whitmore calls for Washington to evacuate in an orderly fashion, but as in *War of the Worlds* we get panic instead. He tells Marilyn to get out of LA too, but she insists on doing the interview first, for fear of alarming people. Hiller gets called back to duty, so he tells Jasmine to move with her son Dylan (Ross Bagley) into Hiller's apartment on base until things calm down. He assures Jasmine there's nothing to worry about—nobody's going to come light-years across space to start a war. Proving him wrong, the ship over Washington ray-blasts the helicopter Whitmore sent up to make first contact.

David finally reaches Whitmore and explains the alien ships' positions prevent line-of-sight communications, so they've hijacked our satellites. Conveniently they use hours and minutes just like humans, so David has figured out they plan a coordinated attack at 6 p.m. Whitmore wisely has everyone evacuate the White House before zero hour. When 6 p.m. comes, the ship fires a Death Star–like blast at the White House, blowing it up—the money shot in the film's trailer—and sending a destructive wave of energy over the city. Air Force One gets the White House team, plus David and Julius, off the ground just in time.

The same thing happens in Los Angeles, where partygoers waiting to welcome the aliens are the first to die. Leaving the city, Jasmine and Dylan ditch their car because of evacuee gridlock, but they find shelter from the blast.

Things aren't any better July 3. The American counterattack can't penetrate the enemy ships' force fields. Russell drives his family into a makeshift refugee camp but they have to evacuate when an alien ship approaches. Jasmine, traveling in a found vehicle, picks up the injured First Lady and takes her to Hiller's base, but it's already destroyed.

Hiller successfully takes down an enemy ship by entangling it in his plane's parachute, though he crashes alongside it. When the alien pilot crawls out, Hiller decks it—"Welcome to Earth"—and drags it behind him as he heads out of the desert. Eventually Russell and his family, traveling with the others fleeing the camp, pick Hiller and his captive up.

Back on Air Force One, Secretary of Defense Nimziki (James Rebhorn) suggests we nuke the invaders, but Whitmore can't accept the death toll if we go nuclear over American soil. Julius suggests studying the spaceships at Area 51 to find a weakness. Whitmore assures him Area 51 doesn't have a stockpile of alien spaceships, but Nimziki admits it's true. He explains to Whitmore that not telling him, and presumably his predecessors, gives the White House plausible deniability.

When they reach Area 51, top researcher Dr. Okun (Brent Spiner) is as jubilant as Forrester about the scientific potential in the invasion. He admits they've never been able to master the tech from the crashed Roswell spaceship, but the lab has studied the ship and the alien corpses. The research shows they travel in biomechanical suits and have no vocal cords, possibly because they're telepathic. Whitmore directs David to work on the tech: "See if you're as smart as we hope you are."

The contrast between the two geniuses is notable. Okun comes off like his Ph.D. is in Mad Science. He's apparently spent decades at Area 51 without leaving, lives for his research, cares nothing for people. David, by contrast, is a regular guy. Sure, he's a genius, but he doesn't come across like one. No airs, nothing to suggest he's brilliant until the moment arrives for him to save the world.

The refugee caravan also reaches Area 51 where Hiller turns over the alien. As Ogun studies the creature, Grey reports that the ships are moving on to fresh targets. Within 36 hours they'll have wiped out every major Earth city. He grumbles that Nimziki should have given them whatever information Okun had developed before sacrificing pilots in a futile attack.

The alien under Ogun's knife suddenly wakes up and seizes the scientist. Imposing telepathic control on Okun's vocal chords it demands its freedom. When Whitmore asks what its people want humanity to do, the answer is "die." The alien backs that up with a telepathic blast into Whitmore's brain before an officer puts a bullet in its head. The telepathic attack conveniently shows Whitmore that the aliens plan to annihilate humanity, strip-mine Earth and move on to the next planet when they're done. With no other option, he tells Grey to go nuclear. The military drops a nuke on the saucer over Houston. It has no effect on the ship, but Whitmore realizes everyone under the saucer is now dead.

Meanwhile David and Connie rehash an old argument about her moving to Washington for the job with Whitmore. She saw it as the chance of a lifetime; David felt that when she criticized his lack of ambition, that meant his love wasn't enough for her. Then David, who's come down with a mild cold, has an insight: he can infect the alien computer system with a virus, spreading through the hijacked satellite network to shut down their force fields.

Hiller leaves the base, finds Jasmine and Dylan and flies them back with Marilyn to Area 51. The First Lady dies telling Whitmore that if she'd only left Los Angeles when he told her to, she'd have survived. Hiller pops the question to Jasmine, followed by a quick ceremony. Watching, Connie sees David still wears his wedding ring and takes his hand, clearly ready to reconcile.

David demonstrates that his virus will work, but only if he gets inside the alien mother ship to download it. Hiller volunteers to fly him in one of the alien ships. Connie's horrified ("*Now* he gets ambitious?") but David tells her with a grin that he'll finally be able to save the world.

Word goes out to the Middle East, China and Russia that "the Americans are planning a counter-attack." "About time!" On July 4, Whitmore delivers a rousing speech to the entire world: instead of being divided, nation against nation, we're now united against a common foe. Humanity will stand together and survive, making the Fourth of July Independence Day for the entire world! Whitmore then gets into fighter pilot gear to join the attack.

Hiller flies into the mother ship and docks, after which David attaches his Mac laptop to the alien system (generating many IT jokes from reviewers, as Macs in those days were not compatible with anything). Once the virus is in the mothership's computers, David alerts Earth. Whitmore fires a missile, becoming the first human to hit an alien ship. The battle initially goes against the invaders, but one ship is in position to wipe out the American high command at Area 51 and none of the nearby planes have any missiles left. As the ship charges its ray-blaster, Russell Casse arrives but with his lone missile locked in its cradle. He dives inside the ship and detonates it, sacrificing his life with a shout of "In the words of my generation—up yours!" The ship crashes to Earth, demonstrating to other pilots how to destroy them. The president returns to Earth to the sound of thunderous applause.

Hiller and David initially find it difficult to disengage their ship from the docking bay, let alone make it out, but they succeed in the nick of time, blowing up the vessel behind them; the film conveniently forgets Gray's warning about the damage when it crashes. Landing on Earth, they stand in the desert, smoking cigars—Hiller lights one up at the end of every successful mission—while a jeep brings their women to rush out and embrace them.

Independence Day is a great spectacle that benefits from a talented cast. Julius is a grouchy Jewish stereotype, constantly kvetching, but Judd Hirsch makes the role way better than it could have been. The movie is also an example of the random, chaotic way in which film sausage gets made. It began with Roland Emmerich wanting to make an alien-invasion film. After reading *War of the Worlds,* he decided it was dated. He opted to use disaster movies as a template instead.[6]

Despite Emmerich disliking the Wells novel, *ID4* includes many of its tropes—evacuees fleeing disaster, unstoppable aliens, men searching for their women. Killing the enemy with a virus could be seen as a Wells riff. *ID4*, however, is heroic where Wells is bleak. America can save the world without any help from bacteria. And we are clearly the good guys; the ending is a moral triumph.

Emmerich and Dean Devlin hadn't planned to tie the film to July 4. When they heard that Tim Burton's parody *Mars Attacks!* was coming out, they worried that if Fox released their movie after an alien invasion parody, the audience would just laugh at it. They settled on the *Independence Day* title as an incentive to get it released ahead of *Mars Attacks!* They wrote Whitmore's speech to cement the connection so the study couldn't just change the title and release it later in the year.[7]

While there have been many films about the U.S. being invaded—*The Battle Cry of Peace* (1915), *Invasion USA* (1952) and *Red Dawn* (1984), for instance—that wouldn't have been believable in the 1990s. The Soviet Union was gone and no other adversaries were on the horizon; we'd fought Iraq but they were hardly up for a counter-attack. An alien invasion, though? That was doable.

The end of the Cold War and talk of cutting the military budget was, to some Americans, a mixed blessing. Instead of finding new threats to fight or exerting our influence to shape the rest of the world, Americans seemed content to live happy, peaceful lives, enjoying the 1990s economic boom. Conservative pundits worried we were becoming too happy, too soft, too peaceful. By contrast, 9/11 was a welcome return to the status quo of perpetual war.[8]

Independence Day shows that despite being at peace, America hasn't lost its mojo. We get brief glimpses of the war overseas, including a ship downed near the pyramids after the final battle, but this is much less a world war than Pal gave us. It's America we see attacked, American monuments smashed and America that fights back and saves all the lesser countries. Whitmore's inspiring speech effectively makes the American national holiday something for the world to celebrate.

The film also reassures us that peaceful 1990s America is still stuffed to the gills with manliness. Whitmore proves he's not a wimp and David proves he's man enough to get Connie back. Women have no more of a role fighting the aliens than Sylvia in Pal's *War of the Worlds.* Their duties are limited to supporting their men and doing what they're told; the First Lady literally dies because she didn't do what her husband told her. Men can't be heroic rescuers if women don't wait to be rescued.

The way the script treats Whitmore reflects some of these 1990s gender and masculinity anxieties. There's a long history of presidents with military service on their CV—Theodore Roosevelt, Harry Truman, JFK, Eisenhower, George H.W. Bush—but Bush is the only president since Jimmy Carter who can claim that. Bill Clinton, president for most of the 1990s, had legally avoided the draft, as later Republican presidents George W. Bush and Donald Trump did. Many Republicans despised Clinton as the "pot-smoking, draft-dodging president," not to mention having a feminist wife with a law degree.

Whitmore has many of Clinton's qualities. He's young—Clinton was the youngest president next to JFK—good-looking and has an independent wife. What he doesn't have are Clinton's negatives: no womanizing, no draft-dodging, no pot smoking that we know about. It's surprising to learn the original template for Whitmore wasn't Clinton but Richard Nixon: rather than prove he was not a wimp. he'd have to prove he wasn't the crook people thought. Devlin and Emmerich had hoped to cast Kevin Spacey for the role; when the studio objected and Pullman got the role, they rewrote the part.[9]

Whitmore's heroism under fire redeems him from his earlier image as a wimp. According to the press, his inability to get bills through Congress and his willingness to use negotiation and favor-trading make it look like he's begging instead of deciding. That's how politics works, but films often fantasize about a president who transcends real-world politics. In 1993's *Dave*, for instance, Kevin Kline is an outsider thrust into the Oval Office. He sets out to do what's right and finds ways to overcome all opposition. Whitmore isn't in that sort of fantasy, so he's stuck not getting things done.

Then the invasion happens, and Whitmore proves that like Harrison Ford in *Air Force One* (1997) and Jamie Foxx in *White House Down* (2013) he's a president who can kick butt. He also delivers a rousing speech, modeled on Henry V's speech before Agincourt in Shakespeare's *Henry V*. Shakespeare's king ties together heroism and a national holiday, St. Crispin's Day; the play shows the Welsh, Scottish and English overcoming their internal frictions to fight together. In *Independence Day* the holiday is the Fourth of July, and we see black and white, Jew and gentile uniting against their nation's foe.

As film scholar Jeanine Basinger says, that kind of unity was a staple of World War II films. Over and over films showed us a diverse platoon—Texan, New York Italian-American, intellectual, roughneck from Brooklyn—coming together under fire to form a tight team. It's also a popular theme in alien-invasion films. The 2016 sequel *Independence Day: Resurgence* shows that two decades after the invasion, Earth is still united. The end of the TV series *Roswell Conspiracies: Aliens, Myths and Legends* (1999–2000) has humanity and various alien species calling Earth their home come together to stop an invasion.

In *The Lathe of Heaven* (1980), a psychiatrist uses a man's reality-warping powers to improve the world, but things never work as planned. The psychiatrist wants to end war between nations, so his patient (Bruce Orr) dreams up an alien invasion. Earth unites against them but almost loses until another dream turns the aliens peaceful. In the bizarrely goofy children's film *Santa Claus Conquers the Martians* (1964), the Martians kidnap Santa, which brings humanity together in a heartbeat—"Never in the history of mankind have the world's nations reacted with such unanimity and cooperation."

It's a small step to thinking that faking an alien invasion might unite humanity. In the *Outer Limits* episode "The Architects of Fear," a group of scientists try to end war by giving humanity a fake alien menace to fight against. The British 1965 series *Object Z* used a similar trick.

In the real world, unity is hard, even during wartime. Lots of nations in history have united against a common foe such as Napoleon or Hitler only to resume hostilities afterwards. Nor did the fight against the Axis suspend America's internal conflicts: segregationists didn't give black GIs any better treatment than in the pre- or post-war years.

The classic *Twilight Zone* episode "The Monsters Are Due on Maple Street" may be truer to human nature. Aliens stage a flying saucer landing, then perform a few tricks to convince the Maple Street residents that one of them is an alien—but which? Before long, the residents are killing each other out of fear and suspicion. As one alien observes to a colleague, there are Maple Streets all over the world....

Still, given humanity's long history of warfare, I can understand the feeling that it would take an alien apocalypse to make us act decently towards each other.

OTHER FILMS AND TELEVISION

The Adventures of Buckaroo Banzai Across the Eight Dimension (1984) Peter Weller plays Buckaroo Banzai, a pulp-style hero who thwarts an other-dimensional invasion. John Lithgow, Christopher Lloyd and Jeff Goldblum co-star.

Alien Invasion Arizona (2007) The survivors of a Marine team join forces with a crew of escaped convicts to battle the aliens hunting them—but can they do it before the military eliminates the threat by bombing the town?

The Atomic Submarine (1960) The crew of a submarine and a pacifist scientist must put aside their differences to stop an alien monster scouting Earth for an invasion.

The Avengers (2012) The heroes of the Marvel Cinematic Universe form a team to stop Thor's brother Loki and the invading Chitauri from conquering Earth.

Battle Los Angeles (2011) On the brink of retirement, Marine staff sergeant Aaron Eckhart must lead his platoon against alien invaders. Also known as *World Invasion: Battle Los Angeles.*

Battleship (2012) Taylor Kitsch plays a low-ranked officer who takes command of a naval vessel when an alien attack wipes out his superiors. Can he prove himself, save the world and get the girl?

Captive State (2019) In a world under the control of the alien Legislators, detective John Goodman investigates a resistance terrorist plot.

Chicken Little (2005) Aliens invade a community of anthropomorphic animals, but it turns out to be a big misunderstanding.

Earth Vs. the Flying Saucers (1956) UFOS animated by Ray Harryhausen attack Washington.

Edge of Tomorrow (2014) As Earth's forces crumble against an invincible invader, Tom Cruise suddenly starts time-looping, giving him an edge in fighting them. Can he and war hero Emily Blunt save the day?

End of the World (1977) Aliens led by Christopher Lee decide to wipe out Earth before it contaminates the galaxy. They disguise themselves as nuns and a Catholic priest.

Extinction (2018) A man fighting an alien invasion discovers he's an android. The invasion is really a repressed memory of humanity's attempt to destroy all androids.

Falling Skies (2011–2015) Aliens conquer Earth. Noah Wylie leads a group of freedom fighters to overthrow our new overlords

Independence Day: Resurgence (2016) A new generation of heroes must step up when the aliens return. Mediocre box office killed plans for a subsequent sequel.

Invasion (2021–) Apple TV series about how multiple protagonists each deal with an alien invasion.

Invasion Earth (1998) Sci-Fi Channel/BBC joint production involving a battle against alien invaders that starts in World War II and runs to the present.

Invasion Earth (2016) A group of addicts have their therapy disrupted by invaders.

Edge of Tomorrow (2014). Even Tom Cruise haters have been known to like this one maybe because Cruise keeps dying? Based on the Japanese novel *All You Need Is Kill*.

Invasion Planet Earth (2019) UK. Low budget film in which invading aliens kidnap a therapist and his patient, subjecting them to alternate realities. Can the insight they gain save the rest of the world?

Invisible Invaders (1959) Invaders try to intimidate us by raising the dead to perform acts of sabotage.

Justice League (2017) Superman and other DC heroes form a team to stop the alien invader Steppenwolf. Later released in the four hour "Snyder cut."

Killers from Space (1954) Aliens with ping-pong balls for eyes (literally) force Peter Graves to commit acts of sabotage, preparatory to their invasion.

Mars Attacks! (1996) Tim Burton parody based on a legendary line of bubble-gum cards. Martians invade, kill the all-star cast and generally wreak havoc.

Returner (2002) Japanese. After invaders conquer Earth, a woman travels back to kill the alien who summoned the alien armada. The alien turns out to be a helpless child. Saving it from a brutal gangster saves the world.

Signs (2002) M. Night Shyamalan story in which crop signs presage an alien invasion. Lucky for Mel Gibson that the aliens die when exposed to water.

Silent Warnings (2003) *Signs* knockoff in which teenagers discover crop circles once again foreshadow an invasion.

Skyline (2010) Two couples find themselves in deadly danger when aliens attack Los Angeles. Followed by *Beyond Skyline* and *Skylines*.

Slither (2006) An alien parasite begins infesting and controlling denizens of a small town.

Taking Earth (2017) One boy on Earth has the power to destroy an alien race. The aliens attack Earth to find him.

Them (1996) Electrical invaders attack Earth to gain access to our DNA.

Time Runner (1993) When an alien invasion overwhelms future Earth, Mark Hamill travels back in time to avert the catastrophe.

Trancers 6 (2002) In this unsuccessful reboot of the *Trancers* franchise, a scientist turning humans into monstrous Trancers turns out to be an alien paving the way for conquest.

Transformers (1984) Animated series in which alien Autobots (good) and Decepticons (evil) crash-land on Earth. They battle each other with their weapons and shape-shifting powers in this series, several later series, and the movie franchise that started in 2008.

Transmorphers (2007) Knockoff of *Transformers* in which humanity strikes back against Earth's robot invaders after being driven underground for 300 years.

Tripods (1984–5) BBC series based on John Christopher's young-adult trilogy about a future world dominated by alien conquerors.

27th Day (1957) Rather than attack us themselves, aliens give five humans weapons capable of wiping out millions. They wait to see if we'll use them to kill ourselves off.

Ultimate Avengers (2006) An animated film pitting Marvel's Avengers against alien invaders.

Wild Blue Yonder (2005) Brad Dourif plays an alien who reveals how inept all his plans to conquer Earth have been. Meanwhile, an Earth space expedition heads to his planet.

X-Men: Dark Phoenix (2019) After the mutant Jean Grey becomes the cosmically powerful Phoenix, the alien D'Barri try to enlist her to wipe out the Earth so they can colonize it.

War of the Worlds (2019) A BBC series, unusual for setting events in Victorian England rather than the present.

War of the Worlds: The True Story (2012) "Bertie Wells" recounts his experiences in the Martian invasion.

Without Warning (1994) A TV news studio covers reports of asteroids striking the Earth that turn out to be alien spaceships. As the government's covering things up, it's hard to tell if the aliens are invaders or came in peace and took umbrage at the human response.

Zombies of the Stratosphere (1952) Movie serial in which Martians plot to blow up Earth and relocate their world into our orbit. Re-edited into the feature *Satan's Satellites* (1958).

THREE

They Come in Peace

Friendly Alien Visitors

"The universe grows smaller every day. The threat of aggression
by any group, anywhere, can no longer be tolerated."
—*The Day the Earth Stood Still* (1951)

Not every alien comes here offering destruction. Some offer their hand in friendship. Some even offer to help. They're here to save us from ourselves, or from unfriendly aliens or they'd just like to hang out with us.

The possibility of friendship with other worlds has been a common one in print science fiction. Multiple stories imagined future humanity in an alliance with the other worlds of the Solar System or perhaps even a fellowship stretching across the galaxy, as in *Star Trek*. Many alien-visitor films are more pessimistic about peaceful relationships with other worlds.

Sure, we feel important and accomplished staring around our little world but compared to aliens who can cross light years to reach us, our sophisticated technology is no better than a savage chipping at flint. Kreton's (Jerry Lewis) teacher in *Visit to a Small Planet* (1960) scoffs at the absurdity of his student spending time on a primitive world such as ours. The galactic empire in *Lilo and Stitch* (2002) regards Earth as special but only because they see it as a wildlife sanctuary for mosquitoes.

Alien visitors in *The Day the Earth Stood Still* (2008) and *Falling Skies* place a high value on our planet's resources, not us. The aliens in *Meet Dave* (2008) and *V* (1983) want to steal our water. In *Liquid Sky* (1982) and *I Come in Peace* (1990) the aliens only interest in us is draining our brains of endorphins.

Other films assert that primitives though we may be, we're still something special. As the *Starman* (1984), Jeff Bridges can work miracles, but he envies our species' music, cooking and sex. In *Eternals* (2021), Ajak (Salma Hayek) says despite participating in the destruction of hundreds of worlds, our species is so special she wants to spare Earth.

The Space Children (1958) doesn't say we're special, but it could be inferred. The story involves an alien brain working with human children to avert a nuclear apocalypse. Doesn't the fact a creature so much wiser and more powerful than we are wants to save us imply we're exceptional? Then again, there's no suggestion the brain wants to stick around or open an embassy for Earth/Brainworld diplomatic relations.

The difference between Raymond F. Jones' novel *This Island Earth* and the film version is instructive. In the novel, Jones' protagonist, Cal, discovers an alien alliance slowly losing a cosmic war has outsourced some engineering work to Earth without revealing the alien aspect. One of the aliens compares it to the Allies in World War II paying natives on a tropical island to build a military base: you give them what wages they ask for and don't worry about explaining the geopolitical situation. At the end of the book, however, Cal convinces the aliens that Earth is part of the interplanetary community, even if most of humanity isn't aware of it yet.

The aliens of Metaluna in the 1955 film *This Island Earth* are considerably less moral: if they lose the war, they intend to take Earth as a consolation prize. When their enemies wipe Metaluna out, it's a win for us. We get to stay on our own uncomplicated island, safe and sound.

Films with friendly aliens are more upbeat. They fall into several categories.

Saving Us from Ourselves

Human progress has been a mixed bag. The 20th century saw amazing, positive transformations in the world—antibiotics, heart transplants, powered flight and the Internet. We also faced massive pollution problems, global warming, the possibility of nuclear war and unresolved older problems such as racism and misogyny. The aliens in *The Day the Earth Stood Still* (1951), *The Cosmic Man* (1959) and *The Space Children* all want to help.

They're not necessarily nice about it. Klaatu warns us that if we're still making war when we venture into space, we'll be annihilated. The alien brain in *The Space Children* knows adults won't listen so it recruits children. Dramatically, this has the advantage of keeping their motives ambiguous. We don't know what *The Space Children* are doing for the brain until the finish, for instance. The aliens in *We Can Be Heroes* (2020) appear to be hostile, battling the misfit children of Earth's greatest superheroes. It turns out they're forcing the kids to step up and take over from the old guard.

Some TV shows keep the helpful aliens off-stage, employing human agents to act for them. The "Assignment: Earth" episode of *Star Trek* is an example. The Enterprise crew travels back in time to the present of the late 1960s and encounters Gary Seven (Robert Lansing), a human possessed of amazing skills and unbelievably advanced technology. It turns out aliens abducted his ancestors from Earth millennia ago, breeding them to create perfect human specimens. They've sent Seven back to Earth to prevent us destroying ourselves, in this case by the U.S. launching a nuclear-armed space platform (I guess we didn't learn our lesson from *The Space Children*). It was a backdoor pilot for a series, under the incorrect assumption *Star Trek* wouldn't come back for a third season.

Gene Roddenberry revisited the idea in a 1974 pilot movie, *The Questor Tapes*. Questor (Robert Foxworth) is the last in a series of androids that aliens created to help nudge humanity along the right path. Questor's mission is to guide us through the nuclear age but a glitch in his creation has left him completely emotionless. When human companion Jerry Robinson (Mike Farrell) learns the stakes, he agrees to work with Questor, providing the emotional intelligence that will help him achieve his missions.

Like Questor's creators, friendly aliens sometimes play the long game. Rather than prevent immediate catastrophe, they hope to save us from an apocalypse far in the future. The 1997 TV movie *When Time Expires* has an alien alliance's agent (Richard Grieco) testing projections of Earth's future, preparatory to inviting our world to join. He discovers a cabal within the alliance is arranging Earth's destruction and tries to alter the timeline to prevent that.

That same year the TV series *The Visitor* starred John Corbett as Adam MacArthur, abducted by aliens decades earlier. Now he's back with amazing powers—to heal, talk to animals, read minds, memorize books instantly—that he uses to help people as he travels the country. It turns out that the aliens who abducted him have discovered Earth is doomed. Defying his alien mentors, Adam wants to avert that future; in the final episode, the extraterrestrial Elders sign off on his mission.

Cleaning Up Their Own Mess

In some alien visitor stories, the only thing that can stop a bad alien with unbelievable powers is a good alien with unbelievable powers. Vol, the flying brain of justice in *Brain from Planet Arous*, is one such, visiting Earth to destroy Gor, the flying brain of evil.

In *The Hidden* (1987), Beck (Michael Nouri) is a detective dealing with a string of cases involving law-abiding citizens suddenly becoming ruthless killers. Gallagher (Kyle MacLachlan), a federal agent on the case, eventually reveals the real killer is an alien parasite using and discarding human bodies. Gallagher himself is an alien law-enforcer, passing as a human to hunt the parasite, which killed Gallagher's mate. In *Alien Trespass* (2009), an alien accidentally lets a monster escape to Earth and borrows the form of a human scientist (Eric McCormack) to recapture it.

In the *Transformers* cartoons, the eponymous robots from the planet Cybertron crashed on Earth centuries ago, waking in the present. The Decepticons are evil Transformers who want to strip-mine Earth of its energy sources; the heroic Autobots fight to protect Earth from their evil kin. The backstory was altered for the movies, but the two sides divide up the same way.

They Like Us! They Really Like Us!

Some aliens are just plain nice. The Beta Lyrae inhabitants of *Moon Pilot* (1962) are one example. They send one of their number (Dany Seval) to help NASA fix a flaw in its space capsules that will otherwise drive astronauts insane. Their motive is simple: the sooner we get out in space, the sooner they can hang with us.

In *Arrival* (2016), linguist Dr. Banks (Amy Adams) struggles to communicate with the alien heptapods after they arrive on Earth, under the gun as Earth's military forces prepare to start shooting. Eventually Banks discovers the aliens' reason for visiting is to gift us with their language, which has such an alien concept of time it can free our minds from linear time.

In *K-Pax* (2001), Prot (Kevin Spacey) claims to be an alien; Dr. Powell (Jeff Bridges) claims he's delusional. Even as Powell struggles to free Prot from his delusions, he can't but notice the "alien's" insights are rehabilitating his fellow mental patients much better than conventional therapy.

False Friends

Just because aliens say they come in peace doesn't mean it's true. The classic example is the third-season *Twilight Zone* episode "To Serve Man." The alien Kanamits arrive on Earth with superior technology that ends famine and war and provides limitless cheap energy. Any doubts about their good intensions fade when a cryptographer (Lloyd Bochner) decodes the title of a Kanamit text as *To Serve Man*. It's only as he leaves with hundreds of others for the Kanamit homeworld that his assistant screams out the correct translation too late—"*To Serve Man*—it's a cookbook!"

Using alien technology as bait is a standard ploy on stories like this. The alien Visitors offer their technology in return for our help in the 1983 miniseries *V*, but only as a cover for taking over the planet. In *Gene Roddenberry's Earth: Final Conflict* (1997–2002) the alien Taelons have improved life on Earth with their advanced technology but not everyone trusts their agenda. The Taelons' human security chief, Boone (Kevin Kilner) agrees to work with the resistance on figuring out the aliens' real game. Unfortunately their agenda is impossible to explain here due to repeated changes in the series' direction during its run.

Thanos (Josh Brolin), the adversary of *Avengers: Infinity War* (2018) and *Avengers: Endgame* (2019), claims to be acting for our own good and sincerely believes it. However, his idea of helping the universe is wiping out half the intelligent life to stave off a universe-wide population crisis. In the first movie he succeeds; in the second movie the Avengers put right what he put wrong. Some MCU fans argue Thanos was right, making him an antihero more than a villain.

The Overseers of *Childhood's End* aren't evil, but they do have a hidden agenda. Arriving on Earth and taking over, they rapidly create a utopia. What they don't reveal is that the next generation of humanity will abandon Earth to join the cosmic mind the Overseers serve—and at that point, Earth and ordinary humanity will end.

Spotlight

The Day the Earth Stood Still *(1951)*

20th Century–Fox. B&W. 92 minutes. Release date September 18, 1951.

CAST: Michael Rennie (Klaatu), Patricia Neal (Helen Benson), Hugh Marlowe (Tom Stevens), Sam Jaffe (Professor Barnhardt), Billy Gray (Bobby Benson), Lock Martin (Gort) Frances Bavier (Mrs. Barley), Frank Conroy (Harley), Carleton Young (Colonel), Edith Evanson (Mrs. Crcokett), Robert Osterloh (Major White), John Brown (George Barley), Marjorie Crossland (Hilda), Olan Soulé (Krull), Drew Pearson, Gabriel Heatter, HV Kaltenborn, Elmer Davis (themselves), Ray Roope (Major General), Tyler McVey (Brady), James Seay (Government Man), Glenn Hardy (Interviewer), House Peters, Jr. (MP Captain), Rush Williams (MP Sergeant), Gil Herman (Federal Agent), Herbert Lytton (Brigadier General), Freeman Lusk (General Cutler), George Lynn (Col. Ryder), John Burton (British Radio Announcer), Harry Harvey, Sr. (Taxi Driver), Harry Lauter (Platoon leader), Charles Evans (Major General), Harlan Warde (Carlson), Wheaton Chambers (Bleeker the Jeweler), Elizabeth Flournoy (Jewelry Store Customer), Dorothy Neumann (Tom's Secretary), Howard Negley (Colonel), Bob Simpson (Colonel), Medical Corps Captains (Kim Spalding, Larry Dobkin), Medical Corps Major (James Doyle), Sentries (Bill Gentry, Kip Whitman, Michael Capanna, Michael Mahoney), Michael Regan (Army Captain), Men (Jack Daly, Harmon Stevens), Marshall Bradford (Government Man). John M. Reed (Taxi Driver), Ted Pearson (Colonel), John Close (Captain), David McMahon (English Sergeant), boys (Sammy Ogg, Ricky Regan), Gayle Pace (Captain), Grady Galloway (American Radar Operator), John Costello

(Cockney), British soldiers (Eric Corrie, Michael Ferris), Hassan Khayyam (Indian Radio Announcer), James Craven (Businessman), Millard Mitchell (General Cutler), Adam Williams (Army Physician), Government men (Ralph Montgomery, Wilson Wood, Gil Warren, Marc Snow, Bruce Morgan, Roy Engle, Charles Sherlock, Marshall Bradford), Beulah Christian (Secretary), Newsboys (Ronald Dodds, Victor Newell), Jean Charney (Mother), Soldiers (Murray Steckler, Jack Geerlings, Kenneth Kendall), Louise Colombet (Frenchwoman), Pola Russ (Russian Woman), Oscar Blanke (Peddler), Peter Similuk (Russian Pilot), John Hiestand (TV Announcer)

CREDITS: Director: Robert Wise; Screenplay: Edmund H. North, based on "Farewell to the Master" by Harry Bates; Producer: Julian Blaustein; Photography: Leo Tover; Art Director: Lyle Wheeler, Addison Hehr; Set Decorations: Thomas Little, Claude Carpenter; Music: Bernard Herrman; Film Editor: William Reynolds.

Behind the film's opening credits we see shots of space, then the point of view shifts to gaze down at Earth clouds, then the Earth itself. The next few scenes bounce us around the world. An American radar operator spots something incredible; the British military clocks a UFO at 4,000 mph; Calcutta radio reports on the mystery spaceship; an Italian village listens to their national news; and the BBC reports the UFO is now circling the Earth.

American radio news confirms this is the real deal, not just another flying saucer rumor. Even more than in Pal's *War of the Worlds*, people everywhere are listening: at gas stations, at country stores, on porches, in pool halls or simply standing outside a radio store front window. A flying saucer isn't enough to stop Washington, D.C., tourists from checking out the city's monuments … until the flying saucer becomes visible above those same monuments.

As the saucer descends on a baseball field, everyone watching scatters in panic. They immediately return and gawk as police and the military surround the ship. Worried officials speak to the president, alarmed calls overwhelm telephone operators and the newspapers rush out a special edition. Drew Pearson, a real syndicated columnist and radio pundit, reassures worried listeners that contrary to rumor there's been no invasion and no destruction.

A door opens in the side of the saucer and a ramp extends to the ground. The GIs train their guns on the opening while kids squirm through the crowd to get a good view of the spaceman. Klaatu (Michael Rennie) steps out onto the ramp in a shiny spacesuit and helmet, declaring that "we have come to visit you in peace and with good will." The military response is to train more guns on him. When he raises a strange rod a soldier fires, injuring him and shattering the rod. The soldiers move in and surround Klaatu.

At this point Gort, a huge robot, emerges in silence from the ship. The visor on its otherwise featureless face rises, showing a glowing eye slit. A narrow beam vaporizes some of the Army's hand weapons, then melts a tank—the crew have time to jump out—and a couple of artillery pieces. Gort stops when Klaatu barks a command.

Picking himself up, Klaatu removes his helmet, showing he looks perfectly human. He tells the soldiers the rod was a gift, a way for the president to study life on other planets. Chastened, the military men take Klaatu to Walter Reed Hospital for treatment and a meeting with presidential aide Harley (Frank Conroy). Klaatu confirms that he's from another world, having spent five months traveling 250 million miles to reach Earth, though that wouldn't even get him outside the Solar System. "Let's just say we're neighbors," he tells Harley. The official says it's hard to think that way about space; Klaatu says it's time for humans to accept that they're not alone in the universe.

The conversation is not productive. Harley offers a meeting with the president but Klaatu insists on a joint address to representatives of every nation. When Harley lists the political and physical obstacles, Klaatu proposes the UN; Harley replies that the UN doesn't include every nation. When he asks Klaatu if they can't cut out the USSR and other Communist nations entirely, the spaceman snaps back that "my mission here is not to solve your petty squabbles—it concerns the existence of every last creature on Earth." Harley agrees to try for a world summit but he's pessimistic. Klaatu quips that he has more faith in humanity than the human; Harley says that's because he's had experience with Earth politics and Klaatu hasn't.

Back at the baseball field, Klaatu's ship has closed up, leaving Gort standing immobile outside. The military can't move or damage the robot or cut into the saucer. The Walter Reed doctors find Klaatu equally remarkable. He appears to be fully human, and although he's 78 he has the body of a 35-year-old. The doctors discuss his amazingly good health as they light up cigarettes, which looks like irony now.

As Harley predicted, politics work against Klaatu: the Soviets won't meet anywhere but Moscow, Great Britain refuses to meet there and so forth. A frustrated Klaatu says, "I get impatient with stupidity. My people have learned to live without it." He suggests meeting with ordinary Americans as a compromise, so he can understand Earth's perspective better. Harley says the military want Klaatu confined to Walter Reed and locks the door as he leaves. The alien smiles wryly; by the time a nurse checks on him later, he's gone.

The disappearance provokes a new round of news reports and special editions, showing the 24-hour news cycle was around long before cable. Some people are intrigued by the idea a spaceman walks among them; others are terrified. Nobody pays attention to Klaatu, clad in a suit and tie and carrying a briefcase—all stolen from another patient—as he walks down a residential street. He hears a TV in a nearby home talking about the "monster at large" though the speaker assures viewers Klaatu is not "eight feet tall with tentacles."

Using the name from the briefcase—Major Carpenter—Klaatu takes a room in a boarding house to size up the average American. Most of the boarders are terrified of what the spaceman might be planning; some assume it's a Russian plot. Young Bobby Denton (Billy Gray) suspects "Carpenter" is an FBI man hunting the alien. Next morning, Bobby's mother Helen (Patricia Neal) realizes she has nobody to watch Bobby while she spends the day with her boyfriend Tom (Hugh Marlowe) so Klaatu volunteers.

Bobby and Klaatu spend the day touring Washington. Arlington Cemetery baffles Klaatu as his people no longer wage war, but he's deeply moved reading the Gettysburg Address on the Lincoln Memorial. The memorial prompts Klaatu to ask who the deepest thinker in the world is. Bobby replies that it's probably Washington scientist Professor Barnhardt (Sam Jaffe). Klaatu then takes Bobby to visit his spaceship and discusses how it operates. This gets a quiet laugh from the guy next to him, who assumes Klaatu's making it all up.

Their next stop is Barnhardt's house. The professor isn't in but through his glass-paneled study door we can see an imposing equation on the blackboard. Bobby guesses nobody else could understand it; Klaatu replies that even Barnhardt doesn't understand it. The spaceman enters—locks once again are no obstacle—and corrects the equation. He warns the professor's secretary not to erase it and provides her with his address. Sure enough a federal agent shows up at the boarding house that evening and invites Klaatu to meet Barnhardt.

The two men engage in technobabble about the equation ("With variation of parameters, this is the answer.") ending when Klaatu admits he's had practical experience using it in interplanetary travel. The alien tells Barnhardt that if nothing changes, humanity will achieve space travel while still aggressive and warlike. Klaatu's on Earth to call for a course correction, otherwise interstellar civilization will eliminate the threat by eliminating Earth.

Barnhardt says Klaatu could address a scheduled gathering of the world's top scientists but admits they don't have any political clout. Klaatu—who from this point on forget he wanted to meet with representatives from every nation—suggests their words would have more influence if he does something drastic first, enough to show Earth it's a small fish in a galactic pond. He suggests leveling New York, then assures Barnhardt he'll find a non-destructive option.

Back in the boarding house, the residents are increasingly jittery about the spaceman running loose. On top of this, Helen is confounded by Bobby's strange stories about Mr. Carpenter, while Tom sees the man as a romantic rival. That night, Bobby sees Klaatu borrow his flashlight and slip out. Bobby follows him to the baseball field where Klaatu signals Gort. The robot knocks out his guards, allowing Klaatu to enter the ship unobserved; the interior is white and minimalist, but eye-catching. Once inside, Klaatu gives the computer orders in an alien tongue, then returns to the boarding house.

Helen and Tom start believing Bobby's stories when Tom searches Klaatu's room and discovers the diamonds interstellar civilization uses for currency. When Klaatu learns from Bobby that the game is up, he visits Helen at her job. As they chat in the elevator it suddenly stops, the result of Klaatu shutting down all electricity in the world for half an hour. We see road after road lined with unmoving cars as well as inert printing presses, trains, washing machines, milkshake machines, outboard motors and assembly lines. Barnhardt asks his uneasy secretary if she feels worried and is pleased to hear she is. The Pentagon discovers Klaatu's feat is even more remarkable than it appears, as the shutdown didn't affect hospitals or planes in flight.

Back in the elevator, Klaatu tells Helen that if she or Tom bring in the authorities to stop him addressing the meeting, there's no hope for Earth. Once the power returns, Helen heads off to warn Tom against spilling the beans. The military quarantines D.C. off, seals Gort in an indestructible plastic block and sends soldiers into the streets to find Klaatu. Tom tells the government what he knows—he's convinced himself this will make his career—but Helen helps Klaatu sneak past the military to Barnhardt's house. Klaatu warns her that if he's shot, Gort will be off the leash and his destructive power is unlimited. If events fall out that way, she must go to Gort and address him with "Klaatu barada nikto."

The advice proves prescient, as the military ambush and kill Klaatu. Sensing his death, Gort immediately dissolves the restraining plastic, then dissolves the guards. It's the first time he's killed anyone. When Helen arrives, Gort's visor opens ominously for another blast; Helen remembers the command phrase and gasps it out before fainting. Gort carries her inside the saucer, then goes to the jail holding Klaatu's body. He melts the wall and carries Klaatu back to the ship.

As the scientists gather outside the saucer, resisting military orders to disperse, Gort uses the saucer's equipment to revive Klaatu. The spaceman assures Helen that only God can resurrect the dead, so his revival is temporary; he's vague enough, however, that it could be anywhere from 24 hours to fifty years. He emerges from the ship with Gort and Helen as the meeting breaks up. For once the military have the sense not to shoot.

Klaatu tells the scientists that "the universe grows smaller every day. The threat of aggression by any group, anywhere, can no longer be tolerated." Interstellar civilization has created and empowered Gort and his fellow robots to eliminate aggressors automatically, without favoritism or bias, and without mercy. This has not made the galaxy utopia, but it allows worlds to flourish without the fear of war. When humanity steps into space we'll be welcomed if we come in peace or annihilated if not. The choice is ours. Klaatu and Gort step inside and the spaceship vanishes into the night sky.

The Day the Earth Stood Still is based on Harry Bates' 1940 *Astounding* short story, "Farewell to the Master." 20th Century Fox paid $1,000 for the story with Bates getting half. Like most films based on short stories, the script adds a great deal of plot to the original. It also cut the big reveal of the story's ending, that Gort is the master, Klaatu the servant. That worked in the short story; it would probably have been underwhelming on screen. The film as it stands is anything but underwhelming.[1]

The Day the Earth Stood Still came out at a tense time. World War II was six years in the rearview mirror, but instead of peace, the U.S. and the USSR had shifted into the Cold War and perpetual military readiness. The Korean War had just begun. The USSR had detonated an atomic bomb in 1949, which meant they could blast America with the same power we'd wielded against Japan. Duck and cover drills for school children to prepare for nuclear attack became as routine as active-shooter drills are today.

From that perspective, Klaatu's ultimatum is more a lifeline than a threat. In the DVD special features, director Robert Wise describes the film as wish-fulfillment, having someone step in and impose an end to war as we seem unable to do it ourselves. Some critics have complained Klaatu's ultimatum is authoritarian. However, he's clear galactic civilization isn't out to impose dictate how Earth lives, beyond ending war. As Klaatu tells Harley, he has no interest in taking sides in the Cold War, a radical statement in a time when communism ranked slightly below Satanism for millions of Americans. Plus, his own people live under the same "make war and die" rules they're imposing on us. While technologically advanced it seems they're no more immune to the lure of war than we are.

Calling for humanity to beat its swords into plowshares is a Christian message. The script by Edmund H. North furthers Klaatu's messianic image with his adopted name of Carpenter, and having him undergo death and resurrection. That latter detail made the studio uncomfortable, hence the assurance in the script that Klaatu is only temporarily resurrected.[2]

The script does have some flaws. Klaatu's people have been monitoring Earth so he should know handing out diamonds for currency in front of Bobby would draw attention. Why not just exchange a couple at a jeweler? Because that would eliminate the clue that conforms Bobby's stories. Another plot-hole is that Klaatu opens Barnhardt's locked door—his room at the hospital too, presumably—without any device or explanation, making it more like magic.

SF film expert Bill Warren doesn't buy that Klaatu can finish the professor's equation easily: why would a diplomatic envoy be an expert in the science and technology of interstellar travel? It's a fair point, though there's no reason Klaatu couldn't have a well-rounded training. A number of science fiction stories show extraterrestrial or far-future civilizations where calculus and quantum physics are considered so simple they're taught in grade school. In alien-visitor movies it's more surprising when the aliens aren't all technical geniuses. In *The Watch* (2012), for instance, it's a surprise that the one friendly alien doesn't know how to deactivate the beacon triggering the invasion ("I'm not an engineer!").[3]

Michael Rennie gives his best film performance as Klaatu. While he's here to help us, he's not a saint: he's impatient with our politics, often curt and doesn't suffer fools gladly. He also shows a sense of humor and proves a considerate, patient babysitter. He doesn't entirely fit in around humans, but he's not so aloof or awkward as to make people uncomfortable. There's none of the awkwardness of Alan Tudyk in *Resident Alien* (2021) or the wariness of Joe Morton as the *Brother from Another Planet* (1984).

Patricia Neal's role isn't as challenging, but she delivers. As Helen, she likes and trusts Klaatu and she's able to grasp the big picture as much as Barnhardt. Giving them a romance would be the obvious choice—it always is, in movies—but happily the film avoids that. Hugh Marlowe isn't great as Tom, but he has a very limited palette to work with: selfish ambition and superficial charm is about it.

Gort (Lock Martin, a seven-foot-tall Hollywood doorman) is a truly memorable character. Other than his visor, his body is completely smooth metal. The film accomplished this by sewing Martin into the suit each day, then shooting from the side without visible seams. His featureless appearance is extremely unearthly. While he wields devastating power—Klaatu tells Helen that Gort could destroy the Earth if provoked—he's capable of using it with pinpoint accuracy, disintegrating guns without hurting the shooters. The giant CGI Gort in the 2008 remake is much less impressive.[4]

Jaffe does an effective job as the great thinker Barnhardt. As Wise says on the commentary track for one scene, when he and Rennie are talking, it's clear their characters are both smart and using their brains. We never learn any specifics about his field of science, only that it involves writing long equations that take up entire blackboards. It's important for the movie that he's smart; we don't have to know the details.

Alien visitor films have mixed views on science and intellectuals. In his book *Seeing Is Believing* Peter Biskind argues that in many 1950s films there's a subtext about whether to trust the brainiacs or to put our faith in the common man. Liberal films say to trust the smart people; conservative films say ordinary people are more reliable. In *Thing from Another World*, for instance, Hendry (Kenneth Tobey) and his air crew are consistently right about how to deal with the alien monster; Professor Carrington (Robert Cornthwaite) and the military brass are consistently wrong. When aliens contact Fitch (Ben Kingsley) in *Species* (1995) with instructions on how to genetically engineer human/alien hybrids, it never occurs to him this might be a bad idea (spoiler: it's very bad).

The Day the Earth Stood Still puts its faith in brains. Barnhardt, the great human thinker, grasps the big picture. By contrast the American soldiers are trigger happy and Klaatu's boarding-house neighbors, other than Helen, all assume the worst about the alien. In an alien-invasion movie Barnhardt's willingness to trust Klaatu would be a blind spot, a weakness. In a friendly-alien film, it's the right thing to do.

The film is one of several where TV or radio provide the audience with necessary exposition. It's not the only one to use real reporters or pundits to deliver the message. In the *V* TV series (1984) that spun off the two miniseries, each episode opens with Howard K. Smith, a real news anchor of the time, delivering news of the war for the Freedom News Network. The series is set in Los Angeles; Smith's broadcasts give us glimpses of the war in the rest of the U.S. and the rest of the world.

Day the Earth Stood Still does this even better. Rather than focus solely on events in Washington, it shows us Americans in all walks of life following the story, not to mention people around the world. Unlike many movies, there's no attempt to censor the news about Klaatu. In *The Monolith Monsters* (1957), the county sheriff tells the local editor to keep news of the monsters out of the paper. The editor grumbles but he accepts the necessity of not panicking people. In *Day the Earth Stood Still* everything comes out. While the public are terrified, they don't abandon the city in panic or set up torch-wielding mobs. It's safe to let the media inform us.

Ultimately what makes the original *Day the Earth Stood Still* work is that everyone involved treated it as a serious, quality film and proceeded to deliver one. The same can't be said for the two 1950s films that imitated it. The mediocre 1954 *Stranger from Venus,* AKA *Immediate Disaster,* has a Venusian (Helmut Dantine) visit a British pub, offering to reveal the secret of peaceful, safe nuclear power if Earth will give up nuclear war. British officials agree to meet with Venusian envoys but only so they can steal their technology. The Stranger sacrifices his life to prevent this treachery from starting an interplanetary war. Patricia Neal plays the female lead.

The Cosmic Man (1959) has a mysterious sphere appearing in a California canyon. As scientists and the military debate whether it's extraterrestrial and whether the occupants come in peace, the shadowy Cosmic Man (John Carradine) walks around uttering cryptic messages and platitudes about how humanity needs to grow and embrace peace. The military kill him, but not before he heals a terminally ill boy. It's unlikely anyone's heartstrings were tugged.

The 2008 *The Day the Earth Stood Still* remake obviously owes a debt to the original but it's a flop. Klaatu (Keanu Reaves) arrives to destroy humanity for fear pollution will render one of the galaxy's few livable planets uninhabitable. Eventually Klaatu decides to spare us but he also shuts down all electricity, limiting our ability to harm the planet further.

Klaatu was also the inspiration for the two-part 1977 *Wonder Woman* episode "Judgment from Outer Space." An alien arrives on Earth in World War II bearing the message that humanity must either put an end to war or the Earth dies. At the climax he realizes that if Earth holds someone as heroic and noble as Wonder Woman, it deserves to live.

There's a resemblance between Klaatu and Sidney Poitier as *Brother John* (1971), though it's probably coincidental. In this regrettably little seen film, John returns to his Southern hometown and finds it just as racist as when he left. The town doctor (Will Geer) learns John now serves interstellar civilization by evaluating whether it's safe to let humanity expand into space. John's verdict isn't favorable and Gort's equivalent is on the way to end us.

V *(1983)*

NBC. 189 minutes, May 1 and 2, 1983.

CAST: Faye Grant (Juliet Parrish), Marc Singer (Mike Donovan), Jane Badler (Diana), Evan C. Kim (Tony Leonetti), Blair Tefkin (Robin Maxwell), Robert Englund (Willie), Michael Wright (Elias Taylor), Richard Lawson (Ben Taylor), Michael Durrell (Robert Maxwell), Michael Alldredge (Bill Graham), Leonardo Cimino (Abraham Bernstein), Jenny Sullivan (Kristine Walsh), Richard Herd (John), Neva Patterson (Eleanor Dupres), Hansford Rowe (Arthur Dupres), Jason Bernard (Caleb Taylor), Diane Civita (Harmony), Peter

Nelson (Brian), Howard K. Smith (Himself), Andrew Prine (Steven), David Packer (Daniel), George Morfogen (Stanley Bernstein), Rafael Campos (Sancho), Frank Ashmore (Martin), Bonnie Bartlett (Lynn Bernstein), Tommy Petersen (Josh Brooks), Penelope Windust (Kathleen Maxwell), Camila Ashland (Ruby), Michael Bond (Talbot), Viveka Davis (Polly Maxwell), Ron Hajak (Denny), Myron Healey (Arch Quinton), Wiley Harker (Secretary General), Mary Alan Hokanson (Ruth Barnes), David Hooks (Dr. Rudolf Metz), Joanna Kerns (Marjorie Donovan), Jenny Neumann (Barbara), William Russ (Brad), Michael Swan (Officer Bob Briggs), Stephanie Faulkner (TV Studio Assistant Director), Tom Fuccello (Sen. Burke), Dick Harwood (Studio Director), Bonnie Jones (Woman), Eric Johnston (Sean Donovan), Curt Lowens (Dr. Jankowski), Marin May (Katie Maxwell), Mike Monahan (Console Man), Jennifer Perito (Resistance Member), Clete Roberts (Newscaster), Nathan Roberts (LA TV Anchor), Robert Vandenberg (Rebel Camp Leader), Momo Yashima (Band Leader), Denny Miller (Visitor Trooper), Stack Pierce (Visitor Captain), Judi M. Durand (Visitor announcer), Val Stulman (Resistance Fighter), Danny Nero (Trooper), Tom Southwell (Man Drawing on Wall)

CREDITS: Director/Writer/Executive Producer: Kenneth Johnson; Producer: Chuck Bowman; Production Designer: Charles R. Davis; Photography: John McPherson; Production Designer: Charles R. Davis; Art Director: Gary Lee; Costumes: Brienne Glyttov; Music: Joe Harnell; Editors: Jack Schoengarth, Alan Marks, Paul Dixon, Robert Richard.

This two-part TV movie opens with text declaring that "to the heroism of the resistance fighters—past, present, and future—this work is respectfully dedicated." As if to prove the point, we open on news cameraman Mike Donovan (Mark Singer) and his partner Tony (Evan Kim) reporting from a guerrilla camp in El Salvador. At the time, the guerrillas were fighting a right-wing, U.S. backed dictatorship; starting the story there shows the movie's politics as much as Rick Blaine in *Casablanca* having run guns to anti-fascists.

Government helicopters attack the camp. The guerillas fight back. At one point the guerilla leader (Robert Vandenberg) faces off against an attack helicopter with nothing but a handgun. Donovan films the conflict, then has to withdraw from the firefight. An attack helicopter pins him in place. Suddenly it backs off and flies away without taking the kill shot. Turning, Donovan sees a massive flying saucer moving through the sky behind him

As the saucers show up all over the world, we see other cast members reacting to the news: brilliant medical student and biochemist Juliet Parrish (Faye Grant) and black colleague Ben Taylor (Richard Lawson); Ben's brother, burglar Elias Taylor (Michael Wright), who catches the news while breaking and entering; anthropologists Robert Maxwell (Michael Durrell) and Arch Quinton (Myron Healey); elderly Abraham Bernstein (Leonardo Cimino) and his family. The sprawling cast is more closely associated than it first looks, as many of the characters live in the same Los Angeles neighborhood.

As the ships position themselves over Earth's major cities, the media up coverage to 24/7 on all networks. Julie mentions seeing Ray Bradbury and Arthur C. Clarke interviewed though they didn't have any deep insights. As part of the coverage, Mike and Tony end up at the UN, directly under the NYC saucer. There they meet Kristine Walsh (Jenny Sullivan), Mike's former lover, still PO'd that on their last night together, he left her bed without saying goodbye.

A shuttle descends from the saucer and someone inside addresses the UN Secretary General (Wiley Harker) in Swedish, his native tongue. The Secretary General accepts the invitation to enter and emerges a few moments later with John (Richard Herd), the leader of the alien expedition. The Visitors, as they become known, look perfectly human, though their voices sound harsh and mechanical; *V* creator Kenneth Johnson says on the commentary track he wanted to simplify the plot by preventing them posing as Earth people. Robert, watching on TV, marvels that the Visitors' evolution parallels ours so exactly.

John explains his people are native to the Sirius star system. This expedition is their first interstellar voyage and Earth is the first intelligent life they've encountered. Having used unmanned UFOs to monitor us and learn our language, they're now ready to greet us on behalf of their homeworld's wise, benevolent Leader. John proposes a deal: if Earth will manufacture chemicals vitally needed on their own planet, the Visitors will happily share their science with us. Watching, Mike's mother Eleanor (Neva Patterson) tells her husband Arthur (Hansford Rowe) that he should offer his plant for chemical production, ASAP.

By sheer luck, Mike and Kristine are chosen to make the first press tour of the mothership overhead. Later that night, they watch themselves on TV; Kristine teases Mike that he gave John's second in command Diana (Jane Badler) more closeups than Kristine got. Kristine is excited enough to forgive Mike walking out on her before, and the couple end up making love.

In next to no time, the Visitors have been normalized. Toy companies put out model shuttles with Diana and John action figures; when the Visitors arrive at Arthur's plant, they're met by a high school marching band playing John Williams' *Star Wars* theme; Kristine and Mike organize Visitor Friends youth groups. Eleanor, a social shark with an eye for who the cool kids are, throws a big party for them.

First contact has gone swimmingly, but some people have doubts. Abraham, a Holocaust survivor, has a gut feeling the Visitors aren't to be trusted. Robert, meeting them at Eleanor's party, notices they have cold hands and that birds panic when the Visitors are close. Quinton and a biochemist friend of Fay's both disappear mysteriously. Kristine becomes the delegation's press secretary, despite Mike's objections it compromises her reporting. They break up as a result.

At Arthur's plant, the Taylor patriarch Caleb (Jason Bernard) isn't happy working alongside the Visitors. He takes a particular dislike to Willie (Robert Englund), a socially awkward Visitor with mangled English; Willie speaks fluent Arabic but wound up assigned to Los Angeles. Caleb's attitude changes after he's almost killed in an accident only to have Willie drag him out. Harmony (Diane Civita), a waitress working near the plant, strikes up a friendship with Willy while Robert's daughter Robin (Blair Tefkin) begins a tentative flirtation with the Visitor Brian (Peter Nelson).

When Ben and Elias meet, things are not so amicable. Elias, who can switch styles between street punk and middle-class man at the drop of a hat, resents his smart, successful brother and turned to crime as an act of rebellion. Ben's angry that Elias is wasting his potential and doesn't tolerate his brother calling him an Uncle Tom.

Then things take a dark turn. ABC anchorman Howard K. Smith reports the Visitors have uncovered an international conspiracy: a scientific cabal is plotting to seize control of the motherships and gain access to the aliens' tech. Several scientists have confessed; others have admitted to being approached. To appease the Visitors, Earth's governments will now require all scientists register with the authorities and submit to computer monitoring. One official says the investigation has found evidence scientists have suppressed cancer cures and other breakthroughs to keep the government research money flowing.

Abraham sees a direct parallel to the rise of the Nazis back in Germany. His friend Ruby (Camila Ashford) assures him it's nothing to worry about—none of his family or friends are scientists—but Abe is unconvinced. Meanwhile Tony, watching film of one scientist sign his confession, remembers that when he and Mike interviewed the man a few years earlier, he was right-handed. Why is he signing as a southpaw?

The outrage over the scientists' betrayal casts a pall on Julie's life. Her stockbroker husband's clients keep backing out of dinners, very polite, nobody bringing up Julie, but … Julie realizes her husband is starting to see her as a liability, so she leaves. The husband is an odd loose end, never mentioned or showing up again.

Mike successfully sneaks onto a shuttle, then onto the mothership. There he hears Steven (Andrew Prine) tell Diana how pleased the Leader is with her brainwashing process: the scientists who confessed genuinely think they're guilty. Diana's more annoyed than pleased: the Leader thinks she can convert everyone but humans aren't that pliable. After she finishes venting, she and Steven relax with a nice meal of live animals, with Diana extending her jaws like a snake to down a guinea pig in one swallow.

After Diana leaves, Steven spots Mike and attacks him. In their struggle, Mike discovers the Visitors wear human masks over scaled reptilian faces. Mike makes it back to Earth with a videotape of the Steven/Diana conversation. When his station tries to air it, the Visitors shut the broadcast down. With heavy hearts they announce to the world that the constant opposition leaves them no choice but to proclaim martial law. Before long, posters of smiling Visitors declaring Friendship Is Universal are going up all over Los Angeles. Opponents of the new regime disappear. Abraham's grandson Daniel (David Packer) finds the changes thrilling. An aimless, frustrated kid before becoming leader of a Visitor Friends group, his affiliation with the aliens now puts him in a position to throw his weight around.

As the aliens tighten their grip, Julie and Ben meet with some of their friends. Julie proposes forming a resistance cell and reaching out to other groups that feel the same. She's also hopeful science can find some vulnerability in the Visitors, otherwise why would they be targeting scientists? Julie's not only smart, but she also demonstrates she's ready to act while the others still hesitate. Gambling that Kristine might be a sympathetic ally, Julie goes to Kristine's apartment that night to contact her. When she arrives, Mike is inside telling Kristine the truth about the Visitors. Kristine refuses to believe she's been fooled, then the Visitors attack, almost capturing Mike. Johnson says that while this makes Kristine look like a villain, she wasn't in on the ambush.

With Kristine ruled out as an ally, Julie's cell steals some equipment to set up an underground lab. The robbery succeeds, but the plan goes awry, leaving Ben with a fatal injury and Julie walking with a cane the rest of the show. When Elias discovers his brother is dead, his cynical persona cracks and he joins the resistance.

The Maxwell family attempts to flee the city—he's a scientist, it's not safe for them—but when they can't get away, Abraham takes them in. Abe's son Stanley (George Morfogen) protests that it's too dangerous. Abraham shuts him up by revealing that contrary to what he'd told his son, Abe's wife didn't die of a heart attack, she died in a Nazi death camp. Later Abraham sees kids spray-painting graffiti on a Visitors Are Your Friends poster so he shows them how to do it right: with a V for victory.

And that was just the first night.

In Part Two, the Visitors capture Mike and Tony and take them to Diana. Mike learns about the conversion process, but he also learns Diana's a practical woman: if she wants information fast, she has a blowtorch and similar tools for extracting it. It looks bad but Martin (Frank Ashmore), a member of the Visitors' own resistance movement, helps Mike escape.

The resistance settles into an abandoned building as their Los Angeles base. Everyone has accepted Julie as leader without even thinking about it—except Julie. As she's trying to fix a plumbing leak, the size of the job sinks in, and she starts crying. Seeing her break down, Ruby comforts her, assuring her she's up for the job ("Trust yourself as much as the rest of us do"). When she's out of her depth, Ruby adds, just act like she's confident and nobody will realize otherwise.

Mike stumbles across the resistance group but they don't hit it off. He can't believe anyone as young as Julie is fit to lead and they're suspicious he's a double agent—nobody else, after all, has escaped from Visitor custody. To prove his good faith, Mike shows them the videotape. Robert says the Visitors are the kind of intelligent life that might have arisen on Earth if the dinosaurs hadn't died out.

Now that they know what they're facing, the question becomes what to do about it. Hopelessness starts overwhelming everyone so Julie, remembering Ruby's advice, declares confidently that "we need to define our overall plan of resistance." There's instant agreement, then everyone looks at her for more. Nervously, she suggests undermining the Visitors' operations and figuring out what their end game is. Other suggestions follow: coordinate with other groups, show people that the Visitors aren't as human as they look.

Daniel, meanwhile, discovers the Maxwells at his house and uses this as leverage to pressure Robin into marrying him. She refuses; he calls in the Visitors. The family escape but the Visitors subsequently capture Robin. The aliens also take in Daniel's family for interrogation. That upsets him at first, but Brian bucks him up by lying that the family will be back soon (Abraham never makes it home). Brian tops that by promoting Daniel to his second in command as a reward for his loyalty, What little decency Daniel had left dies in that instant. Up in the ship, Diana sends Brian to seduce Robin as an experiment in hybridizing their races.

While the resistance distracts the Visitors with a bombing attack, Mike sneaks on board a shuttle. He reaches Martin in the mothership and learns the chemicals Earth is making for the Visitors are worthless. Their agenda is water: it's rare in the universe and their homeworld is dying of drought. Within a generation, every drop on Earth will be shipped back to the Sirius system.

Humanity won't mind as they'll be gone too. In a chilling visual, Martin shows Mike the mothership's massive storage chamber holding endless rows of bodies in suspended animation. Martin explains some humans will be brainwashed to fight in an interplanetary war against the Leader's alien enemies, the rest will become food. Mike discovers Tony's mutilated corpse but frees another prisoner, Sancho (Rafael Campos), to return to Earth with hm. Martin wants to join them for fear he'll be exposed. Mike convinces him to stay and keep working against the Leader.

After sending his younger daughters and wife to a resistance camp in the hills, Robert goes looking for Robin. The Visitor Isaiah (Stack Pierce) captures him and offers to exchange Robin's freedom for the camp location. He promises Robert will have time to rescue his family before the attack, adding that the Visitors plan to take it without any deaths. The alien's lying on both accounts, but it convinces Robert to give him the intel. Robert tells the resistance, who rush to the camp to save everyone. They find themselves in a vicious firefight with the alien shuttles overhead and the body count starts climbing.

Seeing all the death becomes too much for Julie. She faces down Diana's approaching shuttlecraft with a pistol, mirroring the guerrilla leader from the start of the first episode. Even though she's an easy target, the shuttle's ray blasts all miss (the Visitors are ludicrously bad shots throughout the run of the series). The ship turns for another attack but Mike shows up in the stolen shuttlecraft in time to drive Diana off.

In the aftermath Robert discovers his daughters survived but his wife is dead. Robin returns and later realizes she's pregnant. Mike tells Julie what he's learned. She tells Mike that if they can destroy the motherships, she's willing to sacrifice the prisoners to save the rest of Earth.

Mike reaches out to Eleanor as a possible ally but his mother's a survivor; she's going to suck up to the Visitors, not work against them. Julie and Elias beam a signal into space, hoping to contact the Leader's unknown adversary. However, Julie says, there's no guarantee they'll respond, or that they'll be any friendlier than the Visitors. For now, the resistance fights alone.

As Johnson tells it on the commentary track, the original concept for *V* had no aliens. Johnson's pitch for the miniseries *Storm Warning* involved a homegrown American fascist movement taking power. NBC programming chief Brandon Tartikoff didn't think Americans would buy that and suggested a Soviet or Chinese occupation instead. Johnson said no. He hoped the miniseries would become a regular series and didn't think that premise could last for long. After working on *The Bionic Woman* and *The Incredible Hulk* he'd wanted to avoid science fiction for a while, but he eventually realized alien fascists were the solution.

Having grown up in an antisemitic family, Johnson had been deeply shaken watching *Judgment at Nuremberg* as a kid. He used the Nazi Party's rise to power as the template for the Visitors. The Leader is Hitler; Kristine is Nazi filmmaker Leni Riefenstahl; Diana is a mix of several officials, including the sadistic Nazi scientist Josef Mengele. Julie's role was partly modeled on a real-life World War II resistance leader, DeeDee. The scientists, of course, are the Jews of this setting, scapegoats the Visitors can use to justify extreme measures.

Despite the Nazi analogy, the Visitors are not Othered. Both they and the humans have good and bad individuals among them. Some LAPD cops, for instance, don't see law enforcement any differently with the Visitors writing the laws; other officers resist when they can. The heart and soul of the story, Johnson said, is power: "Who has it, who wants it and who's ignoring it and who wants to fight against it."

The idea of America sliding into dictatorship has a respectable screen history. The World War II short film *Strange Holiday* (1945)shows the Nazis subverting America. It became an anti-communist drama after the war thanks to some judicious editing. The unsuccessful 1968 TV pilot *Shadow on the Land* had America succumbed to homegrown dictatorship. Both 1984's *Red Dawn* and 1987's *Amerika* have the Soviet's taking over; Amazon Prime's *The Man in the High Castle* (2015) has the U.S. under Axis control.

Most of these stories focus on a small group of protagonists: government agent Jackie Cooper in *Shadow on the Land*, a group of teenage freedom fighters in *Red Dawn*. *V* is sprawling, with 56 speaking roles. When drawing up the proposal to pitch to the network, Johnson didn't name them, figuring it would be easier to remember characters if he labeled them THIEF or CAMERAMAN.

V has a lot in common with some of the early 1980s' acclaimed prime-time dramas, such as *Hill Street Blues* and *St. Elsewhere*. They also had large casts, multiple plotlines and multiple character arcs. Squeezing them into a two-night miniseries rather than stretching things over a season was another order of difficulty. Johnson credits *War and*

Peace as his touchstone, learning from Tolstoy how to connect the characters and storylines so that all the diverse elements of his story felt unified.

Johnson says that when NBC gave him the go ahead, he only had two and a half weeks before shooting was scheduled to start. The budget was tight, which led to cutting costs wherever possible. For instance, rather than use models for the motherships, they're paintings.

Given the restrictions, it's amazing how well the show turned out. The Nazi allegory, while obvious, doesn't get so heavy it smothers the story. The cast is strong, particularly Faye Grant as a woman who falls into the leadership role, then grows to fit the job. The resistance includes not only women but blacks, whites, Jews, gentiles, teens and seniors. Early 1980s TV wasn't gay friendly and there's no sign any of the humans are gay. The script strongly implies Diana is bi, with a more-than-professional interest in Kristine.

Despite the grim topic and the deaths of several likable characters, *V* also has its moments of humor, from the Bradbury and Clarke references to a kid complaining the Visitors don't look like Spock. When the ratings came in, *V* set a record for science fiction TV movies. It was also the highest rated prime-time program of any sort that NBC had broadcast in 2.5 years.

That should have led to an amazing *V* series, but NBC decided a series would cost too much. Johnson suggested a series of TV movies instead, but NBC found that approach too radical. The compromise solution was to wrap everything up in a second miniseries, *V: The Final Battle* (1984). Johnson drafted the script, then decided the budget wouldn't be enough for quality work and walked away.

The second miniseries culminates in having Julie develop a bacterium that's fatal to Visitors but not to humans. The aliens have no choice but to flee Earth to survive. Ratings were good enough, however, that NBC finally authorized a series. It turns out the bacteria die off without cold weather so hot areas, such as Los Angeles, are vulnerable to Visitor attack. City leader Nathan Bates (Lane Smith) prevents a full occupation, establishing LA instead as an open city under his control. Visitors are welcome but they aren't in charge. This was modeled on the Nazis and refugees mingling in 1942's classic *Casablanca*; Elias even opens a club analogous to Rick's nightclub in the movie.

The episodes, however, were lackluster as were the ratings. Kenneth Johnson came back to wrap everything up but as NBC decided not to shoot the final episode, the series ended on a cliffhanger. ABC tried a reboot series in 2009 without any better luck.

OTHER FILMS AND TELEVISION

The Abyss (1989) An underwater engineering team rescuing a stranded sub finds an alien vessel of unknown origin complicating their work. More an underwater drama than an alien-visitor story.

The Astounding She-Monster (1957) An alien with a radioactive touch stalks around terrifying people. In what's meant to be an ironic twist, it turns out after she's killed that she was the ambassador from a galactic federation offering to help humanity.

Batteries Not Included (1987) Insufferably cute aliens help inhabitants of a small apartment building stave off a corrupt developer.

Close Encounters of the Third Kind (1977) Richard Dreyfuss has a close encounter that leaves him obsessed with UFOs. After crashing the U.S. government's first contact, the Greys accept him on board their ship.

The Day the Earth Stopped (2008) Another Asylum mockbuster. Giant robots arrive on Earth, giving us one day to prove that humanity is worthy of continued existence.

Doctor Who (1963–) Long-running BBC series about a time-traveler from the planet Gallifrey. In multiple times he helps humans against alien invaders, mad scientists and other threats.

Dollman (1991) An alien cop and his criminal quarry both arrive on Earth, after going through an energy belt that shrinks them in size.

Guess Who's Coming for Christmas (1990) A small town eccentric befriends an alien and builds a landing strip for his UFO. His neighbors think he's crazy until the alien shows up.

Indiana Jones and the Kingdom of the Crystal Skull (2008) Indiana Jones (Harrison Ford) races Soviet agents to a lost citadel of alien archeologists. The Soviets hope to exploit the aliens' powers for world conquest.

Knowing (2009) Nicolas Cage realizes solar flares will wipe out humanity. Extraterrestrials who might be angels evacuate some of humanity in space arks.

The Man from Planet X (1951) An alien arrives on Earth as a friendly visitor, only to be captured and tormented by a scientist who wants its scientific knowledge.

The *Mysterious Two* (1982) Cult leaders John Forsythe and Priscilla Pointer claim to be recruiting people for UFOs to take to the stars—but are they telling the truth or human grifters? Based on the Heaven's Gate cult years before it committed mass suicide.

Odyssey 5 (2002–4) After a mysterious force destroys Earth, aliens send the sole survivors back in time five years to find a way to avert the disaster.

Red Planet Mars (1952) Martians don't set foot on Earth but revealing that they're Christians sparks a worldwide religious revival. This thwarts a Communist scheme that almost destroyed America. If you think that sounds bizarre, the movie is stranger and dumber.

The Rocket Man (1954) For no discernable reason an alien gives a small boy a raygun that can work magic.

Something Is Out There (1988) In the pilot, female alien Maryam D'Abo helps cop Joe Cortese hunt down an escaped, shapeshifting prisoner. The woman stays on Earth to become his crimefighting partner.

Tracker (2001–2) Adrian Paul plays an alien cop hunting down 200 criminals who broke out of space prison and are now hiding on Earth.

Four

Now and Then We All Are Aliens

ET Infiltrators and Body Snatchers

"You'll be born again into an untroubled world."
—*Invasion of the Body Snatchers* (1978)

Stories of alien invasions are war stories. By contrast, stories of alien infiltration—*Brain Eaters, Invasion of the Body Snatchers, Human Duplicators, Annihilator*—are a mix of espionage and horror.

They're espionage in that the enemy are among us, plotting, watching, scheming. You leaders, your neighbors, your family may all be covert enemies working against you and your planet. It's a fear analogous to the political paranoia in stories about ordinary human infiltrators. In *I Married a Monster from Outer Space* (1958), newlywed Tom Tryon is an alien spy plotting against Earth. In *I Married a Communist* (1950) newlywed Robert Ryan is a Red, making him just as monstrous. The pod people in *Invasion of the Body Snatchers* are aliens who can pass for human; in 1942's *Across the Pacific*, Victor Sen Yung's Nisei is a Japanese spy who can pass as a regular American. You'll never suspect it until they strike.

Body snatchers, brain eaters and puppet masters don't just infiltrate, though: they *transform*. They can take your friend, your spouse or your dad and turn them against you; given a chance they can transform you too. Anyone you trust can be converted, which means there's nobody you can trust. When Marge (Gloria Talbot), the wife in *I Married a Monster from Outer Space* tries to get help, there's none to be had. The telephone operator "can't" put her call through. The telegraph office takes her message, then throws it in the trash. When Marge drives out of town, the police block the roads. Every avenue of escape has been cut off.

Films about subversives and spies lurking among us go back to World War I. In science fiction, one of the first examples is John W. Campbell's 1938 short story "Who Goes There?" in which an Antarctic research team must figure out if any of them have been replaced by an alien shapeshifter. Robert Heinlein's *The Puppet Masters* (1951) has slug-like aliens taking over human victims and forcing them to work against their fellow Homo sapiens.

Alien infiltrators arrived on the movie screen with the Martian invader (Roy Barcroft) in *The Purple Monster Strikes* (1945). By replacing a human scientist (James Craven) the Monster gets the inside scoop on what the good guys are doing to stop him. In 1953's *Invaders from Mars*, Martians infiltrate a small town, turning everyone around the kid protagonist—his parents, the cops, his best friend—into enemies. In *It Conquered the World* (1956), a Venusian hitches a ride on a U.S. space satellite, then begins mind-controlling key people once it lands on Earth.

Television loves this approach. Series TV doesn't usually have the budget to show an epic *War of the World*s-scale battle week after week. An invasion where the invaders look just like everyone else and sneak around rather than blowing up the White House is much more affordable. In the *Outer Limits* episodes "Corpus Earthling" and "The Invisibles" alien entities take over humans as their agents. The second season *Twilight Zone* episode "Will the Real Martian Please Stand Up?" plays the idea for laughs: someone in a diner is an alien, but which one? In a twist it turns out there are two aliens, from rival planets.

In *The Invaders* (1967–68), David Vincent (Roy Thinnes) discovers aliens have infiltrated American society. He tries and fails to convince the government of the threat but does succeed in thwarting the aliens' plans week after week. In the 1988 *War of the Worlds* TV series the heroes did have government backing in their fight against the bodysnatching Martians, but they were an anomaly. On *The X-Files* (1993–2020) Scully and Mulder found powerful players in government working against them as they fought against alien infiltrators such as the mind-controlling Oileans.

Several TV pilot movies tried and failed to launch more series, *Annihilator* (1986), *Target: Earth* (1998) and an *Invaders* reboot (1992) among them. Almost all involved a similar set-up to *The Invaders*. Protagonist discovers alien infiltrators. Protagonist can't convince anyone of the threat. Protagonist sets out to wage a lone war.

In many of these stories, everything starts out apparently normal. A few things seem odd, people acting out of character, but nothing the protagonist can pin down. Certainly nothing that suggests people have been brainwashed or replaced. If they ask questions, the aliens have answers. The 1993 *Body Snatchers*, for instance, takes place on a military base. The pods people answer any inconvenient questions with declarations they're just following orders.

Keeping up a patina of normality keeps the protagonist from acting or even figuring out what they should do. It also lets the horror build for the audience. We know something's wrong—when a movie's called *Body Snatchers* the threat's obviously not imaginary—but we have to watch and wait as the characters walk about blind to the threat.

In many films, this slow creeping takeover proves impossible to stop. The original ending for the '56 *Invasion of the Body Snatchers* had the pod people winning; in the 1978 remake, they do win. If humanity triumphs, it's often at a high price. The revised ending for the 1956 version has humanity winning but Miles (Kevin McCarthy) has lost his entire world: the woman he loves is dead and so are the small-town residents he's spent his entire life with.

Whether the story ends well or poorly, getting to the end involves plenty of twists. Anyone, at any point can turn out to be one of Them. A trusted friend can be swapped out for an enemy between scenes. The second season *X-Files* episode, "Colony," introduces a shapeshifting alien bounty hunter (Brian Thompson) hunting down human/alien hybrids. At one point Mulder (David Duchovny) shows up at Scully's (Gillian Anderson) door while she has Mulder on the phone; the guy in the room with her is the shapeshifter. The show's "trust no one" mantra was never more apropos.

A big difference between alien infiltrators and human ones is that Red agents in, say, *I Was a Communist for the FBI* (1951) aren't metaphorical. They're exactly what they appear to be, communist subversives working to undermine America. Aliens invite all kinds of metaphors. Robert Heinlein said *Puppet Masters*' message was that we must be

The greatest asset of *Invaders from Mars* (1953) is the eerie set design by William Cameron Menzies. The visuals subtly set up the big reveal, that the story was a kid's dream all along.

willing to fight all forms of totalitarian tyranny. *Invaders from Mars* (1953) has been seen as a metaphor for Communist propaganda and, according to Patrick Lucanio, a Jungian drama involving "the eruption of the self-archetype into consciousness." *Invasion of the Body Snatchers*, as I'll cover below, has generated all kinds of "what it really means" discussions.

Other films don't invite us to search for subtext. *The Human Duplicators* (1965) is a straight-up spy story in which Martin (George Nader), a secret agent, investigates why several brilliant scientists are turning against their employers, stealing equipment and sometimes showing superhuman strength. Martin's boss assumes it's either China or the Soviet Union subverting America's researchers. Instead, it's an alien agent (Richard Kiel) replacing the scientists with androids. The movie is exactly what it looks like on the surface, a mash-up of James Bond with alien infiltration.

SPOTLIGHT

Invasion of the Body Snatchers *(1956)*

Allied Artists. B&W. 80 minutes. Release date February 5, 1956.

CAST: Kevin McCarthy (Dr. Miles J. Bennell), Dana Wynter (Becky Driscoll), King Donovan (Jack Belicec), Carolyn Jones (Theodora Belicec), Larry Gates (Dr. Daniel Kaufman), Ralph Dumke (Sheriff Grivett), Jean Willes (Nurse Withers), Whit Bissell (Dr. Hill), Richard Deacon (Dr. Bassett), Virginia Christine (Wilma Lentz), Tom Fadden (Uncle Ira), Kenneth Patterson (Driscoll), Guy Way (Sam Janzek), Bobby Clark (Jimmy Grimaldi), Eileen Stevens (Mrs. Grimaldi), Beatrice Maude (Grandmother Grimaldi), Jean Andren (Aunt Eleda), Everett Glass (Dr. Pursey), Dabbs Greer (Mac), Pat O'Malley (Baggage Man), Guy Rennie (Nightclub Proprietor), Marie Selland (Martha), Sam Peckinpah (Charlie Buckholtz), Harry J. Vejar (Grimaldi)

CREDITS: Director: Don Siegel; Script: Daniel Mainwaring; Producer: Walter Wanger; Rewrites: Richard Collins, Sam Peckinpah; Photography: Ellsworth Fredericks; Production Design: Edward Haworth; Set Decoration: Joseph Kish; Editor: Robert S. Eisen.

Despite plenty of competition, Jack Finney's novella *Body Snatchers*—later expanded to novel length and retitled with an added *Invasion Of*—and the first two films based on it remain the definitive work in this subgenre.

The protagonist of Finney's novel, Miles Bennell, is a doctor in Mill Valley, California, his lifelong home (it was also Finney's home at the time). At the start of the novel, Miles gets the news that his high school crush Becky is back in town, divorced and available. Miles, however, is divorced himself, which makes him reluctant to risk his heart again. He's also preoccupied professionally with his patient Wilma. She's irrationally convinced her Uncle Ira has been replaced by an imposter, even though Ira is physically and mentally identical to the man she and Miles know. Becky later tells Miles she's had the same fears about her father.

Miles' friend Jack Belicec shows Miles a body in his basement that looks less like a person and more like a blank template: indeterminate features, no scars, no fingerprints. When Jack's wife Teddy looks at the body later, it's become an exact double of Jack. Miles gets an uneasy sense of what's going wrong in Mill Valley and rushes over to

Becky's father's house. Sure enough, he finds an inert double of Becky in the basement and quickly takes Becky away.

Kaufman, the town psychiatrist, assures Miles everything is normal. Miles, Becky and the Belicecs aren't convinced, and come to believe the threat ties into a strange worldwide meteor shower some months earlier. They're right to be suspicious; when they hide out in the Belicec house they find pods growing into duplicates in the basement. As people are only vulnerable to the pods while sleeping, staying awake keeps the quartet safe.

That's not much of a victory as the pod-born duplicates have seized control of Mill Valley. Miles calls a buddy in the Army—unusually for this sort of story the call goes through—who tells him nobody with the power to send in troops would act on such a crazy report. The only hope is to run, but the quartet love their town and aren't willing to abandon it. The price for that loyalty is that the pod people capture Miles and Becky.

The novel slows down at this point as the pods deliver their backstory. In fairness to Finney, this was published in *Collier's*, a mainstream magazine, so the audience may have needed more explanation than if it had appeared in *The Magazine of Fantasy ad Science Fiction*.

The pods did land in the meteor shower and randomly grew into duplicates of anything nearby, even inanimate objects, disintegrating the original. Some of them became human, putting them in a position to grow more pods which could replace more humans. From their perspective they're the same person as the original, but improved, free of humanity's messy emotions. Eventually they'll duplicate every living creature on Earth, send a new generation of pods off to colonize a new world, then slowly die off, leaving Earth lifeless. It's nothing personal, any more than humanity wiping out the passenger pigeon was an act of malice.

In the original novella, the FBI show up and save the day. In the novel, Miles and Becky escape and set fire to a field where more pods are growing. The pods head back into space, looking for a world where the inhabitants won't resist so fiercely; Miles realizes many other people around the world must have been fighting back too.

Despite the talky patch of exposition, the novel is well-executed and creepy as hell. In contrast to Heinlein's malevolent slugs, the pods don't have any malice towards us. Their complete apathy about wiping out humanity makes them more horrifying. And unlike *The X-Files'* shapeshifter, who steals identities, or Heinlein's puppet masters, who steal free will, Finney's body snatchers steal *us*. They replace us with what they consider superior versions, identical except for the lack of feelings, dreams and humanity. To them that's a trivial price.

As the pod process destroys the original, there's no coming back once a pod replaces someone. Many stories involving mind control or brainwashing show the characters heroically resisting conversion. In Finney, there's no you left to fight. The original is dead, long live the new, improved you.

Finney said in a much-quoted letter to Stephen King that there was no deep meaning to any of this. He simply threw together several ideas—a small-town setting, people insisting their family members have been replaced—and built on that. Nevertheless there is a subtext to his story, about the importance of community.[1]

Many characters in Finney's fiction are searching for an old-fashioned community where traditional values and a simpler way of life are the norm. Mill Valley is exactly the type of community they're looking for. It's a place where everyone knows everyone else and everyone else's business and have for years. The death of the town—the pods let everything go to seed to discourage visitors—is part of the horror for Finney. The community rebuilding as the pod people die off and new residents move in is the happy ending.

Some of this carries over into Don Siegel's 1956 adaptation. Films of the 1950s were ambivalent about small towns. Sure, they were warm, cozy communities where everyone knows your name, but they could also be repressive and conformist. Several movies of the decade, such as *Picnic* (1955) and *The Wild One* (1953) show a town cracking as a sexually charged stranger intrudes and breaks the facade. *Invasion of the Body Snatchers* is the reverse. Santa Mira, the town of the film, is a healthy, vibrant community; it's the intruding pods who want to impose a repressive facade.[2]

The movie opens with a framing sequence set at a mental hospital. Two staff doctors (Richard Deacon, Whit Bissell) meet Miles (Kevin McCarthy), an obvious lunatic babbling that the people of Santa Mira have been replaced by aliens. Desperate to convince the doctors, he tells them his story. It begins as he returns early from a medical conference because his nurse Sally (Jean Willes) called to say several of his patients were desperate to see him. They wouldn't discuss their problem with her, nor with the doctors covering for Miles. When Miles arrives in Santa Mira, he sees one of the town's local institutions, a fruit and vegetable stand, has been boarded up.

None of the worried patients show up for their appointments but Miles' old girlfriend Becky (Dana Wynter) drops in, asking Miles to meet with her cousin Wilma (Virginia Christine). When Miles sees Wilma, she tells him her Uncle Ira (Tom Fadden) has been replaced by an imposter. Sure, he looks physically perfect, but something about his emotions just isn't right. A kid patient (Bobby Clark) similarly claims his mother (Eileen Stevens) is not his mother.

Miles finds these claims unsettling but he's more interested in Becky. They're both divorced—Mrs. Bennell couldn't deal with the life of a small-town doctor—and clearly their high-school attraction remains strong. They go out to dinner but discover the local night spot is empty. Nobody's going out to eat any more or getting a drink at the bar and the owner's laid off most of his staff. They run into Danny Kaufman (Larry Gates), a psychiatrist who tells them he's treated several people with the same delusions as Wilma. He describes it as "a reaction to problems in the world," which in the 1950s could mean the Cold War, nuclear Armageddon, integration, juvenile delinquency or all of them combined.

The choice of Kaufman as the voice of reason is a mark of the times. A couple of decades earlier the character might have been a clergyman, a town official or just an older, wiser Santa Mira resident. A town as small as Santa Mira might not have had a psychiatrist. As Ellen Herman says in *The Romance of American Psychiatry,* nobody consulted psychiatrists except for the mentally ill and those rich and avant-garde enough to want psychoanalysis.

During World War II, however, the U.S. military employed a large body of psychiatrists and psychologists for multiple purposes. After the war, with PTSD bedeviling many veterans, the VA became the country's largest employer in the psychiatric field. Many people became aware of psychiatry and the idea that even if you weren't mentally ill, you could benefit from "mental health" treatments. Kaufman's statements about Wilma and others' delusions would have had the weight of an expert's authority behind them, though, of course, he's wrong.

Despite dining alone, Becky and Miles have a great time renewing their romance. Then Miles' friend Jack Belicec (King Donovan), a mystery novelist, asks Miles to his house for an emergency call. When Miles and Becky arrive, Jack and his wife Teddy (Carolyn Jones) show them a body they found in the basement. It's dead, from no discernible cause; it has no fingerprints; and its features are almost blank. When Jack cuts its hand, the body develops an identical cut. The foursome realizes it's Jack's exact height and weight, and begin to wonder if it will eventually assume his face, like it did the cut.

Despite this strangeness, nobody's panicking yet. Miles drops Becky off at her father's house, returns home and discovers the gas company meter reader has planted some sort of large seed pod in his basement. Miles realizes a similar pod must be the source of the half-formed body; uneasy for Becky he sneaks into her father's house through the basement and finds a duplicate of Becky growing there. Although Becky has a hard time waking up, Miles gets her out of the house and brings her home, after which the Belicecs join them.

The next morning Miles and Becky make breakfast with a casual intimacy—the chemistry between the leads is excellent—that suggests they've slept together (the era's Production Code wouldn't allow the film to say it outright). Despite Miles warning Becky not to get involved with a doctor, she has.

The quartet calls the police to investigate the pods. It doesn't help, as Becky's double and the body at the Belicec house have disappeared. Kaufman drops by and assures them Miles just imagined Becky's double. The body at the Belicec home was someone's practical joke—an ordinary corpse, fingerprints removed with acid. A policeman shows up and confirms they found the body in a haystack where the jokesters presumably dumped it.

Miles and the others swallow this story, even though it makes absolutely no sense. Seriously, who'd go to the trouble of stealing a body, erasing the fingerprints and dropping it in Jack's house for a joke? It's the second-weakest moment in the plot. Nevertheless, it satisfies everyone … until Miles discovers more pods in his greenhouse, growing into duplicates of him and his guests. He destroys the pods but there's no longer any doubt that something monstrous is happening.

Up until this point, the horror has been subdued, but now it kicks into high gear. Miles asks an operator to put a long-distance call through to the state capital—you needed an operator for long-distance back then—but she says the lines are all busy. The Belicecs leave town to get help in person, but Miles and Becky decide to stay and fight. They discover the pods are everywhere. Miles overhears Sally talking about putting a pod in a baby's crib. When Miles gasses up the car, the station owner puts a couple of pods in his trunk.

Miles and Becky head to his office and down some stimulants from his medical supplies to stay awake. Then Miles tells Becky, "I see how people have allowed their humanity to drain away, only it happens slowly instead of all at once. They didn't seem to mind … only when we have to fight to stay human do we realize how precious it is to us, how dear—as you are to me."

That the film's message: feelings, love and humanity are good, and some people don't need to become aliens to give them up. As director Don Siegel put it later, "I am sorry to say I have kissed many pods. To be a pod means you have no passion no empathy, you talk automatically. The spark of life has left you."[3]

Having told Becky how much their love means to him, Miles stares out the window with her. They marvel that everything outside looks like Santa Mira on any typical Saturday … until they realize trucks are bringing pods from local farms to families who have relatives in the region. The infestation is spreading.

As if that wasn't bad enough, Jack and Kaufman show up and they're both pods. They explain to Miles that the transformation has fixed all the problems that used to weigh Santa Mira's people down. Once you're taken, "you have no feelings. Only the instinct to survive. Love. Desire. Ambition. Faith. Without them life's so simple." The men deliver this advice in a calm, fatherly tone, sincerely believing they're better versions of themselves. They assure Miles and Becky that once they change, they'll understand.

In the novel, the Belicecs survived unharmed but Siegel goes darker than Finney from this point on. Teddy was supposed to have been hit by a car while she and Jack attempted escaping town; the scene wasn't filmed and she's never mentioned again. But that fits the pods' emotionless nature: Jack no longer misses her so why would he bring her up? Miles and Becky have other things on their mind.

Miles argues with the two men that while they may escape loneliness and pain, they also give up love. The matter-of-fact response is that "you've been in love before. It didn't last. It never does." From the pod viewpoint, that's a win; Miles and Becky don't agree. Using Miles' pharmacopeia they drug both men and walk out, pretending they've been converted. That ruse fails when they see a truck run over a dog without stopping—pod drivers don't care—and Becky shrieks. The couple nevertheless make it out of town ahead of the pods and hide in a nearby cave.

With the stimulants wearing off, Becky collapses into sleep. Miles hears music and realizes anyone who cares enough to play must be human. When he follows the sound, it's just a radio in one of the pod-transporting trucks. Miles returns despondently to the cave and wakes Becky with a kiss. In that instant he knows she's a pod. His voice-over declares that "I never knew what horror was until I kissed Becky," a line even some fans of the movie find overwrought.

Grief-stricken and shell-shocked, Miles runs away from "an inhuman enemy bent on my destruction," one that would stop at nothing to transform the entire world. The pod people pursue him but hold back when he reaches the highway, full of human drivers. Miles tries flagging down a car for help but looks so insane that nobody stops. Watching him stand in the middle of the traffic, shrieking "You're next!" convinces the aliens that nobody will believe him. They head back to town.

After Miles finishes his story, the two doctors agree that he's fit for the psych ward. Then an ambulance brings in a patient injured in a traffic accident involving a farm truck—a truck carrying strange, giant vegetables. The doctors realize Miles isn't crazy and tell the cops to block all the traffic out of Santa Mira. Miles sags against the wall, relief written on his face.

As detailed on the DVD special features, Walter Wanger, a Hollywood producer then working at Allied Artists, read the original *Body Snatchers* novella, saw the potential and bought the rights. Possibly he connected with the story because he identified with the protagonist. Like Miles, Wanger had gone from a respected member of the Hollywood community to outsider, though in his case, the cause was shooting the man he believed was his wife's lover.

Don Siegel got the nod to direct the film which suffered through a protracted search for a title. Kevin McCarthy suggested *Sleep No More*, a reference to *Macbeth*.

That appealed to Siegel, a chronic insomniac, but along with *Better Off Dead* it lost out to *They Came from Another World*. That title lost out to the thuddingly literal *Invasion of the Body Snatchers*. Possibly they'd have gone with Finney's shorter *Body Snatchers* if Boris Karloff's 1945 film *Body Snatcher* hadn't just been rereleased. The final pick lacks the poetry of *Sleep No More* and gives the audience much more of a clue what's happening. However, like *Snakes on a Plane* or *I Married a Monster from Outer Space*, it may be more memorable for its lack of subtlety.[4]

Struggles over the title were nothing compared to the struggle over the ending. Siegel's original movie ended on the scene of Miles screaming "You're next!" on the highway, but Allied Artists executives didn't like it. The exact reason wasn't given but might have been they thought the ending was too dark. An alternative theory is that it came off as over the top and comical to test audience. Or possibly they responded with nervous laughter at the grim finish, which upset the studio suits—it's a horror film, nobody should be laughing!

Wanger's initial solution was to have Orson Welles, either playing a journalist or playing himself, introduce the film, then wrap it up at the end. Welles, however, was flitting around Europe and the filmmakers were never able to pin him down long enough to film the scenes. The framing sequences with the doctors became Plan B.[5]

Siegel also had to struggle with budget: Allied Artists saw *Body Snatchers* as a B-movie, to be made fast and on a low budget, which killed plans to shoot in Mill Valley. The location shooting took place in Sierra Madre, which was more convenient and affordable.

Despite the struggles, the finished film is very good. McCarthy gives a great performance as Miles and the leads make the Miles/Becky relationship entirely believable. The rest of the cast do well in their roles.

The movie starts in a naturalistic setting and slowly slides into nightmare. At first everything's just a little bit off, then the nightmare builds, culminating in Becky's transformation. While shocking, it makes no more sense than the story about the corpse. Miles only left Becky alone for a few minutes and the pods don't duplicate their targets that quickly. Why would a pod even be left in the cave when the aliens had no reason to think anyone would show up there?

For Siegel the heart of the film, as Miles' speech says, was that some people would sooner shut down and sleepwalk through life than risk being hurt. Initially most critics accepted that as the theme. In 1957, critic Ernesto Laura suggested the film was a metaphor for infiltration by communist, "an inhuman enemy bent on my destruction" (in Miles' words) that turns people into servants of an alien agenda. The idea this was the true message of the film became common. Certainly whoever came up with *Better Off Dead* may have been aware of the parallel; it sounds a lot like the Cold War slogan "better dead than Red."[6]

The eerie premise has encouraged multiple other interpretations, such as anti-fascist or anti-conformist. The 1950s was an era of big government and big business, when the conformist "organization man" could do well but might have to smother his true self to get ahead. Critic Peter Biskind suggests it's outwardly anti-communist to cover up that it's criticizing American conformity. Critic Maureen Corrigan suggest it's the fear of people changing: what if the one you love no longer loves you? Film scholar Michael Bliss suggests the entire story is Miles' imagination. He's a divorced failure, trapped in dead-end, small-town life and so he imagines a reality in which his life has value.

At the time the film came out, nobody worried about looking that deeply. Hollywood thought it a flop more than a classic, and few critics disagreed. That changed after it entered television syndication and found growing numbers of fans. That includes Stephen King, who credits it as an influence on *Salem's Lot*: just like the pod people, vampires slowly convert everyone in town from ordinary humans into hostile monsters.

Invasion of the Body Snatchers *(1978)*

MGM. 115 minutes. December 22, 1978.

CAST: Donald Sutherland (Matthew Bennell), Brooke Adams (Elizabeth Driscoll), Jeff Goldblum (Jack Belicec), Veronica Cartwright (Nancy Belicec), Leonard Nimoy (Dr. David Kibner), Art Hindle (Dr. Geoffrey Howell), Lelia Goldoni (Katherine Hendley), Kevin McCarthy (Running Man), Don Siegel (Taxi Driver), Tom Luddy (Ted Hendley), Stan Ritchie (Stan), David Fisher (Gianni), Tom Dahlgren (Detective), Gary Goodrow (Boccardo), Jerry Walter (Restaurant Owner), Maurice Argent (Chef), Sam Conti (Barker), Wood Moy (Tong), R. Wong (Mrs. Tong), Rose Kaufman (Outraged Woman), Joe Bellan (Beggar), Sam Hiona (Policeman), Lee McVeigh (Policeman), Albert Malbandian (Rodent Man), Lee Mines (Teacher), Robert Duvall (Priest)

CREDITS: Director: Philip Kaufman; Screenplay: W.D. Richter, based on Finney novel; Producer: Robert H. Solo; Photography: Michael Chapman; Production Design: Charles Rosen; Editor: Douglas Stewart; Music: Denny Zeitlin

Remaking a classic is always tricky. If you're too faithful to the original, people may wonder what the point of remaking it was. If you make major changes, you may lose what made the original special. In the 1978 *Body Snatchers*, Philip Kaufman and screenwriter W.D. Richter found the sweet spot.

If we take the Siegel film as a metaphor for enforced conformity, it still isn't endorsing nonconformity. The film is about the right of the conventional, middle-class residents of Santa Mira to live the way they choose. They might not feel the same about beatniks or left-wing activists. In Kaufman's film, instead of a small town, the setting is San Francisco. Instead of a group of successful middle-class protagonists, the core cast are eccentric oddballs and losers. In this film, even they have a right to live the way they prefer.

The film opens on an alien landscape. As the credits roll, clouds of gossamer-like threads rise into the air, then drift into space. Eventually they descend on Earth, then on San Francisco. Settling on leaves and plants, they begin to grow stems and blossoms. Elizabeth (Brooke Adams), a health-department scientist, recognizes one of the plants is unique and plucks it to take home. When Elizabeth arrives, her dentist boyfriend Geoffrey (Art Hindle) pulls her into a clinch, then resumes watching the San Francisco Warriors basketball team on TV. Elizabeth tries to research the plant, which she believes is a hybrid, but Geoffrey thoughtlessly keeps distracting her until she gives up and moves to another room.

Cut to Elizabeth's colleague and best friend, health inspector Matthew Bennell (Donald Sutherland). He finds a rat turd in a dish at an elegant French restaurant and tells them he'll have their permit revoked. When he leaves, he discovers someone on the staff cracked his car front window with a wine bottle. Later that night, Matthew clips out a newspaper article about the strange webs drifting over the city—he's a compulsive collector of such articles—and chats with Elizabeth on the phone. After they hang up,

Elizabeth falls asleep on top of Geoffrey. The flower, sitting in a glass of water by the bed, begins to grow.

Next morning Elizabeth finds Geoffrey slipped out from under her without waking her up. He's already dressed and is sweeping something off the floor, which he takes out to a nearby trash truck. Normally Geoffrey's a physically affectionate lug but now he barely acknowledges Elizabeth's touch. When she walks to the office past neighborhood busker Harry (Joe Bellan) and his dog, she sees an elderly man running past in apparent panic but doesn't pay it much attention. It comes off as a comment on big-city isolation; back in Santa Mira, Miles would have known who the guy was and stopped to see if he needed help. Of course, while it looks like the man was fleeing pod people—the pod warning scream is faintly audible in the background—it's possible he's just worried about missing a bus.

At work, Elizabeth tells Matthew she feels uneasy about Geoffrey but can't pin down why. She becomes more uneasy in the evening when Geoffrey goes to a meeting instead of the big basketball game, telling her he gave away his tickets. Elizabeth hugs her man for reassurance but gets none, nor any reaction. She rushes over to Matthew, telling him Geoffrey's not the same person. Matthew recommends she talk to his friend David Kibner (Leonard Nimoy), a psychiatrist and successful self-help author. Matthew makes it clear he's not dismissing her fears, but he thinks Kibner can help narrow down the possibilities: is Geoffrey acting odd because he has a social disease, an affair, he's realized he's gay?

Odd events accumulate. Matthew's dry-cleaner insists his spouse is not the same person. Elizabeth trails Geoffrey and sees him exchange items with strangers across San Francisco, as if he were part of some conspiracy. When Matthew drives Elizabeth to Kibner's book-signing, a man (Kevin McCarthy) flings himself on the car, screaming "they're here!" then running off with a mob in pursuit. A car kills him a second later. Matthew calls in the accident from the bookshop but even though he saw cops on the scene, the department says no accident has been reported.

At the signing Miles meets his buddy Jack Belicec (Jeff Goldblum) who in this version is a frustrated poet rather than a successful novelist. Jack takes six months to write one perfect line of poetry and looks down his nose disdainfully at Kibner, who can dash off a couple of books a year. Jack also hates that Kibner tries changing people to fit society rather than changing society to better fit people.

Like Dr. Kaufman in the Siegel version, this reflects the movie's era. Psychiatrists in the 1950s and 1960s had indeed seen fitting square pegs into round holes as part of their duties. By the 1970s, Ellen Herman says, there was an "antipsychiatry" critique that argued most of what psychiatry called mental illness was a logical reaction to the world's problems.

On the DVD commentary track, Kaufman describes Kibner as a falsely reassuring authority figure, the guy who assures you everything's fine when you know it isn't. At the signing, Elizabeth sees the doctor comfort a woman (Lelia Goldoni) who's convinced her husband (Tom Luddy) has been replaced by a stranger. Elizabeth tries to talk to the woman, but Kibner shuts her down and convinces the woman to go home with her husband. When Elizabeth recognizes the man as one of Geoffrey's conspirators, she gives the woman her number and invites her to call and talk.

Kibner says he's constantly hearing worries that people are changing and becoming less human. Elizabeth says that's not her problem but Kibner talks over her, saying the issue is people getting into relationships too fast. Matthew objects that Kibner's not listening. The doctor says yes, he is. Just like the woman they were talking to, he's hearing Elizabeth saying she wants to end the relationship; imagining her partner is different is just an excuse. Elizabeth, now doubting her own instincts, agrees to wait before acting. Kibner later tells Matthew this may be another case of a "hallucinatory fugue" going around.

Matthew takes Elizabeth home, where they find Geoffrey's left her a plant—yes, one of the special plants—with a thank-you note. The friends say goodbye, unaware of Geoffrey lurking and listening around the corner. Jack goes home from the signing to the mud-bath spa where he works with his wife Nancy (Veronica Cartwright), a pseudoscience believer who reads books like Immanuel Velikovsky's *Worlds in Collision* and Olaf Stapledon's classic science fiction.

After Nancy discovers a strange, half-formed body at the baths, covered with fine vines, Jack calls in Matthew, who recognizes the body as a crude copy of Jack. Matt calls Elizabeth for her opinion but there's no answer; we see that she's asleep and her body is breaking down. Matthew calls Kibner, then heads off to Geoffrey's place. After he leaves, Jack becomes strangely tired and lies down for a nap, at which point the body opens its eyes. Nancy's scream on seeing this wakes up her husband; the body immediately shuts its eyes again. The Belicecs race out through the lobby, where Kibner is waiting.

In the psychiatrist's first appearance he was effusive, smiling, always quick to explain problems away; now he's somber. The body has vanished so Kibner, like Kaufman in the '56 film, suggests a practical joke. Nancy notices the window is open and there's a trash truck outside but doesn't attach any significance to it. It's obvious to us that after the duplication failed, Kibner had the truck dispose of the body.

Matthew calls Elizabeth but Geoffrey won't let him speak to her. Uneasy, Matthew breaks in while Geoffrey watches the TV test pattern (in the days before 24/7 program, that was what you saw if you stayed up late enough). Matthew finds Elizabeth asleep in one bed, a vine-covered duplicate of her in the other. He gets Elizabeth to safety, then brings the cops back to Geoffrey's house. The duplicate has vanished too, of course, and only Kibner's intervention saves Matthew from arrest. Matthew tells Geoffrey that Elizabeth won't be coming home. Geoffrey accepts this calmly but he and the cops gaze at each other ominously afterwards.

Everyone holes up at Matthew's house and tries to convince Kibner the bodies were real. Jack begins to doubt what he saw but finally Kibner says he trusts Matthew too much not to take him seriously. Matthew suggests they treat it like a quarantine and convinces Kibner to work out a plan with city hall. Kibner agrees, leaves, and gets into Geoffrey's car outside.

Back at the apartment, Jack finds another of the sinister flowers. As the quartet puts things together Nancy suggests it's an invasion and wonders "why do we always expect metal ships?" Jack, a materialist, says he's never expected metal ships. Nancy speculates the plants are transforming us the same way ancient astronauts "could mate with monkeys and create the human race."

Matthew contacts several city officials, all of whom say they're working on the problem and that he mustn't go public prematurely. He wanders the crowded streets, finding himself increasingly uneasy among the people—or are they people? His dry-cleaner and the woman Elizabeth talked to are now perfectly happy, saying they've gotten over those silly ideas about their spouses.

When Kibner drops by again, he suggests that given the foursome's stress, they should take some sleeping pills. It won't surprise you that pods have been placed in Matthew's greenhouse; they start to grow into duplicates, an overlong sequence that serves mostly to show off the special effects, Nancy wakes and snaps the other three out of it. Matthew calls the cops again but the person who picks up knows his name before he gives it. Shaken, he hangs up and tries calling a contact in the federal government. The call doesn't go through. Pod people surround the house and pod electricians cut off the power.

Matthew and the others make a run for it, but the pods are all around and they're watching for the fugitives. When the pods spot the humans, they let out a shrill, alien scream, alerting the rest of their kind. The humans run on through a city that's otherwise unnaturally quiet except for the fugitives' racing footsteps and the noise of the pod mob behind them. The pods hunt them on foot, on police motorcycles and in police helicopters overhead. Finally, the runners reach a dead end. Jack sacrifices himself, rushing off loudly to draw the pursuit away. Nancy follows him.

Elizabeth and Matthew walk away, trying not to attract attention. In an eerie scene they find themselves walking down a street with pod people behind them. Uneasy, the couple move faster which makes the pods move faster—and then Matthew and Elizabeth find they're reached the city's red-light district. They're surrounded by strip clubs and topless clubs with barkers hawking their wares at the top of their voices. It's sleazy, but so human it's a relief.

They hail a cabby (Don Siegel) to get to the airport but he's a pod person and almost delivers them to the police. The couple get away, then stumble over Harry, asleep and in the middle of being podded. He won't wake up, so Elizabeth and Matthew keep running.

The two friends hole up at the health department. Huddled together they kiss, silently expressing feelings they couldn't show when she was with Geoffrey. Staring out the window, they see large crowds of people carrying pods onto buses. It would seem to make more sense to carry flowers, but the visual wouldn't be as obvious. They're both exhausted so they borrow from a colleague's amphetamine stash to stay awake.

A quintet of pods, with Jack, Geoffrey and Kibner enter the lab and capture the fugitives. While Kibner prepares a sedative, Jack assures them nothing will change—they'll have the same memories, wear the same clothes, nothing different but the absence of emotion. Kibner echoes Jack Finney, telling Matthew the duplicates aren't acting from malice: they don't hate, any more than they love. It's about survival, nothing more.

By this point the pods have left except for Jack and Kibner. Matt and Elizabeth take the sedative and fake the effects long enough to get the drop on their captors and lock them in the lab freezer. As they leave, they encounter Nancy's pod duplicate, then she reveals she's faking it. The pods can be fooled.

The three humans join a crowd of pod people boarding a bus for Sausalito, each taking a pod with them. It looks like they'll get away but then they see Harry's head on his dog's body, the result of a botched duplication. Elizabeth loses it, the pods notice, and she and Matt have to race off. Nancy, maintaining her poker face, walks away in another direction.

Escaping their pursuers, Elizabeth and Matthew end up at the harbor, where Matthew tells her he loves her. Elizabeth has hurt her ankle so when they hear *Amazing Grace* coming from one of the ships, Matthew leaves her behind while he sneaks over to see who's human enough to play music. As in the original film, it's just a radio, on a ship laden with a cargo of pods. He returns to find Elizabeth has collapsed into sleep and won't wake up. He takes her in his arm, telling her they're going to escape … and her body crumbles. A new, naked Elizabeth rises, assuring him, "It's painless. It's good. Come. Sleep."

A furious Matthew races into a nearby greenhouse growing more of the pods and wreaks havoc, starting fires and slashing at wires. When the Eliza-pod alerts the others to his presence, he escapes outside while the aliens put out the fire. One of the pods remarks that it's not a problem—he'll have to sleep eventually.

The final scene begins with a stony-faced Matt walking to work as a school trip takes kids somewhere they can be podded. Matt heads into the health department where Elizabeth and her fellow techies are at work. When they don't have a task to do, they simply stand around, waiting, without talking or doing anything. Elizabeth, with no makeup, hair pulled back, is as emotionless as he is. At lunchtime everyone walks out, nobody talking or interacting. Nancy comes up to Matthew, revealing she's still human—and Matthew issues the pod people scream. Game over.

This was one of the first remakes of the 1950s SF movies. Quite aside from the next two Body Snatcher films, there have been two remakes of *The Thing from Another World*, several *War of the Worlds* films, two of *The Time Machine,* three versions of *Not of This Earth* and the 2008 *The Day the Earth Stood Still*. Having Don Siegel and Kevin McCarthy appear in cameos—the kind of Easter egg now standard for any remake—was a novel idea at the time. It didn't sit well with one critic who asked, baffled, if Miles had been running screaming through traffic since 1956.

The pod people here really do see themselves as superior beings, the 2.0 upgrade of the originals. They're perfectly mellow, no worries or stress, completely complacent at work and off the job, perfectly well-adjusted to their role in life. Where the '56 duplicates could fake humanity, these aliens don't even try. They're living life on autopilot the way Miles worried about, as willing to watch a test pattern as a TV show. On the commentary track, Kaufman says this is corporate America's ideal, drones who will do their jobs and buy stuff but won't ever cause trouble or challenge the status quo. From the pods' perspective, the life Elizabeth and Matthew are living in the closing scenes is a happy ending.

The lifelessness of the pods makes a sharp contrast to the core four. Matthew and Elizabeth are working in jobs that protect the public; Jack is a sarcastic, frustrated failed poet; Nancy is sweet, eccentric and stronger than she looks. Elizabeth has a trick rolling her eyes that's delightfully goofy, and that pod-Elizabeth will undoubtedly never perform.

Where Matthew and Becky in the Siegel version are fighting for love, Matthew and Elizabeth are fighting for friendship. They know each other well: Matthew begins a joke at one point, she reminds him he's already told it to her, then they laugh at the unspoken punchline. Even though Matthew's feels more for her than friendship, there's never a suggestion he resents her choosing Geoffrey. Unlike Geoffrey and Kibner, Matthew listens when Elizabeth talks and accepts what she says.

The jump from Santa Mira to San Francisco dissatisfied some viewers who'd seen the original. It works, but in a different way. In the 1956 version, Miles knows everyone in town; part of the horror is looking at Sally, Kaufman, the meter reader and realizing they're now enemies. In the '78, the horror is all the people you don't know. We constantly see people standing around, apparently doing nothing, in hallways, on street corners, outside stores. Are they pods? Are they just standing around and we're reading things into it? We have no way to know. Neither do Matthew or Elizabeth.

San Francisco had been the heart of 1960s counterculture, but by 1978 that spirit had crumbled. Instead of achieving the Age of Aquarius, Ronald Reagan would become president in 1980, kicking off a long conservative pushback against all the social changes of the previous two decades.

Kaufman says in the Making Of features that he watched a great deal of film noir to recreate the feeling of noir in a color film. This was a novel idea at the time—*noir* was associated with B&W and shadow—though 1980s neo-noir films such as *Body Double* and *Blood Simple* would make it normal. The soundtrack helps, from Denny Zeitlin's discordant music to the slow loss of natural noise as the film progresses, in favor of the omnipresent garbage truck.

Sound effect editor Ben Burtt said he used a number of sources to provide the sounds of the pods growing and taking shape. They included the squishy noise of his own baby in his wife's womb and the sound of breathing through a scuba oxygen regulator. Bonnie Koehler, the supervising sound editor, ripped apart vegetables and fruits to get an added effect for the pods busting open. Burtt created the chilling pod scream by using high-pitched pig squeals because they sounded close enough to something a human throat could make.

OTHER FILMS AND TELEVISION

The Aliens Are Coming (1980) A failed pilot about a government scientist leading the fight against bodysnatching energy beings from space.

Annihilator (1986) Another failed TV pilot. A man discovers his fiancée is one of multiple people replaced by super-strong alien "dynamators."

The Beast with a Million Eyes (1955) A family living on an isolated ranch come under attack from an alien with the power to dominate and control both animals and human beings.

Body Snatchers (1993) Gabrielle Anwar battles pods taking over a military base.

The Brain Eaters (1958) Mind-controlling parasites take over a town with Leonard Nimoy's help.

Choker (2005) The authorities release a serial killer from prison to hunt down aliens possessing and controlling humans. Also known as *Disturbance*.

The Day Mars Invaded Earth (1963) Martians plot to replace a space researcher and his family so that they can prevent Earth landing a probe on Mars.

Enemy from Space (1957) In the second Quatermass film, alien invaders land in Britain and take over human being.

First Wave (1998–2001) A security expert pits himself against the alien infiltrators serving as the "first wave" of a conquering alien horde.

Imposter (2001) Forty-five years after an alien invasion, a scientist (Gary Sinise) finds the military hunting him in the belief he's an alien android.

The Invasion (2007) Instead of pods, this fourth adaptation of Finney spreads the transformation by xenobacteria. The film makes the pod people so nice, it comes off as a shame we regain our humanity.

Invasion of the Pod People (2007) A mockbuster by The Asylum released to coincide with 2007's *The Invasion*. Aliens replace sexy models and get frisky with each other.

It Conquered the World (1956) A Venusian alien aided by a misguided human scientist plants mind-control devices on human victims as Step One in its plan of conquest. Remade in 1966 as *Zontar, the Thing from Venus*.

The Puppet Masters (1994) An adaptation of the Heinlein novel. Federal agents discover alien parasites have taken over a small town.

Robin Cook's Invasion (1997) Victims of alien mind control build a space gate that can bring the rest of their people to Earth for conquest.

Seedpeople (1992) A bad direct-to-video *Body Snatchers* knockoff.

Slither (2006) Alien parasite possesses residents of a small town, the first step in colonizing the entire planet.

Stephen King's The Tommyknockers (1993) The occupants of a crashed alien spaceship gain control of the minds of local residents by granting their wishes.

Strange Invaders (1983) In a pastiche of alien infiltrator films, a reporter discovers a small town has been occupied by aliens since the 1950s.

Target Earth (1998) In this unsuccessful TV pilot, a cop discovers alien "Implants" laying the groundwork for an invasion.

They Live (1988) A drifter discovers many of Earth's richest and most powerful people are secretly ETs exploiting the rest of us.

Threshold (2005) An alien energy mutates human DNA, transforming ordinary people into willing alien agents. A covert government agency sets out to stop them.

Under the Dome (2013–2015) TV series about an alien body-stealing species that shuts off a small town from the rest of the world with an impenetrable dome.

FIVE

Might for Right, Not Might Makes Right

Alien Superheroes

"There is one man on Earth who will never bow to you."
—*Superman II*

Alien superheroes—Superman, Supergirl, Thor (in the Marvel Cinematic Universe, Asgard is simply another planet)—take it a step beyond friendly, helpful aliens. Klaatu wants to help but he doesn't want to stay. Superheroes stick around

As the narration to George Reeves' *Adventures of Superman* series says, these heroes fight a never-ending battle. They put their lives on the line for humanity day after day, never giving up. There's always another supervillain to capture, an alien invasion to thwart, an innocent life to save or a cat to get out of a tree.

Superheroes have been subject to a thousand interpretations. They're a power fantasy for adolescent boys, they're Freudian, they're fascist. They inspire us to be heroes. They inspire us to sit around passively, waiting for heroes. They're the dream of shy boys that if a woman could just see behind our glasses, she'd realize we were amazing. As the comics writer Kurt Busiek says, that's part of their appeal. Writers can shape superheroes to fit almost any agenda or metaphor. Power fantasies for girls. A political statement about immigrants. A fantasy of obtaining justice in a world that all too often lacks it.[1]

Like alien infiltrators, the appeal of superheroes isn't primarily what they might symbolize. It's about the sheer spectacle of a man who's faster than a speeding bullet, more powerful than a locomotive and able to leap tall buildings at a single bound. That heroes are shown fighting injustice in what looks like the world we're living in is a plus. It doesn't make much sense—just knowing for certain that alien life 100 percent exists would be a game-changer for science and culture. What would Thor's presence on Earth do to religious studies? But imagining the realistic results of Superman or Thor isn't as engaging as imagining that they could almost be real. That we could be the one looking up at the sky saying, "It's a bird ... no, it's a plane ... it's Superman!"

Comic-book superheroes and alien superheroes both have the same starting point: Superman's debut in *Action Comics* #1. As explained on the first page, his unnamed parents rocketed him away from their planet before it exploded. When he landed on Earth a passing couple, also unnamed, found and adopted him. Because his homeworld's people had evolved far beyond Earth humans, he exhibited amazing strength, speed and invulnerability (later revisions credited his powers to the energy of Earth's sun). Growing to adulthood, he vowed to use his powers for good, as Superman.

The pulps had given America near-superhuman heroes such as Doc Savage, and vigilantes with secret identities such as the Shadow and the Spider. Superman combined elements of both and a whole lot more. None of what creators Jerry Siegel and Joe Shuster gave us was completely new but they threw so many things in the blender the result felt completely original:

- A super-evolved human with amazing powers, a familiar concept in pulp science fiction.
- A circus strongman's costume. There were many musclemen performing on stage in the 1930s, and some of their stunts looked like dry runs for Superman's amazing strength.
- A crusading reporter.
- A crimefighting vigilante, another pulp staple.
- A hero hiding his greatness behind an ineffective cover identity, as Zorro and the Scarlet Pimpernel had done.
- A man from another world.

As Brad Ricca's *Super Boys* details, Siegel and Shuster tried different Superman concepts earlier in their teenage career before they found the one that became a legend. They'd tried pitching Superman as a newspaper strip without success but created and worked on several other characters for the company that became DC Comics. With newspaper syndication a flop, they showed Superman to DC. The company bought all rights and used some of the newspaper strips in the first issue of *Action Comics*.

There'd been many fictional characters who could perform amazing physical feats, but the sight of Superman lifting a car over his head on *Action* #1's cover was a whole new level of awesome. The stories weren't deep—few early comics were—but they provided a steady stream of spectacular super-stunts. Jerry Siegel's scripts also had a ripped-from-the-headlines quality. In early issues Superman battled lynch mobs, corrupt business owners, warmongering arms dealers, reckless drivers—a serious problem in Siegel and Shuster's Cleveland hometown—and representatives of sinister foreign powers.

Countless books on comics have tried to nail down Superman's roots. Philip Wylie's *Gladiator*, about a superman created by in utero drug treatments, is often cited as a probable inspiration. Did Siegel's father's fatal heart attack during a robbery inspire him to dream of a hero who couldn't die? Did the dream that a Superman lay under the boys' shy exterior inspire Clark Kent? Was the golem, a Jewish protector with superhuman strength, an influence? Does his dual identity reflect the pressure on American Jews to assimilate and not seem too ethnic? People have seen all these in Superman at one point or another.

Comic-book publishers didn't care about Superman's origins or any subtext that came with him. What they cared about was that he became a certified hit. Not only did he become the star of *Action*, an anthology comic, but he earned a series of his own, a rare thing in those days. DC and other publishers introduced multiple other costumed crimefighters before superheroes fell out of vogue at the end of the 1940s. Only Superman, Batman and Wonder Woman stuck around until the superhero revival that began in the late 1950s.

A number of later heroes were extraterrestrials such as Supergirl, Hawkman, Martian Manhunter, Captain Marvel, Starman, the Comet and the Silver Surfer (several of these names have been held by multiple heroes and not all of the name-bearers were ETs). Being a strange visitor from another planet was far from the only possible origin but it has undeniable advantages.

For one, the writer doesn't have to explain how the hero got powers if he was born with them. For another, it sets up plenty of potential conflicts. Will the hero feel at home on Earth or feel a perpetual outcast? Will Earth accept them or distrust them? If their own people show up, will the hero choose their side or ours? In the *Justice League* cartoon (2001–06) Hawkwoman is a soldier from the planet Thanagar. When the Thanagarias invade, she winds up siding with Earth against her own people at great personal cost.

While several alien superheroes have appeared on screen in the past quarter-century, for decades it was almost entirely Superman. There hasn't been a decade since the 1940s when the Man of Steel wasn't on-screen in either cartoon or live-action form.

In 1940 Superman debuted on movie screens in a series of cartoons from the Fleischer brothers' studio. The Fleischers were cartoon wizards and the series looked spectacular as it pitted Superman against mad scientists, giant robots and other challenges. Although Superman leaped rather than flew in the comics, the Fleischers thought that looked ridiculous and, like the *Superman* radio series of the era, had him fly.[2]

After Paramount took control from the Fleischers, the studio cut costs and quality both. The 1941 cartoons were visually blander and the villains were mostly non-super Japanese and Nazi spies. Typically for the time, the treatment of the Japanese was painfully racist.[3]

The cartoon killed a Republic Studios proposal to make a live-action Superman movie serial. DC's deal with the Fleischers didn't allow for a competing production. Super-fans had to wait until 1948 for Columbia's *Superman* serial. This had an excellent Superman in Kirk Allyn and the first chapter included a much-expanded origin. Columbia couldn't figure out how to make Superman fly believably, however, so they settled for using a cartoon for flying scenes. Republic, which had done cutting-edge flying effects for the *Adventures of Captain Marvel* (1941) wouldn't have had to go that route. Even so, the serial did well enough to justify a superior follow-up, *Atom Man vs. Superman* (1950), though the flying was still a cartoon.

That was only the beginning for the Kryptonian Crimebuster. The 1950s gave us *Superman and the Mole Men* (1951) starring George Reeves, as well as his successful TV series. In the 1960s Superman had a TV cartoon series, followed by *Super Friends* in the 1970. The 1970s also gave us the definitive Man of Steel in Christopher Reeve's *Superman* and its sequels. Ilya and Alex Salkind, the producers of the Reeve films, later used the rights to launch a good *Superboy* series (1988–92).

Other than *Supergirl* (1984) few alien superheroes made it to the screen until the 21st century. Strange as it seems in an age when the Marvel Cinematic Universe (MCU) is a billion-dollar franchise, superheroes weren't seen as viable big-screen properties. Maybe if they were done tongue-in-cheek, like the 1960s *Batman* TV series and related movies, but serious? No way.

Tongue was definitely in cheek for ABC's *The Greatest American Hero* (1981–84), one of several superheroes who, while not alien, got their powers from aliens. Ralph Hinkley (William Katt) was a schoolteacher that aliens selected to fight evil on Earth, using a costume that gave him super-powers and a grumpy FBI sidekick, Bill Maxwell

(Robert Culp). The idea of aliens endowing a human with crimefighting abilities had been around for years in comic books but it was novel on TV.

The most successful television version of that concept was the *Mighty Morphin' Power Rangers*. When the alien sorceress Rita Repulsa (played by multiple actors) sets her sights on conquering Earth, her ancient enemy Zordon (ditto) gives a team of teenagers the power to morph into Power Rangers when danger threatens. Mixing Japanese footage from the *Super Sentai* series with new American footage, it was a smash hit. The series started in 1993 and never stopped, though some versions, such as the *Power Rangers Time Force*, have nothing to do with aliens.

The 1990s also gave us a live-action TV Superman in *Lois and Clark* and a cartoon version in *Superman: The Animated Adventures*. In the 21st century, Superman's movie adventures have been few but the WB's *Smallville* (2001–11) became one of the hero's most successful television series. He's also appeared in *Superman and Lois* (2021–) and multiple direct-to-DVD animated movies.

The growing number of cable companies and streaming services, plus the success of the MCU, have brought other alien heroes to the screen. Melissa Benoist played the CW's *Supergirl* from 2015 to 2021. DC's Martian Manhunter, last survivor of his dead world, has appeared in the *Justice League* cartoon, *Smallville* and *Supergirl*. Chris Hemsworth has played Marvel's Thor in multiple movies and his brother *Loki* (Tom Hiddleston) got his own series (2021–) on the Disney + streaming channel.

The alien-powered human hero hasn't gone away either. In the first episode of the animated *Ben 10* (2005–08, plus three subsequent series), young Ben Tennyson (Tara Strong) discovers an alien bracelet device inside a meteor. Using it, he can temporarily transform into any of ten alien forms to fight against evil. In *The Middleman* (2008), artist Wendy Watson (Natalie Morales) joins a secret, alien-backed crimefighting agency whose other agent (Matt Keeslar) has no idea who's behind it—he's just the Middleman. Together Wendy and her boss battled gorilla gangsters, zombie flying fish, a cursed tuba and other weirdness.

Superman or Super-Menace?

Despite the massive profits of the MCU, it's unlikely to dislodge Superman from his position in pop culture. He's one of the few fictional characters almost everyone knows. Even his supporting cast—Lois Lane, Lex Luthor, Jimmy Olsen—are familiar to people who've never read a comic book.

Because he's so successful, creators can put their own spin on the Superman concept in complete confidence the audience knows what they're doing. Amazon Prime's *Invincible* (2021) gives us the mighty alien superhero Omni-Man (J.K. Simmons), Superman in all but name, with a devoted wife (Sandra Oh), and an admiring son, Mark (Steven Yuen). In the opening episode, Omni-Man meets with his team, the Guardians of the Globe, and kills them. He's not a hero, he's a sleeper agent sent by his people, the Viltrumites, to lay the groundwork for conquest. Can Mark, using his inherited powers as Invincible, stop his unstoppable father from selling out the planet?

In *Brightburn* (2019), Brandon (Jackson A. Dunn) is a foundling from space adopted by a childless couple, manifesting super-powers as he hits puberty. He's also hearing voices in his head telling him that his mission, like Omni-Man's, is to rule us rather than protect us. Given how many times DC Comics has explored the idea of an evil Superman, this film was nowhere as revolutionary as the creators may have thought.

Some of those evil Superman have shown up on screen. In the syndicated *Superboy* series (1988–92), a third season episode has Superboy (Gerard Christopher) stranded on a parallel world. His counterpart's rocket from Krypton landed not on the Kent farm but a few hundred yards away, on the property of Smallville's wealthiest resident. Kal-El's foster father raised him to become a privileged, arrogant ass-hat. Now, as the Sovereign, he rules the Earth with an iron fist.

In *Superman: Red Son* (2020)—based on a limited series written by Mark Millar—Superman lands not in the wheat fields of Kansas but the wheat fields of the pre–World War II Ukraine. He grows up Communist and eventually shows his powers to Stalin, putting them at the service of the state. It becomes obvious to the U.S. government that nuclear bombs are no longer enough to protect the United States—can American genius Lex Luthor find a weapon to stop the Soviet Superman?

With the growth of the Marvel Cinematic Universe, the Marvel characters are getting in on the alternative timeline action. One episode of the Disney + series *What If …* (2021–) shows an alternate timeline where Thor was an only child, instead of stepbrother to Loki. Without his conniving sibling Thor becomes an irresponsible party animal. When he runs wild on Earth, even SHIELD can't stop him.

Spotlight

Superman *(1978)*

Warner Brothers. 143 minutes. Release date December 15, 1978.

CAST: Christopher Reeve (Superman/Clark Kent), Margot Kidder (Lois Lane), Gene Hackman (Lex Luthor), Marlon Brando (Jor-El), Valerie Perrine (Eve Teschmacher), Ned Beatty (Otis), Jackie Cooper (Perry White), Glenn Ford (Pa Kent), Phyllis Thaxter (Ma Kent), Trevor Howard (1st Elder), Jack O'Halloran (Non) General Zod (Terence Stamp) Maria Schell (Vond-Ah), Jeff East (Young Clark Kent), Marc McClure (Jimmy Olsen), Sarah Douglas Ursa), Susannah York (Lara), Harry Andrews (2nd Elder), Vass Anderson (3rd Elder), John Hollis (4th Elder), James Garbutt (5th Elder), Michael Gover (6th Elder), David Neal (7th Elder), William Russell (8th Elder), Penelope Lee (9th Elder), John Stuart (10th Elder), Alan Cullen (11th Elder), Lee Quigley (Baby Kal-El), Aaron Smolinski (Baby Clark), Diane Sherry (Lana Lang), Jeff Atcheson (Coach), Brad Flock (Football Player), David Petrou (Team Manager), Billy J. Mitchell (1st editor), Robert Henderson (2nd Editor), Larry Lamb (1st Reporter) James Brockington (2nd Reporter), John Cassady (3rd Reporter), John F. Parker (4th reporter), Antony Scot (5th reporter), Ray Evans (6th reporter), Su Shifrin (7th Reporter), Miquel Brown (8th Reporter), Vincent Marzello (1st Copy Boy), Benjamin Feitelson (2nd Copy Boy), Lise Hilboldt (1st Secretary), Leueen Willoughby (2nd Secretary), Jill Ingham (3rd Secretary), Pieter Stuyck (Window Cleaner)

CREDITS: Director: Richard Donner; Screenwriters: Mario Puzo, David Newman, Leslie Newman, Robert Benton; Story: Mario Puzo; Creative Consultant Tom Mankiewicz; Producer: Pierre Spengler; Executive Producer: Ilya Salkind; Associate Producer: Charles F. Greenlaw; Production Designer: John Barry; Photography: Geoffrey Unsworth Editor: Stuart Baird; Music: John Williams

Superman—while it was widely referred to as *Superman: the Motion Picture* that's not the title on screen—opens on Krypton, a cold, sterile world with icy, crystalline architecture. As the film begins, we see Jor-El (Marlon Brando), one of the members of the Science Council, in a robe bearing a coat of arms identical to Superman's S symbol. Jor-El presides over the sentencing of Zod (Terence Stamp), Ursa (Sarah Douglas) and Non (Jack O'Halloran), three criminals who sought to take over Krypton. The Council condemns the trio to the Phantom Zone, a dimensional prison where they'll exist as disembodied wraiths for eternity.

Jor-El's successful prosecution is followed by failure: he can't convince the Science Council that Krypton is about to explode. The skeptical council makes Jor-El promise he won't attempt to leave Krypton ahead of his imaginary apocalypse. Jor-El, however, says nothing about his plans to send his son Kal to the planet Earth, where the environment and solar radiation will make him superhumanly powerful. Kal's rocket launches seconds before Krypton shatters. Some of the fragments turn green as they hurtle away into space.

Over the course of the long trip to Earth, a Jor-El hologram tells baby Kal his history. The ship crashes on Earth, almost smashing into a truck driven by Jonathan Kent (Glenn Ford) with his wife Martha (Phyllis Thaxter) beside him. When Martha discovers the baby, she wants to keep it but Jonathan's less enthused. He changes his mind while jacking up the truck to change a tire. The jack collapses but the baby holds up the truck, saving Jonathan's life.

We leap ahead to Clark (Jeff East) as a teenager. Where Krypton was cold, Smallville is warm and sunny, an idealized American small town. Life isn't all Norman Rockwell for Clark, however, as he's spent his whole life hiding his powers. In a football-crazy community, he can't even try out for the team because it wouldn't be fair. Everyone but his folks sees him as a shy, quiet loser. His only relief is using powers covertly, for example, for a superfast cross-country run. A young Lois Lane spots him from the window of a passing train but nobody believes her.

After Jonathan dies of a heart attack, Clark leaves home and heads to the Arctic, carrying a crystal from his rocket. When he tosses it into the icy waters, it grows into his Fortress of Solitude, with Jor-El's hologram in residence to provide further advice. Jor-El warns his son that while he can live among humanity and help them, he must not alter the path of human history. This provides a rationale why Superman doesn't immediately eliminate world hunger or melt down all our nuclear weapons.

The third act of the film begins at the *Daily Planet* in Metropolis, where Lois Lane (Margot Kidder) and Jimmy Olsen (Marc McClure) work for editor Perry White (Jackie Coogan). To Lois' surprise, Perry hires an unbelievably shy, bespectacled young man named Clark Kent as the newest staff reporter. Perry assures her Clark has a string of good stories under his belt, a snappy writing style and "he's the fastest typist I've ever seen." Clark is immediately smitten with Lois but the feeling isn't reciprocated.

Finally, almost 40 minutes into the movie, the Man of Steel makes his debut. Lois takes a helicopter ride from the roof of the *Daily Planet* to her next assignment but the helicopter snags on a cable, threatening to fall into the street. Lois tumbles out and ends up hanging on one of the runners with a long and fatal drop beneath her. Clark spots the peril, glances at a payphone—but instead of a phone booth, it's sitting in the open on a metal pole. He can't change there so he dashes into a rotating door, emerges as Superman and rises to catch Lois and the helicopter—"Don't worry, I've got you." "You've got me? Who's got *you*?"

The scene with the payphone riffs on the image of Clark changing into his super-suit in a phone booth. This happened occasionally on the 1940s *Adventures of Superman* radio show and very rarely anywhere else. Somehow, though, it became accepted as part of the legend, familiar enough most viewers probably grasped the Easter egg.[4]

After putting Lois and the helicopter down safely, Superman spends the rest of the night busting criminals and helping citizens, like a girl whose cat is stuck up a tree. By morning, the media are going crazy about this new super-man and desperate for information. Superman grants Lois his first interview, a flirtatious scene in which Superman proves his X-ray vision by describing Lois's underwear—her suggestion. He also takes her for a romantic flight over the city.

Everyone's thrilled except for criminal genius Lex Luthor (Gene Hackman). He's watching events from a hidden lair under the city's toniest residential district, where he lurks with his mistress Eve Tesmacher (Valerie Perrine) and moronic, comic-relief henchman Otis (Ned Beatty). Seeing Superman as a threat to his plans, Luthor studies Lois's interview, particularly Superman's account of his origin. From this, Luthor deduces the existence of kryptonite and that it might be fatal to Superman. Luthor locates a kryptonite meteorite in Addis Ababa and steals it. He also steals nuclear missiles from the U.S. military, using Eve's voluptuous charms to distract the guards.

While Luthor schemes, Jor-El fumes: hearing about Superman's activities he chides his son about intervening too much in human affairs. It's a little hard to see how Superman is supposed to help us if the stuff he's done so far is excessive, but that's Jor-El's take. The hologram also warns his son to keep his true identity secret—his enemies would find it too easy to target him otherwise.

Luthor, however, can target Superman without knowing his identity. He lures the Man of Steel to his lair with a high frequency signal, then explains he's invested a fortune in worthless real estate along California's San Andreas fault. The nuclear missile he's just launched at the fault will change that by triggering a quake that drops everything west of the fault into the ocean. Lex will be new owner of the entire California coastline.

The mass destruction and death doesn't faze Luthor in the slightest. When Superman prepares to intercept the missile, Luthor reveals he's launched the second missile to take out a civilian target elsewhere. Not even Superman can stop both missiles; only finding Luthor's hidden detonator and making the missiles self-destruct can save everyone. Superman scans Luthor's lair, spots a hidden lead-lined box and deduces that's where Luthor hid the detonator. When Superman flings open the lid, it's the kryptonite inside, fastened to a metal necklace. As Superman collapses, a gloating Lex slips the chain over his neck, proclaiming this a victory of "mind over muscle." Lex throws him into the lair's pool and leaves to monitor his scheme.

Luthor's one mistake? Aiming the second missile at Hackensack, New Jersey, because Eve's mother lives there. After Lex leaves Superman to drown, Eve removes the kryptonite in return for Superman's promise he'll stop that missile first. He does, then stabilizes the San Andreas fault, then stops the floods and landslides the trembling fault caused. Then he discovers the one landslide he didn't stop crushed Lois. Unable to accept this, he travels back through time far enough to prevent her death, literally changing human history. Superman then brings Luthor and Otis to justice, after which the elegantly coiffed Luthor rips off his wig and hurls it down in fury. It turns out he's just as bald as in the comics.

Like *Independence Day*, *Superman*'s backstory is an entertaining look at the winding paths by which some hit films reach the screen, well documented in Jake Rossen's *Superman vs. Hollywood*. Alexander Salkind and his son Ilya had become successful producers with various low budget projects before hitting the A-list with *The Three Musketeers* (1974) and *The Four Musketeers* (1975). They'd also earned a rep for financial tricks: they'd filmed the Alexander Dumas adaptation as one film, paid the actors for one film, then released it as two. The Screen Actors Guild wrote the "Salkind Clause" into its standard contract to prevent such games.[5]

Looking around for a new project, Ilya, a comic book fan, suggested they bring Superman to the big screen in a major motion picture. By the standards of the day, the idea was insane. The last attempt at a serious Superman picture had been the very low budget *Superman and the Mole Men* (1951). The 1960s *Batman* TV show had convinced millions of people that superheroes were suitable adult fare only if they were campy. The live action *Spider-Man* TV show of the early 1970s had stayed as mundane as possible, favoring terrorists and mobsters over costumed villains. The senior Salkind, an immigrant with zero interest in comic books, didn't think Ilya's idea could work—but when he pitched it to a group of European investors, they liked it.

DC Comics was wary. Superman and Batman were their stars, and the company had a long list of terms limiting what the Salkinds could do with Superman. Warner Brothers, however, was DC's corporate parent, and they had no attachment to the Superman brand. Nor did they think they would ever see big profits from a Superman film, so why hold out for a better offer? For $4 million, the studio signed over the rights to Superman for the next quarter-century.

The Salkinds knew they'd need to bring in some big names to get investors to open their wallets. For the scripting they considered Leigh Brackett, William Goldman and science fiction writer Alfred Bester before striking a deal with Mario Puzo, author of *The Godfather*. Puzo's script came in at 300 pages, filled with super-stunts that would have cost a fortune to realize on-screen in the pre–CGI days. David and Leslie Newman eventually rewrote it into something more manageable, breaking it into two films to be shot together, as the Musketeer movies had been.

The Salkinds made a real catch by hiring Marlon Brando for $3.7 million and 11.75 percent of the profits. Brando's early performances in *A Streetcar Named Desire* (1951) and *The Wild One* (1954) *had* made him a star; his 1972 roles in *The Godfather* and *Last Tango in Paris* had made him a legend. Signing Brando brought media attention; signing for a spectacular paycheck earned with less than a half-hour's work generated even more buzz. According to one long-standing legend, Brando wanted to play the role voice only—have Jor-El look like a suitcase or a bagel!—until director Richard Donner pointed out that every kid in America, including Brando's grandkids, knew Jor-El wasn't a suitcase. Donner confirms Brando said it, but only as a joke.

Landing Brando made it possible to sign Gene Hackman, another highly respected actor who'd given excellent performances in *The French Connection* (1971), *The Conversation* (1974) and *Young Frankenstein* (1974). Director Richard Donner says on the commentary track that Hackman balked at playing the entire film in a bald skullcap but was willing to do it for the final scene.

The Salkinds initially picked Guy Hamilton for director, shooting the film in Italy to save money. Brando's casting made that impractical. An Italian court had ruled *Last Tango in Paris* obscene, which could mean legal trouble for Brando if he entered the

Superman (1978). A beautifully simple, striking poster for the film that made flying look real. It's depressing to see how bad the flying scenes are in Christopher Reeve's final low-budget turn in *Superman IV: The Quest for Peace.*

country. The alternative was England, but under English tax laws Hamilton would suffer a huge tax bill if he stayed in the U.K. long enough to shoot the film. Hamilton dropped out; Donner stepped in.

Casting for Lois came down to Stockard Channing and Margot Kidder. Donner opted for Kidder, feeling Channing was so forceful she might overpower whoever they picked for Superman. Filling the lead role proved a real challenge: they needed someone who looked the part physically but could also play both Clark and Superman credibly. Finding the right person was beginning to look impossible until Christopher Reeve came along; Donner said on the DVD that he didn't find Reeve, God sent him.

While Reeve's later movie career never matched up to his impact in the Superman films, in them he was perfect. He's totally believable as the klutzy, shy Clark, but he also radiates power, confidence and compassion as Superman. Many good actors would later don the costume but nobody inhabited it as naturally as Reeve.

One of the taglines for the film was "You will believe a man can fly" and the film delivered. As detailed in another of the DVD special features, Zoran Perisic developed the "Zoptic" optical projection system to give the feeling Reeve was zooming towards or away from the camera. A fiberglass tray supported his body in some scenes; others used traditional wire work, vibrating the wires fast enough the camera couldn't catch them. A network of remote-controlled rods manipulated his cape so that it looked as if it were blowing in the wind.

Making *Superman* was not a smooth process. Donner pushed for perfection and costs steadily mounted up beyond what the Salkinds had budgeted for both films combined. Once it hit the screen, though, it paid off. The movie was a smash hit generating glowing reviews. The horrifying $55 million budget generated returns of $134 million domestically and $300 million worldwide.

It also generated lawsuits: Kidder, Donner and Brando all sued over their share of the profits; Brando asked for an injunction banning the use of any his screen footage until the suit was settled, though the court said no. The Salkinds responded by replacing Donner with Richard Lester to complete shooting on *Superman II*; replacing Brando with Susannah York's Lara in a key *Superman II* scene; and dropping Kidder from *Superman III*.

The film worked out much better for Superman's creators. By the late 1970s, Siegel and Shuster were living on the edge of poverty, their contribution to DC's success rarely acknowledged. With the movie putting a massive media spotlight on DC Comics, Superman and his creators, Siegel and Shuster's situation because an immense black eye for the company. Eventually, Rossen says, that led to a $20,000 annual payment to both men and a "created by Jerry Siegel and Joe Shuster" credit on movies, comics and other Super-material going forward.

Despite everything that went on backstage, the film is first-rate and remains amazingly entertaining. It has an odd structure, partly because it's an origin story and Superman's origin had grown over time. *Action* #1 tossed off the destruction of Krypton in a single panel. Krypton wasn't named until *Superman* #1; Jor-El and Lara not until 1948, to fit in with the first Superman movie serial. Superman himself didn't learn he came from Krypton until 1949's *Superman* #61. Over time, however, his alien origins assumed more importance. Other Kryptonian survivors showed up; pieces of Kryptonian technology kept landing on Earth and falling into the wrong hands.

In comics' Silver Age (roughly 1956 through 1970), the Superman stories greatly expanded Krypton's role. Readers learned about its culture, its prominent landmarks and Jor-El'sscientific achievements. Starting the film with Superman on Earth would have disappointed a lot of people.

The Kryptonian scenes are cold, emotionally as well as physically. Brando's Jor-El clearly cares for his son, but it's unlikely he'd ever have cuddled him. The Kryptonians are an example of the science fiction trope that the smarter you get, the less emotions you feel (see Chapter Eleven for more). After a 1986 reboot of the Superman comics by writer/artist John Byrne, the movie's version of Krypton became the comics version too. The idea that Superman's S symbol was an El family crest took much longer to become comics canon.

After Krypton comes the much friendlier world of Smallville. It's warm and inviting but by the time we see teenage Clark, Smallville's become too small for him. He's restless, ready to show the world what he can do. As Donner says, the transition from Smallville to Metropolis is a transition from Andrew Wyeth to a comic strip. Things have a slightly tongue-in-cheek tone, but not enough to make it 1960s-*Batman* camp.

It's to the creative team's credit that even though it takes a while to get to Metropolis, let alone see Superman in action, it doesn't become boring. The three different tones all work together. Superman's feats look utterly believable; moviegoers who've grown up with CGI may not realize how astonishing they were at the time. The core cast are excellent. Margot Kidder makes a lively Lois, high on nervous energy, though that may partly reflect her mental health issues. She and Reeve have a good chemistry together; she's clearly taken with Superman and shows a big-sister fondness for his alter ego. Reeve does a remarkable job shifting from quietly confident Superman to nervously awkward Clark. Hackman makes an amazing villain, jovial and witty while plotting the deaths of millions.

The weakest part of the film is the climax. Donner had originally planned to have Superman rewind time at the end of the second film, but nobody had a good idea for finishing the first one. The Salkinds' solution was to move up the ending of *II* and think of a different conclusion for that film down the road.

They should have tried harder because the ending doesn't work, though I don't know it would have worked on the second film either. If Superman can turn back time, then nothing can stop him. It would be easy to rationalize that—the effort is so demanding, nothing short of his massive grief could make him push his limits this way—but the film doesn't even bother.

Superman II *(1981)*

Warner Brothers. 127 minutes. Release date June 19, 1981.

CAST: Christopher Reeve (Superman/Clark Kent), Margot Kidder (Lois Lane), Gene Hackman (Lex Luthor), General Zod (Terence Stamp), Nom (Jack O'Halloran), Sarah Douglas (Ursa), Valerie Perrine (Eve Teschmacher), Ned Beatty (Otis), Jackie Cooper (Perry White), Susannah York (Lara), E.G. Marshall (President), Leueen Willoughby (Leueen), Robin Pappas (Alice), Roger Kemp (Spokesman), Roger Brierley (Terrorist), Anthony Milner (Terrorist), Richard Griffiths (Terrorist), Melissa Wiltsie (Nun), Alain Dehay (Gendarme), Marc Boyle (C.R.S. Man), Alan Stuart (Cab Driver), John Ratzenberger (Controller), Shane Rimmer (Controller), John Morton (Nate), Jim Dowdell (Boris), Angus McInnes (Prison Warder), Antony Sher (Bell Boy), Elva May Hoover (Mother), Hadley Kay (Jason), Todd Woodcroft (Father), John Hollis (Krypton Elder), Gordon Rollings (Fisherman), Peter

Whitman Deputy), Clifton James (Sheriff), Bill Bailey (JJ), Dinny Powell (Boog), Hal Galili (Man at Bar), Marcus D'Amico (Willie), Jackie Cooper (Dino), Richard Parmentier (Reporter), Don Fellows (General), Michael J. Shannon (President's Aide), Tony Sibbald (Presidential Imposter), Tommy Duggan (Diner Owner), Pamela Mandell (Waitress), Pepper Martin (Rocky), Eugene Lipinski (Newsvendor) Cleon Spender (kid), Carl Parris (Kid)

CREDITS: Director: Richard Lester; Screenwriters: Mario Puzo, David Newman, Leslie Newman; Story: Mario Puzo; Creative Consultant Tom Mankiewicz; Producer: Pierre Spengler; Executive Producer: Ilya Salkind; Production Designer: John Barry and Peter Murton; Photography: Geoffrey Unsworth; Editor: John Victor-Smith; Music: Ken Thorne, from original material composed by John Williams

After a recap of the first film, we open with Clark discovering there's a hostage situation in Paris, where terrorists claim to have a nuclear bomb. Lois is a terrorist captive so Superman flies to Paris, saves her, takes down the terrorists and hurls the bomb into space. It strikes the Phantom Zone and frees the three prisoners. The trio arrive on the moon where they kill the members of a joint U.S./Soviet space mission, then head to "Houston," which they gather from the astronauts is the name of the planet below.

The opening is one of the major differences in the Donner cut of the film, which is now available on DVD. There we see the Phantom Zone—less a zone, apparently, than some kind of energy prison—drawn from Krypton to our solar system in the wake of Kal-El's rocket. One of the missiles Superman hurls into space at the climax of the first film strikes the Zone and frees the villains.

In Metropolis, Perry assigns Clark and Lois—who's just registered how much Clark looks like Superman—to check into a Niagara Falls honeymoon hotel allegedly scamming newlyweds. To test her theory about Clark, Lois throws herself out of Perry's window to her death. Clark saves her of course, but in a fashion that convinces her she was wrong. In the theatrical release, they cut all that and go straight to Niagara Falls as one of the three parallel tracks both movies follow.

In one track, Luthor escapes from prison with Tessmacher's help, though Otis winds up left behind. Luthor's scientific genius lets him locate the Fortress of Solitude where he learns much from Jor-El's hologram, including the existence of the Phantom Zone prisoners. Lex and Tessmacher then head back to Metropolis.

In the second track, Zod and his acolytes arrive on Earth. They explore their new powers by demolishing a country town, crushing the military sent to stop them and destroying the required iconic landmark. In the theatrical release they resculpt Mt. Rushmore with heat vision; in the Donner cut it's the Washington Monument. They smash into the White House—a much more vicious attack in the Donner cut—and demand the president bow to Zod. He does, but the general realizes no true leader would kneel so easily. The real president (E.G. Marshall) steps forward and kneels with a despairing "God." The general replies, "No—Zod!"

After repeatedly hearing that Superman will stop him, Zod's ready for a clash of titans but there's no sign of the Man of Steel. Enter Luthor, who reveals Superman is the son of Jor-El, and that Lex can help the Kryptonians find him. In return, oh, how about giving him rulership over Australia? Zod agrees.

In track three, we're back with Lois and Clark. During the fake honeymoon, Clark awkwardly tries bringing up his real feelings for Lois, then accidentally sticks his hand on the fireplace in the middle of their suite. When Lois realizes he hasn't burned, she realizes the truth. She suggests his accident was a Freudian slip to reveal what he couldn't say. In the Donner cut, she takes a more drastic step, firing a revolver into Clark's chest, then revealing the gun was loaded with blanks once he confesses the truth. In both cuts they follow the big reveal by flying to the Fortress for a night of romance.

After dinner, Superman goes to the hologram projector. Instead of Jor-El, it's Kal's mother Lara (Susannah York) who appears, telling her son Jor assigned her to talk about the mushy stuff. As Lois eavesdrops, Lara tells Clark that to be with a woman of Earth he must become fully human. After confirming this is what he truly wants, she directs him into a chamber in the Fortress charged with red-sun energy, the light of Krypton's sun. In a matter of seconds, Clark's powers are gone.

The Donner footage with Jor-El, filmed before the Salkinds decided to axe Brando from *II*, works better as it builds on the established father/son relationship. Jor-El is much less understanding than Lara, objecting that loving one person goes against Clark's mission to care for everyone on Earth. Clark protests that he's given so much already he's entitled to some happiness for himself. It's a turning point in the father/son relationship; creative consultant Tom Mankiewicz describes it on the Donner DVD as a "god and Jesus" moment. Reluctantly Jor-El accepts his son's wishes and tells him about the red sun chamber. The power the chamber requires shuts down Jor-El's hologram.

Logically, Clark and Lois are now stranded somewhere in the Arctic. Nevertheless, we see them returning to Metropolis by car without explanation. When they stop at a diner, a bullying trucker, Rocky (Pepper Martin) hits on Lois, then beats up Clark when he objects. Reeve gives the moment a palpable shock as Clark discovers what it's like to hurt. Worse, Clark sees Zod on television, issuing his challenge, and realizes he's made a mistake. The world needs Superman more than Superman needs to be with Lois.

Clark somehow hitches a ride to the Fortress, which must be much closer to a major highway than it's ever seemed. In the Donner cut Clark reactivates the hologram, apologizing for failing Jor-El and the world. Jor-El's hologram touches Clark, restoring his powers at the cost of the hologram's own existence. In the theatrical release Clark sobs out his apology, picks up one of the holo-crystals … and that's all the explanation the film could give us without Brando.

Back in Metropolis, the Kryptonians attack the *Daily Planet* to force a confrontation with Superman. When he doesn't appear, Zod decides he might as well kill Luthor, then Superman arrives for a showdown. Superman goes mano-a-mano with Zod, Ursa and Non with everyone hurling chunks of buildings and buses at each other alongside super-punches. Zod realizes Superman's worried about the civilians watching the fight so the general rains destruction on them to keep Superman off-balance. In a great moment, the villains take Superman down but the crowd steps up to fight for him. Zod and Ursa scatter them with super-breath but that buys Superman the chance to turn and flee.

Luthor proves he's worth not killing by directing the Kryptonians to the Fortress of Solitude. When the battle resumes, both sides suddenly demonstrate new powers such as teleportation and Superman creating holographic doubles of himself (the Donner version skips this bit). Zod plays his trump card—Ursa has Lois by the throat—so Superman tells Luthor to get the trio into the red sun chamber where Superman can depower them. Luthor tells Zod, who forces Superman into the chamber. When Superman emerges, he kneels before Zod, takes the general's hand—and crushes it. Knowing Luthor would backstab him, Superman set the chamber to irradiate the rest of the Fortress. Lois takes the opportunity to punch Ursa cold.

It's a happy ending, except Lois is miserable: she can't be with the man she loves but she has no way to turn off her feelings. Clark solves things by kissing her, which magically erases all memory of their romance and his identity (in the Donner cut, rewinding time prevents her learning the truth and keeps the Zone from reaching Earth). Clark goes to pick up some food for Lois at the diner, encounters Rocky again, and beats him up.

No question the Salkinds, the cast and their behind-the-scenes team pulled it off again. Stamp and Douglas make impressive, cold-blooded villains. Zod in the comics had been only one of many Phantom Zone villains; after this film he was the definitive Kryptonian foe. Although the theatrical cut has too many silly moments, the romance and the epic climactic fight make up for it. While 2013's *Man of Steel* had a much bigger, more spectacular battle with Zod (Russell Crowe) and his army, neither the script nor Superman showed any concern for the Metropolis residents caught in the crossfire. Superman's efforts to shield them in *Superman II* are much truer to the character.

Alas, the ending makes even less sense than turning back time. There's no reason kissing Lois should erase her memories; contrary to Internet legend he's never displayed this power in the comics either. It's a cheat to get out of an otherwise insoluble situation.

The dynamic between Lois and Clark was much more interesting than between Lana Lang (Annette O'Toole) and Clark in *Superman III* (1983). In the *Superboy* comics, Lana filled the role that Lois did for the adult Superman. In *III* her relationship is entirely with Clark. Superman was irrelevant to their romance, which doesn't work for a Superman movie.

It was, however, the least of the film's problems. The Salkinds had kicked around several ideas for a third film including an evil counterpart for Superman or having him battle the humanoid computer Brainiac, one of his comic book arch-foes. When stand-up comic Richard Pryor, a white-hot entertainer at the time, said he'd like to perform in a Superman film, Warners directed the Salkinds to build the third film around Pryor.

Pryor plays Gus Gorman, a loser who takes a computer course and discovers a flair for computer hacking, a new concept at the time. He loots several hundred thousand dollars from his employer, Ross Webster (Robert Vaughn), a less interesting version of Luthor. When Webster discovers the truth, he hires Gorman to manipulate computers for him, for example, using weather satellites to create catastrophic storms. When Superman thwarts Webster's plans, Gorman uses a computer to create artificial kryptonite. Instead of killing Superman it turns him evil: a scowling, unshaven Superman straightens the Leaning Tower of Pisa, blows out the Olympic flame, beds Webster's mistress and generally acts like a jerk. Eventually Superman's evil side splits off and loses to the good side, freeing Superman up to stop a super-computer built by Gorman from wreaking havoc.

Reeve gives it all, as usual, and he's more engaging as evil Superman than *Brightburn* was. Pryor, however, became the center of the film so Warners could get the most bang for the buck out of him. It's a tedious performance, unrelated to the biting standup Pryor was famous for.

Superman IV: The Quest for Peace (1987) was a cheap, disastrous mess with uninspired fights and embarrassing flying special effects. In this film Superman does destroy the world's nuclear weapons, which brings him into conflict with Luthor's latest scheme. *IV* killed off Superman at the movies until 2006's *Superman Returns*, a sequel to *Superman II* that wisely ignored *III* and *IV*. While Brandon Routh did a decent job, the film did not rejuvenate Superman's movie fortunes. Superman has however, appeared in more direct-to-DVD features than I can hope to list here.

OTHER FILMS AND TELEVISION

Animorphs (1998–99) An alien shares its shapeshifting powers with a group of teenagers so that they can fight against the mind-controlling alien parasites threatening Earth.

Batman vs. Superman: Dawn of Justice (2016) Superman and Batman clash, then join forces. The first live-action film to show them both together.

Green Lantern (2011) In this DC comics adaptation, Hal Jordan (Ryan Reynolds) becomes a member of the Green Lanterns, an interplanetary police force. Can a man without fear save Earth from the fear entity Parallax?

Lois and Clark: The New Adventures of Superman (1993–97) Superheroics take a back seat to the romance between Lois (Teri Hatcher) and Clark (Dean Cain) in this version.

Man of Steel (2013) An origin story showing Henry Cavill's Superman from the destruction of Krypton to a battle with Zod (Russell Crowe). A very clumsy effort to make Superman dark and gritty.

The Man with the Power (1977) Dull TV pilot about a man who discovers he's half-alien, which gives him telekinetic powers. He uses them to fight crime.

Max Steel (2016) Teenage boy with uncanny powers becomes symbiotically fused with an extraterrestrial, creating a new superhero.

Sailor Moon (1992–97) Anime in which teenage girls discover they're reincarnated warriors from an ancient lunar empire. Using their powers, they defend Earth from a multitude of apocalyptic threats.

Smallville (2001–11) "No flights, no tights." A look at Clark's (Tom Welling) adventures before he finally embraces the Superman mantle.

Supergirl (1984) Superman's cousin (Helen Slater) arrives on Earth and battles a wealthy woman (Faye Dunaway) with an evil agenda.

Superman and Lois (2021–) Clark and Lois move to Smallville with their two sons, one of whom has inherited Clark's powers. The first season involved yet another Kryptonian plot to conquer Earth.

Superman Returns (2006) After several years in space Superman comes back to Earth to discover Lois is raising his son and Luthor (Kevin Spacey) has a new evil scheme.

Thor (2011) Thor (Chris Hemsworth) is cast out of Asgard for defying his father. Forced to live on Earth, he learns to become a hero. Followed by *Thor: The Dark World* (2013), *Thor: Ragnarok* (2017) and *Thor: Love and Thunder* (2022).

Tomorrow People (1973–79) British kidvid. Human mutants protect Earth with the help of technology provided by the Galactic Federation.

Wordgirl (2007–2015) PBS educational series about an alien superhero, Wordgirl, whose vocabulary is almost as impressive as her powers.

Six

The Invasion Has Already Happened
UFO Abductions

"The presence of the Greys is now a fact of life,
like death and taxes."
—*Dark Skies*

UFO abduction films are a very different kettle of fish from *Independence Day* or *Invasion of the Body Snatchers*.

Abduction stories are the darkest, most pessimistic subgenre of alien visitor films. The aliens in *War of the Worlds* devastate the Earth but humanity wins. In many alien abduction movies, we've already lost. Aliens can take us, anally probe us and experiment on us at will. Neither we, the military nor the government can stop them. In 2013's *Dark Skies*, a researcher (J.K. Simmons) scoffs at the *Independence Day* concept of aliens coming in with guns blazing. "The invasion has already happened," he tells a worried couple (Keri Russell, Josh Hamilton). Earth is occupied territory and our new owners can do with us what they like.

In many of these movies, the government does its best to cover up that terrible truth. In *Official Denial* (1993), the government knows about alien abductions but won't admit to the public that aliens can kidnap U.S. citizens with impunity. Crawford (Joel Gretcsh) in the 2002 miniseries *Taken*, makes the same point during the Cuban missile crisis: if the threat of nukes in Cuba throws American into a panic, how can they handle the truth about aliens?

In *The Forgotten* (2004), the NSA hunts Telly (Julianne Moore) down as a security risk after she learns abductions are real. The feds can't tolerate public protests because if we resist the aliens, the spacemen will annihilate us. In *The X-Files*, Agent Mulder discovers a shadow syndicate within the government actively collaborates with the aliens.

The protagonists in these films frequently come to bad endings. In *Visitors of the Night* (1995), a mother and daughter (Markie Post, Candace Cameron) help the aliens achieve their goal of understanding emotion. In the last scene, the aliens return and abduct them anyway. In *Dark Skies*, the aliens kidnap the protagonists' son. A character in *Communion* (1989) talks about having her baby stolen out of her womb. Jillian McWhirter in *Progeny* (1998) is abducted, impregnated by tentacle rape and then dies. In many stories the abuse has been going on for years: the female lead (Jordan Hinson) in *Beyond the Sky* (2018) has been abducted every seven years since childhood and understandably dreads her upcoming 21st birthday.

Alien visitors in film were abducting humans long before extraterrestrial anal probes became a trope. In 1952's animated short *Hasty Hare*, Mars sends one of its agents—later christened Marvin—to bring back an Earth creature for study. Picking Bugs Bunny does not go well for the alien. In 1964's infamously bad *Santa Claus Conquers the Martians*, the Martians kidnap Santa so that he can bring joy to their listless children the way he does to Earth. Similarly, in 2011's *Mars Needs Moms*, the Martians kidnap an Earth woman to drain her mind and create AI mothers for their own children.

A more memorable example is the 1964 *Outer Limits* episode "Fun and Games." The alien Senator (Robert Johnson) abducts weaselly gambler Mike Benson (Nick Adams), who's running from a murder rap, and Laura Hanley (Nancy Malone), who's running from a foundering marriage. The alien explains that his planet, Andera, amuses itself by gladiatorial matches. Benson and Hanley have been picked to battle a male/female pair of reptilian humanoids to the death—and if the humans lose, Earth will die in five years.

Despite the stakes, neither human wants to play. Hanley's too conflict-averse and Benson would sooner enjoy five years of fun than risk certain death. In the end they wind up playing, successfully defeat their adversaries and return home. Benson clears his name and Hanley, accepting her marital problems were partly her fault, returns to her husband. It's one of the show's best episodes and gives a simple reason for the abduction: they do it for kicks.

In another episode, "Second Chance," a fake space ride at an amusement park turns out to be the real deal. The aliens behind it need humans to save their world, and carefully selected individuals whose lives suck, figuring they'll be grateful. When it turns out most of them aren't willing to relocate, the aliens return them to Earth and agree to solicit volunteers.

These kidnappings have none of the elements now associated with UFO abductions such as missing memories and anal probes. The films were released when abduction wasn't a big part of real-world ufology. Some UFO believers claimed to have ridden in spaceships, but consensually. Most close encounters of the third kind portrayed them as a positive experience with friendly spacemen.

This kind of old-school alien visitor story didn't disappear when anal probes came into vogue. *Space Jam* (1996), for example, has Bugs Bunny and other Looney Tunes characters kidnapped to work as slaves in an extraterrestrial amusement park. With their freedom hinging on beating an alien team at basketball, they recruit Michael Jordan to help them win. It's an uninspired film—Bugs should be able to outwit these aliens as easily as he did Marvin the Martian—but it *is* an abduction tale.

The first real-world account of UFO abduction came from a Brazilian, Antônio Villas Boas. In 1957 he claimed he'd been abducted against his will, then forced to have intercourse with a beautiful woman. His account became a sensation, but it was Betty and Barney Hill's story in 1966 that really made UFO abductions part of the paranormal zeitgeist. Perhaps the difference was that they were Americans, or the lack of a sexy element. A lot of people still look on a man being coerced into a sex with a beautiful woman as fantasy more than assault.[1]

The Hills say they saw a UFO behind them during a drive in Massachusetts in 1961. Barney also claimed to have seen Nazi-looking aliens inside it. Suddenly it was two hours later, and the couple were on a different road, closer toward home, with no memory of the intervening time. Betty began suffering nightmares about what had happened in the missing hours, which led the Hills to undergo hypnotherapy. They remembered being captured by a flying saucer, subjected to experiments and having their body probed, though not anally. Depending on your worldview, the hypnotherapist either dredged up repressed memories of the Hills' abduction or caused them to fabricate memories.

The 1975 TV movie *The UFO Incident* dramatizes the Hills' experience. "Dramatize" might be too strong a word as it's notably non-dramatic. Most of the film focuses on the everyday life of the Hills (James Earl Jones, Estelle Parsons—yes, the real couple were interracial) and their gradual, growing awareness that something happened to them that night. Then come the hypnotherapy sessions, with Barnard Hughes as the psychiatrist. Even Jones, despite his immense talent, can't bring the film to life.

This may reflect that the movie is supposedly telling a story taken from real life. The Hills, like most other abductees, didn't have an exciting life before the abduction. Most peoples' lives aren't exciting. As critic Todd Gilchrist says, showing that ordinariness suggests the movie is grounded in reality rather than science fiction. Because we know their stable, normal world is about to be overturned, even the ordinary scenes can feel ominous if they're well done.[2]

After the Hills went public, other individuals began reporting similar encounters. The stories reached the public in the form of newspaper articles, ufologist reports, allegedly nonfiction books and documentaries. By the early 1990s, believers had added to Allen Hynek's three classes of close encounters a Fourth Kind—abduction. Recurring motifs in abduction accounts include stretches of missing time, multiple abductions since childhood, physical abuse (anal probes, removal of sperm or ova) and physical evidence in the form of scars or implants. The elements are familiar enough for the sitcom *People of Earth* or Philip Powell's short "Non-Alien Abductees Anonymous"—a support group for people who feel inadequate because no UFOs have abducted them—to parody them and be confident viewers would get the joke.

Believers cite the similarity between the different accounts of abduction as proof the phenomenon is real. Skeptics argue it's because so many of us have been exposed to the stories: everyone knows what a Fourth Kind encounter is supposed to involve. David Clarke, writing about the history of UFO beliefs, points out that Barney Hill's description of the alien leader, while unique in "real" encounters at that time, resembles the ET in an *Outer Limits* episode, "The Bellero Shield."

Like so much about UFOS, there's a resemblance between alien-abduction scenarios and older more supernatural folklore. People taken by faeries could disappear for years with no sense more than a night had passed. Ghosts, demons and night-hags can inflict torments upon sleeping people. In the 1950s-set *The Vast of Night* (2020), the protagonists interview a woman whose missing child began speaking in a strange, alien tongue; eventually the aliens took him. With a little tinkering that could be a story about faerie changelings. *Dark Skies* starts out with aliens disrupting a household—refrigerator raids, tampering with furniture—like the early manifestations of the ghosts in *Poltergeist*.

One difference between older kidnapping stories such as "Fun and Games" and more recent UFO abduction movies is that the older ones didn't claim to be based on a true story. A number of recent ones do, no matter how many liberties they take with the facts. Even films that don't tie themselves to specific cases still deal with what many people believe is a real phenomenon. That puts them in a different category from, say, *ALF* or *Superman II*.

The very existence of the aliens in abduction films is often uncertain. In most alien visitor films, characters may be initially skeptical that the falling star was a UFO, but once the aliens start blowing things up, it's obvious. The audience often knows what's coming before the heroes realize it. In alien abduction films, even at the end of the movie the abductees may face a wall of skepticism. It's possible they don't know themselves what happened, and neither do we.

The UFO Incident is ambiguous about whether the Hills had a real experience or imagined it. In *Fire in the Sky* (1993), based on the Travis Walton abduction, the movie comes down on the side of It's Real but investigator Watters (James Garner) remains convinced it's all a hoax. Scully (Gillian Anderson) insists on finding a rational explanation for Mulder's (David Duchovny) alien abduction accounts for most of the run of *The X-Files*; the show itself is often unclear about what exactly happened in any given episode.

On the other hand, accounts we'd write off as delusions if we heard them in the real world get presented as absolute truth. The 2016–17 TV series *People of Earth* focused on members of an abductee therapy group. One episode shows they all have psychological reasons for fantasizing they were abducted. Richard (Brian Huskey), for instance, is jealous of his brother's turn on a reality show and thinks being abducted makes him equally special. In real life, that would suggest he's fantasizing; on *People of Earth,* it's just a coincidence. In *Beyond the Sky,* residents of a ufologist tourist trap are faking alien abductions to keep up the tourist trade. Nevertheless it turns out some abductions are the real deal.

One of the standard critiques of real-world alien abduction accounts is to ask what possible reason aliens could have for abducting and probing people over and over? Alien-abduction films often don't provide one. *Fire in the Sky* tells us nothing about the whys of Travis' (D.B. Sweeney) abduction. *Communion* opts for murky, mystical speculation that perhaps the aliens are an aspect of the divine. Even in *Close Encounters of the Third Kind* we get no explanation why the Greys abducted some humans and held them for years, a detail that gets ignored in the feel-good climax.

Some comedies suggest it's because the Greys are sickos. In TV's *Resident Alien*, Harry (Alan Tudyk) repeatedly talks about how gross he finds the Greys and their anal obsession. Harry (Gary Shandling) in *What Planet Are You From?* likewise assures one human that he's nothing like those creepy perverts.

A more serious answer is that it's for science. In *The Forgotten,* an alien researcher has kidnapped a planeload of children, then erased all memories and proof of their existence. When Telly (Julianne Moore) refuses to let go of her memories, the researcher goes all out to see if he can break the mother/child bond. Aliens in *The Recall* (2017) endow abductees with strange powers. A former abductee (Wesley Snipes) compares it to testing new industrial chemicals on lab rats.

In *Visitors of the Night* and *Taken*, the aliens want to understand human emotion. That's the mission in *Beyond the Sky* too, but with a twist: the aliens are our time-traveling descendants, trying to recover the emotions that evolution has bred out of them.

The idea UFO abductors come from our future crops up in other films. In *Official Denial,* future humanity is sterile. The Greys are collecting genetic material from Parker Stevenson and other abductees in the hopes of changing that. In the 2004 TV series *The 4400*, the "aliens" abduct, yes, 4,400 people over the decades, then return them to modern-day Seattle. The goal: endowing abductees with superhuman abilities will change history and avert the slow collapse of human civilization in the abductors' future.

In other stories, such as *The X-Files* and *People of Earth*, the scientific study is just a prequel to the actual invasion.

Alien abduction has become such a well-known trope, some elements have seeped into other subgenres. In 1950s films such as *War of the Worlds* or *Target Earth*, the aliens settle for blasting us with death rays. In the 2005 *War of the Worlds*, Ray witnesses humans undergoing imprisonment and torture akin to many alien abduction films.

SPOTLIGHT

Fire in the Sky *(1993)*

Paramount. 109 minutes. Release date March 12, 1993.

CAST: D.B. Sweeney (Travis Walton), Robert Patrick (Mike Rogers), Craig Sheffer (Allan Dallis), Peter Berg (David Whitlock), Henry Thomas (Greg Hayes), Bradley Gregg (Bobby Cogdill), Noble Willingham (Sheriff Blake Davis), Kathleen Wilhoite (Katie Rogers), James Garner (Frank Watters), Georgia Emelin (Dana Rogers), Scott Macdonald (Dan Walton), Wayne Grace (Cyrus Gibson), Kenneth White (Buck), Robert Covarrubias (Ray Melendez), Bruce Wright (Dennis Clay), Robert Biheller (Ellis), Tom McGranahan, Sr. (Dr. Wilson), Julie Ariola (Dr. Cayle), Peter Mark Vasquez (Ramon), Gordon Scott (George), Mical Shannon Lewis (Mary Rogers), Courtney Esler (Emily Rogers), Holly Hoffman (Cathy), Marcia MacLaine (Nurse), Glen Lee (Geiger Counter Man), Vernon Barkhurst (Bill Grant), Jerry Basham, Teresa Fox, Travis Walton (Citizens), Susan Castillo (Anchorwoman), Jane Ferguson (Lurae Jenkins), Nancy Neifert (Cathy's Mom), Charley Lang (Jarvis Powell), Lyn Marie Sager (Ida), Mari Padron (Thelma), John Breedlove (Building Man), Frank Chavez (Orlando), Louis A. Lotorto, Sr. (Paramedic), Ronald Lee Marriott (Digger), Shinichi Mine (Japanese Reporter), Scott M. Seekins (Emergency Room Doctor), Eric Wilsey (Claude)

CREDITS: Director: Robert Lieberman; Screenplay: Tracy Tormé, based on *The Walton Experience* by Travis Walton; Producers: Joe Wizan, Todd Black; Co-Producers: Tracy Tormé, Robert Strauss, Nilo Rodis-Jamero; Executive Producer: Wolfgang Glattes; Photography: Bill Pope; Production Designer: Laurence Bennett; Editor: Steve Mirkovich; Music: Mark Isham.

The film starts on an Arizona night in 1975. As the credits roll, a pickup truck drives recklessly along a rough forest road, stopping at a bar on the outskirts of Snowflake, Arizona. As the shaken men in the truck enter the bar, the server starts to tell them the kitchen is closed. She shuts up and walks away when she sees their faces. Mike Rogers (Robert Patrick) reminds the other to stick to the story "no matter how rough it gets." Another guy, Greg (Henry Thomas) assures Mike they have his back, then tells him to make the phone call.

Cut to Lt. Frank Watters (James Garner), an investigator famous for closing every case he's worked on. As he drives, UFO lights appear to descend behind his car but it's a fake-out—they're on a descending railroad crossing gate. Watters gets a call on his car phone to head for Snowflake, where Sheriff Davis (Noble Willingham) is in over his head. When Watters arrives, Davis introduces him to Mike and his logging crew: Greg, David (Peter Berg), Bobby (Bradley Gregg) and Allan (Craig Sheffer), a drifter new to the area and allegedly a bad apple. Rather than synopsize, Davis asks Watters to hear their story firsthand.

When Watters sets up a tape recorder, Allan freaks out ("We already told that Barney Fife of a deputy everything we know!") but Watters insists. As they start their narrative, we flash back to the previous morning, full of sunlight and mundane reality. The focus is on Travis Walton (D.B. Sweeney), a fun-loving, slightly reckless guy with a mischievous streak, demonstrated by driving his motorcycle on the sidewalk. He and Mike are lifelong best friends; Travis works as a logger on Mike's crew and hopes they can open a motorcycle shop together someday. Travis is also in love with Mike's sister Dana (Georgia Emelin).

Mike, married with kids, is more responsible than his buddy, but he's foundering. His crew is behind on their current government logging contract; the company won't give Mike an extension; and as Mike's wife Katie (Kathleen Wilhoite) keeps reminding him, their mortgage is on the line. Travis tells Mike he shouldn't worry—they'll meet the deadline—but with a family to take care of, Mike can't help worrying.

Traveling up into the mountains for the day's work, Mike, Travis and the crew bicker amiably over what to play on the radio. Travis and Allan are much less amiable when they disagree. Allan's a jerk and during the logging, he almost drops a tree on Travis. Only after it misses does Allan yell "timber!"

When work ends, Mike begins the drive back to Snowflake only to see a fire light up the sky, blocking their path. They drive toward it to see if their path down the mountain is blocked. Instead of a fire, they see a UFO veiled by glowing red mist, with a faceted eye at the center. Travis recklessly leaves the truck to approach it. The eye lifts him up with a ray beam, then flings him to the ground, apparently dead. His friends peel out in terror, then Mike's loyalty reasserts itself. The others get out of the truck, he drives back—but there's no flying saucer, and no Travis.

Watters doesn't buy a single word. He assumes the guys made up the story to explain Travis's death, but he admits to Davis he can't see what they'd gain by such a bizarre alibi. By next morning the story has spread through town; the local radio station treats it as a joke while Dana is horrified her brother abandoned Travis.

Law enforcement, accompanied by a mass of volunteers, searches the area, watched by an Apache from the nearby reservation. There's no trace of Travis, no sign of a UFO and Allan has vanished. Travis' brother Dan (Scott Macdonald) blames Allan, though he also faults Mike for letting it happen. The town's consensus is that Mike's either a killer or a liar. The government cancels his logging contract, which leaves him and Katie broke. Mike isolates himself at a local motel, otherwise full of curiosity seekers, UFO hunters and reporters.

Next morning the reporters hound Mike for interviews. Ufologist Jarvis Powell (Charley Lang) offers his help, which Mike declines. The eyes watching Mike and his crew at breakfast are accusatory, and one belligerent man demands Mike confess. When someone suggests the guys take a polygraph test to confirm—or disprove—their truthfulness, they refuse. Watters no longer believes they're murderers "but for the life of me I can't figure out what you're covering up."

Mike eventually figures out Allan is hiding on the reservation with the Apaches and confronts him. Allan admits he's afraid that as the non-local on the crew, the cops will happily pin all the blame on him for Travis' death. He suspects Mike will go along to get himself off the hook.

Fear consumes the Snowflake community. Kids worry they'll be abducted; parents worry Snowflake's no longer safe; and the town's getting an unsavory reputation in the media. Mike agrees to resolve things by taking the polygraph test. The rest of his crew are wary—what if the polygraph guy just lies about the results—but they agree to participate. Polygraphs can't accurately separate truth from lies—there's a reason they're no longer called lie detectors—but everyone in the film takes their accuracy as fact.

After the test, the polygraph expert, Cy (Wayne Grace), says Allan's results are ambiguous but the other guys are completely truthful. Watters lies to the guys that all the results were inconclusive, hoping to shake their story. He doesn't succeed, nor can he talk them into another round of polygraphy.

That night, Mike is shell-shocked to receive a phone call from Travis, pleading for help. Mike and Dana find Travis at a gas station outside a nearby town, curled up fetal by the ice dispenser. He's shivering and shaking and lets out an animalistic scream when he's touched. Rather than call the cops, Mike takes Travis to Jarvis Powell. The UFO researcher questions Travis without getting any information, but Travis has a flashback to his nightmarish experience and passes out.

Travis wakes up in hospital, still traumatized. Mike sneaks in to see him and apologizes for leaving him behind. That shocks Travis, who didn't remember being abandoned, but Mike points out it was Travis' own damn fault for running into danger.

Travis leaves the hospital but remains tense and subdued, saying nothing about his experiences. He does give his autograph when some local kids ask ("You're famous. You've been to space") which inspires Watters to a new theory. Maybe the guys are staging a publicity hoax to get their fifteen minutes of fame plus a supermarket tabloid check for Travis' first-person account.

Travis is not making it up. During his family's big welcome home party, his memories come rushing back and Dana finds him hiding from them under a table. In Travis' flashback we see him waking up, confused, inside a bubble. He tears it open and climbs out into a vast, gravity-free chamber holding more bubbles. Floating or clinging to the walls—a tether keeps him from drifting off—Travis explores the cyclopean architecture and discovers some tethered Greys. Then he realizes they're empty ET spacesuits—except one of them isn't empty. The alien and its companions strip Travis naked, strap him down and perform the usual body-horror experiments, all without a word. The flashback ends as they drive a needle into his eye.

Travis wakes up in local physician Dr. Cayle's (Julie Ariola) office with his family and Dana there. He shares what he remembers but Watters still isn't convinced; he figures Travis' five-day absence just gave him five days to rehearse the story. Watters tells Travis that he'll slip up eventually and then the investigator will have him.

Doesn't happen. In the final scenes, several years later, Travis is married to Dana, with a kid and a steady job. Mike, by contrast, is a divorced, embittered recluse who hasn't seen his former buddy in two years. Travis goes to visit Mike and take him up to the abduction site to talk. Travis apologizes for his foolishness in staring down the saucer and the two guys make up. Mike wonders what will happen if the aliens come back, but Travis says they won't: "I don't think they liked me."

A text crawl informs us that the guys eventually took polygraph tests again and they *all* passed this time.

Travis Walton's 1975 abduction, which he wrote about in *The Walton Experience*, is one of the best-known cases. Depending who you talk to it's overwhelmingly persuasive the phenomenon is real or it's a well-executed concoction. Possibly Mike Roger made up the story to excuse falling behind on the logging contract. Possibly, as Watters suspects, it was for money and publicity via the tabloids. Some skeptics have pointed out that *The UFO Incident* aired shortly before the Walton abduction allegedly took place.[3]

Walton's account was considerably less horrific than in the movie: he woke up, surrounded by aliens, then fought back hard enough they threw in the towel (no wonder they didn't like him). That wasn't considered exciting enough for the film so screenwriter Tracy Torme threw in more nightmarish material.[4]

The movie account is well-executed, but a good example of emphasizing the mundane side of the story. Anyone thinking they'd get an *Earth vs. the Flying Saucers* level of excitement is out of luck. The UFO is only on screen for a small, though intense part of the running time. The alien abduction shapes the story, but if it had been a hoax, the movie wouldn't require much rewriting.

To the extent the film is fun, it's because of the cast. It's a solidly acted film and Sweeney gives an effective performance as the traumatized Travis. Whatever happened in real life, seeing the abduction through his eyes makes it real for the purposes of the movie. The default assumption for flashbacks is that they're real memories.

The Fourth Kind *(2009)*

Universal, Chambara Pictures, Gold Circle Films, Dead Crow Pictures. 98 minutes. Release date November 6, 2009.

CAST: Milla Jovovich (Abbey Tyler), Charlotte Milchard ("real" Dr. Tyler), Sheriff August (Will Patton), Hakeem Kae-Kazim (Awolowa Odusami), Corey Johnson (Tommy Fisher), Enzo Cilenti (Scott Stracinsky), Elias Koteas (Abel Campos), Eric Loren (Deputy Ryan), Raphael Coleman (Ronnie Tyler), Mia McKenna-Bruce (Ashley Tyler) Daphne Alexander (Theresa), Alisha Seaton (Cindy Stracinski), Tyne Rafaeli (Sarah Fisher), Pavel Stefanov (Timothy Fisher), Kiera McMaster (Joe Fisher), Sara Houghton (Jessica), Juliay Vergov (Will Tyler), Yoan Karamfilov (Ralph)

CREDITS: Director, Screenplay: Olatunde Osunsanmi; Story: Osunsanmi, Terry Lee Robbins; Producers: Paul Brooks, Joe Carnahan, Terry Lee Robbins; Executive Producers: Scott Niemeyer, Norm Waitt, Ioana A. Miller; Photography: Lorenzo Senatore; Production Design: Carlos Da Silva; Editor: Paul J. Covington; Music: Atli Orvarsson

Fire in the Sky presents Walton's abduction as something rooted in the real, mundane world. *The Fourth Kind* doesn't waste its time on plausibility. It works in alien abduction, government cover-ups, ancient astronauts and a nightmare horror scenario reminiscent at times of *The Exorcist*. In one scene, an abductee's alien implant lifts him off the bed and twists his neck around just like Linda Blair's. Only as this is not a supernatural film, his neck snaps and he's paralyzed.

The movie opens by emphasizing the story we're about to see is very much based on truth. Milla Jovovich introduces herself as the actor playing Dr. Abigail Tyler, a real psychologist in Nome Alaska; she says the other characters are real but their names have been changed to preserve their privacy. The movie will mix dramatizations of events, found footage of Tyler's therapy sessions with abductees, and interviews between Tyler and the film's director, Olatunde Osunsanmi.

Osunsanmi is actually pulling a *Blair Witch Project*, basing the film on a true story that doesn't exist. The Tyler in the interviews and the found footage is Charlotte Milchard, a professional actor. It's an effective trick. While I assumed the movie had little to do with the real Tyler's experiences, it never occurred to me there was no real Tyler.

We open with Tyler (Jovavich, not Milchard) in Anchorage, in therapy with fellow

The Fourth Kind (2009). Why would an ancient Sumerian astronaut torment people in Nome, Alaska? Don't look for answers in this ingenious but over-the-top film from Olatunde Osunsanmi.

shrink Dr. Abel Campos (Elias Koteas). Several months earlier, an intruder broke in and killed her husband Will (Juliay Vergov) while Tyler lay next to him. Since that night her daughter Ashley (Mia McKenna-Bruce)has suffered blindness due to the psychological trauma. Campos suggests that's also the reason Tyler can't remember the killer's face.

Tyler returns to Nome, where she and her late husband moved to research the abnormally high rate of disappearances and deaths in the community. In hypnotherapy, several patients talk about repeatedly seeing a creepy owl—a common motif in alien abduction stories—outside their bedrooms at night. Tommy (Corey Johnson) says he's seen the same owl since childhood; Scott (Enzo Cilenti) claims the owl got into his room once, even with the doors and windows closed.

At home, Tyler not only has to deal with Ashley's blindness but her son Ronnie's (Raphael Coleman) sullen resentment over his father's death. Ronnie tells his mother that for a healer, it's ironic she can't help herself, and that she needs to accept his father's death and move on. In one of the interview scenes, Tyler (Charlotte Milchard) tells Osunsanmi that Ronnie blamed her for Will's death.

Probing the mystery of the owls, Tyler puts Tommy under hypnosis again. Although he can't describe the owl, he remembers it opening his bedroom door—and before he can remember further, he starts struggling and smashing furniture, desperate to keep the memories at bay. Tragically, it doesn't work. That night he takes his family hostage, threatening to kill them. When short-tempered Sheriff August (Will Patton) calls Tyler in, Tommy tells her that if she knew what he'd seen, she'd understand why he can't bear to see it again. He cries out "Zimabu Eter!" and demands to know what it means, then shoots his family, then himself.

In the aftermath, August demands to know if Tyler's hypnotherapy triggered Tommy's murder-suicide. And why didn't she warn the sheriff's department he was unstable? Tyler replies that he didn't seem unstable and that whatever her therapy dredged up would have come out eventually. Tyler says her research will continue, which infuriates August. When Tyler reminds the sheriff he never solved Will's death, August replies cryptically that she knows what happened.

When Tyler hypnotizes Scott again, he freaks out too, saying that "they" have been visiting him for years. After the session Scott realizes the owl he saw wasn't an owl, but he can't describe the reality any more than Tommy could. He does remember its smell—putrid cinnamon—and that the "owls" can communicate by both spoken word and telepathy. Tyler tells Campos this is textbook alien abduction stuff, adding that the evidence abductions are real is overwhelming: "When something boasts 11 million witnesses, that would win any court case in the world" (this is an estimate of reported UFO sightings, not reported abductions).

Tyler routinely dictates notes into a tape recorder for her assistant to transcribe. Listening to her notes on the current case the doctor realizes they're accompanied by weird breathing, a scream and some strange foreign words. Much as she hates to believe it, it's her voice screaming. She tells Osunsanmi that a burn on her skin and scratches on the floor from her fingernails prove she was taken, even if she can't remember it.

After recovering from her shock at the revelation, Tyler tries to identify the foreign words. She discovers clues in Will's book of Sumerian myth, and calls the author, Odusami (Hakeem Kae-Kazim). He says Will also contacted him to ask about ancient languages. When Odusami hears the tape, he confirms the words are Sumerian and translates the phrase as "Our creation … examine … ruin … destroy." He says the second voice sounds inhuman; as Tyler's voice sounds normal, it's not a distortion caused by a tape glitch. Odusami mentions Sumerian artifacts that show images resembling space suits and space capsules. He's not drawing any conclusions of course, just pointing out incontrovertible facts.

After Tyler discovers Scott has the same shoulder mark that she does, he reluctantly lets her put him under hypnosis again. In his trance, he tells her "they" implanted something in his head. Cue up found footage of the "real" hypnosis session, in which the implant levitates Scott off the bed before the videotape becomes completely scrambled. We hear the Sumerian voice on the tape, saying something to the effect that he's here and he's ending his research. Later the film reveals Scott twisted his head so far around it snapped three vertebrae and paralyzed him.

August, furious, puts Tyler under house arrest, though it's not clear for what. In another interview scene, Tyler tells the director about the abnormal number of missing people and deaths in Nome since the 1960s, and that the FBI is very active in the area. She adds that abductions are happening all over the world, but many victims don't realize it because they've been forced to forget.

As Deputy Ryan (Eric Loren) watches the Tyler house that night, he sees something pulling Tyler and Ashley out of the house into the night sky. By the time August gets there, Tyler is back, sobbing, but Ashley has vanished. August blames her for the disappearance, lies that Ryan didn't see anything, and removes Ronnie from the house.

At Tyler's insistence, Campos places her under hypnosis. She sees the owl, then the aliens take her; we see memory flashes of her inside a UFO with sinister medical instruments penetrating her body. The found footage of her session suddenly goes blurry as a voice roars in Sumerian that Ashley is gone forever: "I … savior … Father I am … god … Zinabu Eter!" Tyler tells Osunsanmi that she remembers the entity's presence inside her, and it felt like utter hopelessness. Therefore it isn't God, only an imposter.

The Sumerian/alien implant twists Tyler's neck like Scott's, but only enough to put her in traction. Afterwards August confronts her with the truth about Will: he killed himself and she made up the attacker rather than accept it. Campos tells Tyler that whatever truth Will uncovered about the abductions must have broken him.

In the interview, Osunsanmi asks why we or August should believe Ashley's story when she hallucinated her husband's killer. Tyler replies that it wasn't a hallucination, just a coping mechanism. Besides, the recordings don't lie and don't hallucinate. Ashley remains missing; Scott's back remains broken. Tyler breaks down in tears, telling the director she still prays that someday she'll see her daughter again.

Jovovich wraps up by telling us the FBI have made 2,000 visits to Nome since the 1960s, compared to 353 to Anchorage, which has 76 times the population. Then follow details on the "real" people the film's characters were based on, what they're doing now and whether they participated in the film.

Olatunde does a remarkable job making this look like a real if unbelievable docudrama rather than pure fiction. The promotional campaign did likewise, putting out multiple fake online articles from the Alaska papers to bolster the based-on-truth aspect. The Alaska Press Club sued on behalf of seven of the newspapers; Universal agreed to a $20,000 settlement.[5]

Other than the skilled fakery, the film comes up short. The staging is static, with characters sitting and talking way too much of the time. Tyler and Osunsanmi sit and talk in their interview; Tyler sits and hypnotizes people sitting with her; August interrogates Tyler; and so on. The level of acting isn't comparable to *Fire in the Sky*, though Patton gives a solid performance as August.

The found-footage, based-on-truth aspect is supposed to justify the lack of clear answers or explanations. It's not Osunsanmi's fault that Tyler never learned what happened to Ashley, or what the Sumerian alien/demon/ancient astronaut/scientist was doing. This kind of vagueness is common in found-footage movies, but it makes for an unsatisfying film. Why is a Sumerian extraterrestrial visiting Alaska? Why does August lie about what his deputy saw? What kind of alien experiments justify this insanity? *The Blair Witch Project* left viewers with questions but it's a much superior film. In *The Fourth Kind* it feels like found footage is just an excuse for lazy plotting.

OTHER FILMS AND TELEVISION

Alien Abduction (2014) A vacationing family encounters aliens who want to—well, you can guess.

Alien Abduction (2016) After being abducted, a young woman and her friends find themselves locked up in an asylum by government agents.

Alien Exorcism (2011) Italian. A hypnotherapist researching alien abductions battles an entity possessing one of his entranced patients.

Communion (1989) Based on novelist Whitney Strieber's book about his experiences as an abductee. A tedious film that slides into muddled mysticism at the end.

Darkening Sky (2010) Another abduction horror film. A grad student working on a thesis about UFOs as modern mythology discovers evidence alien abductions are real.

Intruders (1992) Psychiatrist Richard Crenna comes to realizes his patients' delusions of alien abductions are not hallucinations.

Official Denial (1993) The government recruits repeated abductee Parker Stevenson to communicate with a Grey they've captured.

People of Earth (TBS, 2015–16) After a strange experience a reporter begins investigating a UFO abductee group, then begins to suspect he might be one of them. A comedy.

Taken (Syfy, 2002) Miniseries involving families targeted by alien abduction for three generations, and a family of military officials determined to capture the aliens.

This Island Earth (1955) Rex Reason and Faith Domergue are unwittingly hired to do scientific research for aliens. When they try to escape, they're abducted to another planet.

SEVEN

Strangers in a Strange Land

The Alien Immigrant

"You're amazing but so few of you live up to the ideals you set."
—*Alien Nation*

Some aliens arrive on Earth because they have nowhere else to go.

Their planet blew up and they alone survived. Their ship crashed and now they're stranded. They're seeking asylum on Earth or hiding here until they can liberate their planet. They're here because their own planet kicked them out.

Alien immigrants and refugees have been around as long as alien visitors have appeared on screen. The first Fleischer Superman cartoon, *The Mad Scientist* (1941), opens with a couple of minutes detailing Superman's escape from Krypton and his arrival on Earth—though, unlike the comics, it implies he grew up in the orphanage without being adopted. Superman has often been cited as an illegal/undocumented immigrant, but under the law at the time, a foundling would have been a legal citizen.[1]

Kal-El was the first screen alien to arrive here fleeing a disaster. The aliens of *It Came from Outer Space* (1953) became the first of many peaceful alien visitors stranded on Earth when their ship crashed. Looking more alien than Superman, they were considerably less welcome, but they only stayed briefly.

Ray Walston's spaceman in *My Favorite Martian* (1963–66) wasn't that lucky After covering the launch of an experimental plane, reporter Tim O'Hara (Bill Bixby) found a flying saucer that had crashed to avoid the jet. The injured Martian inside it convinced Tim to give him shelter rather than publicize his presence. The reporter let "Uncle Martin" stay with him, hiding his saucer in the garage until Martin could repair it.

Although Martin has antenna, they're retractable. Without them looks perfectly human so it's easier for him to pass as human than the Newcomers of *Alien Nation*. His powers would flare up occasionally, such as when he got stuck in invisibility mode. In other episodes, some quirk of Martin's behavior would draw unwelcome attention. In one episode, Martin levitates to the top of a water tower to enjoy a cool breeze during a heat wave. Passersby assume he climbed up to jump and he's assigned to a psychiatrist. In another he duplicates another man's fingerprints so he can apply for a driver's license— Martians have no fingerprints—and discovers too late the man is a wanted jewel thief.

My Favorite Martian was the first of the 1960s' multiple paranormal sitcoms (*Bewitched, I Dream of Jeannie, The Munsters*, etc.). Media historian Lynn Spigel argues that as stories of ethnic families went out of fashion on TV in favor of white suburban settings, these sitcoms reintroduced the Other into the community. They didn't fit. They struggled to assimilate. Det. Bennett (Alan Hewitt), who joined the *My Favorite*

Martian cast in the second season and instantly distrusted Martin, represents the fear that suburban Eden has a snake.

As an ethnic metaphor, Martin's pretty bland. He doesn't have major trouble fitting into American society. Despite Bennett's suspicions, most people he meets accept him as one of them. The protagonists of later alien sitcoms such as *Mork and Mindy* (1978–82), *ALF* (1986–90) and *Marvin Marvin* (2012–13) aren't as lucky. ALF (voiced by Paul Fusco) doesn't even remotely look human; he's like a cross between a monkey and an anteater. Det. Bennett only suspected Martin; ALF knows the federal government is hunting him and in the show's final episode, they capture him. (Don't worry—he escaped and wins his freedom in a 1996 sequel film *Project ALF.*)

As Mork from Ork, Robin Williams looked human, but the concept of how Americans behave—heck, how anyone human behaves—constantly eluded him. For instance, after his human roommate Mindy (Pam Dawber) explains that humans don't lie, she and Mork attend the funeral of a loathsome acquaintance. When Mork hears Mindy telling the man's family how wonderful he was, Mork decides she really liked him and resurrects the guy. The alien researchers of *3rd Rock from the Sun* (1996–2001) had similar trouble fitting in. When a minister announces a group is gathered together before God, Dick Solomon (John Lithgow) asks which of the people is God because he has some questions.

The third season of *Mork and Mindy* made the immigration/assimilation subtext into text. The second season had become increasingly bland, damping down Williams' laugh-a-minute performance. At the start of the third season, Mindy shows her father (Conrad Janis) that Mork has become completely Americanized, calling himself Morey because he finds Mork too ethnic. It takes Mork's homeworld arranging an "eggsorcism"—eggs are very important on Ork—to restore him to himself.

Not every immigrant wants to move into suburbia, though. After *The People*'s (1972) spaceship crashed on Earth, they opted for isolation. Living in an isolated, rural community, they raise up their children to pass for normal, which requires suppressing their psychic powers. When a new human teacher moves to town and learns the truth, she convinces them to embrace their abilities and use them to help others.

Zenna Henderson's stories of The People may have influenced Alexander Key's alien-refugee children's novel, *Escape to Witch Mountain*. Many of Henderson's stories involved a lost, lonely member of the People finding a way home to their kin. Key's novel likewise concerned two alien kids, survivors of a spaceship crash, making their way to the Witch Mountain colony despite a Soviet agent hunting them. In *Escape to Witch Mountain* (1975), the hunters are corrupt millionaire Aristotle Bolt (Ray Milland) and his evil scientist lackey Deranian (Donald Pleasance, always an engaging villain). The film did well enough to generate a 1978 sequel, *Return from Witch Mountain*, an unsuccessful spinoff TV pilot and two remakes.

A big difference between the People and sitcom aliens is that one alien, or even four in the case of the Solomon family, has a shot at passing unnoticed. With an entire community, it's hard to impossible. *Alien Nation* (1988) deals with the social impact of having several thousand alien slaves land outside Los Angeles. The "Newcomers" can't fit in physically—they don't look human, they don't have a human diet—but there are far too many of them to ignore.

SyFy's *Defiance* (2013–15), 1997's *Men in Black* and the 1999 TV cartoon *Roswell Conspiracies: Aliens, Myths and Legends* make things more complicated by adding multiple species of refugees. In the *Men in Black* franchise there are thousands of ETs living on Earth, discretely, many of them famous; a standout scene in the movie shows Sylvester Stallone, Newt Gingrich, and other public figures who are secretly nonhuman. The MIB agency is dedicated to keeping the truth a secret and intervening whenever some immigrants turn out to be bad apples.

In *Defiance*, aliens arrived on Earth in 2013 thinking it was uninhabited, fit for terraforming (xenoforming?). Eventually a war erupted between humans and the various alien races, with the xenoforming technology remaking the Earth. Most governments collapse in the chaos. The story is set in 2046 in the community of Defiance, where aliens and humans live side by side, but not always peaceably.

The underlying message in most of these stories is that immigration is a good thing, or at least acceptable. We can adapt to them, even if they look strange to us. We don't have to Other them no matter where they come from. In *It Came from Outer Space,* protagonist Putnam (Richard Carlson) points a spider out to the local sheriff (Charles Drake). Spiders freak us out, Putnam says, because they're so alien—eight legs instead of four, mouth moving side to side instead of up and down—but does that make them evil? Of course not (though I've known several arachnophobes who'd say otherwise)—so why assume the aliens are evil because they look monstrous to human eyes?

Just as anti-immigrant voices have become increasingly loud in 21st century politics, movies and TV have taken a darker turn. The insectoid aliens of *District 9* (2009), derisively known as "prawns," aren't given any opportunity to merge into human society. They aren't even treated with decency. They're penned up and segregated in a shit-hole community, struggling to make do, many of them hooked on drugs. As the movie begins, they're told that to reduce conflict with nearby humans, they're being relocated from their shantytown to an even worse hell-hole.

The 2014 TV series *Star-Crossed* opens with alien refugees landing in the U.S. Where the Newcomers were greeted peacefully, the military attack the Atrians, assuming they're an invading force. Ten years later the government keeps the Atrians segregated in a separate community, though a much nicer one than the Prawns got. In the series' first episode, the government promotes assimilation by enrolling a handful of teens, "the Atrian Seven," in a human high school. Human and Atrian extremists alike are unhappy, particularly when cross-species dating and sex begins.

While the kids in the *Alien Nation* TV series faced discrimination in schools, the opposition here is much more belligerent and organized. It feels close to the outrage segregationists felt over 1954's *Brown vs. Board of Education.*

On the other hand, the CW's *Supergirl* (2015–21) has repeatedly taken a pro-immigration stance. Like *Men in Black*, multiple aliens have come to Supergirl's (Melissa Benoist) Earth home of Capitol city and settled in. Agent Liberty (Sam Witwer), a character in the fourth season, is a xenophobic racist but he's also the villain.

Alien Exiles

Not all the alien immigrants are huddled masses yearning to breathe free. A handful of them are exiles, sent to Earth because their planet doesn't want them. The Great Gazoo (Hans Conried) in *The Flintstones* is an example. His world's most brilliant scientist, he invented a machine capable of destroying the universe—not to use, just because it was cool. Exiled to prehistoric Earth (the "modern stone age" in the words of the theme song), he's obligated to help whoever finds him first, which happens to be Fred Flintstone and Barney Rubble. Gazoo appeared in less than a dozen episodes before the series ended.

The TV series *Hard Time on Planet Earth* (1989) gave us another exile. Trained from birth as a warrior, he wasn't prepared for life away from the battlefield. After rebelling against his government the alien was exiled to Earth in human form (Martin Kove) until he could learn to master his violent instincts. Accompanied by a control AI (Danny Mann), "Jesse" wandered around, trying to figure out human society—he and Control had to learn ATMs aren't supposed to give money to just anyone—and helping people in trouble in hopes of redeeming himself.

Other exiles are here not because they've been cast out but because they're chosen ones, figures of destiny. Matthew Star (Peter Barton) in *The Powers of Matthew Star* (1982–83) is a prince on his homeworld, which has been overrun by alien conquerors. On Earth he poses as a typical teen, watched over by his guardian, Walt (Louis Gossett, Jr., an actor who really deserved a better show). After years of running from alien assassins, Matthew is finally getting to put down roots and even get a girlfriend (Amy Steel).

While Walt trained Matthew to master his telekinesis and other powers, they got involved in the lives of Matthew's fellow students. When that didn't catch many viewers, the show switched to having Matt and Walt take on special assignments for the government, but that didn't juice the ratings any more than Gazoo did.

Benji, Zax and the Alien Prince (1983) was an equally unsuccessful Saturday morning show that combined the appeal of Benji, a popular canine movie star, with *Star Wars*. Prince Yubi (Chris Burton), like Matthew Star, has come to Earth following the conquest of his homeworld, accompanied by Zax (Ric Spiegel), a droid meant to draw in the George Lucas fans. Alien assassins were on their tail but just like Lassie, Benji was more than heroic enough to get Yubi and Zax out of danger, week after week.

Although based on a successful series of Y/A novels, *I Am Number Four* (2011) comes off like *Powers of Matthew Star—The Movie*. The teenage protagonist, John (Alex Pettyfer), is one of nine superhuman ETs hiding on Earth from the aliens who wiped out their world. John and his guardian are drifters like Matthew and Walt until John meets a girl at his new school and wants to stop running. Then the alien assassins show up to eliminate Number Four as they've already done with one through three.

Immigrant Threats

Some immigrants in alien-visitor films turn out to be villains. Every Kryptonian who survived Krypton's destruction is a refugee just as much as Superman and Supergirl. Unlike the heroes, they usually arrive on Earth with the intention of conquering it. That's been the case in *Superman II, Lois and Clark, Smallville, Man of Steel* and *Lois and Clark*.

It's not just Kryptonians. In *Roswell Conspiracies,* vampires—reptilian fanged aliens rather than bat-based—are power-hungry schemers who've amassed great power in Silicon Valley. The Aesir in the same show are super-strong, indestructible sadists. Some of the Atrians in *Star-Crossed* are involved in a scheme to bring their people to Earth and go from immigrants to conquerors.

SPOTLIGHT

Brother from Another Planet (1984)

A-Train Films. 108 minutes. Release date Sept. 7, 1984.

CAST: Joe Morton (The Brother), Darryl Edwards (Fly), Steve James (Odell), Leonard Jackson (Smokey), Bill Cobbs (Walter), Dee Dee Bridgewater (Malverne), Edward Baran (Vance), Fisher Stevens (Card Trickster), Tom Wright (Sam), Ren Woods (Bernice), Herbert Newsome (Little Earl), John Sayles (Man in Black), David Strathairn (Man in Black), Michael Albert Mantel (Lowe), Jaime Tirelli (Hector), Liane Curtis (Ace), Rosanna Carter (West Indian Woman), Ray Ramirez (Hispanic Man), Yves Rene (Haitian Man), Peter Richardson (Islamic Man), Ginny Yang (Korean Shopkeeper), Maggie Renzi (Noreen), Olga Merediz (Noreen's Client), Minnie Gentry (Mrs. Brown), Reggie Rock Bythewood (Rickey), Alvin Alexis (Willis), Caroline Aaron (Randy Sue), Rosetta Le Noire (Mamam), Chip Mitchell (Ed), David Babcock (Phil), Randy Frazier (Bouncer), Sidney Sheriff, Sr. (Virgil), Copper Cunningham (Black Hooker), Marisa Smith (White Hooker), Ishmael Houston-Jones (Dancer), Kim Staunton (Teacher), Dwania Kyles (Waitress), Carl Gordon (Price), Leon W. Grant (Basketball player), Anthony Thomas (Basketball Player), Andre Robinson, Jr. (Pusher), John Griesemer (White Cop), Ellis Williams (Watcher), Josh Mostel (Casio Vendor), Deborah Taylor (Vance's Receptionist), Herb Downer (Floor Buffer)

CREDITS: Director/writer/editor: John Sayles; Producers: Maggie Renzi, Peggy Rajski; Photography: Ernest R, Dickerson ; Production Designer: Nora Chavooshian; Score: Mason Daring; Art Director: Stephen J. Lineweaver; Costume Designer: Karen Perry

In the opening scene we see flashing lights and electronic displays, then an astronaut; the displays and lights are the console of his space capsule. After a glance at Earth below, he launches from the mother ship, landing in New York Harbor. He climbs out onto Ellis Island with his space suit gone, his right foot torn off and blood dripping from the stump. For the first time we see his face, and he's black (Joe Morton). The Brother's hands glow as he touches the wound; the bleeding stops. He hops into the island's immigrant processing center in a scene almost devoid of background noise. Touching the walls, the Brother "hears" the voices of some of the immigrants who passed this way before him.

Come morning his leg has regrown; with three toes and talon-like nails, it's his only non-human feature. The Brother studies the city thoughtfully, jumps into the water, gets picked up by a boat and reaches the mainland. A helicopter passes by during the trip and the Brother crouches low, as if it were hunting for him.

The Brother wanders through the city, staring around like a tourist, but an uneasy one who flinches at any suspicious sounds. When a man asks him for charity donations, the Brother can't quite figure out what he's supposed to do. At a Korean grocery he eats fruit from a stand without paying for it, then learns from the angry owner (Ginny Yang) that was a mistake. Watching her accept money from another customer, he figures it out. As he has no cash of his own, he turns his powers on the register, making it open, then hands her all the bills inside. When a cop answers the owner's call, the Brother bolts— the symbols and weapons of authority are obvious even to an alien.

A few minutes later he passes a religious store and stares uneasily at the crucifix graphically depicting an agonized Jesus with nails driven into his hands and feet. The Brother looks from the icon to the young man getting frisked by the cop across the street, wondering if breaking the law means you get crucified.

Finally the Brother wanders into a Harlem bar, almost taking a seat until his empathic sense warns him someone was once murdered on that barstool. He sits at a table, his body language screaming discomfort while casual, random conversations swirl around him ("The first thing that happens in leprosy—your prick drops off"). Smokey (Leonard Jackson), one of the regulars, compares the Brother to a fugitive from a chain gang; bar owner Odell (Steve James) dismisses the alien as a drunk with an "internal malfunction." Walter (Bill Cobbs) grumbles to everyone about the dangers of space satellites bringing xenobacteria back to Earth, though it's clear he's got no scientific knowledge of this topic.

Smokey speculates that the Brother is either deaf, insane or a drunk. The Brother does respond to sudden sounds and can't stand alcohol so they settle on crazy. When Sam (Tom Wright), a social worker, drops by, everyone looks to him to help the stranger out. Sam offers his hand but the Brother mirrors the gesture rather than shaking. As the Brother's empathic abilities let him sense what Sam wants, they have a halting conversation until the spaceman senses one patron's frustration with a malfunctioning arcade game. When the Brother fixes it with a touch—by his powers, not technical knowledge—the guys realize he has skills.

Sam arranges for the Brother to rent a room with Bernice (Ren Woods), a constant talker who's delighted to have such a quiet boarder. This becomes a running element of the Brother's life: his cautious silence makes people see him as a good listener they can rant or chat to about anything. The Brother proves a good boarder, healing Bernice's son Earl (Herbert Newsome) of a small cut and fixing Bernice's broken TV with a touch.

The next day Sam lands the Brother a job with Lowe (Michael Albert Mantel), an arcade owner. Lowe is baffled the Brother didn't bring tools or parts and makes a racist assumption that as a black man, he's too disorganized. After Lowe's assistant Hector (Jaime Tirelli) shows the Brother the dead machines, the alien begins his healing work.

Meanwhile two of the slavers (David Strathairn, John Sayles) get a report that the Brother has escaped. After reaching Earth they enter the bar with body language even stranger than his, but they know Earth culture enough to fake it, asking Odell for beer.

When Smokey lets slip he recognizes the photo they're showing around, Odell demands to see the men's badges. They reply they're with immigration, hunting an "illegal alien"—apparently, they have a sense of humor—to which Fly (Darryl Edwards) snaps that half the city is made up of illegals. Sayles' hunter responds by asking for Fly's green card, an intimidation tactic that pisses Fly off ("You ever been to South Carolina? My people built that!"). The slavers finish their beers and leave, though they don't know Earth currency well and shortchange Odell until he calls them on it.

Lowe is blown away to discover the Brother somehow brought all his defective machines back into condition. While steps away for a minute, leaving the Brother in charge, the alien listens to arcade hotshot Ace (Liane Curtis) grumble the games aren't fast enough to challenge her level of skill. The Brother's response is to accelerate the Space Chaser game she's playing, giving her the challenge she's itching for. Riding the subway back to Bernice's, the Brother encounters an amateur magician (Fisher Stevens) who shows him an elaborate card trick. As the conversation has no emotional context, the Brother's empathic skills fail him. He just sits there uncomprehending what he's supposed to do.

The next day, two white guys from Indiana visiting the Big Apple for a "self-actualization conference" wind up in lost in Harlem without even a clue how to get back to the subway. They're slightly on edge surrounded by blacks ("There weren't any black people in my town—at least I don't think there were.") but make it into the bar and wind up chatting to the Brother. He's slightly uneasy, as he associates whiteness with his former masters, but the guys take his enigmatic silence as a reason to unburden themselves. Eventually Odell decides he's had enough and gives them directions to the subway.

A couple of junkies mug the Brother as he walks home from the bar but after one of them loses it and cuts him, they freak out and run. He heals himself. It's a seemingly random event that leads to other developments later, as does a poster of Malverne Davis (Dee Dee Bridgewater), a singer performing at a local night club. Something stirs in the Brother's heart when he sees her image, to the point he buys one of her albums. Rather than playing the LP, he tries using his empathic powers on it. When he doesn't get any feeling for her from the vinyl, he throws it away but keeps the cover with her image.

After catching her act at the club, the Brother walks home and discovers a dead junkie in the street. Studying the man's drug paraphernalia, he winds up injecting himself and collapses, shaking. He spends the night wandering around witnessing sex workers, men chatting on stoops, dancers—and also tries a joint. He wakes up the next morning with his shoes stolen but otherwise unharmed. On the way home he takes a strange interest in a graffiti covered wall and add some symbols by painting in his own blood.

In between doing odd jobs and repairs to earn money, the Brother takes Earl to an art museum. When they see an exhibit on slavery, the Brother explains his backstory to Earl in mime and gesture. Meanwhile the slavers continue the hunt. They question Hector, who pretends to speak no English, and Bernice, who refuses to help them. Sam's coworker Noreen (Maggie Renzi) intimidates them with a massive pile of paperwork she says they have to fill out before she's authorized to speak about clients. Bernice, however, tells the Brother when he gets home that he needs to move out. She doesn't want him bringing any trouble near Earl.

The Brother finally meets Malverne and shows he can communicate by gestures very effectively when motivated. They go to her apartment and make love; Morton's expressions and body language while experiencing kissing are delightful. Malverne tells him, however, that he really needs to trim those toenails before they share a bed again.

Walking home the next morning, the Brother spots a couple of drug dealers heading into a brownstone. A white rookie cop tries to strike up a conversation but for once the Brother's too distracted to be a good audience. Walking away, he removes one of his eyes and places it where it can watch the entrance. He recovers it later and it replays everything it witnessed. This gives him a trail he eventually follows to white businessmen Vance (Edward Varan) but the man's secretary (Deborah Taylor) refuses to let the Brother in. Sensing she won't budge, he heads back to the bar.

The slavers show up at almost the same time but the bar regulars rally around their friend. The slavers are incredibly strong—one of them snaps the baseball bat Odell keeps behind the bar—but the Brother manages to escape. He returns to Vance's office that night and confronts him. Vance assumes he's working for a rival gang and makes him an offer, assuring him the company's only dealing drugs temporarily to solve a cash flow problem. The Brother doesn't answer which moves Vance into a rant about how blacks can't see the big picture. During his rant the alien calmly opens a bag of heroin Vance offered him and places it over Vance's face.

The slavers catch the Brother as he leaves, implanting a control module that enables them to manipulate him physically. As they walk him back through Harlem, something in the strange graffiti inspires the Brother to pop the control unit out and run. The slavers pursue, calmly confident—but when they catch up, the Brother is standing with a dozen other people, all fellow runaways. Now the tables are turned, the hunters the hunted; when their former victims corner them, the slavers incinerate themselves. In a conversation-by-gesture the other escapees tell the Brother that the Hunters didn't escape, they died—though other viewers have given other interpretations.

The Brother no longer needs to run. In the final scene, he rides the subway and stares through a chain fence at a large government building. He turns around to face the camera and smiles. He's calm. He's happy. He's still on an alien world, but now it's home.

On the commentary track, writer/director Sayles says his film started with a literal dream about an extraterrestrial in Harlem, feeling alienated from everything around him. In developing the dream into *The Brother from Another Planet*, he drew partly on Ralph Ellison's *Invisible Man* and on a desire to capture the immigrant experience: "You could be Polish or come from Nigeria—you have to learn, to assimilate." He stuck with Harlem as the setting because while it's a real place, it's also "an iconic place in our imagination." However, he notes, the Brother knows less about Harlem than most white Americans do.

The alien slavers were based on research Sayles made on the Men in Black when it looked like he'd be writing Steven Spielberg's *Night Skies* (see Chapter Twelve). They show up, threaten, demand information, but never provide any ID or authorization.

While confusion about Earth life and customs is a staple in alien-immigrant stories, it's played more realistically than in, say, *3rd Rock from the Sun*. The Brother has no idea how things work, and he has to learn fast to make a life for himself. Trouble is, he's clueless about what a life in New York would look like or what he wants it to look like. He doesn't know the rules; he's worried about breaking them, even unintentionally; and he has no friends. By the end of the film, he's confident. He's not the person he used to be, but he likes the person he's become.

Sayles made a deliberate choice to minimize special effects and keep it low-tech. The Brother's powers help with that: he doesn't need any sort of tools or equipment to work with machines. Like Klaatu unlocking doors or the Starman's miracle-working spheres (see Chapter Eleven)—his powers are as much magic as science For the most part Sayles keeps the powers consistent, but the Brother's ability to detach his eye and use it as a hidden camera comes out of left field.

The film does have its flaws. The exaggerated barfight with the superhuman slavers feels out of place in the film. The drug plotline isn't horrible, but feels like it wandered in from a 1970s blacksploitation film. Still, *Brother from Another Planet*'s merits outweigh its weaknesses. Morton's performance as the alien runaway slave is a wonder. This is one of several films that rely heavily on the star's ability to convey alienness by acting (*Starman*, TV's *Resident Alien*), but nobody else does it mute.

As Sayles says, Morton's acting has a moment-to-moment quality. The Brother's constantly struggling to learn, deal with what he's learned, and course-correct accordingly. He starts as an obvious fish out of water but by mid-movie he comes across more shy and socially awkward than strange. He's jubilant when Malverne starts kissing him, calmly methodical when giving Vance an OD on his own supply.

The rest of the cast don't get the spotlight the Brother does but they're all good in their roles. Sayles, as in some of his other films, is excellent playing hard and mean. It helps that while the humans take an interest in the Brother, he's never the center of their world. For Vance's secretary, he's nothing but a distraction from the phone conversation she's having. While the Brother's in the bar, life goes on around him in assorted, random conversations. Odell, for instance, has an argument with his girlfriend about whether he'll take her out for dinner or she'll cook him something.

Like most of Sayles' indie films, this one is both excellent and different from anything else you'll run into.

Alien Nation (1988)

20th Century–Fox. 91 minutes. Release date October 7, 1988.

CAST: James Caan (Sgt. Matthew Sykes), Mandy Patinkin (Sam Francisco), Terence Stamp (William Harcourt) Kevyn Major Howard (Kipling), Leslie Bevis (Cassandra), Peter Jason (Fedorchuk), George Jenesky (Quint), Jeff Kober (Strader), Roger Aaron Brown (Bill Tuggle), Tony Simotes (Wiltey), Michael David Simms (Human Dealer), Ed Krieger (Alien Dealer), Tony Perez (Alterez), Brian Thompson (Trent Porter), Frank McCarthy (Capt. Warner), Keone Young (Winter), Don Hood (Maffet), Earl Boen (Duncan Crais), William E. Dearth (Coroner's Technician), Robert Starr (Coroner's Attendant), Bobby Sargent (Coroner's Driver), Bebe Drake-Massey (Computer Operator), Edgar Small (Minister), Thomas Wagner (O'Neal), Abraham Alvarez (Mayor), Diana James (Ortiz), Frank Collison (Bentner), Tom DeFranco (Detective), Angela O'Neill (Kristin Sykes), Seth Marten (Helicopter Pilot), Kendall Conrad (Mrs. Francisco), Brian Lando (George Jr.), Tom Morga (Raincoat), Reggie Parton (Porter), Jessica James (Mrs. Porter), Tom Finnegan (Natuzzi), Doug MacHugh (Victor Goldrup), Lawrence Kopp (Human Cop #1), Alec Gillis (Newcomer in Bar), Shuko Akune (Police Secretary), Stephanie Shroyer (Female Cop), Frank Wagner (Derelict), Clarence Landry (Old Man Driver), Newcomers on TV (Van Ling, Mark Murphey), Kirsten Graham (Kid at Burger Stand), George Robotham (Boat Captain), Debra Seitz (Harcourt's Girlfriend), James De Closs (Detective), Douglas Cameron (Photographer)

CREDITS: Director: Graham Baker; Screenplay: Rockne S. O'Bannon; Producers: Gale Anne Hurd, Richard Kobritz; Production Designer: Jack T. Collis; Photography: Adam Greenberg; Art Director: Joseph Nemec III; Music: Curt Sobell; Editor: Kent Beyda. Aliens created at Stan Winston Studios

It's Los Angeles, 1991, the opening text tells us, and "they have landed ... and now they are among us." This comes from a TV news retrospective showing three-year-old footage of a large flying saucer. After it crashed near LA in 1988, humans discovered the saucer was a slave ship from space: the inhabitants were alien slaves, genetically engineered to adapt to hard labor under almost any conditions.

The federal government interned the "Newcomers," then eventually released them and granted them American citizenship. As their own names are hard to translate or pronounce, the immigration officials processing them assigned them Earth names. Initially they went with ordinary ones but the sheer mass of Newcomers eventually leads to handing out monikers such as Rudyard Kipling or Sam Francisco. This presumably reflects the longstanding legend that immigration inspectors at Ellis Island routinely misspelled or willfully Americanized foreign names. That's more myth than reality, though. It was far more likely to be an error in the ship's manifest when the immigrants left their homeland, or a conscious decision by the immigrants themselves to take American names.[2]

The decision to release them on California soil wasn't popular. One interviewee in the broadcast recommends shipping them to Russia instead. Another says he's worried about his job: how can humans compete when Newcomer 10-year-olds can do college-level work? President Reagan, however, came down on the side of granting them citizenship and made it happen.

Backstory filled in, we return to 1991 as LAPD detectives Matt Sykes (James Caan) and his black partner Tuggle (Roger Aaron Brown) cruise through "Slagtown," named for the racial slur "slag" often applied to the aliens. It's a typical night with Newcomers playing sports—something that looks like lacrosse—giving dance classes to humans and catching *Rambo 6* at the local cinema.

Sykes views it all with a jaundiced eye. He doesn't like or trust the aliens and he's even less pleased when a Newcomer, drunk on sour milk, begs for change at the car window. Sykes explains to Tuggle he's in a lousy mood because his daughter Kristin (Angela O'Neill) is getting married, and her mother's wealthy second husband is paying for the whole affair. The divorce is still a raw wound for Sykes and much as he loves his daughter, he's reluctant to attend.

When the detectives see some Newcomers holding up a drug store, they switch to cop mode. The crooks are playing hardball: one Newcomer guns down an alien named Porter inside the store, another fires at the cops with rounds powerful enough to punch through a lamp post. A volley from the super-gun goes through the car Tuggle is hiding behind, killing him. A furious Sykes chases the shooter, coming to grips with him, but the alien fights Sykes off and escapes.

Sykes is still dazed on the ground when the uniformed cops show up. When Sykes sees a Newcomer with him, he attacks the man before realizing he's a cop too. Sykes still recoils when the Newcomer, Sam Francisco (Mandy Patinkin) attempts to help him up. Back at the crime scene, Francisco mentions another Newcomer, Hubley, was killed recently by a similar high-powered weapon.

A dour, bitter Sykes returns home, which like Ray's in *War of the Worlds* is a mess. His bills are overdue and all he has in the refrigerator is sour milk. Over a drink, Sykes listens to Kristin's message on the answering machine, pleading with him to come to the wedding. She tells Sykes she loves him, then laughs that she shouldn't have said that—now he'll pull out the tape to keep and replay later. He does.

Next morning Sykes learns Detective Fedorchuk (Peter Jason) has been assigned to Tuggle's murder. Fedorchuk jokes it'll be tough learning anything, given "the list of Newcomer informants is as long as a list of Mexican war heroes." Which earns a glare from his Latino partner Alterez (Tony Perez). Then the precinct captain (Frank McCarthy) announces that as part of a federal program, they're promoting a Newcomer to detective third grade, so someone needs to step up and become his partner. Sykes stares with a bittersweet smile at Tuggle's desk, then realizes the new detective is Sam Francisco. Sykes volunteers to partner with him, suggesting they investigate the Hubley murder. The captain thinks that's an excellent idea, unaware Sykes sees it as a roundabout way to hunt Tuggle's killer.

Sykes makes it very clear to Francisco that they aren't friends: "We are not married, we are not pals, we are not taking long moonlight walks together." He balks at using Francisco's punning first name, calling him George instead. Stung by Sykes' attitude, George mentions that in his language "Sykes" translates roughly into "shit head."

The detectives learn Hubley worked at a local refinery—a common Newcomer job as they aren't affected by methane—and died high on drugs. Checking out his possessions, they find a condom and Sykes explains to his partner how it's used. They talk to Hubley's supervisor, but the man says he could barely recognize Hubley—they all look alike—let alone know about his personal life. After the cops leave, the supervisor frowns ominously.

Sykes and Francisco also meet prominent Newcomer businessman William Harcourt (Terence Stamp) at a banquet in his honor. Harcourt identifies Hubley as part of a Newcomer real-estate investment group and compliments Francisco on his promotion.

As the investigation progresses, the film emphasizes that in classic buddy cop-movie style, the two detectives are polar opposites. Francisco wears a suit and tie, Sykes goes for T-shirt and jacket. Sykes is divorced, Francisco is happily married; the mushy goodbye he gives his wife when Sykes picks him up annoys the human. When they stop for fast food later, Sykes is disgusted to find he has his partner's raw beaver wrap (Newcomers can't absorb nutrients from cooked food). After they swap meals, George mentions in passing that he learned English in just three months; the genetic improvements made by their masters make Newcomers fast learners.

The detectives try to force information out of a Newcomer lowlife, but the man shrugs off Sykes' punches; Francisco explains his people's vulnerable pressure points are under the upper arms. They eventually learn Hubley had ties to Strader (Jeff Kober), a Newcomer who runs Encounters, a club with both Newcomer and human exotic dancers. Strader is currently taking a meeting with Harcourt, who wants Strader to distribute *jabluka*, a Newcomer drug, to his club's patrons. Strader refuses so Harcourt's henchmen throw him in the ocean. As saltwater affects Newcomers like acid, this eliminates one loose end in Harcourt's schemes. All that remains is taking out Francisco and Sykes.

At Encounters, the detectives talk with the dancer Cassandra (Leslie Bevis), Strader's girlfriend, who intimidates Sykes by flirting with him ("You could tie me up.... I have my own ropes"). Afterwards they stop off at Sykes' house where he pours himself booze and Francisco discovers the sour milk. As they drink, they begin a slow night of bonding, and trying, with moderate success, to understand each other's culture.

At one point George says what baffles his people is that "you invite us to live with you in equality, give us ownership in our own lives," in contrast to the slavery they've known. "You're amazing but so few of you live up to the ideals you set." Sykes' drunken response is "Don't count me, George, I never had any ideals." By the time Francisco leaves he's too drunk to get home and goes to sleep in Sykes' car instead.

When Francisco wakes the next morning, he finds one of Harcourt's people wiring up a bomb to the car; George removes it, but the hood escapes. Our heroes catch up with Fedorchuk and Alterez on the waterfront, where they're investigating Strader's death; it turns out Harcourt's people conveniently left Strader's ID on the corpse. When Fedorchuk mocks Francisco for not coming near the water, Sykes snaps, slams the detective's face into his steering wheel and throws his car keys in the ocean. He and Francisco are becoming a team—but when they see the forensic report on the drugs in Hubley's system, Francisco suddenly turns sullen and uncommunicative.

Finally he tells Sykes about *jabluka*. The Newcomers' overseers used the drug as a reward for hard work. *Jabluka* was the only taste of pleasure in their grim lives, inspiring them to work even harder for more of the drug. Eventually the drug kills—Francisco lost his best friend that way—but the added work it produces means the slavers come out ahead. Francisco's horrified of what will happen to his people if they have access to *jabluka* again. He's also worried of the human reaction if the Newcomers lose their image as the model minority. Sykes replies that "all you had to do was tell me" and makes it clear he has his partner's back.

Francisco says one question that baffles him is where Hubley could have gotten *jabluka*, as there was none on the ship when it crashed. With a little research the detectives put it together: during the initial quarantine, Harcourt, Hubley, Strader and Porter all bunked together. Porter, a chemist, recreated the formula; Hubley manufactured it at the refinery for Strader to distribute through Encounters. Harcourt eliminated them to seize the profitable trade for himself. At the refinery, Francisco threatens Hubley's supervisor while Sykes plays the good cop role ("I saw him actually pull out a guy's spine once and show it to him"). They learn Harcourt's convening an underworld meeting at Encounters that night which prompts Francisco to drive off alone. Destroying the *jabluka* matters more to him than waiting for warrants or following procedure.

Francisco and Cassandra burst in on the meeting, with the cop carrying the bomb Harcourt's man placed on Sykes' car. Harcourt sneers that Francisco doesn't have a legal leg to stand on: *jabluka* doesn't affect humans and it's not covered by Earth's drugs laws so "it might as well be twelve kilos of grape jelly." Francisco's ready to go suicide bomber if it eliminates *jabluka*, but when Cassandra realizes her lover is dead, she freaks out and gets in his way. That gives Harcourt's muscle a chance to overcome George. Before they can finish him, Sykes busts in and shows he's learned his lesson about where to hit Newcomers.

Harcourt's underlings get busted but the boss man escapes in a stolen cop car. After a car chase, Sykes corners him, but the Newcomer takes an overdose of *jabluka* and dies. As an ambulance takes the corpse to be autopsied, Sykes tells Francisco that with the case closed, it's time to end their partnership. He likes George, he respects George, but the Newcomer's a straight arrow and needs a partner just like himself. During the conversation, Sykes mentions the overdose. An alarmed Francisco says they need to catch up with the ambulance, ASAP. By the time they do, Harcourt has revived as a hulking brute and killed the driver. As they pursue the fleeing felon to the waterfront, Francisco tells Sykes this is another reason he's worried: seeing what a *jabluka* overdose does to Newcomers could make humans fear them.

The partners split up to hunt Harcourt and Sykes catches up with him first. Harcourt breaks the detective's arm, but Sykes pursues the Newcomer onto a getaway boat. As Harcourt steers it out into the harbor, Sykes, realizing he can't beat the man-brute in a fight, throws himself at Harcourt so they both go over the side. The saltwater eats away at Harcourt's flesh but his pumped-up physique lets him keep Sykes underwater.

George, arriving in a police helicopter, overcomes his fear of salt water and orders the pilot down. As Harcourt finally dies, George thrusts his arm into the water, screaming in pain as he pulls Sykes out. In response to the pilot's question, Sykes says he can't identify the man they were fighting—"he looked like every other Slag to me."

The film ends at Kristin's wedding a couple of days later. Both men are still injured so Francisco has to knot the tie around the neck of his broken-armed partner. Their partnership is a go after all, though Sykes says he's "going to apologize in advance for all the rotten things I'm going to do and say to you over the years." Francisco replies, "You're only human."

No question, *Alien Nation* is a boatload of cop-movie clichés. Mismatched partners who grow into mutual respect and friendship. A cop wanting revenge for his dead partner. A burned-out, divorced cop. The seemingly respectable businessman/politician who's dirty as can be—anyone in this sort of film who gets a testimonial banquet is invariably a bad guy. A car chase. A villain who cheats death at the climax because he's just that tough. There are also plot holes a-plenty. Why did Strader refuse to work with Harcourt when he's already planning to deal drugs? And what about the super-guns of the opening, which drop completely out of the plot?

For all of which, the film has two advantages the written script doesn't—James Caan and Mandy Patinkin. They're amazingly talented actors and they sell their respective roles. Caan gives his bitter, pissed-off Sykes an emotional depth that makes him less of a cliche. Patinkin, playing a nice guy who just wants to fit in, has a tougher role, less obviously dramatic, but he pulls it off. Regrettably Stamp, who made *Superman II*'s Zod a memorable villain, can't do the same for a crook as generic as Harcourt.

The film's tackling of immigration, assimilation and racism in a science fictional setting is what makes it stand out from the pack. Unlike the Brother, the Newcomers are an entire new minority suddenly existing in the U.S. Unlike the People, they're not in hiding. They have their own community and customs, their own problems. Like many immigrants, some of them turn to crime. They're conscious of how they come across to humans and like many minorities they carry names that don't sit well on American tongues.

Using extraterrestrials to reflect real-world refugees has an obvious metaphorical power: instead of making a statement about Somali immigrants or Latin American immigrants an alien immigrant can stand in for all of them. The racism they face is the racism and xenophobia all immigrants face. What's not to love?

For some people, quite a bit. *Los Angeles Times* reviewer Kevin Thomas strongly objected to portraying immigrants as literally inhuman: "By now it should be obvious that the Newcomers are convenient stand-ins for any minority—blacks, Latinos, Vietnamese—to make points about the folly and immorality of racism … it's disturbing to consider that an unthinking audience could be given the impression that members of such minorities are somehow inhuman."

On the other hand, Walter Chaw, writing in *Decider*, said he found *Alien Nation* strongly reminiscent of the Asian-American experience. Sykes, for example, is comfortable partnering with a black man and working with Alterez, but like some anti–Asian bigots Chaw has known, he can't give Newcomers the same tolerance. Chaw says he also sees parallels between the Newcomer experience—names nobody in the U.S. can pronounces, food humans think is disgusting—and similar reactions to Asian-American names and food.

In 1989, an *Alien Nation* TV series debuted on Fox, following up on the film with Gary Graham and Eric Pierpoint in the Sikes [sic] and Francisco roles. The series fleshed out the struggles of the "Tecktonese" in more detail, showing that some Newcomer women, like so many immigrants, wound up in sex work. In one case George has to deal with his conflicted feelings when the victims in a serial killing turn out to be Overseers, Newcomers who controlled the other slaves in return for greater privileges.

Along with solving crimes, Matt strikes up a tentative relationship with Cathy (Terri Treas), a Newcomer neighbor, complicated by Matt feeling dirty about the interspecies attraction. George had to cope with his teenage son Buck (Sean Six), a rebel frustrated that his father is so willing to assimilate.

To series fans' dismay, the series ended on a "we're sure we'll be renewed" cliffhanger: Sykes and Cathy split up, Sykes and Francisco do too and a hate group is targeting Newcomers with a deadly bacteria. Surprisingly the story didn't end there: show-runner Kenneth Johnson reunited the cast for a 1994 TV-movie, *Alien Nation:*

Dark Horizon that wrapped up the cliffhangers. Several more movies followed, wrapping up everything else. Buck gains fresh respect for his father and becomes a cop; Matt proposes to Cathy; and a Tecktonese defeats a human xenophobe for a position on the Los Angeles City Council, proof that the Newcomers, like the Brother, have finally made a home here on Earth.

OTHER STORIES

ALF (1986–90) Gordon Chumway, an obnoxious alien, crashes his spaceship into the Tanner family's home. With the military eager to dissect the Alien Life Form, the family agrees to hide him until he can repair his ship.

Amanda and the Alien (1995) A young woman (Nicole Eggert) helps a bodysnatching alien stay out of the clutches of federal agent (Michael Dorn).

The Cat from Outer Space (1978) A telepathic cat asks a scientist (Ken Berry) for help repairing his spaceship. They have to say one step ahead of a buffoonish general (Harry Morgan) who thinks the cat is a security threat.

Earth to Echo (2014) Earth teenagers help a crashed alien robot return to the stars despite the government's determination to capture or destroy it.

Galactica 1980 (1980) In this sequel series to the original *Battlestar Galactica*, the Galactica reaches Earth in the present day. The crew have light-hearted adventures on Earth while keeping their presence secret.

Halfway Across the Galaxy and Turn Left (1994) Australian TV series based on a book about a refugee alien family living on Earth.

Jupiter Ascending (2015) Earth woman Mila Kunis discovers she's the clone of an alien queen and therefore inherits all her possessions, including Earth.

The Man Who Fell to Earth (1976) David Bowie plays Thomas Newton, arriving on Earth from his dying planet. His efforts to obtain enough water to restore his world run afoul of ruthless government officials.

Marvin Marvin (2012–13) Aliens send their son to Earth to keep him safe from evil invaders. Like other sitcom immigrants, Marvin suffers comical struggles getting used to Earth life.

Phantom from Space (1953) A terrified, invisible alien tries to stay alive after landing on Earth.

Samurai Jack (2001–04, 2017) In this animated series, a samurai trapped in the future and seeking to return to the path wanders across an Earth full of alien immigrants.

Stepsister from the Planet Weird (2000) A teenage girl discovers her peculiar new stepsister and stepdad are refugees hiding on Earth from an alien tyrant—whose agents finally catch up with the fugitives.

Suburban Commando (1991) Alien warrior Hulk Hogan causes chaos after his ship crashes on Earth. That's nothing compared to the chaos unleashed when his enemies find him.

EIGHT

Cuckoos from Space

Spacemen, Rape and Human/Alien Hybrids

"It isn't a matter of hate. It's a biological obligation."
—*Village of the Damned* (1960)

Taking over a planet by invading, British author John Wyndham once wrote, is quite conventional.

The Martians in *War of the Worlds*, Wyndham wrote in *The Midwich Cuckoos*, did exactly what an Earthly army waging war on Britain might do: "They simply conducted a straightforward campaign with a weapon that outclassed anything that could be brought against it." That's true of most alien invaders in movies: their victory relies on death rays or impenetrable force-fields shielding them from human attack.

What if they didn't have that technology? What if their spaceships couldn't transport an army across light years? What if they got here and discovered, as Wells' Martians ultimately did, that they couldn't live in Earth's environment?

One solution is to grow a new generation of colonists here on Earth. In *Species* (1995), Earth establishes contact with an alien race. Along with valuable technological breakthroughs, the aliens show Fitch (Ben Kingsley) how to splice their genetic code into a human embryo. Fitch decides this is a cool idea and goes ahead. In a matter of days, the resulting hybrid child grows into Sil (Natasha Henstridge), a beautiful woman who can shapeshift into an unkillable monster. Her mission is to find a man to impregnate her so she can breed more of her kind and begin colonizing Earth.

Species is one of several films where aliens adopt the tactics of the British common cuckoo (*Cuculus canorus*). The female lays eggs in other birds' nests, with shell patterns resembling the other species' real eggs. The cuckoo fledgling hatches, kills the other eggs or fledglings, then lets its stepparents feed it and care for it until it's ready to leave the nest. As an "obligatory brood parasite," cuckoos expend no effort feeding their young which enables them to lay more eggs per year than other birds. It's why Wyndham used *The Midwich Cuckoos* as the title of his 1957 novel about aliens colonizing Earth by impregnating human women.

Using Earth's women as breeders—or in *Species*' case, using the clueless Fitch's lab—lets the aliens take over without an invading army. Their kids grow up here, and over time will push *Homo sapiens* out of the nest. This invokes, intentionally or not, several old tropes. For example, there's the "great replacement" theory that immigrants or minorities will outbreed and eventually replace white Americans. There's also the old, ugly belief that men of color want nothing more than to violate the precious beauty of white women.

Some films invoke the "captivity narratives" of the 19th century, about white women kidnapped by Native Americans (John Wayne's 1956 film *The Searchers* draws from the same well). For instance, in *Mars Needs Women* (1968) and *Frankenstein Meets the Space Monster* (1965), the aliens aren't out to conquer Earth, just drag some nubile young women back to their own planet.

Like so many beliefs and stories about alien visitors, this echoes older folklore, in this case about coupling with nonhuman things, such as the succubus and incubus of medieval legend. In Greek myth the Minotaur resulted from the Queen of Crete having sex with a bull. The Jersey Devil of American folklore supposedly resulted from a woman cursing her own child during agonizing labor pains. Mixed-race children in American fiction were often imagined as a dangerous blend of racial qualities, such as the supposed fiendish cunning of Asian minds enhanced by the supposed superior intelligence of the white race. And of course there are fathers' fears that their children are not, in fact, theirs by blood.

The uncanny quality of pregnancy, with a stranger growing inside a woman's body, also plays a role. There's a long fictional tradition of fetal horror in print and at the movies. Ray Bradbury's short story "The Small Assassin" involves a fetus that's fully conscious from the moment of conception, and angry as hell at being confined to the womb for nine months. It became an episode of the anthology *Ray Bradbury Theater* in 1988. The novel and movie *Rosemary's Baby* (1968) have Rosemary (Mia Farrow) raped by Satan to bear the devil's child; *Demon Seed* (1977) has a supercomputer artificially fertilize a woman so that it can transplant its consciousness into the baby.

Hybridization plays a role in real-world UFO beliefs too. In Antônio Villas Boas' story of sexual assault by a beautiful alien (sec Chapter Six) the woman implied afterwards that she was pregnant. Human/alien hybrids should be impossible but advanced EBE science can handwave many things. Multiple ufologists such as Bud Hopkins and David Jacobs have speculated aliens need our genes to supplement their damaged DNA or, like Wyndham's novel, to create surrogates to colonize Earth for them.

Based on Hopkins' same-name book, the TV miniseries *Intruders* (1995) is one of several films that takes the optimistic approach: aliens are impregnating women and taking the babies "to start a new world. Or to save an old one." Despite the aliens going through the usual abduction cruelties over the course of the film—experiments, implanted technology, kidnapped babies—Mary (Mare Winningham) learns at the end that the aliens have good intentions, though the movie doesn't explain what they are. The book was more pessimistic.

In 1993's *Official Denial*, Paul (Parker Stevenson) learns the aliens who've abducted him and others for years also have good intentions. They're our descendants, coming from the distant future when humanity has become sterile. By extracting 20th century DNA, they hope to restore their genetic vigor.

The X-Files goes with the cuckoos-for-conquest approach. As Scully and Mulder (Gillian Anderson, David Duchovny) learn over several seasons, a handful of human conspirators are working with alien colonizers to create a hybrid human/ET race. Similarly, in *What Planet Are You From?* (2000), the disguised alien Harry (Garry Shandling) impregnating Susan (Annette Bening) is key to conquering Earth though the film never gets around to explaining how. As the film is primarily a rom-com ("You made love to me while we ate. If I'd known you were going to do that, I'd never have ordered the soup"), the big and evil plan doesn't really matter.

The 2002 miniseries *Taken* falls between the two poles. The aliens, so evolved they've lost the capacity for emotion or compassion, start by experimenting on humans purely for science. The more they know us, the more they envy our emotions and our morality. The end result of their breeding experiments, Allie (Dakota Fanning), is a hybrid possessing alien psionic power but also human emotion. In the final episode she agrees to join the aliens so that neither they nor government alien-hunters will harass her parents any longer.

A common trope in many stories of hybrid pregnancies is the fetus, then the child, growing at an accelerated rate. While Allie grew up normally, Sil in *Species* matures rapidly, as do the children in *Village of the Damned*. Elizabeth—the child of a human/Visitor coupling in *V*—pops out of Robin's (Blair Tefkin) womb much faster than normal, then grows into a small child (Jenny Beck) in a matter of days. In the follow-up TV series Elizabeth ages into a teen (Jennifer Cooke) in the first episode.

Aging so fast marks the hybrid kids as something superhuman but it's also a plot convenience. There's only so much you can do with a baby, even one with psi-powers. Once they grow, it's much easier to tell stories about them. In *Species*, having Sil undergo normal growth would mean waiting years before she could start mating and killing.

V's Elizabeth has phenomenal abilities—TK and superhuman computer skills—that neither her father nor Robin possess. That's not how hybridization works—the child doesn't just get new abilities—but Elizabeth is also a child of destiny. A birthmark on her hand, the Mark of Zon, identifies her as one fated to overthrow the Visitors' Leader and bring about peace. The series promptly forgot about this, but it would have played a role in the final episode if NBC hadn't pulled the plug.

Scully's (Gillian Anderson) son on *The X-Files* is another hybrid chosen one. Prophecies implied he would either save Earth from alien invasion or lead the invasion himself. He might be a perfect human with no flaws, an alien messiah or a human born with the powers of the aliens' super-soldiers. Scully decided he'd be safer raised by adoptive parents and didn't see him again until the 2016–18 revival series. In his appearances there, William (Miles Robbins) demonstrates mental abilities including telepathy, illusory disguise powers and the ability to make people explode. This may have less to do with his mixed-species status than heavy genetic engineering, as detailed in Chapter Fourteen.

By contrast with William or Elizabeth, Scott Hayden (C.D. Barnes) in *Starman* (1986–87) was an underachiever. Conceived in the theatrical film *Starman* (1984), he'd been abandoned at an orphanage by his mother to keep government agents from dissecting or exploiting him. When his father returned to Earth and reunited with his son, he began training him to use the same powers Dad possessed. Scott didn't show any powers his father didn't also have.

Rape, Reproduction and Maternal Agency

Women obviously play a large role in stories involving human/alien pregnancy, but not necessarily an active role or one with any agency. In many of these stories the women are pawns or victims, helpless to stop what's happening to them.

What's happening to them is rape, but the films rarely acknowledge it. In *The X-Files,* Scully learns William resulted from the sinister Cigarette Smoking Man

(William B. Davis) impregnating her—technologically, not physically—while she was unconscious. Nobody says aloud that he raped her, even if it wasn't with his penis. It's the second time something like this happened to Scully, who conceived another child during an earlier abduction.

At least Scully gets to be horrified at the violation. In *The Midwich Cuckoos* the sardonic scientist Zellaby says the women of Midwich don't really mind being impregnated against their will because all women care about is having babies. They don't care how that bun got in the oven. In the 1995 *Village of the Damned* remake, Venker (Kirstie Alley) quips that "first they knocked them out, then they knocked them up," but it's tossed off as a smart-ass joke. In the 1964 *Children of the Damned*, the one woman who does get angry about her inexplicable pregnancy ends up in a serious traffic accident. It feels like a punishment for not wanting motherhood.

Marge (Gloria Talbott) in *I Married a Monster from Outer Space* (1958) is horrified to realize the man she thinks is her husband Bill (Tom Tryon) is an alien imposter. His people's women have died out so he and his cohorts in the first wave of invaders are trying to impregnate human women. If they succeed—their scientists are working on it—they'll conquer Earth and use human women as breeders to rebuild their species. It's not surprising a 1950s film didn't call this rape, but the 1998 remake, *I Married a Monster*, doesn't acknowledge it either.

The Astronaut's Wife (1999) makes it clear that the alien impersonating Spencer (Johnny Depp) impregnated Jillian (Charlize Theron) by sexual assault. Jillian does get to feel horror at learning she has an alien embryo in her womb. Even so, the film seems to revel in her suffering. The assault is brutal, and at the climax of the film Spencer brags to Jillian about it. He killed her husband, impregnated her and she still can't live without him! *Progeny* (1998) lingers on the graphic tentacle rape that impregnates one of the protagonists, Sherry (Jillian McWhirter). Having blocked out the memory, she remains happy and hopeful about the baby until she gives birth and dies. It comes off as the most misogynistic of the films in this chapter.

Mars Needs Women (1968) opens with Fellow No. 1 (Tommy Kirk) and his Martian raiding party teleporting women to their ship to make up for the 100/1 male/female ratio on Mars. A teleporter glitch kills all the women, so the Martians start asking for volunteers instead. Nobody on either world seems to care about the women who died.

The 1974 film *The Stranger Within* makes Ann's (Barbara Eden) pregnancy a traumatic event. The trauma, though, is that because her husband (George Grizzard) had a vasectomy, everyone assumes Ann cheated. When a hypnotherapist (David Doyle) probes Ann's mind and learns she's been impregnated by aliens, he suggests it's a wonderful and exciting thing. That Ann's been turned into a surrogate mother against her will doesn't mar his enthusiasm.

What Planet Are You From? is comparatively enlightened by comparison. The Harry/Susan relationship is built on a lie—Susan has no idea Harry's an alien—but it's consensual otherwise. Eventually Harry comes to love his family, siding with them against his own people.

These movies almost never bring up the possibility of abortion, a topic Hollywood is often squeamish about. In *The Astronaut's Wife* and *The Stranger Within*, Jillian and Ann do try to terminate the pregnancy but the fetus in both cases is able to stop them. In the 1995 *Village*, Venker offers $3,000 to every woman if she goes through with her pregnancy. They all do.

While women are the targets of the alien sexual assault, the agency in the films belongs to the men. This was also an element in captivity narratives, where—in contrast to the actual history—the women abducted by Native Americans can do nothing but resist their captor's lustful assaults until a big strong white man arrives to save them. Women's lack of agency also shows up in *The Midwich Cuckoos*, which is an English novel, so possibly I'm reading a subtext that isn't there.

In Wyndham's novel, it's the men of Midwich who figure out how to keep the women from panicking and slut-shaming each other. The 1960 adaptation focuses less on the women's trauma and more on the men sitting and brooding about what's happened to their wives and daughters. In the 1995 remake, the only mother to take action is Jill (Linda Kozlowski), who's protecting her son, David. In the two *I Married a Monster* films, the protagonist relies on the town doctor to find men who haven't been replaced and organize a posse. The doctor knows all the local women are human, but neither film lets them fight.

The bizarre 1958 film *Night of the Blood Beast* uses some of the same tropes on a male victim. Aliens unable to enter our atmosphere implant a human astronaut with embryos that can grow up on Earth. The astronaut (Michael Emmet) is surprisingly comfortable with this, although it's implied the alien might be controlling him. The alien claims their people destroyed their world when they developed "the ultimate power"—which in the 1950s probably meant atomic energy—and they want to help humanity avoid their error. The astronaut becomes convinced the real agenda is colonization and turns against them. Unusually, we never learn for sure what the truth is.

Other stories about aliens using men for their sperm such as *Species* and *Devil Girl from Mars* (1954) don't push the same buttons as alien impregnation films. In *Species*, the horror for the men is the same as in *Fatal Attraction* (1987) and *Play Misty for Me* (1971), that the woman you had a one-night stand with turns out to be a dangerous psycho.

Spotlight

Village of the Damned *(1960)*

MGM. 77 minutes. Release date October 28, 1960.

CAST: George Sanders (Gordon Zellaby), Barbara Shelley (Anthea Zelaby), Martin Stephens (David Zellaby), Michael Gwynn (Major Alan Bernard), Laurence Naismith (Dr. Willers), John Phillips (General Layton), Richard Vernon (Sir Edgar Hargreaves), Jenny Laird (Mrs. Harrington), Richard Warner (Harrington), Thomas Heathcote (James Pawle), Charlotte Mitchell (Janet Pawls), Keith Pyott (Dr. Carlyle), John Stuart (Prof. Smith), Bernard Archard (Vicar), Sheila Robins (Nurse), Peter Vaughan (Constable Gobby), Tom Bowman (Pilot), Susan Richards (Mrs. Plimpton), Rosamund Greenwood (Miss Ogle), Sarah Long (Evelyn Harrington), Pamela Buck (Milly Hughes), Alexander Archdale (Coroner), Anthony Harrison (Lieutenant), Gerald Paris (Sapper), Diane Aubrey (WRAC Secretary). Children (June Cowell, Linda Bateson, John Kelly, Carlo Cura, Lesley Scoble, Mark Mileham, Roger Malik, Elizabeth Munden, Theresa Scoble, Peter Priedel, Peter Taylor, Howard Knight), Village Children (Brian Smith, Janice Howley, Paul Norman, Robert Marks, John Bush, Billy Lawrence)

CREDITS: Director: Wolf Rilla; Screenplay: Stirling Silliphant, Wolf Rilla, George Barclay, based on John Wyndham's *The Midwich Cuckoos*; Photography: Geoffrey Faithfull; Art Director: Ivan King: Editor: Gordon Hales; Music: Ron Goodwin; Photographic Effects: Tom Howard; Producer: Ronald Kinnoch

"One of the luckiest accidents in my wife's life is that she happened to marry a man who was born on the 26th of September." So says Richard Gayford, the narrator of Wyndham's *The Midwich Cuckoos*. Because September 26 was his birthday, the couple left the small, quiet village of Midwich to celebrate in London. Returning home, they found the town cordoned off by the military. Everyone within a mile of Midwich has fallen asleep. Anyone who enters the affected area joins the victims in slumber but wakes if dragged back out. Aerial photographs suggest a spaceship has landed in the village.

Suddenly everyone wakes up, apparently unharmed. When the military moves in there's no sign of a spaceship or anything out of the ordinary. A couple of months after the "Dayout," though, every fertile woman in Midwich—single, married, virgin, lesbian—is pregnant.

The village vicar, the doctor and Professor Zellaby worry this could lead to an outbreak of gossip, slut-shaming and guilt among the women so they make a pre-emptive strike. They have Zellaby's wife Anthea gather the women together and make it clear that whatever happened affected them all. Nobody's at fault. This tactic works, and only a few women leave town. Eventually they give birth, all on the same day, to golden-haired, golden-eyed infants. Anthea's son is an exception. She'd already conceived before Dayout so her child is normal.

The other infants are anything but. Even before they can speak, the babies whose mothers took them from Midwich compel the women to return. When one woman accidentally jabs her baby with a diaper pin, the baby retaliates by making mommy stab herself with the same pin, over and over. Zellaby figures out that the children belong to two hive minds, one male, one female, giving them powerful psi-abilities, though they still retain some individuality.

The British government realizes this is a colonization attempt by an alien race. Even so, it takes no action against the children, hoping to exploit their powers. Gayford learns another Dayout took place in the USSR. The Soviet government also hoped to exploit the children but decided the risk was took high. The government wiped out the village with a bombing raid, sacrificing the human residents too. There was no other way to prevent the children's telepathy from sensing what was coming.

The Midwich children sense their kindred's deaths and realize they're more vulnerable than they thought. From that point on, they retaliate much more violently against anyone who attacks them. Finally they tell Zellaby they're ready to leave town and begin growing other colonies, though it's left unclear how—seduce other humans? Reproduce with each other? Zellaby agrees to arrange their departure but instead he carries out a suicide bombing, wiping the children out.

In the 1950s, Wyndham was a highly successful English novelist whose science fiction, like Michael Crichton's was popular with mainstream, non-genre readers. *The Midwich Cuckoos* is one of his best-known books. The novel's great strength is that it's very low key. Mundane details of life in Midwich ground the story in reality. Even though the children are clearly unnatural, they don't pose an overt threat, so everyone delays acting. Wyndham makes a point of contrasting the story with the action and heightened emotion of a Hollywood invasion film where the scientist hero comes up with a "deus ex laboratoria" to defeat the menace.

Midwich Cuckoos does get extremely talky in the last quarter, as the children discuss their goals with Zellaby and recycle stock Cold War clichés. England, you see, is just too darn *nice* and too democratic to deal with them as ruthlessly as the

Soviets did. It almost feels like a commie villain sneering at the weakness of "decadent capitalists."

Throughout the book, the women are acted upon rather than acting. Zellaby explains at one point that they're not scared because their simple, placid minds can't conceive how dangerous the children are. Besides, once they had babies in their arms, trivial issues like extraterrestrial sexual assault became irrelevant. Wyndham apparently liked this line of thought as he makes a similar argument in *The Day of the Triffids*.

The film opens with a pastoral scene of sheep being herded and tractors in motion. Inside a nearby stately home, Professor Gordon Zellaby (George Sanders) is chatting on the phone to his brother-in-law, Major Alan Bernard (Mark Gwynn). Then the professor suddenly collapses to the floor. His dog goes to sleep too, as does the tractor driver.

The camera pans over Midwich to show everyone, everywhere—on the street, at the telephone switchboard, in the general store—is dead to the world. Irons burn clothes, sinks overflow. The only sound is the town clock striking 11 a.m., but nobody's listening.

An hour later, Alan reports to General Layton (John Phillips) that not only is Zellaby not answering, neither is anyone else in town. Alan points out there are military exercises in the area and while it's unlikely there's any sort of threat in Midwich—well, could he start his leave early and head home?

As Alan approaches Midwich, he sees a local bus has run off the road into a ditch. When Constable Gobby (Peter Vaughan) bicycles up to take a closer look he immediately falls asleep and tumbles off his bike. Alan calls Layton and gets authorization to organize a military response. The military soon establishes that anyone who crosses an invisible boundary around Midwich, even wearing a gas mask, falls asleep. Pull them back out and they wake up, no worse for wear but feeling chilled. Neither Alan nor Dr. Willers (Laurence Naismith), returning to Midwich from an outside call, can explain the cause or how the effect is confined precisely within the boundary. Alan sends a plane over the village to see if the effect extends upwards. It does; the plane crashes and the pilot (Tom Bowman) dies.

Suddenly, the "Timeout" ends and everyone wakes up. Zellaby and his wife Anthea (Barbara Shelley) can't figure out what happened to them. When Zellaby learns the entire village went to sleep he joins the military researchers hunting for a cause. Discussing the lack of answers with Alan and Layton later, Zellaby says that "until we know what happened, we won't know what to expect."

Two months later, Anthea's eating for two with a penchant for anchovies. Mrs. Plimpton (Susan Richards), who runs the general store, knows what to expect but Zellaby's too caught up in his research to notice. When Anthea tells him she's pregnant he's initially reduced to befuddled idiocy, then thrilled to the core. He tells his wife that at his age he appreciates how wonderful this is.

That's not the mood elsewhere in Midwich. Milly (Pamela Buck) freaks out when Willers tells her she's pregnant, insisting she's a virgin (though not using the word). Janet Pawls (Charlotte Mitchell) has to tell her husband (Thomas Heathcote) she's pregnant; given that he's been at sea for a year, he suspects his brother Edward (uncredited actor) is the father. Willers tells Zellaby and the Midwich vicar (Bernard Archard) that one woman's already attempted suicide. The vicar reluctantly violates the confidence of his flock by disclosing other women have told him about impossible pregnancies. Put it all together and it's clear every fertile woman in Midwich got pregnant during Timeout.

Five months after that dark day, Dr. Willers X-rays Anthea and confirms the baby's perfect, except for the trivial fact it's seven months along. Zellaby, still excited about having a late-in-life baby, assures Anthea they have nothing to worry about. She assures him there is, and that she's lain awake night after night wondering where the baby came from. Is it truly theirs? And if not, whose? Her husband's far more upbeat than most of the village men, who spend their nights marinating in misery at the pub. Harrington (Richard Warner) mutters darkly that he hopes none of the babies live.

No such luck. All twelve mothers deliver within a day or so, with all the babies around 10 pounds weight and possessing golden eyes. Anthea's blissfully happy now that she's able to hold her son, David (Martin Stephens), though Zellaby's dog Bruno takes an instant dislike to the infant. Animals sensing alien evil is a staple film plot—the alien in *I Married a Monster from Outer Space* kills Marge's dog because it's so hostile—but Bruno's reaction never comes up again.

Zellaby and Willers soon discover the babies' hair and nails, like their eyes, are abnormal, plus the kids are growing freakishly fast. While they're discussing this, they hear a cry from upstairs and run up to see David's nurse (Sheila Robins) trying to stop Anthea from thrusting her hand into boiling water. Anthea calms down after Zellaby slaps her out of it. It turns out she didn't check David's bottle: the milk scalded his mouth, after which she felt the urge to scald herself. Anthea doesn't know the reason but stares uneasily at her son. He stares back, ominous and still.

By the time David is one year old, he looks five and can spell his own name. Zellaby demonstrates a Chinese puzzle box for David, who instantly understands how to open it himself. More remarkably, the other children know without any demonstration; what one child knows, they all share. One golden-eyed boy's brother snatches the puzzle box away from him; his little brother's eyes glow gold and the boy hands it back.

Before long, the kids look seven or eight and they're creepy as hell. Walking to Mrs. Plimpton's store with their blonde hair and immaculate black overcoats, they look less like kids and more like tiny Hitler Youth or possibly Men in Black. The other kids in Midwich don't like them. When one bounces a ball off one girl's head she turns and stares at him ominously, but David tells her not to do anything. The cuckoos go on to pick up their weekly supplies from the store. David can tell Mrs. Plimpton's afraid of them; he assures that while they're not a threat, they'll have someone else do the shopping from now on. The film never explains what they need food for, as they're all still living with their parents.

Unlike the rest of the village, Zellaby's more buzzed about the children than afraid. As he and Alan head off to a high-level conference on the situation, Alan tells his brother-in-law there's good and bad and the kids fall on the bad side. The professor replies that children must be taught morals; as they're so smart, teaching them will be easy. Alan says Zellaby's seduced by dreams of his son becoming the next Einstein. Zellaby says David could be greater than Einstein—but the professor adds that he isn't David's father.

While the men are away, we see Anthea acting maternal with David, trying to straighten his tie before he goes out. David insists on doing it himself and brushes off her other nurturing efforts with cold detachment.

At the conference General Layton reveals Midwich wasn't the only Timeout that day. One in Australia misfired so the babies were born dead; an Eskimo village left the babies out on the ice to die; a Mongolian village killed the babies and the mothers. In the USSR, however, the children lived and are receiving the best state education.

One scientist suggests the kids are mutants, but that wouldn't explain the Time-out. Another proposes that if Earth can bounce an electrical beam off the moon, there's no reason another planet couldn't accurately aim a ray at Midwich. That's as close to an explanation as we ever get.

Zellaby opposes taking any action against the children, including imprisoning them. Layton points out there have been multiple suspicious accidents and even a death among the normal children of Midwich but Zellaby pooh-poohs the threat. Combined into a hive mind, the children have an intellect twelve times normal—given how badly humanity has failed to solve its problems, isn't it worth seeing what such a genius can do? He proposes the government let him move the children into a common home, apart from others, and give him a year to work with them.

Returning to Midwich, Zellaby asks the children if they know of life on other planets. They respond with suggestive silence. They do admit they can read minds, but for now only surface thoughts. That will change, just as they've recently grown strong enough to affect minds in planes overhead.

The kids walk to their new group home, Anthea accompanying David. Edward Pawls' car accidentally hits one of the children, although she isn't hurt. The children force Edward to kill himself by driving into a wall. Martin looks at his mother a moment later and almost smiles. At the inquest, Anthea tries to say what she thinks happened, but the children's will power keeps her from testifying. The verdict is accidental death.

That's not good enough for Pawls, who comes after his brother's killer. Zellaby tries to save Pawls by talking him out of attacking but that's not good enough for the children. They force Pawls to kill himself. Afterwards Zellaby admits to Alan and Willers that he blames himself for underestimating the threat; the children's minds are sealed off by a brick wall he can't reach through. Alan gets word from Layton that the Russians, realizing they were losing control of the children, wiped out the entire village with artillery. Evacuating the normal humans would only have warned the kids, so everyone died. While England isn't that ruthless, it's clear something must be done.

The village men agree. A classic torch-wielding mob attacks the kids' home to burn it down. The children freeze the men where they stand; Harrington drops his torch and unconvincingly burns to death. The children tell Alan that what happened in Russia "will not happen to us because we have to survive—no matter what the cost." They mind-blast Adam, giving him an extreme case of shock and hysterical blindness.

Seeing his brother-in-law's condition, Zellaby realizes anew how dangerous the children are, but he has no idea what to do. When David drops in, Anthea tries appealing to his non-existent decency. Wherever he came from he's part of the human race now: can't both races learn to live together? David cuts the conversation short to talk to his father. He's impressed that despite everything, Zellaby still doesn't fear the cuckoos; he tells his father if his mind wasn't clouded by emotion, it could be as powerful as theirs.

The time for parents is done, however. David says it's safest if the children leave town and split up, preparatory to forming new colonies. Zellaby agrees to make the arrangements and to detail them at their Friday night lesson. Come Friday Zellaby has Anthea drive the still-blind Alan back to London. Once they're gone, he brings out a bomb, sets the timer and places it in a satchel. As he stares at the wall of his study, he reminds himself to think of it—a brick wall—and nothing else.

On the road, Anthea begins to figure out her husband's strange mood and drives back. By this point, Zellaby's at the classroom where the kids pick up that he's worried.

They start probing his mind but all they find is a wall. As they focus, we see the wall and then see it slowly, gradually start to crumble. It falls apart, revealing his secret and as one they stare at the satchel. Too late: the bomb goes off (I really love this whole scene). Anthea watches in dismay as the building collapses, then we see several sets of disembodied golden eyes in the ruins. Silently they fly away.

In the book *Keep Watching the Skies!*, Bill Warren says MGM snapped up the rights to the novel, photocopying the pages as fast as Wyndham typed them, then sending the copies to screenwriter Stirling Silliphant. As North American cuckoos don't reproduce the way the British cuckoo does, MGM decided the title would be incomprehensible in the U.S. and changed it to the blander *Village of the Damned.* An early draft of the script did explain the cuckoo reference, but very clumsily; the title change was a better choice.

Given MGM's interest, the three-year gap between the novel and the screen is surprising. The DVD commentary track says when MGM looked closer at the story there were concerns it came off like a parody of the virgin birth. They put the script away and only gradually overcame their discomfort. The script gets around that by being as vague as possible. Nobody says the word "pregnant" in the film and there's no hint the women were physically impregnated. The theory the aliens did it with a pregnancy ray reduced the risk of offending anyone in the audience but it makes the Timeout pointless. Why not just fertilize the women as they slept? Why not start hundreds of colonies rather than a handful?

While this version follows Wyndham's plot, it trims the cast and the wide-angle view of the Midwich community to focus on Zellaby, Alan and Mark. There's much less sense of village life. A lesbian couple from the book—not named as such, but quite obviously one—never appears, though they were in one of the earlier drafts of the script. Still, the three leads are good in their roles. Sanders, who usually played villains, cads or cynics, makes the most of a rare sympathetic role. As Anthea, Shelley doesn't have much to do beyond look beautiful, sympathetic and occasionally worried. Once David's born, the worries stop and maternal love takes over. We see much more discomfort and rage from the men in the film than any of the women are permitted.

The children, particularly Stephens, are creepy as hell. Rilla said he achieved that by keeping them still and never letting them fidget on camera. Stillness is most unnatural in kids. It's clear their attitudes are unnaturally grown-up too: Stephens conducts himself like an adult, serious and businesslike about everything. It's a great, chilling performance.

The cuckoos are more murderous than in Wyndham's novel. In the conference, Layton's discussion of mysterious deaths includes a strong swimmer who drowned suddenly. This was explained more in an earlier draft: the boy splashed water on a book one of the cuckoos was reading and they retaliated. Unlike the finished script they're full of pride and anger which prompted responses like that. The emotionless children of the finished film are more effective. When they act against the humans it's not from childish rage or fear but calculated. Like pod people, they have no malice, only the will to survive. The best way to do that is to exact a price from anyone who threatens them.

This is one of those alien visitor movies where heightened intelligence is a bad thing. The children have a mentality twelve times greater than ours but they're also sociopaths, devoid of feeling. Like so many evil aliens they look on emotion as a weakness because, as David tells his father, it gets in the way of reason and developing mental power.

Zellaby has similar exalted view of intellect. He's a brain himself, though we never learn what, exactly, he's a professor of. It's enough to know he's amazingly smart and values smartness in others. Despite knowing he's not David's biological father, at first he takes as much pride in David's genius as if the boy carried Zellaby genes.

It's not just pride, though. Zellaby sees the potential if the children's intellect can be channeled for good, but like Uncle Matthew in *War of the Worlds* or Carrington in *The Thing from Another World* he can't see that's impossible. Uncle Matthew assumed a more advanced race must be closer to God. Zellaby assumes superior intellects must find it easier to grasp moral law. He thinks the problem is immaturity, not that they have no use for human morality.

In this film it's the smart people who are wrong, the average folk who are right. Zellaby thinks we can co-exist with cuckoos; the military and government leaders are reluctant to wage war on children, reluctant enough they let Zellaby talk them out of it. The Midwich men who try to kill the children know what needs to be done and try to do it but they're punching out of their weight class.

The film is devoid of special effects except for the glowing eyes. In the novel, the eyes have a lambent, almost glowing quality but MGM wanted the science fiction film to have a visual hook. Special effects man Tom Howard used matte inserts of the irises of the kids' eyes, then reversed them, positive for negative. It's visually striking and MGM, according to Bill Warren, believed it was the money shot that sold the film; the posters emphasize "the eyes that paralyze."

The ghostly eyes flying off at the end are a striking image too but not a logical one. The children weren't possessed by demons, they were physical, flesh-and-blood human/alien hybrids. Blow up their brains and their minds presumably go with them. In any case, the film doesn't need gimmicks. It's smart, well-made and absolutely chilling.

Children of the Damned *(1964)*

MGM. 89 minutes. Release date January 29, 1964.

CAST: Ian Hendry (Dr. Lllewellyn), Alan Badel (David Neville), Barbara Ferris (Susan Elliott), Alfred Burke (Colin Webster), Sheila Allen (Diana Looran), Ralph Michael (Defense Minister), Patrick Wymark (Commander), Martin Miller (Prof. Gruber), Harold Goldblatt (Harib), Patrick White (Davidson), Andre Mikhelson (Soviet Official), Bessie Love (Mrs. Robbins), Clive Powell (Paul), Lee Yoke-Moon (Mi Ling), Roberta Rex (Nina), Gerald Delsol (Ago), Mahdu Mathen (Rashid), Frank Summerscale (Mark)

CREDITS: Director: Anton M. Leader; Screenplay: John Briley; Executive Producer: Lawrence P. Bachman; Associate Producer: Ben Arbeid; Photography: Davis Boulton; Art Director: Elliot Scott; Music: Ron Goodwin; Edior: Ernest Walter

We open in London where psychologist Dr. Llewellyn (Ian Hendry) is making intelligence tests on children as part of a worldwide research study. He shows geneticist David Neville (Alan Badel) that the young mute Paul Looran (Clive Powell) is phenomenally intelligent. Paul is also composed and still in the manner of the Midwich cuckoos. Curious about Paul's upbringing, the scientists meet Paul's mother Diana (Sheila Allen). She's crass, working class and clearly Paul didn't get his brains from her, nor does she encourage him in his studies. Diana flinches when they bring up Paul's father and refuses to say anything about him.

After the scientists leave, Diana taunts Paul that the men are stronger than she is, so he won't be able to escape when they come after him. Paul stares silently back at her, which prompts his mother to add she wishes she'd never been born, or that she'd smothered him the first time she held him. Paul's response is to put her in a trance and send her walking into traffic. His mother ends up hospitalized with multiple fractures and other injuries. When the two scientists check up on her, she tells them Paul can't be her child because she's a virgin—though as in *Village*, the word itself isn't used. With Diana laid up, her sister Susan (Barbara Ferris) takes over parental duties.

Neville suggests Paul is a mutation. He's astonished when he learns five other children—Russian, American, Chinese, Indian, and Ghanan—are arriving in London for a conference on the research study. The choice of Ghana may reflect that it was the first British colony in sub-Saharan Africa to declare independence (1957), which made it a bigger deal in England than, say Uganda. When Neville and Llewellyn meet the kids, they're all quiet, silent and still, like Paul. Asking the mothers about the fathers causes everyone around the kids to clam up. The mother of Rashid (Mahdu Mathen) freezes when the men ask if Rashid makes her do things against her will.

Neville's friend Colin Webster (Alfred Burke), a British spy, asks the two scientists if a half-dozen mutants cropping up simultaneously by chance is possible. Could they be parthenogenetic births—no father involved—and could radiation induce such a thing? This may be a roundabout reference to the children in Midwich, justifying the film's claim to be a *Village of the Damned* sequel. In any case, Neville replies that parthenogenesis is a very long shot. Llewellyn tells Webster what matters is that the fathers are absent while the kids' mothers are unstable.

Shortly afterwards, British agents gather on the street outside Diana's flat. An entranced Susan calls to ask Llewellyn for help. Webster shows up instead, telling Susan that Llewellyn sent him to take her and Paul somewhere safe. When Llewellyn and Neville arrive in response to the phone call it's obvious Susan has no memory of calling them. It's also clear Webster was lying. He explains that the scientists snooping around has made the six governments aware of how valuable these geniuses will be for military research. The other five nations are sending jets to bring their prodigies home, and the Secret Service assumes if Paul isn't in British custody, he'll end up kidnapped. In any case, Webster has Diana Looran's authorization to take the boy so it's a done deal.

Paul, however, is not amenable. On the street outside he telepathically compels a driver to crash his car (not dangerously), then disappears while everyone's distracted. Going from embassy to embassy he collects the other kids along with the American boy Mark's (Frank Summerscale) dog. They hole up in an abandoned church and Paul summons Susan to join them. She doesn't like being recruited as involuntary den mother, but the children won't let her leave. She soon discovers they can talk if they choose and each child knows everything the others know.

A couple of British agents try to corral the children. The dog protects the kids aggressively so one of the agents shoots him. The children retaliate by forcing the man to shoot his partner, then kill himself. When Llewellyn arrives, the children, speaking through Susan, request food, which the psychiatrist arranges. Illogically the government never attempts to drug them, or for that matter to gas them.

Webster tells the two scientists the kids can't be allowed to stay free. As one American puts it later in the film, their genius makes each of them a potential Manhattan Project; the military threat if they're in the wrong hands is too great. Llewellyn protests they may not be interested in science or the military—"What if all the want is to become poets or lovers or even tramps? You remember Shakespeare and Casanova?" "These days," Webster replies, "we'd find a better use for Shakespeare or even Casanova." If Britain can't use them, Webster wants them destroyed.

With the five other nations watching, Britain can't openly go after the kids. Instead a delegation from all six countries meets to ask them to come home. The children don't want that as their powers are strongest when they're together. They discourage the delegates' plan by demonstrating their shared knowledge: if one of them learns government secrets, the other five can reveal them.

The delegates back off but the efforts to control the children continue. Foreign agents distract the military cordon, then charge into the church. The children fight them off by converting the church organ into a solar-powered sonic weapon. Its effects are agonizing but one of the men stays on his feet long enough to shoot. A bullet kills Rashid.

Neville collects a sample of Rashid's blood and shows that if you put it on a slide with a regular blood cell, Rashid's cell will engulf and absorb the other. Webster suggests this is how the children were created, by taking over an egg in the womb; Neville isn't sure about that but says his experiment proves they're non-human.

This is little more than a tentative hypothesis, but Neville's convinced enough he urges the government to wipe the kids out; they're the superior race, we can't co-exist. Unusually for an alien visitor movie, Llewellyn rejects that: the children haven't hurt anyone except in self-defense and humans co-exist with lots of weaker species. Neville counters that we have no defense against their telepathic powers. Besides, if they reproduce it will be their descendants who inherit the Earth, not ours. Another scientist says that even if the kids aren't a threat, the potential for a hostile government to exploit their genius is too great.

Llewellyn goes to the church and tells the children that even though they're only killing in self-defense, they're making the authorities afraid. Speaking through Susan, the children reply that being hunted is terrifying for them too. Llewellyn asks what their goal is—why are they even here?—but Paul says they don't know.

Shortly after that trip, Susan shows up at Llewellyn's apartment to say the kids have vanished. Neville tries to call in an alert but Llewellyn refuses to let him. The furious geneticist says the children could easily control the mind of someone flying a nuclear bomber—what right does Llewellyn have to put millions of lives at risk? The children never laugh, never play—they're not children at all!

It turns out the kids did not listen to Llewellyn's urging to play nice. Mark returns to the American embassy to meet with a trio of officials. While they assure Mark they want him to come home, each of them is preparing to kill him. They attack, but Mark makes them turn their weapons on each other. The same thing happens at the other five embassies. From the government perspective, it looks like a string of unprovoked killings, more than enough reason to destroy the children.

A military task force gathers around the church, then Llewellyn shows up with another geneticist, Dr. Gruber (Martin Miller). Contrary to Neville, Gruber says Rashid's blood cells are human, just a million years ahead of us. Neville says that changes nothing: we're a million years ahead of the apes and look how we treat apes. Llewellyn, however, convinces the civilian officials on the scene to approach the kids and talk. Paul and a couple of the children emerge from the church. Paul says the children are ready to die: humanity has chosen the path of violence, the children are rejecting it. As he speaks, the two remaining children emerge with Rashid, alive again.

For a second it looks like both sides will step back from the brink. Instead, a loose

THEY COME TO CONQUER THE WORLD...

...so young, so innocent, so utterly deadly!

METRO · GOLDWYN · MAYER presents
A LAWRENCE P. BACHMANN production
Starring IAN HENDRY
CHILDREN OF THE DAMNED X
with ALAN BADEL · BARBARA FERRIS · Screenplay by JOHN BRILEY · Produced by BEN ARBEID · Directed by ANTON M. LEADER

Children of the Damned (1964) is the only sequel to 1960's *Village of the Damned*. The films *These Are the Damned* and *School of the Damned* are only connected by the name.

screwdriver in the command center slides down a console and accidentally triggers the signal to attack. Despite people screaming and barking commands to stop, the military, once in motion, can't course-correct. The children, and several civilians from the look of it, all die. This time, no glowing eyes go flying away.

Screenwriter John Briley says on the commentary track that he saw the film as a Cold War metaphor. Governments around the world had come to see intelligence and science strictly as weapons and they evaluate the kids in that light. The question of what the children want is irrelevant; if they're not assets, they're threats. In that situation all it takes is an accident like the screwdriver to set off a war, a serious real-world fear in the nuclear age. Briley meant the film as a call for peace: the kids start out with an eye-for-an-eye response to human violence but by the end of the film they've risen above that. They reject brute force, even if it costs them their own lives.

Trouble is, the film doesn't deliver on this premise. Even given that Diana's words to Paul were cruel, forcing her into a potentially fatal accident is hardly a proportionate response. If he acted out of anger, there's no sign he ever regretted it. And Diana has reason to be angry too—discovering she's pregnant with no awareness how, had to have been traumatic, to say nothing of the slut-shaming she must have received. It feels the film's punishing her for being less than a perfect loving mother.

Forcing Susan to serve as their spokesperson isn't violent but it is coercive. It's also pointless as they can all speak for themselves and for that matter could communicate with telepathy. Their motives for taking her are left unexplained. Nor does the film explain how Rashid came back to life; like Klaatu's ability to open locked doors it seems to be "aliens are magic" thinking. The plot holes are true to Briley's theme, in a way—nobody but Llewellyn cares about the kids' motives—but they're still annoying.

Gruber's theory suggests that the sextet aren't alien visitors at all but simply mutants. But as Neville says early on, the chance of six parthenogenetic births coincidentally producing the same mutation is hard to swallow. Alien intervention makes more sense. But not a lot more sense: unlike Midwich the children don't know why they're here and they clearly aren't looking to replace us. Nor is it likely the cuckoos would ever have become pacifists.

There simply are no good answers. But I'll give Briley credit for trying a new variation on a theme, rather than the flat Carpenter remake of 1995.

Village of the Damned *(1995)*

Universal, Alphaville Films. 99 minutes. Release date April 28, 1995.

CAST: Christopher Reeve (Alan Chaffee), Kirstie Alley (Dr. Susan Verner), Linda Kozlowski (Jill McGowan), Michael Paré (Frank McGowan), Mark Hamill (Reverend George), Meredith Salenger (Melanie Roberts), Peter Jason (Ben Blum), Constance Forslund (Callie Blum), Pippa Pearthree (Sarah) Karen Kahn (Barbara Chaffee), Thomas Dekker (David), Lindsey Haun (Mara), Cody Dorkin (Robert), Trishalee Hardy (Julie), Jessye Quarry (Dorothy), Adam Robbins (Isaac), Chelsea DeRidder Simms (Matt), Renée René Simms (Casey), Danielle Wiener (Lily), Hillary Harvey (Mara at 1 year) Bradley Wilhelm (David at 1 Year), Jennifer Wilhelm (Mara/David at 4 months), Buck Flower (Carlton), Squire Fridell (Sheriff), Darryl Jones (CHP), Ed Corbett (Older Deputy), Ross Martineau (Younger Deputy), Skip Richardson (Deputy), Tony Haney (Dr. Bush), Sharon Iwai (Eye Doctor), Robert L. Bush (Mr. Roberts), Montgomery Hom (Technician), Steve Chambers (Trooper), Ron Kaell (Trooper), Lane Nishikawa (Scientist), Michael Halton (Station attendant Harold), Julie Eccles (Eileen Moore), Lois Saunders (Doctor at Clinic), Sidney Baldwin (Labor Room Physician), Wendolyn Lee (Nurse), Kathleen Turco-Lyon (Nurse), Abigail Van Alyn (Nurse), Roy Conrad (Oliver), Dan Belzer (Young Husband), Dena Martinez (Young Wife), Alice Barden (Woman at Town Hall), John Brebner (Man at Town Hall), Ralph Miller (Village), Rip Haight (Man at Phone)

CREDITS: Director: John Carpenter: Screenplay: David Himmelstein, based on *Midwich Cuckoos* and the original *Village of the Damned*; Producers: Michael Preger, Sandy King; Co-Producer: David Chackler; Executive Producers: Ted Vernon, Shep Gordon, Andre Blay; Co-Executive Producers: James Jacks, Sean Daniel; Photography: Gary B. Kibbe; Production Designer: Rodger Maus; Editor: Edward A. Warschilka; Music: John Carpenter, Dave Davies

In Carpenter's American remake of the 1960 film, the Timeout sends everyone in a small California town to sleep. Unlike the original film or Wyndham's novel, a couple of men die in accidents as a result. One burns to death falling on a barbecue grill, an example of the higher level of gore in this version.

When it becomes clear that the women in town all became pregnant on that day, chain-smoking government researcher Venker (Kirstie Alley) arrives. In a town meeting, she tells the women that while she can understand some of them wanting an abortion, her research grant will cover all ob/gyn bills with a $3,000 bonus for every woman who goes through with the pregnancy. None of the mothers aborts, but one of them delivers a stillborn baby girl. Venker takes the body.

After the kids are born, it becomes obvious that, like the original, they're more than human. Mara (Lindsay Haun), daughter of local scientist Alan Chaffee (Christopher Reeve), becomes the children's leader. When Mara's mom (Karen Kahn) accidentally scalds her daughter, Mara forces her to burn herself in turn, with much more graphic detail than in the 1960 film. Mara tops this by forcing her mother to walk off a cliff to her death. This is weirdly disproportionate and it's hard to see what Mara gains from it. Nobody knows she's responsible, so it won't even serve as a good object lesson for the other parents.

Chaffee eventually learns the children are designed to pair off and reproduce. The stillbirth threw a spanner in the works because David (Thomas Dekker) no longer has a partner. Without a partner to balance him, he begins to develop human emotions, earning scorn from the other children.

Venker later shows Alan the stillborn girl, a grotesque alien physically unlike any of the other children. Does that mean she died because the hybridization didn't take? It isn't explained. When the children learn later that Venker dissected their sibling, they engage once again in graphic gore, forcing Venker to vivisect herself.

Chaffee, like Zellaby, becomes the kids' teacher. When he learns they're preparing to scatter and breed fresh colonies, he adopts Zellaby's solution and goes to the final lesson with a bomb in his briefcase. First, though, he tries to get David to safety as a favor to his mother Jill (Linda Kozlowski). She and David escape, then Chaffee blows the kids to kingdom come along with himself.

With *John Carpenter's The Thing*, the director gave us a remake that surpassed the original. This time he fell far short. On the plus side, there's a broader sense of the community and the women get larger roles than in the 1960 take. Venker, however, is the only one with much agency and she borders on mad scientist territory. Jill has some agency, but she's fulfilling a traditional female role, protecting her child. Reeve is no Sanders and none of the children have the eerie screen presence Martin Stephens did.

Part of the strength of Carpenter's *The Thing* was that it went back to the original source material. Reincorporating Wyndham's lesbian couple or specifying that the aliens impregnated the women physically might have helped this film stand out from Wolf Rilla's version. Instead it mostly follows the Rilla film, and when it makes changes, they're for the worse.

OTHER FILMS AND TELEVISION

After the Lethargy (2018) An alien drugs, rapes and impregnates captive women.

Bad Channels (1992) Alien takes over a radio station and captures young women by playing hit songs. Includes a lot of music videos.

Breeders (1986) Monstrous aliens hiding in the New York subways hunt human virgins to rape and impregnate.

Devil Girl from Mars (1954) An alien warrior woman and her ludicrous robot show up at a rural British hotel to select male breeding specimens. If they're suitable, world conquest will follow.

Extant (2014–15) After returning from a space mission, astronaut Halle Berry discovers she's pregnant. The hybrid child's powers make him a valuable prize to some, a terrifying threat to others.

Frankenstein Meets the Space Monster (1965) Aliens who lost their women in a nuclear war arrive in Puerto Rico to kidnap replacements. Frank, an android disfigured in one of their attacks, is the women's best hope to survive.

Monarch of the Moon (2004) In a tongue-in-cheek serial adventure, the World War II superhero Yellowjacket discovers the Empire of the Moon has allied with the Axis to invade America and take its women as breeding stock.

Mutant Swinger from Mars (2009) A parody found-footage film set in the 1950s. Martians compel a human scientist to assist in their scheme to kidnap Earth women as breeders.

The Stranger Within (1974) In a memorable horror/SF hybrid, aliens impregnate Barbara Eden, who finds herself drinking literally gallons of coffee, drowning her food in salt and reading every conceivable topic, all to satisfy the alien growing inside her.

Weird Ones (1962) A randy alien commits violent crimes on Earth. Two press agents employ a sexy woman as bait to trap him. An obscure, lost film.

Zeta One (1969) British spy spoof in which superspy discovers alien warrior women kidnapping women from Earth to regrow their population.

NINE

When Ancient Astronauts Attack
Gods from Outer Space on Screen

"We owe our human condition here to the intervention of insects?"
—Quatermass and the Pit

What if Sodom and Gomorra were destroyed by nuclear weapons?

What if Adam and Eve were the product of extraterrestrial genetic engineering on primitive ape men?

What if spacemen built the pyramids or the Nazca carvings?

What if the reason gods of ancient myth live in the heavens is because they really came from outer space?

The idea that a hypothetical superscience can explain mythology, history and religion has a long history. Following H.G. Wells' *War of the Worlds,* one Garrett P. Serviss published *Edison's Conquest of Mars* in which the great inventor defeats a Martian invader. The "Edisonade," as they called such adventures back then, includes the reveal that it was Martians who built the Egyptian pyramids and the sphinx.

Many more stories followed in the 20th century. Edmond Hamilton's *A Yank in Valhalla* identifies the Aesir as a mutant race whose advanced technology convinced our ancestors they were gods. The Henry Kuttner/C.L. Moore collaboration *The Mask of Circe* has a descendant of Jason of the Argonauts battle against Apollo, a rogue AI created by Olympian science. Jack Williamson's *Darker Than You Think* shows that witches, vampires and werewolves are all mutants with super-psionic powers.

Other science fiction writers went with spacemen. Nelson Bond's 1942 short story "The Cunning of the Beast" has an alien create Adam and Eve through genetic engineering, only to have them rebel against him. In Arthur C. Clarke's 1953 *Childhood's End*, the alien Overseers look like the classic image of devils, with batwings and horned heads. It turns out that because they've arrived on Earth to manage the last years of human existence, humanity unconsciously projected a psychic vision of them back through time as a warning. Jack Kirby's 1970s comic book series *Eternals* credits the Greek gods, belief in Satan, the creation of humanity and Noah's flood to the intervention of the cosmically powerful Celestials.

While some fiction and pseudoscience assumes the space gods are long gone, others assume they're still around or will return. Charles Fort, an early 20th century paranormal writer, suggested in his *The Book of the Damned* that many of the incidents he reported on could be explained by Earth being "owned" we're farm animals and Earth is the paddock in which we're allowed to graze. At least for now. Kirby's *Eternals* was built around the return of the Celestials to judge how well we've lived up to their standards.

Most screen explorations of the ancient-astronauts concept have been in the form of pseudoscientific documentaries such as *Chariots of the Gods* (1970) and more than a dozen seasons of *Ancient Aliens* on cable TV. While Von Daniken's theories have been ripped to shreds by serious science, they are superficially persuasive; I found them fascinating as a tween. They rely heavily on the assumption that, as *Plan Nine from Outer Space* says, "You can't prove it didn't happen!" We cannot conclusively show aliens didn't arrive on Earth and tinker with our DNA, therefore it's just as plausible as evolutionary theory, right?

Wrong. That's not how science works. And in some cases, there is evidence it didn't happen: despite spacemen supposedly building the pyramids, centuries of Egyptian archeology have not turned up any traces of advanced technology.

Ancient astronaut theories are another example of a science fiction and pseudoscience echoing older traditions. Many old earthworks in England have been nicknamed "grim" (e.g., Grimm's dyke, Grimm's ditch), an old name for the devil, implying a supernatural origin. The massive mounds built by Native Americans cultures such as the Hopewell and the Adena have been credited to Romans, the lost tribes of Israel and others. White Europeans simply couldn't conceive that the natives they thought of as sub-human primitives could have created anything so remarkable.[1]

For some of Von Daniken's critics, the implied racism of his concepts is as big a problem as the scientific errors. Nobody claims the Romans needed help to build the Coliseum or that medieval Europeans couldn't have built Notre Dame Cathedral and similar structures. With rare exceptions such as Stonehenge, ancient-astronaut theories always focus wonders outside Europe—Angkor Wat, pyramids, the Nazca lines in Peru. The *Chariots of the Gods* documentary focuses on ancient Egyptian and pre–Columbian architecture, not European. It mentions the Romans but only to suggest they built their temples on foundations that had once been launch pads for UFOS, not that they needed help with the temples themselves.

Several Von Daniken-influenced films follow this line of thinking, associating ancient non–European cultures with space gods. A line in *The Thing*, for instance, asserts that everything the Incas knew, they learned from the little green men. *Hangar 18* (1980) says the aliens interbred with our ape ancestors to breed humanity; apparently bestiality is acceptable when it's alien/ape sex.

Killer Klowns from Outer Space (1988) mentions the ancient-astronauts idea but for laughs. In the middle of the fight against the extraterrestrial clowns, someone asks why aliens would show up looking like that. One suggestion is that it's the other way around: clowns look like them because of race memories formed by past encounters with the creatures.

And of course, *2001: A Space Odyssey* (1968) opens with primitive ape men encountering a mysterious black monolith that sparks their mind to use weapons, the first step towards modern tool-using man.

Although there are documentary films aplenty, relatively fiction films put ancient astronauts front and center. The first to show Von Daniken's influence was the unsuccessful TV pilot *Search for the Gods* (1975). After a drifter, Willie (Stephen McHattie), protects an elderly Native American from a couple of thugs, the old man hands over his greatest treasure, a strange medallion. It turns out to be part of a larger device that will reveal ancient secrets. Willie and his new buddy Shan (Kurt Russell) set out to gather the other parts ahead of a mysterious millionaire who wants them all. The TV movie is bizarrely vague, constantly hinting at cosmic secrets but avoiding details. It's as if the filmmakers were afraid talking about gods from outer space would turn the audience off.

By contrast *The Phoenix* (1981) has the courage of its convictions, referring to "electric batteries thousands of years old. Maps in the 16th century that could only have been chartered from the air." Judson Scott, better known for *Star Trek II*, plays Bennu, an ancient astronaut discovered in an Egyptian-style sarcophagus in Latin America. Taken to the U.S. and revived, Bennu refuses to spend his life as a lab specimen: he escapes and becomes one of the era's countless vagabond TV protagonists. He demonstrates a variety of psychic powers as well as a deep spiritual understanding of everything. The opening narration also makes him sound like a messiah figure: "The gods sent to Earth a child of their so that he might teach men the knowledge of the greatest of gods." This pilot went to series, but it died after a few episodes.

The animated series *The Roswell Conspiracies: Aliens, Myths and Legends* (1999) reveals that vampires, werewolves and yeti, among other myths, are aliens who've been living on Earth for centuries.

Alien vs. Predator (2004) tells viewers that millennia in the past, the Predators secured dominion over various cultures by presenting themselves as gods. They commanded their worshippers to become hosts for Xenomorph (as the monster of *Alien* is designated) eggs so that when the aliens hatched, they'd give the Predators the ultimate prey to hunt. If the battle went against the Predators, they'd nuke the civilization to wipe out the Xenomorphs, which explains why some cultures suddenly vanish from history.

The most successful take on the idea to date was 1994's *Stargate* which led to TV's *Stargate: SG-1* and four other spinoff series. In the film, an archeologist in 1920s Egypt discovers a mysterious artifact. In the present, archeologist Daniel Jackson (James Spader) translates the inscriptions on the artifact and figures out it's a gateway to another world. He accompanies a military team headed by Col. Jack O'Neil (Kurt Russell) to see what's on the other side.

What's on the other side is Ra (Jaye Davidson), the last of a dying alien race. When Ra found Earth, he was able to sustain his life by occupying human bodies. With his advanced technology he became ruler of Egypt and brought many of its people through the Stargate to serve him on another world. The Egyptians back on Earth eventually buried the Stargate so that Ra could never return. Now it's up to O'Neil, Jackson and their team to defeat Ra and liberate his slaves.

In *Stargate: SG-1* (1997–2007) it turns out Ra's species, the Gou'ald, isn't dead. Other Gou'ald controlled different parts of Earth as other gods—Amaterasu, Anubis, Ares, Ba'al, Balor, Indra, Kali, Marduk, etc.—and like Ra control other worlds populated with slaves exported from Earth. They'd also like to regain control of Earth, so the battle is on.

SPOTLIGHT

Quatermass and the Pit *(1967)*

Known as *Five Million Years to Earth* in U.S. release.

Associated British-Pathe Limited /Hammer Films. 97 minutes. Release date November 9, 1967.

CAST: James Donald (Dr. Roney), Andrew Keir (Bernard Quatermass), Barbara Shelley (Barbara Judd) Julian Glover (Col. Breen), Duncan Lamont (Sladden), Bryan Marshall (Captain Potter), Peter Copley (Howell), Edwin Richfield (Minister), Grant Taylor (Police Sergeant Ellis), Maurice Good (Sgt. Cleghorn), Robert Morris (Watson), Sheila Steafel (Journalist), Hugh Futcher (Sapper West), Hugh Morton (Elderly Journalist), Thomas Heathcote (Vicar), Noel Howlett (Abbey Librarian), Hugh Manning (Pub Customer), June Ellis (Blonde), Keith Marsh (Johnson), James Culliford (Corporal Gibson), Bee Duffell (Miss Dobson), Roger Avon (Electrician), Brian Peck (Technical Officer), John Graham (Inspector), Charles Lamb (Newsvendor)

CREDITS: Director: Roy Ward Baker; Producer: Anthony Nelson Keys; Story and Screenplay: Nigel Kneale; Music Composed by: Tristram Cary; Musical Supervisor: Philip Martell; Photography: Arthur Grant; Supervising Art Director: Bernard Robinson; Supervising Editor: James Needs; Editor: Spencer Reeves

The best film about gods—or more precisely devils—from outer space came out before Von Daniken. That's typical for Britain's Nigel Kneale, whose ideas were often out ahead of everyone else's. The film reworks his third Quatermass serial, also called *Quatermass and the Pit*, which the BBC broadcast in 1958. In the first two serials and the movies based on them, Quatermass—the head of British rocket research—battled threats to Earth coming from space. In this film the invaders are here and the enemy is us.

The film opens as workers on the London Underground rebuild and expand the Hobbs End station. One of them digs up an odd-looking human skull, then the crew discover skeletons in the wall, equally odd. The newspapers soon report the discovery of, in the words of one headline, *UNDERGROUND APE MEN*.

Dr. Roney (James Donald) and his assistant Miss Judd (Barbara Shelley) take charge of the excavation. Roney tells the press that the skeletons indicate humans walked the Earth five million years ago, earlier than anyone had imagined. That would have been even more startling then than it is now—the australopithecine fossil Lucy pushed our ancestry back to 3.2 million years but that wasn't until 1974. Although the authorities want to restart the construction ASAP, Roney insists on waiting until the site has been thoroughly studied. Further excavation turns up an unexploded World War II bomb—not uncommon in London—which a puzzled bomb expert reports isn't made of any sort of steel.

Cut to Quatermass (Andrew Keir), learning from a cabinet minister (Edwin Richfield) that the rocketry group is no longer a civilian operation: the professor and his team now answer to Col. Breen (Julian Glover). Quatermass' mission going forward is to help the military establish a nuclear-armed lunar base before any other nation, giving Britain a decisive advantage. Quatermass objects to dragging Earth wars out into space but the minister tells him to get out of the ivory tower and confront the real world.

Quatermass reluctantly takes Green to his office, but on the drive over, the professor can't resist detouring to the dig to see what's going on. Roney happily shows Quatermass that the skulls are not only human, they're closer to modern human brain size than any ancestors that far back should be. Roney isn't as happy to talk to Green, taking an instant dislike to him and vice versa.

Exploring the Hobbs End excavation, Quatermass and Judd visit a neighboring house known for poltergeist phenomena and grotesque dwarven ghosts. The two researchers discover old claw marks on the walls of the house, and a policeman who drops by can barely stand being inside. Judd points out a sign showing the street's original name was Hob's End, referencing an old name for the devil. Looking at newspapers in the local library later, Judd discovers stories of supernatural phenomena going back to 1927, when the station was first dug.

The supposed bomb turns out to be a metal ship which feels freezing yet isn't physically cold. When workers open the ship up, the inside is smooth, glassy metal, with a walled-off section marked with a pentagram. One worker screams, claiming he saw a hideous dwarf come through the pentagram wall, but nobody else saw anything. Quatermass rules out the rocket coming from Germany, adding the minister can contact Werner von Braun in the United States for confirmation.

As more phenomena accumulate around the excavation, Quatermass, scientist though he is, decides they might as well use the word "ghost." After all, ghosts don't have to be supernatural—perhaps they're natural phenomena, badly observed. Archival research shows anything that disturbs the ground in Hob's End, from felling trees to digging wells, triggers hauntings. They present their theory to Breen, but he's a rationalist terrified of anything paranormal. He dismisses their concerns and has a man drill into the sealed compartment.

Even though the drill doesn't penetrate, the attempt causes everything around them to vibrate and move. Then Roney sees a hole in the bulkhead, too big to have been caused by drilling. Cracks form around the hole, then the wall shatters. On the other side lies a crystalline hive-like structure full of large insect-like creatures. They start to decay at once, much to Quatermass' disappointment. He suggests they and the ship are as old as the skeletons but Breen once again denies anything unusual is happening.

Quatermass, Roney and Judd saw enough of the aliens before they disintegrated to recognize there are similar images everywhere in human culture, from horned masks to gargoyles. Is it possible humans have a common racial memory of these creatures? Quatermass takes it a step further, theorizing the aliens were Martians ("A name that's been nearly worn out before anything turned up to claim it") evacuating their dying world. When he announces this publicly, the press have a field day. The government has fits: how dare he bring this up without authorization? Quatermass replies that science isn't subject to government approval.

Breen objects that Mars is obviously lifeless but Quatermass has factored that into his theory. The Martians knew their world was dying so some of them evacuated to Earth. They couldn't survive here but they took our ape ancestors and transformed them through surgery and selective breeding, giving the apes an intelligence comparable to their own. It was colonization by proxy, and probably happened all over the world. The other ships returned to Mars to die but for whatever reason, the London ship suffered a failure to launch.

Breen, stubbornly proposes an alternative explanation: the entire thing was an Axis psy-op from World War II. Germans gambled that launching an experimental rocket with fake bodies would create a panic, weakening British morale. The minister likes the colonel's theory much better than the professor's and prepares to tell the press the great Quatermass was bamboozled by German special effects.

You don't need me to tell you Breen is dead wrong. When Judd goes down into the station, it triggers a poltergeist storm of wind and flying objects. Sladden (Duncan Lamont), who's working on the ship, panics and flees with the wind pursuing him— down the tunnel, into the next section, up onto the street, with telekinetic effects hitting objects and people around him. Sladden collapses in a church graveyard, with the gravel under him quivering from the mysterious force.

Judd brings Quatermass to the church a few hours later. Sladden is still on the edge of hysteria and the Vicar (Thomas Heathcote) believes he's been touched by spiritual evil. The Vicar warns against stressing Sladden any further but Quatermass forges ahead and presses Sladden to say what he saw. He does: "I had to run, to get away, they were coming—them! Them! … They were alive, hopping—I knew I was one!" He adds that the sky overhead in this vision was brown.

Quatermass concludes the vision triggered a latent telekinetic ability, probably another part of our Martian heritage. The vicar objects to Quatermass explaining away evil with science. Quatermass replies that no, he fully believes the ship down in the pit—"the pit" is also a euphemism for hell—and the forces emanating from it are evil.

Roney has already shown Quatermass an experimental mind-scanner he's working on. They try using it on Quatermass near the ship without any results. Judd, however, walks towards the ship in a trance. When they place the scanner on her head, the scanner visualizes buried Martian memories like the ones Sladden saw.

Quatermass shows the images to his superiors, explaining the swarming Martians are engaging in a ritual purging of their society, attacking and killing the unfit and the abnormal. This is a complete guess—there's no way he can deduce it from what we see on the video—but he's a genius, so it's correct. Quatermass also guesses that our Martian racial inheritance includes similar directives to purify the population. The minister dismisses the images and hallucinations and announces the dig will open to the public for a press conference that night. That will show everyone Quatermass is full of it!

At the conference, Breen says they're working with Germany to identify the missile. Quatermass finds he can't stomach the party line and calls Breen out, saying he's rationalizing the truth away because he's afraid. As they argue, a worker accidentally touches an electric cable to the ship. Energy flows through the metal, making it glow. Quatermass rushes everyone out but Breen stands frozen, watching until the energy kills him.

The energy, unfortunately, is now free of the excavation. Everyone around Hobbs End, Quatermass included, runs wild, and poltergeist phenomena manifest everywhere. Roney is an exception. Unaffected by the madness he drags Quatermass into an empty pub and snaps him out of it. Out on the street, the rest of the mob begins attacking people, either with TK or with brute force. Quatermass almost succumbs to the impulse to kill Roney and realizes this is the Martians' final triumph—as the purging spreads, everyone whose genes have mutated away from the Martian template will be eliminated.

Overhead in the sky, the accumulated psi-energy takes the form of a Martian head, looking like a horned devil. Quatermass realizes the manifestation is the Martian Achilles heel: a mass of metal plunging through it might discharge the energy, like legends that cold iron negates magic. The men settle on a nearby crane as their best shot, but Judd confronts them as they approach the crane. While Quatermass grapples with her, Roney climbs the crane and swings its arm into the devil-head. The touch of steel grounds the power, freeing the humans from their Martian compulsions. Roney, however, is caught in the surge and dies. The film ends with Quatermass and Judd standing around, shaken.

Kneale's Quatermass serials were head and shoulders above anything American television was doing in science fiction at the time, in acting, story and ideas. They still hold up well; Kneale's in the top tier of television science-fiction writers. *Quatermass and The Pit* boasts a solid cast and a much more intelligent approach to the "aliens made us" concept than, say *Hangar 18*. It's another variation of the *Midwich Cuckoos* approach to colonization—rather than colonize physically, the Martians made us their surrogates.

The first two Quatermass films suffered from Brian Donlevy playing Quatermass as an overbearing bully. Keir's Quatermass is simply hot-tempered and lacking any talent for diplomacy. Julian Glover does excellent work as Breen. He plays arrogant and tough yet when he cracks and shows his hollow core it feels entirely plausible.

The film sides with Quatermass over Green every step of the way. The rocket scientist is right; the military and the government bureaucracy are wrong. Green can't deal with the concepts Quatermass is proposing; the government just wants everything to stay calm.

Eternals *(2021)*

Marvel Studios. 157 minutes. Release date November 5, 2021.

CAST: Gemma Chan (Sersi), Angelina Jolie (Thena), Richard Madden (Ikaris), Kumail Nanjiani (Kingo), Lia McHugh (Sprite), Brian Tyree Henry (Phastos), Salma Hayek (Ajak), Lauren Ridloff (Makkari), Ma Dong-seok (Gilgamesh), Don Lee (Gilgamesh), Barry Keoghan (Druig), Kit Harington (Dane Whitman), Harish Patel (Karun), Bill Skarsgard (Kro), Haaz Sleiman (Ben), Jack (Esai Daniel Cross), Patrick (Alan Scott), Sandra (Hannah Dodd), Eros (Harry Styles), David Kaye (Arishem, voice only), Patton Oswalt (Pip the Troll, voice only)

CREDITS: Director: Chloé Zhao; Screenplay: Zhao, Patrick Burleigh, Ryan Firpo, Kaz Firpo; Story: Kaz Firpo, Ryan Firpo; Based on *The Eternals* by Jack Kirby; Producers: Kevin Feige, Nate Moore; Co-Producer: Mitch Bell; Executive Producers: Kevin De La Noy, Louis D'Esposito, Victoria Alonso; Photography: Ben Davis; Editing: Dylan Tichenor, Craig Wood

Comics legend Jack Kirby created and co-created a long list of characters: Captain America, the Fantastic Four, the X-Men, Marvel's version of Thor and the Black Panther. On Thor, he showed a flair for working with mythology and cosmic themes, the same talents he brought to his 1976–78 Marvel series *Eternals*.

In the first issue, Professor Damien and his daughter Margo discover an ancient Inca ruin holding carvings that, just as Von Daniken claims, show familiarity with space travel. The Damiens' guide, Ike Harris, then reveals he's Ikaris, one of the immortal race known as the Eternals.

Millions of years ago, the cosmically powerful Celestials took Earth's most advanced ape species and genetically engineered them into three races. The Eternals are immortal, beautiful and powerful. The Deviants' unstable genes cause them to breed generation after generation of freaks and monsters. And then there's humans, the middle ground. The Deviants are the monsters and devils of our religion and folklore; the Eternals are gods and heroes; Celestial intervention has caused many events in myth and religion such as Noah's flood.

Now the Celestials have returned to evaluate Earth's progress. If we fail to pass their tests, they'll destroy us, and no world has *ever* passed. The odds are against us, even without the Deviants scheming to attack the Celestials and regain dominance over humanity.

The series had an epic sweep and some clever touches. Where many comics keep this kind of cosmic battle hidden from the world, Kirby has the Eternals go public, with their activities covered in the press. The comic also had problems, such as nobody pointing out that the Celestials are cosmic genocides. While the series gives lip service that

In *The Eternals* (2021), Gilgamesh arrives on Earth in Babylonian times 7,000 years ago. That's not far enough for Gilgamesh as his legend goes back earlier, to ancient Sumer.

the Deviants' monstrous appearance doesn't prove they're monsters, multiple scenes suggest that yes, they are inferior and vile because they look vile.

Another problem was that Marvel overrode Kirby's intentions and insisted the series tie in with the Marvel Universe. That misses the point. As Kirby conceived it, Makkari, Zuras and Thena are the truth behind the myths of Mercury, Zeus and Athena (this mixes up Greek and Roman gods but that's a common comics mistake). In the Marvel Universe the Greek gods are real. Makkari, Zuras and Thena are simply powerful beings who get confused with the gods of Olympus a lot.

The opening text crawl of *Eternals* (2021) gives them a different origin. The immortals of the planet Olympia have served the Celestials for millennia, traveling from world to world to protect the inhabitants from the monstrous Deviants. Seven thousand years ago, the Celestial Arishem (David Kaye) sent a band of Eternals to Earth for that purpose:

- Ajak (Salma Hayek), the team leader.
- Ikaris (Richard Madden), her trusted right hand. He can fly and blast energy beams from his eyes.
- Sersi (Gemma Chan), Ikaris' lover, with a limited transmutation ability. Earth is her first mission.
- Thena (Angelina Jolie), a fighter who manifests weapons of solid energy.
- Kingo (Kumail Nanjiani), a skilled marksman and as we later learn, a gifted actor.
- Sprite (Lia McHugh), physically in her early teens and a mistress of illusion.
- Phastos (Brian Tyree Henry), a mechanical genius.
- Makkari (Lauren Ridloff), superhumanly fast and also a deaf-mute.
- Gilgamesh (Don Lee), skilled warrior and great cook.

We see Ajak receive her band's assignment from Arishem, then they transport to Earth. We find them there in 5000 BCE, battling against the Deviants, who in the MCU are monstrous creatures composed of what looks like interwoven living wire.

Primitive tribes watch as Makkari saves Ikaris from one Deviant, which frees Ikaris to blast another of the monsters out of the sky. As the battle ends, Sersi picks up one of the tribe's flint knives and transforms it into a beautifully made dagger.

Jump ahead to modern London where Sersi sees the dagger on a billboard, promoting a museum exhibit about artifacts that altered history. She's not pleased, but she has no time to do anything but rush to the history class she's teaching. She arrives late, but fortunately her boyfriend, fellow teacher Dane Whitman (Kit Harington), has filled in for her. As he doesn't know her field, the lecture has wandered into a discussion of how the alien Thanos wiped out half the world's population before the Avengers reversed things.

The students are amused to realize Dane and Sersi are a couple, then Sersi takes them into a discussion of apex predators; this seeds a later revelation about the Deviants but makes no sense in a history class. The discussion ends when an earthquake shakes the building, bringing down a piece of wall that Sersi disintegrates to save one of the students. Outside a Deviant rises from the water of the Thames, but nobody sees it except for a dog. A news broadcast announces the earthquake was a worldwide one, something the report treats as less remarkable than it would be; earthquakes don't hit the entire world. Then again, given events in the MCU to date, maybe it's not that startling.

After school wraps up, Sersi meets up with Dane and gives him a gift, an old ring with his family crest on it. He's thrilled but then blurts out that he thinks she's a wizard, like Dr. Strange. Sersi assures him she's not a wizard, but he next asks about her former boyfriend—why does her roommate Sprite mention them breaking up a century ago? Why does Sprite claim the guy flew? Sersi replies that he was a pilot but Dane's not convinced. This sets up a running element of the film, that way more people know about the Eternals than are supposed to.

As Sprite joins the couple, the Deviant suddenly attacks. Dane is in danger but Sersi liquifies the pavement the Deviant is standing under, then solidifies it. This delays it long enough to save Dane but no longer than that; Sprite's illusions add to the delay but can't hurt the creature. The battle finally ends when Ikaris shows up and blasts the Deviant, leading Dane to quip "I guess this must be the pilot."

Sersi then explains they're Eternals, not wizards, and that they thought they'd wiped out the Deviants five centuries ago. Dane asks the big questions: why didn't they help in the battle against Thanos? Why are they still here if the Deviants are gone? Sersi replies that they only get involved when Deviants attack, otherwise humanity would never learn to take care of itself. And they haven't received orders to relocate, so where else would they go? In response to another question, Sersi says Sprite made up the story that Ikaris—the Greek Icarus—was a failed flier.

Sersi and Sprite wonder why the Deviant was stalking them, where it came from and how it was able to heal its injuries—Eternals can do that, but not Deviants. Clearly it's time to get the band back together and find out. We flash back again to Babylon as the Eternals rack up yet another victory against the Deviants. After the battle the Eternals party with the Babylonians while Ajak communes with Arishem. She tells him people are flocking to Babylon because of their protection, making it Earth's largest city. Ajak adds that she thinks Earth is something special but Arishem orders her to focus on the prime directive, protecting humans from Deviants.

The next day the engineer Phastos—obviously the basis for the later Greek myth of Hephaestus—shows off a steam engine that will enable the Babylonians to farm more effectively than they do now. When Ajak warns him it's too advanced and will terrify the humans, a disgruntled Phastos goes with plan B: "Ladies and gentlemen, I present to you—the plow." Thena is less enthused with their triumphs, as there's nothing currently to battle. Ikaris is feeling great: he finally shares how he feels about Sersi and she reciprocates.

Back in the present, Sersi and Sprite drop in on Ajak only to find the Deviants have killed her. The Deviant they battled was able to heal because it drained Ajak's abilities. A ball of energy jumps from Ajak's body and into Sersi. It's the connection with Arishem, which means Ajak chose Sersi to succeed her as leader. In the brief glimpse Sersi gets of the Celestial, Arishem only conveys one message: "It's almost time."

As Sersi returns to herself, we enter another flashback. It's Tenochtitlan, the scene of the final battle against the Deviants. As the Eternals destroy the last of the monsters, they witness the conquistadors massacring the Aztecs. Ajak reminds them their duty is not to interfere in human wars, but Druig protests that what they're seeing is genocide.

Suddenly they have a more pressing problem, Thena descending into "madweary" as her millennia of memories overwhelms her. In Thena's case she's having confused flashbacks to countless past battles and acting them out by attacking her fellow Eternals. After the madweary fit passes, Ajak says the only way to cure it is by erasing Thena's memories. Thena shrinks from the thought of losing herself, despite Ajak's assurances that she's not defined by her memories.

The butchery in Tenochtitlan has gotten worse during this and Druig is disgusted Ajak won't let him use his mind-control powers to end it. When she reminds Druig of the rules, he replies that they're as much pawns of the Celestials as humans are of their leaders.

Ajak then says that as they have no further duties until the Celestials recall them, they should separate, following whatever path brings them happiness. Gilgamesh volunteers to watch over Thena as an alternative to a memory wipe, accepting the risk that she might kill him in a madweary attack. Ikaris protests they should stay together but Ajak insists there's no reason not to enjoy themselves.

Back in the present we learn Kingo's enjoying himself as a superstar of Bollywood films, the third generation of an Indian movie royalty. In reality, of course, all three generations are him. His fellow immortals are flummoxed, however, when his valet Karun (Harish Patel) tells them how honored he is to meet Kingo's fellow Eternals. Kingo laughs that Karun at first thought his employer was a vampire—the lack of aging, I assume—and attempted to stake him through the heart.

Karun knows enough to guess that the Eternals are here because the Deviants are stirring again. Kingo isn't thrilled about being called back into action. He's making the first of a trilogy and if the production pauses, a lot of people don't get paid. Karun, however, reminds his boss that "life affords no greater duty than to fight for your family," a quote from one of Kingo's movies.

Kingo charters a plane for the next step of their journey, which allows Karun to come along with them and film a documentary. When he interviews Sersi, she admits her transmutation powers are ineffective—she can turn rocks to powder or metal to flowers but nothing more complex. Sprite mocks Kingo for going into movies. Kingo replies that catching movies with Sprite and seeing how much she enjoyed them is what inspired him to become an actor.

After the plane touches down in Australia the Eternals travel out into the desert to meet Thena and Gilgamesh. The Eternals warn Karun that Gilgamesh is the most fearsome warrior of all time, a buildup undercut when he comes to the door in a "kiss the cook" apron. He's delighted to see his kin and invites them in for a meal. Thena, however, is sitting under a tree, painting obsessively, her way of fighting down a madweary attack. Sprite helps her calm down by creating an illusion of the Celestial chamber in which they started their voyage.

Over an excellent dinner and Gilgamesh's home-made booze, the Eternals banter and catch up. Kingo says he could use his connections to turn Gilgamesh's brew into a major micro-brand. Gilgamesh replies that he makes it out of homegrown corn which he ferments by chewing each kernel, so mass production isn't practical. Kingo spits his mouthful out.

Sprite abruptly wonders who'll lead the Avengers with Captain America and Iron Man gone. It feels more like product placement for the next *Avengers* film than a natural topic of conversation.

After the meal Sersi tries and fails to contact Arishem. Gilgamesh suggests she relax and not force it, which proves the magic recipe. To Sersi's dismay, she learns their mission on Earth is not what she believed. Arishem has planted a seed at Earth's core which will eventually grow into the Celestial Tiamut (an idea introduced in Marvel's series

Earth X). The Eternals weren't sent to Earth to protect humanity but to ensure the seed blooms. This requires a large human population so that Tiamut can drain off their life force to fuel her birth process. The Deviants had to be destroyed because their attacks were keeping human population too low.

Arishem explains Celestials shepherd new planets, new stars, new galaxies into being. The universe has to lose one world to birth a new Celestial but that leads to fresh life on a thousand others. The Eternals exist to ensure it happens. There is no Olympia: the Eternals are androids manufactured in the Celestial world forge. After a new Celestial is born, Arishem summons the Eternals back, erases their memories and sends them out again. Sersi assumed this was her first mission for the Celestials but she's been on many more—she just doesn't have the memories.

The Deviants, Sersi learns, have a similar origin. Arishem designed them to kill off the apex predators who would otherwise keep intelligent life on chosen worlds from achieving a high enough population. The android monsters gained intelligence and went rogue (presumably that's when they started being called Deviants), targeting the intelligent life the Celestial seed would need to feed on. Arishem created the Eternals to deal with their renegade predecessors.

After a shell-shocked Sersi tells her crew the truth, Gilgamesh declares that instead of heroes, they've been villains all along. The group also realize what made Thena crack up is that her last memory wipe was ineffective, leaving her bogged down with far more than 7,000 years of memories. Kingo, however, still trusts that Arishem is working for the greater good, even if it doesn't seem that way. If Earth has to end, so be it.

The shaken Eternals find Druig living in a small village where he maintains peace and prosperity with mind control. He's horrified to learn he's "been on a suicide mission for 7,000 years" and vents by smashing Karun's camera. The valet has a spare, but Sprite later smashes that one too. Druig is ready to fight against Tiamut's birthing but Sersi worries that she's not up for leading the team against the Celestials.

Ikaris joins them and almost immediately Ikaris/Sersi seems to be a thing again. Sprite watches moodily and Kingo informs her it's like *Peter Pan*: Ikaris is Peter, Sersi is his Wendy and Sprite is Tinkerbelle, who loves Peter but can never have him. Sprite wonders why Arishem made her as an Eternal child who can never grow up, but we never get an answer.

Ikaris is about to tell Sersi why he left her so long ago but the Deviants attack first. Sersi exerts more power than before, successfully turning one Deviant into a tree. One of the others, Kro, drives its spike-headed tentacles into Gilgamesh, draining his life force and his powers. Kro (Bill Skarsgard) says the Deviants are retaliating against the Celestials for using the monsters to help destroy countless worlds. The Eternals have the same blood on their hands when they serve the space gods.

Kro leaves, Gilgamesh dies and Thena collapses in tears. Sersi comes up with a long-shot plan, hinging on Druig using mind-control to send the Celestial back to sleep. That's beyond Druig's powers but Phastos' devices might be able to enhance them. Phastos, however, gave up on the mission in 1945, after Hiroshima: he concluded that advancing human technology had brought Earth into the nuclear age, swore off using his gifts, and vanished.

The Eternals track Phastos to suburbia where he's living with his husband Ben (Haaz Sleiman) and their son Jack (Esai Daniel Cross), who recognizes Ikaris from footage of the London fight. Hearing Sersi's story, Phastos understands why they weren't allowed to stop human wars or power struggles. War takes lives but it also accelerates technology, leading to longer lifespans. He swears he no longer uses his powers beyond fixing his son's bike. Ikaris proves that's a lie by firing an energy blast into the window without effect; Phastos has rendered the house invulnerable. Ikaris demonstrates the dinner table is just as indestructible but it breaks—it was standard IKEA.

Phastos figures out that he can repurpose some of the Eternals' tech to channel their powers into a group "Uni-Mind," a Kirby coinage the film mocks ("That's a terrible name"). Combined, they could fuel Druig's telepathy and possibly beat Tiamut. That'll take some added tech so the Eternals head to Phastos' lab in their old flying base, the Domo, which looks like the monolith from *2001*. Makkari's been living in the Domo for decades and Phastos winces at the mess.

Sersi explains the details of her plan. They can't keep Tiamut asleep forever but perhaps they can buy enough time to build space arks and save some of Earth's people. Ikaris flashes back to six days ago, when he met with Ajak for the last time. She had always known the Celestial agenda and shared it with him long ago. Living among humans has led her to doubt the mission, though: if humans could save the universe from Thanos, doesn't that indicate they're something special? She's traveled among them, seen what they're capable of, and no longer believes sacrificing them to birth Tiamut is a good trade.

Ikaris' answer is to fly Ajak to an icy cliff. Down below, a half-dozen Deviants, frozen in ice centuries ago, have thawed out. Ikaris throws Ajak off the cliff, telling her he will not betray Arishem. Kro drains her life-force after which Ikaris returns the body to Ajak's home, knowing the others will blame her murder on the Deviants.

Returning to the current moment, Ikaris tells Sersi that going against the Celestials defies the natural order. She counters that it's not just one planet: once Tiamut is born, they'll be rebooted and sent out again, killing more worlds, never knowing rest. Ikaris drops the pretense and swears he'll stop them. He flies out of the Domo; Sprite goes with him. Kingo assures the others she's acting from love, not loyalty to Arishem. He's surprised nobody else picked up on her feelings.

Sersi still isn't confident about leading the team to victory. Thena speaks up and says, yes, Sersi can: she loves humans passionately, which makes her the right leader for a fight to save them.

A massive volcanic eruption tells them where Tiamut is rising. A gargantuan figure begins to emerge out of the sea as the Eternals arrive to battle Ikaris and Sprite, with Kro lurking around to drain more power if he can. The Deviant battles Thena and almost breaks her will but pays with his life for the "almost." Meanwhile Makkari hammers Ikaris with super-fast punches, then Phastos chains Ikaris so Makkari can pummel him more. Ikaris breaks free, driving the others back, but at the climactic moment he can't kill Sersi. She activates the Uni-Mind, drawing enough power to transmute even a Celestial into stone. Sersi realizes that was only possible because the Uni-Mind drew on Tiamut's energy too.

Using the remaining Celestial energy, Sersi turns Sprite into a human, free to grow up as she's always wanted to. Ikaris immolates himself in the sun as punishment for his failure; Makkari and Druig head into space in the Domo to find other Eternals. Phastos returns to his family.

Then, as typical for MCU films, the ending sets up future movies. As Sersi reunites with Dane, Arishem captures her, announcing that scanning her memories of Earth will decide whether the planet deserves to live. Dane, determined to save Sersi, contemplates using his family's accursed black sword—Dane Whitman in comics is the superhero the Black Knight—while Makkari and Druig encounter Thanos' brother Eros (Harry Styles) and his sidekick Pip the Troll (Patton Oswalt).

While Marvel superheroes have been appearing on-screen since their various Saturday morning cartoons in the 1960s. the current MCU launched in 2008 with *Iron Man*. Marvel's owner Disney was hardly the first company to launch an interconnected film series—Universal tied together its various classic horror film characters back in the 1930s—but this time the interconnectivity was planned. One film led to another; the introduction of Captain America, Thor and Iron Man in their own movies led to the Avengers and so on. This culminated in *Avengers: Endgame* (2019) in which the Avengers defeat Thanos, Steve Rogers retires as Captain America and Iron Man dies.

Eternals is one of the building blocks for the next phase. The film plays down the mythological aspects compared to the Kirby comics: there are passing mentions of them as myths—Thena appeared at King Arthur's court—but it's not as important as it was in the comics.

The Deviants are much blander than Kirby's version. For most of the movie they're nothing but special-effects monsters with no personality. While they're not the main villain of the story, they play that role for too much of the film to be so dull. It is a nice visual touch that their wire design resembles the wires of energy that make up a lot of Celestial tech and Eternal power manifestations.

Director and co-screenwriter Chloé Zhao had been on the short list for directing Marvel's *Black Widow* (2021) but directing *Nomadland* (2020) required her to drop out. This was probably a smart move, as she became the second woman and first woman of color to take home a Best Director Oscar. *Eternals*, however, strongly appealed to Zhao due to a childhood immersed in manga, anime and Chinese wizard stories, plus a fondness for Marvel Comics' superheroes. While working on *Nomadland*, she lobbied to direct *Eternals*.[2]

The film departs from the previous phases of the MCU. It's an entirely new set of characters with no connection to the Avengers or Spider-Man, and a much more complicated mythology than the Guardians of the Galaxy. The film worked for me but many people found the script bogged down from the amount of backstory it required. For that matter, many people also found Kirby's original series one of his least impressive creations.

The strengths of the film include an excellent cast and a much greater diversity than the original comic or most Marvel movies. It's striking to look at: Zhao is known for beautiful landscape shots and whether it's London or the Australian outback, she delivers. Kingo and Karun are delightful characters who steal any number of scenes.

On the downside, the film doesn't offer any reason for Ajak to turn against the mission. The flashbacks show humanity either butchering their enemies or standing around while the Eternals protect them. No acts of decency or kindness that would suggest we stand out from the other races Ajak has helped destroy.

While the Eternals are upset by the "needs of the many" dilemma they face, they never question that Arishem is on the level. We have only his word for it that stopping Tiamut's birth will be a tragedy for worlds yet unborn—is that good enough? Could he be lying, or simply wrong? Perhaps the sequel will have the answers.

The "gods from outer space" aspect is much weaker than Kirby's original series.

Even though we only met Zuras, Thena and Makkari of Olympia, we could reasonably extrapolate that other Olympians corresponding with the other gods were out there. Here, we know they're not: the Eternals we see are all that we are. Did Sprite just make up the entire pantheon? Did the Greeks extrapolate? The Celestials didn't evolve MCU humanity so they don't get credit for *Genesis*. They are, in a sense, more mundane.

The movie generated a lot of negative reviews, becoming the first Marvel movie to rate under 50 percent positive on the Rotten Tomatoes review aggregator site. This may reflect that it's a departure from earlier films or that for some critics the flaws outweigh the merits. Or that Zhao is a woman entering the male-dominated genre of superhero action films. Or that critics were uncomfortable with Zhao opting to make a massively mainstream, commercial film instead of more indie work. It's too soon to tell if the views will change over time, as happened with the '56 *Body Snatchers* or *The Thing* (covered in the next chapter).

TEN

Destroy All Monsters Before
They Destroy Us

Monsters from Space

"It sounds as though you're describing some sort of super-carrot."
—*The Thing from Another World*

Monsters and monster movies go back long before anyone ever heard the term "unidentified flying objects."

Kong. Frankenstein. Dracula. Dinosaurs lurking in some cryptozoological lost world. And starting in the 1950s, Ymir (*20 Million Miles to Earth*), giant destructive meteor crystals (*The Monolith Monsters*), murderous animated plants (*The Day of the Triffids*), blind predators that hunt humans by sound (*A Quiet Place*) and a potential alien pandemic (*The Andromeda Strain*). Japan has an even more spectacular history with kaiju such as *Ghidrah, the Three-Headed Monster*.

It's no surprise that alien monsters have a long track record. Monsters are a great fit for the screen. Print fiction can do its best describing monstrous creatures but it can't match the visceral body horror of the shapeshifter in *The Thing* (1982).

Of course, if the film is cheap and unimaginative, a monster that might have worked on the printed page can turn out laughable. The Gargan in *Teenagers from Outer Space* looks like little more than a large lobster. The Venusian invader in *It Conquered the World* (1956) resembles an eight-foot-tall cucumber with arms and a mouthful of fangs. It's even worse on screen than it sounds (see page 161).

Monster movies also provide many of the same thrills and spectacle as alien invasion films. 2013's *Pacific Rim* has monsters emerging through a dimensional portal, met by humans piloting Jaegers, giant anime-style mecha. Monster films can also provide intense terrors and suspense. In one scene in *A Quiet Place* we see a character bringing their foot down on a loose nail, knowing they're going to cry out and that will bring the monsters—but there's nothing we can do to warn them.

A lot of ink has been spilled discussing the definition of a monster. It's even trickier in alien visitor films where monstrous aliens may be peaceful creatures with the best of intentions. The invaders of *Independence Day* and *War of the Worlds* (both the 1953 and 2005) are physically monstrous but the films aren't monster movies, they're war films. The look of *ID4*'s invaders doesn't matter as much as them being militaristic, organized and wielding advanced technology. Conversely, Carpenter's *The Thing* is horror even though the monstrous alien has the potential to take over the entire planet.

In some cases it's obvious. *The Blob* (1958) doesn't have intelligence enough to do anything but absorb any animal creatures it touches; it's a monster. But what about *The Thing from Another World*? It isn't as monstrous as Carpenter's *Thing*; it seems ready to colonize the planet; and it's fighting a contingent of Air Force men. Even so, the film feels closer to horror than an invasion film, which is why it's in this chapter.

Some monsters are mindlessly destructive. Like the Blob, *The Monolith Monsters* (1957) are literally mindless. They're meteorite crystals that grow when exposed to water, collapse and fracture when they get too big, then the pieces start growing again. The meteorite landed up in the mountains, their growth/collapse/growth cycle is moving them downwards and there's a helpless small town right in their path. How do you stop something that can't be killed or reasoned with?

Other monsters are more sympathetic. The Venusian Ymir in *20 Million Miles to Earth* (1957) isn't malevolent. Earth's first Venus expedition brought the tiny creature home with them for experimentation only to have it escape and start growing. Facing a world it doesn't understand, it lashes out at anything that seems to be a threat. In many ways the Venusian's plight resembles *King Kong* when he's trapped in New York. Given that Ymir's creator Ray Harryhausen is a diehard *King Kong* fan, that may not be coincidental.

Some alien visitors rework classic horror concepts. *Not of This Earth* (1957) has a vampiric alien from a race that subsists on blood. With his world's supply tainted, the alien hopes to find fresh sources on Earth. The mix of aliens and vampires apparently worked as the movie was remade three times. There are also ET vampires in *Roswell Conspiracies* and the 1996 TV movie *Vampirella*.

Other monsters are simply weird. *Under the Skin* (2013) has alien Scarlett Johansson inviting men back to her apartment for sex, after which she dissolves them in a pool for reasons not easily apparent. She seems to be a monster but a singularly incomprehensible one.

In many films, nobody believes the first stories of the monster until it's too late. That gives the creature more time to wreak havoc and gain strength. When the creature's existence is confirmed, the usual response is to meet it with guns blazing or search for a weakness.

If neither one is an option, it's usually best to run. In some films, survival is the most the characters can hope for. In *Alien vs. Predator* (2004) and *Alien vs. Predator: Requiem* (2007) humans are caught between the two hostile, deadly extraterrestrial races. Even getting out alive is a long shot.

Just as some alien invasion films show what life is like after the aliens win, a few monster films present a world where the monsters are a fact of life. In *A Quiet Place* civilization has collapsed under the attack of the impossibly fast, super-sensitive-to-sound monsters; our protagonists' goal is just to find somewhere they can exist without being heard and devoured.

In *Monsters* (2010), a crashed NASA probe brings tentacled aliens to Earth. By the time of the film, they've come to dominate much of the Southwestern U.S. and Mexico. Nobody freaks out at their existence or assumes we're doomed; the military and everyone else simply adapts.

In the years since *The Thing from Another World* gave us the movies' first alien monster, the biggest change has been technology. Movie special effects and makeup have steadily improved. In the 1950s, stop-motion animation was standard. By 1982, according to the *The Thing*'s special features, Carpenter cut a scene because he'd done it in stop motion and it didn't look believable. A decade later and computers could have fixed the problem bits.

Imagination, however, remains more important than tech. Rob Bottin worked on Carpenter's film without the digital enhancements so common today but he still created a spectacular journey into body horror. The monster makers in the 2011 *The Thing* had thirty years of technical advances to work with, but all they did was imitate where Bottin broke fresh ground.

SPOTLIGHT

The Thing from Another World *(1951)*

Winchester Pictures, released by RKO. B&W 86 minutes. Release date April 29, 1951.

CAST: Kenneth Tobey (Captain Patrick Hendry), Margaret Sheridan (Nikki Nicholson), Douglas Spencer (Ned "Scotty" Scott), Robert Cornthwaite (Dr. Arthur Carrington), Dewey Martin (Bob), James Young (Lt. Eddie Dykes), Robert Nichols (Lt. Ken "Mac" MacPherson), William Self (Cpl. Barnes), John Dierkes (Dr. Chapman), James Arness (The Thing), Eduard Franz (Dr. Stern) Sally Creighton (Mrs. Chapman), Paul Frees (Dr. Voorhees), George Fenneman (Dr. Redding), Norbert Schiller (Dr. Laurenz), David McMahon (Gen. Fogarty), Edmond Breon (Dr. Ambrose), Everett Glass (Dr. Wilson), William Neff (Olson), Robert Stevenson (Captain Smith), Robert Gutknecht (Cpl. Hauser), Robert Bray (Captain), Ted Cooper (Lieutenant), Allan Ray (Lieutenant), Nicholas Byron (Tex Richards). Eskimos: King Kong, Charles B. Opunui, Riley Sunshine. Cooks: Lee Tung Foo, Walter Ng

CREDITS: Director/Producer: Howard Hawks; Co-Director: Christian Nyby; Screenwriter: Charles Lederer; Additional Script: Ben Hecht; Associate Producer: Edward Lasker; Art Directors: John J. Hughes, Albert S. D'Agostino; Photography: Russell Harlan; Music: Dimitri Tiomkin; Editor: Roland Gross; Makeup: Lee Greenway; Special Effects Cinematography: Linwood Dunn; Special Effects: Donald Steward

In 1938, John W. Campbell, Jr., published "Who Goes There?" a science fiction short story in which humans encounter an alien shapeshifter. Sometime before the story's opening, an Antarctic research base discovered a spaceship buried in the ice; an earlier version of the story, published decades later as *Frozen Hell*, shows the discovery. This being 1938, it's not a flying saucer. MacReady, the second in command at the base, describes it as a submarine without a conning tower.

The ship, made of a magnesium-based alloy, burned up when the researchers melted the ice with thermite. As compensation, they found the ejected, frozen corpse of the pilot nearby and brought it back to base. After recapping all that, the researchers debate whether it's safe to thaw and dissect the alien. Could it carry dangerous bacteria? Could it still be alive? Pretty much every action in the story requires more debate; for all its merits, the story is incredibly talky. Characters don't experience things as much as they talk about experiencing them.

One objection raised against thawing the creature is that its expression is evil. The pro-thawing side points out the absurdity of judging an extraterrestrial's facial expressions by human standards, particularly when it was on the brink of death. A perfectly logical point that's also perfectly wrong: the creature *is* evil.

It's also formidable. Once it thaws out, it shows it's both a telepath and a shape-shifter. It can digest and replace another living creature or bud off a clone of itself to take the victim's shape. By the time the men realize this, they also realize some of them have already been replaced. The creature's thoughts telepathically penetrate the researchers' nightmares, revealing its intention is to reach the outside world and eventually replace all humanity. The humans act quickly to confine it by smashing their helicopters and other escape options.

MacReady figures out that the alien's clones are independent creatures; neither the original nor the clone will risk itself for the other. If they take blood samples from a duplicated human, the blood will become a separate organism too. Threaten the blood with heat and it will try to escape, thereby revealing the donor was an alien. This method smokes out most of the aliens. One man, however, has stayed isolated from the rest of the company. It turns out he's the last clone, hiding so he can build an anti-gravity device and escape. Killing him saves the world and the device he built can take us to the stars. MacReady concludes as we haven't seen any of the shapeshifter's kin in the millions of years since the crash, we're probably safe from them.

The cast of the story is larger than either the Howard Hawks or Carpenter films, with more than 30 guys on base. As Campbell doesn't have to pay actors or worry about blocking them in a scene—something Carpenter says on the DVD commentary track was a real challenge with just seven men—this makes sense. It also allows for a higher body count before the end.

The 1951 movie adaptation switched Campbell's title out for the simpler *The Thing*, probably adding *From Another World* to distinguish it from a then-current novelty song, "The Thing." Like many alien-visitor films, it's the military versus an alien menace. Instead of America's full military might, however, it's a single Air Force crew stranded at an Arctic base with no outside help available.

The film begins with a black screen, then letters of light burn through the dark to deliver the title. The credits roll in front of a snowbound landscape, then we find ourselves on an equally snowbound Anchorage Air Force base as Scotty (Douglas Spencer) enters the Officer's Club. A reporter frustrated at having nothing to write about, Scotty joins Captain Hendry (Kenneth Tobey), copilot Lt. Dykes (James Young) and navigator Lt. MacPherson (Robert Nichols) as they play poker. Dykes and Mac are less interested in the cards than mocking Hendry's love life. He's pining for Nikki Nicholson (Margaret Sheridan) who works at a research base 2,000 miles further north. Their last date ended badly but Hendry's still stuck on her and winces under the guys' needling.

Professor Carrington (Robert Cornthwaite), the head of the lab where Nikki works as secretary, calls the base to report a crashed aircraft and request assistance. Carrington is a Nobel prize-winning genius who formerly worked in nuclear-weapons research, so he gets what he wants. Hendry and his crew go north, with Scotty riding along in hopes of a story. The plane reaches the base without incident, but Mac notices a strong magnetic force drawing their compass away from true north.

No sooner do they land than Hendry meets Nikki again. We learn they had a good time in Anchorage but their last date before she left involved Hendry "making like an octopus" before passing out from booze. Hendry's impressed that Nikki matched him drink for drink and stayed conscious; he's embarrassed that he woke up with her good-bye note pinned to his chest, and that a half-dozen guys read it while he was sleeping. Nikki's still wary of Hendry's wandering hands but she agrees they can start over.

Carrington reports that something massive came out of the sky and smashed into the icecap recently. It's now giving off the magnetic signal that MacPherson noticed. Hendry says it sounds like a meteor; Carrington says a meteor couldn't have briefly flown upward before crashing back to the ice.

What they find at the impact site is a flying saucer, buried in the ice except for a fin sticking out. An awed Scotty proclaims it "the biggest story since the parting of the Red Sea," but Hendry says it's official military business so he can't report it. Scotty's inability to report on the earthshaking events of the film become a running joke. If radio static isn't making it impossible, the military's imposing a news blackout.

As in the Campbell story, melting the ice with thermite burns the alien ship along with it. Again as in Campbell, the men find the pilot's frozen body and bring the ice block holding it back to the research station. Hendry refuses point blank to let Carrington thaw it out, smashing the lab window to keep the air below freezing. He also posts MacPherson on guard on the door.

With the alien dealt with, Hendry finally convinces Nikki to have a private talk. She ties up his arms to prevent another round of groping, but they flirt and kiss despite that. Nikki finally admits she's attracted to him, at which point Hendry shows he's had his hands free for a while.

When Corporal Barnes (William Self) takes up guard duty over the lab, he's unnerved enough seeing the creature through the ice to cover it with a blanket. He doesn't notice it's an electric blanket, plugged in and turned on. An hour later the sled dogs outside start barking, then Barnes rushes into the mess and tells Hendry the Thing lives. The men rush back to the lab, but the Thing (James Arness) has escaped, rushing out into the snow and killing some of the sled dogs when they attack it.

The dogs managed to tear off the Thing's forearm, which bears thorns as well as claws. Carrington discovers it's made of plant tissue, still alive and moving despite having no body attached. He suggests they're dealing with an intelligent humanoid plant, which doesn't go over well ("I'm not going to say you're stuffed full of blueberry muffins …"). The great thinker concludes that in addition to its advanced technology, an intelligent plant must be free of the emotional and sexual drives that interfere with the human intellect. This doesn't particularly follow—if a plant can be intelligent, why can't it have emotions?—but it fits the recurring idea in these films that intelligence and emotion are antithetical.

Carrington points out that the spaceman's (spaceplant's?) aggression is understandable: first it crashed, then it froze, now it's unfrozen but trapped on an alien world by alien creatures. Plus the idea of communicating with animal life must seem as absurd to the Thing as we'd find talking to cabbages. It's a sensible observation, but this is the kind of film where giving the alien the benefit of the doubt is a mistake. Carrington believes "there are no enemies in science, only phenomena," but events prove the Thing is indeed an enemy.

Carrington discovers the Thing, which has regrown its missing hand, has deposited the body of a dead dog in a greenhouse storage bin. Instead of telling Hendry, he settles for posting a guard. The Thing returns, kills two men and uses their blood to nourish seedlings. Hendry and his men manage to confine it to the greenhouse but have no way to kill it.

Carrington's shaken by the deaths and tells his team that they're facing a war such as Earth has never known. At the same time, he can't stop seeing the Thing as both a superior being and a scientific puzzle. Taking seeds from the severed arm and plasma from the base's blood bank, he starts growing seedlings of his own. He ignores the warnings from his own researchers that the alien might be on Earth to grow a conquering army.

When Hendry learns about Carrington's experiment, he puts an end to it, and also manages to destroy the seedlings in the greenhouse. He wants to kill the Thing too but the military sends a radio directive to preserve the alien at all costs. Nevertheless, when the Thing stalks into the base looking for more blood, Hendry doesn't hesitate to ambush it, blasting it with a Very pistol, then tossing kerosene on it. The Thing smashes out the window, screaming. They've found a way to hurt it.

The Thing retaliates by shutting off the oil flow to the heating system. When Nikki notices their breath is visible, they realize the Thing plans to freeze them to death; if they turn the oil back on, it'll find another means of attack. The solution is to withdraw to the generator room and set up an electric arc to kill the Thing when it comes for their blood. When the Thing arrives, Carrington tries to talk the men out of this but fails. The professor then attempts a Hail Mary play, warning the Thing away while appealing to its better nature: "They think you mean to harm us all … you're wiser than anything on Earth."

The alien has no better nature: it slams Carrington to one side, leaving him unconscious and injured, then charges the other humans. This brings it into the arc, which fries the Thing until there's nothing left to regrow. Nikki and Hendry finally acknowledge they belong together, and Scotty finally gets to file his story. Before getting into the details of Earth's first battle against an invader from space, Scotty warns everyone listening to his broadcast to "keep watching the skies!"

Officially this film was directed by Christian Nyby, a film editor and protégé of Howard Hawks. SF expert Bill Warren cites on-set accounts that say Hawks was the real director but wanted to give his friend the on-screen credit. Nyby said in an interview that people simply couldn't believe he was that good his first time out.

The film certainly feels like a Hawks production. There's a handful of tough men against the odds, with no chance of cavalry riding to the rescue. It's a situation familiar from countless war films—can the outpost hold out?—and Hawks Westerns such as *Rio Bravo* (1959). Here, though, they're holding the line against an enemy from space. If they fail, it's not the base alone that's lost but possibly the world.

It's a taut film with pressure that ratchets up steadily and sharp, sometimes snarky dialog. The characters aren't deep or complex but they're strong enough stock characters, well enough acted, to feel real and recognizable.

The alien's appearance isn't that horrifying, simply Jim Arness in a monster suit. Even so, the Thing's savagery and the tension of the film make it feel formidable. In the best Othering tradition, it's completely malevolent, extremely aggressive, with no redeeming features outside of its intelligence. Possibly it realizes we're intelligent too, just as a human confronting ambulatory, clothes-wearing cabbages might suspect intelligence. It doesn't care, though. Humanity's a blood bank to the Thing, nothing more.

In Peter Biskind's film analysis (see Chapter Three) this is a right-wing movie. Hendry and his crew, the regular guys on the front lines, see what must be done. Carrington and his scientific underlings don't, though one or two of them have qualms. Neither does the Air Force brass; the cluelessness of generals is a running joke in the film. Early on someone mentions the Pentagon sending ten crates of pith helmets to the

The Thing from Another World (1951). There's a legend that Howard Hawks shot scenes where his "intellectual carrot" looked more like the monster in John W. Campbell's "Who Goes There?" Nineteen-fifties SF film expert Bill Warren says nobody's ever found such footage.

Anchorage base. Returning from the saucer crash site, the crew laugh at a news article in which the Air Force announces flying saucers don't exist. Scotty jokes that the Pentagon will probably make Hendry a general for burning up the contrary evidence.

Carrington's hardly the only character in an alien-visitor film to misread alien intentions but he takes it to an extreme. He doesn't simply try to make peace with the Thing, he actively subverts Hendry's efforts to destroy it. Some reviewers see Carrington as a communist figure: cold, ruthless, intellectual, willing to sacrifice human lives for the greater good. Wearing a fur hat in one scene, he even looks like Lenin.

The metaphor doesn't work, though. The military brass gives Hendry the same instructions as Carrington, to keep the Thing alive at all costs. It's not a case of Carrington vs. Hendry but men on the front line vs. eggheads and pencil-pushers.

Carrington does have the classic mad-science viewpoint of valuing knowledge over human survival. He tells Hendry at one point that "we've only one reason for existing—to think, to find out, to learn!" But his ultimate error is simply misunderstanding the enemy. He convinces himself the Thing must have the calm, dispassionate nature of *Star Trek*'s Vulcans, not realizing its lack of emotion makes it a coldblooded killer. At the end of the film, Hendry and Scotty hide the truth about Carrington's actions, indicating they see him as misguided, not an enemy.

As in the later *Independence Day* and *Predator*, manliness and toughness mean a great deal here, as they often do with Hawks. Unlike the later films, it's taken for granted: Hendry and his people never have to prove they're tough, they simply act. Scotty confirms his toughness by reminding Hendry he covered the action at El Alamein and Okinawa during World War II. Case closed.

Nikki doesn't have much to do but she's clearly tough too. She can drink Hendry under the table—a measure of character by the standards of the times—and she's not a shrieker or a fainter. The closest she comes to losing it is repeatedly, nervously tapping her cigarette in one scene. She often chooses to stay up close near the action rather than retreating somewhere safe. She's a stronger character than any of the women in *Independence Day*.

The Thing *(1982)*

Turman-Foster Company, Universal. 109 minutes. Release date June 25, 1982.

CAST: Kurt Russell (MacReady), A. Wilford Brimley (Blair), T.K. Carter (Nauls), David Clennon (Palmer), Keith David (Childs), Richard Dysart (Copper), Charles Hallahan (Norris), Peter Maloney (Bennings), Richard Masur (Clark), Donald Moffat (Garry), Joel Polis (Fuchs), Thomas Waites (Windows), Norbert Weisser (Norwegian), Larry Franco (Norwegian with Rifle), Nate Irwin (Helicopter Pilot), William Zeman (Pilot)

CREDITS: Director: John Carpenter; Screenplay: Bill Lancaster; Producer: David Foster, Lawrence Turman; Co-Producer: Stuart Cohen; Associate Producer: Larry Franco; Photography: Dean Cundey; Production Design: John Lloyd. Special Make-up Effects: Rob Bottin; Special Visual Effects: Albert Whitlock; Editor: Todd Ramsay; Music: Ennio Morricone

Carpenter's fondness for the original Hawks version shows almost immediately: after seeing the alien spaceship reaching Earth millions of years ago, the movie title burns through the screen just like the previous film. The effect was created by stretching black plastic in front of a light, then burning away strips. The script, however, looks to Campbell for guidance.

After an establishing shot showing the empty Antarctic landscape, we see two guys flying a helicopter over the snow, one of them sitting half outside the cabin. A sled dog running across the ice turns and watches the chopper, then resumes running. The helicopter crew starts shooting at the dog as it approaches the American base.

Inside the base, guys are playing ping-pong, reading or drinking. MacReady (Kurt Russell), the base pilot, is matching wits with a chess-playing computer (sophisticated tech for the time). When the computer's female voice announces checkmate, Mac pops it open and shorts it out with a shot of booze ("Cheating bitch").

The helicopter circling the base draws the Americans out into the snow. The dog immediately runs up and shelters with them as the helicopter lands, the men on board calling a warning. They're heavily armed, but the pilot blows himself and the helicopter up with a dropped grenade. The second man (Larry Franco) storms forward, shooting at the Americans until Garry (Donald Moffatt) drops him with a bullet through the eye.

The events baffle everyone, but radio operator Windows (Thomas Waites) can't raise the Norwegian base or anywhere else to get answers. While the dog explores, Nauls (T.K. Carter), who roller-skates around the base, quips that maybe we're at war with Norway. Although the Norwegian crew have only been stationed there for two weeks, Nauls says it only take a few minutes to go nuts. He offers the pot-smoking Palmer (David Clennon) as proof.

MacReady flies some of the men to the Norwegian base where they find frozen, murdered corpses and a grotesquely deformed corpse that's been burned to death. There's also a block of ice that looks as though something had been cut out of it. When they bring the deformed corpse back to their own base, scientist Blair (A. Wilford Brimley) checks it over and confirms it's human. Oh, and the Norwegian with the rifle had no alcohol or drugs in his system.

That night Clark (Richard Masure), who manages the sled dogs, puts the new dog in the kennel. The dogs take an instant dislike to it, following the horror tradition that animals can spot evil. The Norwegian dog quivers, then tentacles emerge from its widening mouth while its body sprouts insect legs and more tentacles, with which it impales some of the dogs. Clark calls the others, telling them whatever he's looking at is "weird and it's pissed off!" The other men arrive to find the Thing has killed or absorbed the other dogs and budded off a clone of itself. The men unleash a flame thrower, destroying the duplicate. The original Thing smashes out the roof.

Examining the dogs' bodies, Blair concludes the creature was converting them into duplicates of itself, though Clark stopped it before the process could finish. Then Blair realizes not only was Clark alone with the Norwegians' dog, the creature spent the entire day wandering through the camp.

A videotape MacReady brought from the Norwegian bay shows the base crew out on the ice, setting off thermite charges to unearth something, a scene modeled on the 1951 film. MacReady and a couple of the guys visit the location and find a half-buried spaceship. The thermite exposed it, but ruined it beyond hope of flight. Nearby, the guys see a block of ice has been removed. They deduce the pilot ejected or was hurled out, then froze instantly.

When MacReady spells out his theory back at the camp, Childs (Keith David) asks how the pilot could possibly be alive. MacReady replies that "it's not like us. It's from outer space." Childs doesn't buy it but Palmer cites *Chariots of the Gods* and tells him the aliens "practically own South America—they taught the Incas everything they know."

Meanwhile, Blair carries out a computer projection that shows a 75 percent chance at least one of his colleagues has been transformed. Worse, if the creature gets beyond the Antarctic, it could replicate itself and replace all of humanity within three years. The DVD special feature *Terror Takes Shape* acknowledges there's no way Blair can work this out, but it was a short cut to establishing the stakes. The computer's conclusion horrifies Blair, who gets a gun from his desk and locks himself in his room.

Fuchs (Joel Polis) discovers one of Blair's notebooks and shows Mac a rant about how even the burned corpses may be able to regenerate. One of the other men spots Bennings (Peter Maloney) battling the creature outside, but by the time they reach him he's alone, unconscious and turning monster. Using a spilled oil can nearby, Mac burns Bennings so thoroughly there's nothing left. They do this with the other corpses.

While they're thus occupied, Blair smashes the helicopter and tractor, kills the remaining dogs and wrecks the radio. "Nobody gets in or out of here, nobody!" he tells the others. "You guys think I'm crazy, well that's fine!" Blair, distrusting everyone, shoots when the other guys get close but they disarm him and lock him in the tool shed. Blair warns Mac to watch Clark, as he was alone with the dog-thing for a while.

The thinking among most of the men is to wait until spring when their replacements arrive. Mac points out that by then they could all have been killed and replaced; the only way to survive is to figure it out as fast as possible. Dr. Copper (Richard Dysart) proposes taking blood from each of them and mixing it with his plasma supply: if anyone's been turned, the mix will trigger a reaction. By the time they go to get the blood, the supply has been destroyed. Garry's the only one with a key and nobody believes it could have been stolen off his key ring without him noticing. Windows and Garry draw guns on each other, but the rest of the men talk them into disarming. Garry steps down as leader until he's proven human.

The group picks Mac as their chief. He assures them he's human and adds that at least some of them are too. If he was the only human the Things would gang up and kill him, but they aren't willing to expose themselves if they can avoid it. Mac has Norris shoot up Clark, Garry and Copper with morphine, then watch for their reaction. Mac assigns Fuchs to find new techniques for detecting duplicates.

Forty-eight hours later nobody's figured out anything. Mac, recording a tape for whoever might show up, says the creature can't duplicate clothing. They've found one ripped-up set of long johns but they can't tell whose they were.

By this point everyone's suspicious of everyone and nobody's on nobody's side. Fuchs realizes even eating a few cells of the Thing could let it take someone over; everyone should prepare their own meals, eating out of unopened cans. Later Fuchs discovers torn long johns in the snow belonging to Mac. Fuchs doesn't return so Mac tries sending out teams to search for him. Everyone refuses, knowing that if they go out with the wrong partner, they won't return. MacReady checks in on Blair, who now has a noose hanging in the shed. He assures Mac he's fine, though he'd like to come back in with the others.

Searching in a group, the men find Fuchs, who apparently burned himself to death rather than become a duplicate. Mac goes to check on his shack after he sees a light burning there. While he's gone, Nauls finds the long johns. Mac must be a Thing—or could it be a trick?

By the time Mac returns, they're ready to burn him just in case. He's anticipated that, so he comes in with a blowtorch in one hand, dynamite in the other. Everyone reluctantly puts down their guns. Norris collapses, apparently of a heart attack, so Copper applies CPR. As he's pressing on Norris's chest, the man's body opens like a mouth and bites Copper's forearms off. The other men burn Norris's body, but his head grows legs and runs away. Mac burns it too.

Watching the head scurry away without trying to save its former body gives Mac an idea. He orders the other men to tie each other up, threatening to shoot whoever refuses. He's not bluffing; when Clark jumps Mac from behind, Mac shoots him dead. Clark, it turns out, was human.

Mac explains his plan. The Thing's body parts can exist independently, and they have zero team spirit. If he draws blood from a Thing and heats the blood cells, the cells will try to escape even though that exposes the disguised Thing. Blood from Mac, Windows and Clark passes the test. Palmer's blood, however, scurries off the lab dish—nobody thinks to burn it—and Palmer breaks free from his bonds. Mac's flamethrower conveniently goes on the fritz. By the time he gets it going, the Thing has eaten and duplicated Windows, but Mac burns them both.

When Mac, Nauls and Garry go out to test Blair they discover he's not in the locked shed. A tunnel from the shed into a cavern in the ice shows Blair has been cannibalizing parts from the smashed helicopters to create a one-Thing flying saucer. The men blow up the ship but Blair Thing destroys the camp generator. The Thing will freeze along with the men, but unlike them it can survive.

The three men decide the one way to stop the Thing is to burn down the entire base. With breathtaking stupidity they split up to plant bombs across the base; sure enough, the thing kills Garry. Nauls goes to investigate, which is the last we see of him.

A few minutes later, the Thing charges through the ground like a mole, heading for MacReady. It emerges from the Earth in full monster form, but he successfully destroys it. As Mac sits in the ruins of the burning base Childs appears, claiming he got lost in the snow hunting Blair.

So now what? Can the men trust that neither one is a Thing? What will they do when the fire dies down and the temperature drops? After a quick discussion, Mac shrugs: "Why don't we just wait here for a little while? See what happens." And both men chuckle as the film comes to a grim, ambiguous end.

In the DVD's commentary and special features, director John Carpenter says he's a great admirer of the 1951 film, which he describes as "so terrifying, my popcorn flew out of my hands." When the studio contacted him about remaking the film, Carpenter agreed, and decided a more faithful adaptation of Campbell would distinguish the new film from its predecessor. The studio gave him a year to work on it.

Scriptwriter Bill Lancaster says he was less than thrilled by the plot of "Who Goes There?" but intrigued by the ambience, the Antarctic isolation and the paranoia. While there were women working at Antarctic bases in 1982, Carpenter thought it would be more novel to make it completely male. It also simplified the plot by eliminating any possibility of sex or romance.

Kurt Russell, who'd starred in Carpenter's *Escape from New York* (1981), helped him with casting but neither man could find a good MacReady. Carpenter asked Russell to take the role, conceiving it as first among equals in an ensemble. That changed, Russell says "once we discovered that we had these makeup and wardrobe problems where everybody looked the same." Once the cast had been signed, the men began holding group rehearsals to figure out the dynamic between them.

Rob Bottin, who'd worked with Carpenter on *The Fog*, was fascinated by the potential in a shapeshifting monster. Carpenter, realizing how elaborate the F/X would have to be, directed Bottin to work with storyboard artist Mike Ploog on a scene-by-scene breakdown of transformations and effects. Bottin did so, though he had no idea at the time how he'd make some of his ideas work. Today's computer effects weren't an option in 1982.

To create the Things, Bottin's team used a variety of tricks. Sometimes it was a simple as photographing rubber figures carefully, so there'd be no sign of the seams or wires. Norris' body for the arm-biting chest was a fake, carefully modeled on actor Charles Hallahan's body down to the hair pattern. For the arm-biting scene they replaced Dysart as Copper with a man missing both his forearms and wearing a rubber mask of Dysart's face. When the mouth slams shut it tears the man's two fake forearms off.

For the first manifestation in the kennel, Bottin asked for help due to the sheer number of effects he was working on. Stan Winston stepped in, using an animatronic puppet operated by someone inside it: "We literally built a really cool hand puppet with an animatronic face."

The final showdown between Mac and the Thing initially had a stop-motion creature on a scale model of the set, done by animator Randy Cook. Carpenter decided the stop motion was too obvious, so the footage was never used. Surprisingly it's not even an extra on my DVD.

The end results are amazing. Whatever Bottin's technical limits, he showed a tremendous imagination that more than made up for them. The creature, carrying the template of every life form it's ever duplicated, is a freakishly bizarre thing. I half wonder if it isn't the reason aliens in several 21st century movies look like a random mix of tentacles and legs with no evolutionary logic behind them. Here, though, it works.

The film is very different in tone from Hawks' film. In Hawks, everyone but Carrington works against the Thing, bonding and working smoothly as a team. In Carpenter's version, there's more friction than teamwork. No trust. No remorse from Mac when he kills Clark. The humans are almost as ruthless as the Thing. Even before the paranoia begins, there's no sign any of them are friends or do more than tolerate each other. Where Hawks' Air Force guys become stronger under pressure, here the men crack. This may reflect that, as Nauls says, being stuck in the Antarctic for several months isn't the best thing for mental health.

The end results are a first-rate film but that wasn't the reaction in 1982. The film got mixed reviews and only adequate box office. The bleak ending didn't help. In Hawks' film, we win. Here, either one of the men is an alien or they're both human and going to die in the snow. Editor Todd Ramsay says they shot a second ending in which Mac survives and is confirmed human, but Carpenter decided to tell the story his way, regardless of the audience reaction.

The audience reaction was to make *E.T.* the king of science fiction cinema that year and *Poltergeist* the king of horror. Where *Poltergeist* was PG, the Carpenter film was an R. Perhaps the intense body horror made it the wrong film at the wrong time.

All that's changed. As with the 1956 *Invasion of the Body Snatchers*, *The Thing* found new viewers on home video, then streaming, and many of those viewers became ardent fans. I'm personally fonder of Hawks' take but Carpenter's film has surpassed it as the definitive version of the story. Perhaps even more definitive than Campbell's original short. There's a devoted fan base online, happy to engage in debates about the minutiae, such as when particular characters turned.

The film's completely masculine cast has fueled plenty of online debate. The one female voice we hear is the chess computer: is MacReady shorting it out and making the film a sausage fest a sign that the film is fundamentally misogynist? Or is the film making a statement, however unintentionally, about how quickly men left to themselves will turn on each other—that masculinity in an all-male environment is inherently toxic? That depends on part on how you see the cast—were they stressed out by their isolation before the Thing appeared, or did they use to be a tight cohesive group?

Some critics' gender analysis is shaped by the possibility the Thing is a woman or at least a female metaphor. Are her tooth-filled openings vagina dentata? Is her spawning new Things a kind of birthing process? Is her taking over the men a metaphor for male fears of being domesticated? Are her presence and the men's reactions a sign of what happens when a woman penetrates an all-male space?

Some of the analysis compares Carpenter's film with the 2011 prequel, *The Thing*, which has Mary Elizabeth Winstead in the leading role. The Norwegian base recruits scientist Kate Lloyd (Winstead) to study an alien corpse they've found in the ice. The alien thaws out and begin the usual round of paranoia, terror and death. Lloyd survives to the end but then we cut without explanation to the opening of the Carpenter film, showing the Norwegians lost to the Thing after all.

One view of the film is that it shows Carpenter was right to go with an all-male cast. With Lloyd there, the paranoia doesn't develop to the same degree. As a woman—not the only one in the cast, though the woman researcher on base dies early on—she bonds with the men in a way MacReady couldn't. The tension is gone.

But then again, that could be because the filmmakers on this version simply aren't as good as Carpenter. It has none of the tension and horror his *Thing* did; the special effects are more spectacular but they're not as novel or shocking as the original. Nor does the movie have the energy and crackling dialog of the '51. It mostly shows that 21st century film studios will mine every bit of value from their intellectual property.

The Andromeda Strain *(1971)*

Universal. 131 minutes. Release date March 12, 1971.

CAST: Arthur Hill (Dr. Jeremy Stone), David Wayne (Dr. Charles Dutton) James Olson (Dr. Mark Hall) Kate Reid (Dr. Ruth Leavitt), Paula Kelly (Karen Anson), George Mitchell (Jackson), Ramon Bieri (Major Manchek), Kermit Murdock (Dr. Robertson), Richard O'Brien (Grimes), Peter Hobbs (Gen. Sparks), Eric Christmas (Senator from Vermont)

CREDITS: Director/Producer: Robert Wise; Screenplay: Nelson Gidding, based on the novel by Michael Crichton. Production Design: Boris Leven; Photography: Richard H. Kline; Special Photographic Effects: Douglas Trumbull, James Shourt; Technical Advisors: Dr. Richard Green, George Hobby, William Koselka; Scientific Background Support: Cal Tech, Jet Propulsion Laboratory; Art Director: William Tuntke; Editors: Stuart Gilmore, John W. Holmes; Music: Gil Mellé

Even before we went into space, alien visitor stories worried about what we might bring back.

The 1953 *Quatermass Experiment* series on the BBC has the UK putting the first men into space When they return, they're not alone. They've been contaminated by an extraterrestrial life form that eventually fuses them into a combined hive mind. Now it's ready to explode and spread its spores around the world.

Andromeda Strain (1971). Having a non-sexy middle-aged female scientist in the film was an anomaly in 1971 and still is. The two female scientists in the 2008 *Andromeda Strain* miniseries were both better looking.

The *Outer Limits* episode "Specimen Unknown" likewise has a research team pick up alien spores that grow into deadly flowers. They take root on Earth but fortunately die when rain hits them. In *Monsters*, the tentacled monsters came down on crashed probe. In *Invasion* (2007), the third remake of *Invasion of the Body Snatchers*, the threat isn't pods but bacteria that fuse human beings into a hive mind.

The most effective film about returning from space with a monster aboard remains the 1971 adaptation of Michael Crichton's novel *The Andromeda Strain*. The monster here is a xenobacterium with the potential to start a pandemic.

Crichton's 1969 novel opens with a claim the book was based on a real incident, backing it up with details such as non-existent scientific papers cited as sources. The film takes the same tone, opening with a text crawl declaring, "This film concerns the four-day history of a major American scientific crisis." It thanks the many people who encouraged the filmmakers to tell the story and assures us the information it reveals doesn't compromise national security. As the credits role we see shots of classified files and other data to drive the point home.

Two Army men sent to recover a crashed space satellite find it in Piedmont NM, population 68. When they reach Piedmont, they spot vultures circling overhead in the night sky. One man says to his companion the diurnal birds wouldn't be out at night if they didn't have a feast.

A few minutes later, Scoop Mission Control at Vandenburg AFB receives a call from the men that the entire town is dead. Their expressions of horror intensify, then the call ends. After an overhead flight confirms corpses are sprawled everywhere, Major Manchek (Ramon Bieri) unlocks a security phone and calls a Wildfire alert. The meaning of Wildfire and Scoop Mission Control are not yet clear.

Once the alert goes out, military officers arrive at Dr. Jeremy Stone's (Arthur Hill) elegant cocktail party, much to his wife's (Susan Brown) annoyance. They inform Stone "there's been a fire" and escort him out over his wife's protests. She tries calling her father, a U.S. senator, but the government cuts into the call to tell her she won't be talking to anyone.

Things are urgent enough that the government has rented an entire passenger jet to transport Stone to Wildfire as fast as possible. The plane is empty so he can read the top-secret material on the current crisis without anyone catching a glimpse.

Wildfire also calls Dr. Charles Dutton (David Wayne) away from his home, despite his family's disapproval of him working with the "germ warfare people." Surgeon Mark Hall (James Olson) and bacteriologist Dr. Ruth Leavitt (Kate Reid) get interrupted in the middle of their work, neither one pleased about it. During a helicopter ride with Stone, Hall admits that he never reads Stone's periodic Wildfire briefings, dismissing them as science fiction. Perhaps it's understandable Hall wasn't the first choice for the team but the backup—the top pick isn't available. Stone tells Hall that in addition to his medical skills, it's important that he's single. He doesn't explain further.

The film shifts forward in time to a Senate committee hearing. The back and forth with one witness reveals that Stone proposed Wildfire to the government because he believed NASA precautions against extraterrestrial contamination weren't adequate. Stone had no idea the Scoop program for gathering extraterrestrial biological matter existed until Wildfire activated him.

The helicopter flies Stone and Hall over Piedmont. Fearing the birds eating the corpses could become disease vectors, they kill them with gas bombs, then don hazmat suits and descend by rope. The film adopts a split-screen effect to show both the scientists peering into homes and the dead bodies they're finding inside. Some victims died where they stood, but a few committed suicide. Hall notices that although some bodies are marked with cuts or vulture bites, none of the cuts are bleeding.

The two men find the Scoop satellite open in the town doctor's office, with the doctor dead next to it. Hall discovers all the blood in the doctor's body has turned to powder, and protests there's no organism on Earth that can do that. Stone grimly replies, "there didn't use to be."

The scientists locate two survivors, an old derelict named Jackson (George Mitchell) and a hungry baby. Stone has them both transported to Wildfire, then contacts presidential aide Robertson (Kermit Murdock) to recommend sterilizing Piedmont with a nuclear strike. In the situation room, Robertson and his colleagues discuss how to explain this to the USSR. Above-ground nuclear tests have been banned by treaty but telling the Soviets it's not a test will raise questions the White House would rather not answer. Ultimately the president decides to wait 48 hours, using the National Guard to cordon off Piedmont in the meantime.

The four researchers arrive at the Wildfire underground complex, hidden in the desert beneath an agricultural research station. They undergo intensive sterilization treatments to purge anything that could be a growth medium for xeno-bacteria. Leavitt has to give up her cigarettes; meals are scientifically prepared to minimize available sugar. If worse comes to worse, Stone says, Wildfire sits on top of a nuclear bomb. If it looks like something might escape, they start a five-minute countdown. If it's a false alarm, Hall has a deactivation key he can insert into any of Wildfire's computer workstations. The reason it matters that he's single is that studies indicate a single man is the most likely to let the bomb go off if necessary.

Once sterilization is done, Stone breaks the mission into three stages: detect the cause of the deaths in Piedmont; identify the organism responsible and how it works; then control or exterminate it. Dutton warns against exterminating too quickly, on the ground intelligent alien life could exist in microbial form.

Over the next couple of days, the team struggles to crack the mystery. They establish the killing agent—eventually code-named Andromeda—spreads by air, and that it came to Earth as green slime on a small meteorite embedded in Scoop. Leavitt and Dutton begin to suspect Scoop was collecting bacteria that might become biological warfare weapons. That's the case in Crichton's novel but only a high probability here. Stone reminds them that in any case, their job is to fix the problems, not point fingers.

The big question is why two unrelated, extremely different individuals—a healthy baby and a senior with a taste for drinking cheap sterno—both survived Andromeda. The team determines Andromeda kills by clotting the blood in our veins. The speed with which it works depresses Hall. It won't be easy to treat and it's too fast to explain why it drove some people to suicide. With a slower effect, blood clots developing first in the brain might explain it.

Back at Piedmont, a plane flies overhead—there's no way to cordon off the air space without drawing attention—then crashes when the pilot's oxygen mask dissolves. Gen. Sparks (Peter Hobbs) insists the crash is a coincidence, but Manchek's team discovers all plastic on the plane had dissolved into slime. Manchek's puzzled that the Wildfire team hasn't pushed the president to follow through on nuking the town.

We learn the reason why via another trip to the Senate committee. Wildfire gets government messages by teletype, with a bell ringing when a message arrives. A strip of paper came loose and blocked the bell, so nobody knew the messages have been coming in. The maintenance crew assumed any problem would be electronic, so they looked for short circuits, not paper jams.

The Wildfire team discovers the green slime has no proteins, DNA or amino acids; as the phrase goes, it's life, but not as we know it. They aren't worried as the destruction of Piedmont means there's no urgent danger. Hall keeps studying his two patients; Leavitt analyzes Andromeda growth projections. Because she's epileptic—something seeded in earlier scenes—a flashing red light triggers a brief fugue so she misses key information.

As if the slow pace of science wasn't frustrating enough, one of the maintenance crew discovers the problem with the bell. When Stone learns Piedmont is still standing he convinces the White House to go nuclear, then returns to the research. They learn Andromeda has a crystalline structure, separating biochemical functions into different facets. It's near indestructible, able to adapt to any environment, feed on any substrate and even absorb nuclear radiation—at which point Stone rushes to cancel the nuclear strike. Without that, however, they have no way of stopping Andromeda, which is mutating and growing and could spread across the entire southwest.

As they're projecting the outcomes, Dutton realizes the computer maps they're using were designed for bio-warfare projections. He and Leavitt realize that yes, Scoop was looking for weapons, not research. Stone insists the maps are purely hypothetical, for dealing with an enemy WMD attack. They're not convinced.

When Dutton returns to one of the labs, the seal breaks, exposing him to Andromeda. He sits hyperventilating in terror while Stone pumps in oxygen to slow Andromeda's growth. Hall suddenly tells Stone to stop feeding the lab oxygen: forcing Dutton to breathe harder and faster will make his blood, like Jackson's, more acidic. Hall's found the key: Andromeda can only survive at a neutral pH. Highly acidic environments like Jackson's blood or alkaline like the baby's will kill it. Better news: the rat in the lab with Dutton is alive because Andromeda has mutated into a non-infectious form.

The celebration is short-lived. The current mutation, like the one that hit the plane, feeds on plastic so all gaskets in Wildfire are melting down. Faced with a breach, the lab's computers have activated the nuclear countdown. Not only will they all die if Hall can't shut it down, but the bomb will also trigger a massive Andromeda growth spurt. Some of the resulting mutations will be lethal ones again. As if that wasn't enough, the security doors have trapped Hall in a section without a workstation. He has to climb through the core of the base, where the security devices almost kill him before he completes the shutdown.

With Andromeda no longer an immediate threat, it's safe to let the westerly winds carry the organisms from Piedmont over the Pacific. Stone arranges to trigger a rainstorm by cloud-seeding, washing Andromeda into the ocean where the pH levels will kill it. Talking to the Senate committee in the conclusion, Stone tells them the question remains—how will we deal with this when it happens again?

Andromeda Strain established Michael Crichton as a science fiction writer who was never classified as science fiction. His work held a sheen of realism that got him shelved in general fiction, read by people who'd never look at Asimov or Heinlein. *The Andromeda Strain* was the right novel at the right time, the same year man walked on the moon. The space race was huge and exciting and made the idea of our bringing back life from space that much more plausible. The presentation as a based-on-truth dramatization didn't hurt.

The book's great strength, which carried over to the movie, is its approach to science. Fiction dealing with science or medicine tend to focus on groundbreaking discoveries and dramatic breakthroughs, including the "deus ex laboratoria" that brings victory in alien-invasion films. Real science is slow, plodding work, repeating the same thing over and over again. Leavitt, for instance, studies a long, endless string of Petri dish cultures, looking to see which ones Andromeda grows on and which retard growth. Hall researches endless aspects of his patients' blood chemistry, looking for the common factor that let them live. When they don't get usable results, they try, try again, over and over. This fits with Crichton's approach to make this a "howdunnit"—even after identifying Andromeda, they still have to figure out how it causes death.

Robert Wise says in a DVD Making Of feature that Universal offered to buy the rights to the novel if he wanted to direct it. He said yes. Rather than ask Crichton to write the screenplay he turned to Nelson Gidding, who'd written several films for Wise before. Wise believed that novelists adapting their own work resist making changes for the screen, even when they're necessary.

It was a wise choice. While the film follows Crichton's plot with very little changed, Crichton didn't give his science team much personality. They're interchangeable characters except for their scientific specialties. Gidding's script gives them personalities. Stone's a reliable member of the establishment. Dutton's more cynical and left-wing. Hall's impatient and a bit of a skirt-chaser. Leavitt is tart-tongued and irascible. The book's Leavitt says he avoids flashing lights because they remind him of his World War II ambulance service. Movie Leavitt jokes about working in a red-light district.

Wise added to the realism by casting four good actors who weren't big names ("I figured it would be less believable if we had someone like Gregory Peck"). Reid is a particularly pleasant surprise, going against the tradition of young, beautiful female scientists. Several reviews compared her favorably to Raquel Welch as a scientist in *Fantastic Voyage* a few years earlier. By contrast, the 2008 miniseries, which was much less faithful to the book, has two women scientists, both good-looking.

The movie also looks good. Wildfire is an impressively cool, futuristic lab that appears more expensive than it was; the set only had one hallway, but they repainted it different colors to represent different levels. The ultimate strength of the film, though, is the tense script and the solid cast.

OTHER FILMS AND TELEVISION

Alien Factor (1978) A spaceship crash leaves alien creatures intended for an intergalactic zoo running loose on Earth.

Alien Hunter (2003) A crashed spaceship threatens to unleash a worldwide pandemic.

Alien vs. Predator (2004) A group of researchers exploring an ancient Predator base in the Antarctic find themselves trapped between the Predators and the Xenomorphs.

Alien vs. Predator; Requiem (2007) This time the battle between the two species takes place in a small Colorado town. Can a military veteran keep her family safe?

The Alien Within (1995) Made-for-cable *Alien* knockoff involving Americans battling a chest-bursting monster in an underwater base.

Almost Human (2013) A missing man returns to his hometown. It turns out he's been infected by an alien parasite that drives him to kill.

Beasties (1989) Extraterrestrial time-traveling monsters wreak havoc on a small town.

The Crawling Eye (1958) Alien eye monsters lurk on an Alpine mountain top, attacking humans who come too close.

The Creeping Unknown (1956) The crew of an experimental space flight transform into an alien monster that threatens to spread its spores worldwide. The first of three Quatermass films.

Critters (1986) Vicious, furry little aliens terrorize a farm community.

The Day of the Triffids (1962) A meteor shower leaves most of humanity blind and brings monstrous carnivorous plants to Earth. Based on a John Wyndham novel.

The Deadly Spawn (1983) Another wave of monsters lands on Earth and begin eating people.

Flame Barrier (1958) A satellite that crashes to Earth carries an oozing monstrosity with it. Bill Warren rates this as a complete mess.

The Giant Claw (1957) Absurd-looking giant bird terrorizes the world. It's extraterrestrial, prehistoric and protected by an anti-matter force field to boot.

The Giant Spider Invasion (1975) Giant alien spiders arrive on Earth through a black hole.

High Desert Kill (1989) A telepathic alien torments and tortures humans as part of an experiment (but without abducting them first).

Iron Invader (2011) Xenobacteria animates an iron statue and sends it on a rampage.

Killdozer (1974) An alien intelligence takes over a bulldozer and turns it against a construction crew working on an isolated island. Based on a Theodore Sturgeon short story.

Kronos (1957) Giant, very cool looking robot attempts to drain off all forms of manmade energy.

Little Shop of Horrors (1986) Science fiction musical in which a nerd (Rick Moranis) becomes a celebrity after he discovers a unique species of plant. It turns out the plant is an intelligent, talking alien that needs human blood to grow.

Metamorphosis: The Alien Factor (1990) An alien transforms a human scientist into a monster.

A Quiet Place (2018) and *A Quiet Place II* (2020) Alien predators with uncanny hearing force humanity to stay silent or die in these nail-biting films.

Space Master X-7 (1958) A Mars probe returns to Earth bearing a deadly and rapid-growing fungus.

Sphere (1998) Dustin Hoffman leads a team of scientists exploring a mysterious spaceship. The ship turns out to come from the future but it contains an alien entity that alters reality in response to the research team's fears.

Threshold (2003) During repairs of the Hubble space telescope, an astronaut becomes infected by alien insects. Now he's back on Earth and they're ready to swarm.

Vampirella (1996) A sexy vampire (Talisa Soto) from the planet Drakulon helps Earth fight of an invasion of evil vampires.

Virus (1999) An alien computer virus seizes control of a ship with an intention of eventually eliminating humanity. Jamie Lee Curtis, William Baldwin and Donald Sutherland are in the cast.

The X from Outer Space (1967) Aliens spray an Earth spaceship with spores in this Japanese film. One of them develops into a kaiju or giant monster.

Zarkorr! The Invader (1996) Aliens decide to test humanity by unleashing an unstoppable monster and challenging an ordinary human to find Zarkorr's weakness.

ELEVEN

Loving the Alien

Interplanetary Love Stories

"I like to watch you sleep. I don't know why."—Starman

Romance is a staple in modern film and television. In any movie or series of any genre—war, crime, horror—there's a good chance some of the characters will fall in love or at least hook up. It's no surprise the same is true of alien-visitor stories. Lots of these films have romances between the human protagonists, such as Forrester and Sylvia in *War of the Worlds*, David and Connie in *Independence Day* or Mike Donovan and Julie Parrish in *V*.

Other alien-visitor stories find more potential in love or lust between humans and aliens. Love stories thrive on obstacles to keep the lovers from finding their happy ending before Act One is over. Interspecies romance offers plenty of obstacles. They come from different races on different worlds. They may find each other's attitudes towards sex, dating and gender incomprehensible. Sometimes they're in a war and on opposite sides. Yet they'll keep fighting for their love because they're drawn to each other like magnet and steel. Or occasionally moth and bug zapper.

For many aliens, one major obstacle is that they don't feel love, or don't believe that they do. As I've covered in previous chapters, screen aliens often conform to the stereotype that the smarter you are, the less emotion your brain has room for. Even human emotions are often seen as a relic of our primitive past, as in all the references our "lizard brain" causing us to behave badly. Alien visitor stories routinely assume that if the aliens have better tech than we do, they must also be smarter, therefore devoid of emotion.

In most cases, rather than making aliens detached and contemplative like an enlightened human mystic, lacking emotion makes them mean. They aren't capable of compassion, but they have deep wells of cruelty. In the *Outer Limits* episode "Keeper of the Purple Twilight" (a title that has nothing to do with the story), the alien Ikar (Robert Webber) explains his world runs on perfect rationality. That doesn't stop them from being aggressive and warlike and it also makes them misogynists. On Ikar's world, woman have no role other than "breeder." Apparently, the writers didn't think judging women by their intelligence or other abilities would be rational.

Plenty of humans, such as Carrington in *The Thing from Another World* think getting rid of emotions would be a plus. Most films assume the audience will know this is a bad idea; a few films make it a point of debate. Miles arguing with the pods in *Invasion of the Body Snatchers* is one example. Another is 1956's *It Conquered the World*.

The film's human villain, Tom (Lee Van Cleef), is a brilliant scientist embittered because his ideas have never brought the recognition he thinks he deserves. He's made

Capable actors Beverly Garland, Peter Graves and Lee Van Cleef got the lead roles in *It Conquered the World* (1956). Unfortunately they co-star with a Venusian invader that looks like a zucchini with fangs.

contact with the last of the dying Venusian race, who've flattered his genius until he sees them as friends. With Tom's help, one of the Venusians has reached Earth. It proceeds to take over several key officials using control devices that destroy emotions. With no loyalty or love, the human victims are puppets. Even though Tom dearly loves his wife (Beverly Garland), he looks forward to the day the Venusians purge all emotion from all of humanity.

Tom's former best friend, Paul (Peter Graves), doesn't see it that way. After the Venusian takes over Paul's wife, he's forced to kill her, then he goes over to confront Tom. Even at gunpoint Tom won't betray his alien friend. Paul says that's because Tom's able to feel emotions such as loyalty and courage; one of the Venusian's human robots would logically conclude survival is the top priority and answer all questions. Without emotion, community and civilization would be impossible.

The aliens are often unsure their loss of emotion is a good thing. Raw physical passion is frequently a game changer. Jamarcus (Richard Ayoade) in *The Watch* admits one reason he's siding with Earth against his own people is the pleasure of having a woman lick his testicles. In TV's *The First Wave* (1998–2001), the pleasures of human bodies are an open secret on the aliens' homeworld, to the point there's a waiting list to serve on Earth.

An uglier version of this takes place in *The Brain from Planet Arous*. When the alien brain Gor possesses Steve (John Agar), it feels an intense arousal looking at Steve's fiancée Sally (Joyce Meadows). When Steve kisses her with more passion than usual, she likes it. Then he shoves her down on a deck chair and starts tearing off her blouse, which horrifies her—not because she's a prude, as some reviews claim, but because it's sexual assault.

In many alien/human romances, the human half has no idea who they've really fallen for. In *Night Slaves* (1970) Clay (James Franciscus) takes a vacation with his wife Marjorie (Lee Grant) as a last-ditch effort to stave off divorce. Stopping in a small town, Clay discovers everyone, including Marjorie, driving off in the night except for flirtatious Naillil (Tisha Sterling). It turns out an alien ship has crashed nearby; as the aliens are pure mind they've borrowed human bodies to make repairs. Naillil is one of them.

Joey (James Spader) in *Starcrossed* (1985) falls for Mary (Belinda Bauer) under the impression she's a Soviet defector chased by the KGB. She's really a refugee from the tyrants who've conquered her peaceful planet. The people pursuing her are agents sent by the conquerors, who want to prove nobody can escape them.

In TBS's 2016–17 TV series *People of Earth*—a comedy about a support group for abductees—Don (Bjorn Gustafsson) is a White (pale-skinned, human-looking alien) who's fallen in love with Kelly (Alice Wetterlund), whom he once abducted. He eventually poses as a human to be with her and wins her heart. When she realizes most of what he's told her is a lie—though not that he's an alien—she breaks up with him.

Once the big reveal takes place, the next challenge is for the alien to prove it. In *Starcrossed*, Mary convinces Joey with telekinesis. In a comedy, the human may stay clueless. Characters in *Pajama Party* (1964) never grasp that the Martian Go-Go (Tommy Kirk) is anything but an oddball guy with a flair for stage magic.

Knowing the truth doesn't solve all the problems. In *Earth Girls Are Easy* (1989), Valerie (Geena Davis) falls for Mac (Jeff Goldblum), a furry alien who looks handsome once all his hair is gone. But how can she be with a spaceman when she's already engaged to a human, Ted (Charles Rocket)? Sure, sex with Mac is amazing and Ted's a sleazeball cheater ("Just because I'm getting married to her doesn't mean we can't date") but still…

In the *Alien Nation* TV series, Detective Sikes (Gary Graham) meets and falls for Cathy Franklin (Terri Treas), an alien Newcomer neighbor living across the hall. Despite being partnered with another Newcomer, Francisco (Eric Pierpoint), Sikes has a lot of bias against them to get past. There are also cultural differences: Cathy, like a lot of Newcomers, loves Earth clowns whereas Sikes can't stand them.

And what happens when the two sides are divided by war? In the TV series *Star-Crossed* (2014), human Emery (Aimee Teegarden) and the Atrian teen Roman (Matt Lanter) are mutually attracted to each other. With the Atrians confined to a military controlled zone—Roman is one of the Atrian Seven attending a human high school—relations between the species are not good. Militants on both sides disapprove of mixed-race relationships, particularly as Roman's the son of the murdered Atrian leader. Can their love survive? In *Mars Needs Women*, Dop (Tommy Kirk) has to bring Earth females to Mars as breeders; after falling for Dr. Bolen (Yvonne Craig), he gives up his mission and tries to save the kidnapped women.

The physical issues—two alien species are unlikely to find each other attractive, let alone physically compatible—usually gets hand-waved. Superman and Lois Lane have been lusting for and loving each other for decades, even though, as Larry Niven's short story "Man of Steel, Woman of Kleenex" points out, it's unlikely they'd be biologically compatible. Although given that Superman has never been written as a realistic alien bound by the laws of science, it's a silly hill to die on.

Handwaving the science is probably the right call. I doubt anyone who watches *Earth Girls Are Easy* is anticipating xenobiological insights into human/alien mating. Most films don't even bring it up. *Starcrossed* does: when one of Joey's friends asks how Mary can look human, Joey reminds him we're made in God's image—how many images do you imagine he's got?

Do the lovers always get a happy ever after? No. Mary of *Starcrossed* flies back to her planet to fight for her people leaving Joe here on Earth. Dop dies at the military's hands as he's trying to do the right thing. The show runner for *Star-Crossed* told the TV Addict website that if the series had lasted, Emery/Roman wouldn't have.

The format—film or TV—plays a role here. A film needs to wrap everything up within a couple of hours or so, whether the lovers get together or part forever. A TV series needs to structure relationships for the long haul. That often means moving slowly—by the end of *Mork and Mindy*'s first season they'd just about reached the "more than friends" point. A *Star-Crossed* movie would have had to move much faster on Emery/Roman; an *Earth Girls Are Easy* TV series might have kept Valerie wavering between Mac and Ted for an entire season.

SPOTLIGHT

Starman *(1984)*

Columbia Pictures. 115 minutes. Release date December 14, 1984.

CAST: Jeff Bridges (Starman), Karen Allen (Jenny Hayden), Charles Martin Smith (Mark Shermin), Richard Jaeckel (George Fox), Robert Phalen (Major Bell), Tony Edwards (Sergeant Lemon), John Walter Davis (Brad Heinmuller), Ted White (Deer Hunter), Dirk Blocker (Cop #1), M.C. Gainey (Cop #2), Sean Faro (Hot Rodder), Buck Flower (Cook), Russ Benning (Scientist),Ralph Cosham (Marine Lieutenant), David Wells (Fox's Assistant), Anthony Grumbach (NSA Officer), Jim Deeth (S-61 Pilot), Alex Daniels (Gas Station Attendant), Carol Rosenthal (Gas Customer), Mickey Jones (Trucker), Lu Leonard (Roadhouse

Waitress), Charlie Hughes (Bus Driver), Byron Walls (Police Sergeant), Betty Bunch (Truck Stop Waitress), Victor McLemore (Roadblock Lt.), Steven Brennan (Roadblock Sergeant), Pat Lee (Bracero Wife), Judith Kim (Girl Barker), Ronald Colby (Cafe Waiter), Robert Stein (State Trooper), Kenny Call (Donnie Bob), Jeff Ramsey (Hunter #1), Jerry Gatlin (Hunter #2), David Daniell (Letterman), Randy Tutton (2nd Letterman)

CREDITS: Director: John Carpenter; Writers: Bruce A. Evans, Raynold Gideon; Producer: Larry J. Franco; Co-Producer: Barry Bernardi; Executive Producer: Michael Douglas; Production Designer: Daniel Lomino; Photography: Donald M. Morgan; Music: Jack Nitzsche; Editor: Marion Rothman

As the Columbia Pictures logo appears on screen, we hear sounds from the 1977 Voyager 2 launch. The probe was the second human craft to enter interstellar space, carrying information, music and videos from Earth, including a tape-recorded invitation to aliens to come visit us. As the credits roll, we watch the probe's journey into space and glimpse some of its contents.

Jump to present day, in Jenny Hayden's (Karen Allen) rural Wisconsin home. She's sitting with a cigarette and a glass of wine, watching home movies of herself and her deceased husband Scott (jeff Bridges). Being 1984, the movies are actual film strips playing back on a home projector. Watching them only makes Jenny's grief for Scott more raw. Finally, with a tear-streaked face, she drags herself to bed.

Elsewhere in the night, a small spaceship approaches the Earth. When the U.S. government detects it overhead, planes go up and security official George Fox (Richard Jaeckel) gets called in. The military tell Fox the intruder isn't Russian, nor do the Russians know about it. The planes attack without provocation, bringing the ship down in the forest near Jenny's house. Fox calls in Mark Shermin (Charles Martin Smith) of SETI, the Search for Extraterrestrial Intelligence. Shermin's on a large government retainer precisely for situations like this; he compares it later to national security checking him out of SETI like a library book.

A blue light rises from the wrecked ship. We see through its eyes as it crosses the woods to Jenny's home, studies her car, then goes inside and studies her house. It replays the film strip; studies the carpet at such close range it can see the details of the weave; and pages through Jenny's photo album. It turns one of the photographs of Scott into a hologram, then discovers a lock of Scott's hair taped to one page. It slips inside a strand of hair, which begins flashing with light.

The glow from the living room wakes Jenny. She finds a grotesque baby on the floor, growing rapidly older, dropping a handful of spheres on the floor as it elongates, alters and ages into adulthood. Jenny grabs a gun as the figure gets to its feet and turns, showing Scott's face. When he walks towards her, she can tell it's not Scott—the body language and facial expressions aren't at all normal—but she's shaken enough to let him take the gun. He points it at her, not threateningly but obviously unaware of the risk.

The Starman addresses her in multiple languages, freaking her out enough she starts reciting the Lord's Prayer. Then he suddenly declares "as Secretary General of the United Nations…. I send greetings." Jenny faints. The alien walks awkwardly to the mirror, studies his face, then reruns the film strip. Watching Scott teach Jenny how to shoot, the Starman mimics the actions and fires a bullet through Jenny's window. The film also shows Jenny being nice to a stray raccoon, establishing her kind heart.

The sound of a helicopter overhead stops the Starman cold. He raises his hand, summoning the spheres to his palm. Stepping outside, he uses one sphere, floating in the air, to send a message: *Observation craft destroyed. Environment hostile. Rendezvous third day Landing Area One.*

Jenny wakes and tries to slip away to her car. She bumps into the alien outside and screams; he screams in imitation, then tells her they both need to leave. Jenny gets into the car with him but the car engine won't turn over. The alien touches the starter and it goes. They drive off with the gun in his lap. One of his spheres projects a map showing their destination, which Jenny thinks is in Arizona. She tells him to go alone but he insists, in his odd, alien way, that she drive him. As they head down the highway, he's fascinated by everything, from the movement of the windshield wipers to the way Jenny races through a yellow light before it turns red.

As the military fly Shermin to the crash site he asks them to monitor police bands for anything "freaky. Bizarre." A research team is already at the site when he arrives and has established there's no radiation or infectious material on the meteorite. Shermin tells one researcher the meteorite changed direction twice before impact which is why he was called in. The crew drilling on the meteorite discovers it's hollow. Shermin says that's impossible, then vapor gushes out through the drill hole from the interior.

Jenny hears about the meteorite strike on the car radio and realizes that was the Starman's spaceship. She peppers him with questions—where are they going? What does he want? Why does he look like Scott?—but his response is to sing the Rolling Stones' "Satisfaction," which was included in Voyager 2's cultural material. Jenny snaps and drives into the left lane, playing chicken with an oncoming van. The van steers off the road, then Jenny brakes her Mustang to a stop. Leaping out of the car she tells the other driver (John Walter Davis) she's being kidnapped.

The Starman, unfazed, approaches the driver, declaring "I send greetings." When the man advances, wielding a lug wrench, one of the spheres turns it red hot. The man drops it before the heat makes it explode into molten metal, which is enough to send him running. Scott leads a dismayed Jenny back to the car.

As they resume driving, Jenny asks Scott to put the gun away because it makes her jumpy. "Define jumpy" (his catchphrase throughout the film is asking her to "define—"). She does, then asks if he understands. He replies that he understands Earth greetings in 54 languages, then rifles through the glove compartment from curiosity. He tries to smile but it comes off like a death's head grimace. Eventually he tells Jenny he cloned Scott's form in the belief she wouldn't be jumpy around him.

Shermin's team sets up a lab and begins studying the spaceship. He reports to Fox that "the balloon has just gone up" then one of the soldiers assigned to him reports the driver's story of the lug wrench—is that the sort of freaky bizarre thing you were looking for? When the researchers find the Voyager 2 materials inside the spaceship, Shermin realizes someone responded to our invitation.

Back on the highway, Jenny convinces her companion the car needs refueling. At the gas station, she goes into the women's room, making it clear he mustn't follow, and writes a plea for help on a paper towel. The alien occupies himself gawking at a bird, visiting the men's room—his strangeness pisses off the other man in there—and then returns to the women's restroom. He sees the note but doesn't understand so he takes it with him. When he asks Jenny to define "kid-nap-ed" and shows the note, she brakes the car and angrily tells him, "it's being dragged out of your house in the middle of the night by some—whatever you are," with no idea why, or where they're going. She tells him to shoot—she'd sooner be dead than constantly scared.

The Starman puts the gun to her head. Jenny closes her eyes, but the gun clicks, empty: "I mean you no harm, Jenny Hayden." It's their first turning point, though she's still not happy about being "kid-nap-ed." Still, she allows the Starman to drive while she sleeps. When she wakes up, he's singing along to the radio; in answer to her question he says that yes, his planet has singing. She asks if his people get hungry, which baffles him. Jenny explains and he realizes yes, his body is hungry. To reach a restaurant fast, he speeds through an intersection, almost getting hit by a truck. He assures Jenny that's what he learned watching her—"Red light stop. Green light go. Yellow light go fast." This is a very old joke, but it works.

Shermin updates Fox and reveals the alien's current physical form, to which an incredulous Fox replies "You expect me to tell the president an alien has landed and has assumed the identity of a dead house painter?" Fox finds it hard to believe cloning from a lock of hair is possible, but Shermin points out the aliens are way, way ahead of Earthly science. He suggests that the alien's "I send greetings" might be a sign he's friendly; Fox retorts, "It is also what the cannibal said to the missionary just before he ate him." Shermin: "The question in this case is, who is the missionary and who are the cannibals?"

The Starman finally answers Jenny's question about their destination: three days after the crash, at noon, the mothership will descend to collect him. If they don't make it, he'll be stranded and die. When they park at a bus station to get another meal, the neighboring car has a dead deer strapped to the hod. The Starman is astonished a human would kill an animal that isn't a threat; the hunter (Ted White) mocks him for being upset someone shot Bambi.

Over dinner at a bus stop, Jenny figures out their destination is the Meteor Crater, a mile-wide landmark near Winslow Arizona. The Starman confirms the meteor was another ship from an earlier visit by his people. Jenny doesn't want to travel any further but she knows he needs to, so she makes out a map and gives it to him along with her car keys and a credit card. She pulls a honeymoon photo out of her pocket in the process which leads to her explaining love—"It's when you care more for someone else than you do for yourself.... When someone you love dies—oh, shit." Fortunately the waitress arrives with their meals to end the conversation. The alien eats his Dutch apple pie with a strange, ecstatic expression.

Jenny pays the bill, then tries to slip out the back to catch a bus. The waitress points out the Starman will see her doing it because he's already out in the parking lot. Jenny looks and sees him expend one of the spheres to resurrect the deer, after which he unties it and helping it to stand. The outraged hunter runs over and punches the alien out. The Starman punches back but the hunter's buddies pile on until Jenny gets the gun from her car and fires it into the air. The hunters go running. The waitress comes out and offers to hold the bus for Jenny. Jenny tells her no and gets back in the car.

They drive off but the hunters drive in pursuit. Jenny narrowly steers around a bus while the other car crashes into it. That stops the pursuit but the police put an APB out on the Mustang. Shermin's people alert him to the incident so he flies there quickly to interview the eyewitnesses. He's bemused to learn Jenny's now traveling with the Starman voluntarily.

In the car, Jenny tells the story of how she and Scott met ice-skating and how beautiful it felt, then defines beautiful ("Beautiful is better than terrific. Better than Dutch apple pie The best"). They stop at a motel, unaware a couple of cops have recognized them from the APB. The trigger-happy men aren't happy at being told not to use force unless it's life or death. One cop says to the other that perhaps they can make that happen.

Up in their room, Jenny sleeps while the alien watches TV. After catching the classic scene in *From Here to Eternity* where Burt Lancaster and Donna Reed make out in the surf, the Starman goes over and snuggles close to Jenny, as if he wants to do the same. At that instant, a guy knocks on their door to warn them the cops are trying to jimmy the lock on their car. The guy cheerfully distracts the cops long enough for Jenny and the Starman to get in the car and go.

When the police catch up, the Starman ignores Jenny's warning and threatens them with the gun. One of the cops fires first, shooting Jenny in the gut. The horrified alien accelerates the car away from the police, ignoring the warning signs that there's a wrecked fuel tanker on the road ahead. The Mustang smashes into the tanker, making both vehicles explode in fire. The Starman emerges from the fireball on foot, carrying Jenny and shielding them with an aura of blue light.

The alien carries Jenny into a small prefab house being transported across country by truck. He sacrifices one of his two remaining spheres to gradually restore Jenny to life. A couple of days later, when the truck pulls up at a truck stop, it's done. The Starman leaves Jenny while she sleeps and gets a lift from one of the restaurant staff for the next leg of his journey

Jenny wakes up and goes into the truck stop, assuming she'll find the alien there. She also calls Shermin—there's no explanation how she knows his number or even who to call—and begs him to leave her alone. When she learns the alien is already on the road, she asks another driver to help catch up. Ahead of her, the Starman chats with his companion, a Southerner, imitating his accent reflexively and accepting a cigarette. Smoking it does not go well.

Both cars end up stuck at a military roadblock, with soldiers requiring everyone get out of their cars and line up for inspection. The guy carrying Jenny distracts the military by using his gas can as a Molotov cocktail, then driving off (given she's a total stranger, this seems remarkably self-sacrificing). With the soldiers focused on him, Jenny's able to pull the Starman out of the queue and runs with him until they reach a different highway. They hitch a ride on a pickup truck, joining a woman and her baby in the back.

Jenny's furious with the Starman but he doesn't see why: isn't it obvious now that the trip is too dangerous for her? Jenny says he should have said goodbye first, then has to define goodbye. The other woman's baby prompts the Starman to discuss human reproduction. Jenny reveals she and Scott wanted a baby but she's infertile.

The couple leave the pickup to race through the rain and hop a nearby freight, carrying a blanket the woman gave them so they'd have something to sleep on. Inside the freight car, Jenny peels her companion's sodden shirt off—and they give each other a look of mutual interest. Moments later they're lying on the blanket, kissing. The expression on the Starman's face is strange, as if he's trying to figure out what he's feeling. Next scene, he's on top and the kissing is more intense. Then Jenny's on top again and he's smiling like he understands now; Jenny grins in response and it's adorable.

Jenny drifts into sleep and wakes to find the Starman watching her. She asks if he can stay with her. He says no, then grins and tells her she's pregnant; genetically it's her and Scott's child but "he will know everything I know and when he grows to manhood, he will be a teacher." The Starman adds that he can unmake the pregnancy if she wishes. Jenny just hugs him tight, deliriously happy, and asks him to point out his home star.

It turns out they hopped the wrong freight and end up in Vegas instead of Winslow Arizona. They're almost broke but the alien's powers enable him to win enough cash to rent a car. They have just enough time to reach the Meteor Crater before the deadline. Fox's team, however, have figured out their destination, based on the scout ship's original trajectory. Shermin's blood curdles when he realizes Fox intends to have the alien killed and dissected. Fox dismisses his protests, telling Shermin not to lecture him on morality. Shermin: "Screw morality, what about good manners? We invited him here!" Fox sneers that Shermin's free to return to academia and give up his federal salary if he isn't happy.

Back on the road, the Starman opens up and tells Jenny what it's like on his world: "Only one language, only one people … no war … we are very civilized but we have lost something I think…. I will miss the cooks and the singing and the dancing. And the eating…. And the other things." When they stop for a final meal near the Crater—more pie—Jenny asks if he has a wife on his homeworld. He says no, adding with a longing expression, "I wish…. I wish…." But whatever he wishes is cut short, as local cops show up to detain them.

Shermin shows up before Fox, awed to meet a man from space. Jenny begs him to let them go but Shermin refuses. The Starman confirms Shermin's guess his people have been visiting Earth for a long time: "You are a strange species, not like any other. And you would be surprised how many there are…. Shall I tell you what I find beautiful about you? You are at your very best when things are worst."

It's enough to prod Shermin into listening to the better angels of his nature. He informs the cops it's a case of mistaken identity and tells the couple they're free to go. Jenny kisses Smith goodbye; the Starman kisses him too. When Fox arrives, he's furious at the betrayal. Shermin calmly lights a cigar—Fox can't stand him smoking—and blows smoke in Fox's face ("Much as I hate to stoop to symbolism").

The two fugitives reach the crater and race down inside it, but the alien is now stumbling a lot, as if running out of steam. A fleet of military helicopters closes in, laying down warning fire—then backing off as a sphere the size of the crater descends, pausing over Jenny and the Starman. A ray streams down, as does what appears to be snow, and Jenny begs the Starman to take her. *He:* "You'd die there." *She:* "I don't think I care." *He:* "I care. Now tell me again how to say goodbye." *She:* "Kiss me and then tell me you love me." He does, then gives Jenny the last ball, telling her their child will know how to use it. The Starman walks away and turns to look at her one last time. Rather than show him entering the ship, the camera shows us Jenny's face, sad and a little overwhelmed, gazing up as he rises. Her expression fills with awe.

At the time Columbia offered John Carpenter the chance to direct *Starman*, he was known primarily for horror films such as *Halloween* and of course *The Thing*. He says on the DVD commentary track that he jumped at the chance to do something different and really liked the gentleness of the script. He thought of Bridges as a possible lead; Bridges suggested playing the alien as someone trying to fit in by impersonating a human being. Bridges says normally he tries to look at home in his body when he's performing; now he went the opposite route, modeling the alien's movements on the eccentric body language of a friend of his.

The actor does an amazing job, possibly the best performance of an alien trying to pass for human (Joe Morton's eternally silent Brother might tie him for the honor). *Starman* uses the stock trope of the alien discovering the joys of human existence—sex!

Pie!—and that could easily have become cloying fast. Bridges pulls it off. He earned a Best Actor nomination, a rare thing for a science fiction film.

The alien's powers are borderline magical, but the limited number of spheres keep the magic from getting out of control. It also makes his use of them more meaningful: where Kreton in *Visit to a Small Planet* can perform an infinite number of miracles, resurrecting the deer costs the alien some of his power. He willingly makes the sacrifice.

The script follows the template of many classic road romances such as *It Happened One Night*: two characters, initially antagonistic, developing deeper feelings as they travel together (Carpenter did, in fact, shoot it across country, including at the Meteor Crater). It could very easily have gone wrong. A kidnap victim falling for her abductor feels more like Stockholm syndrome than true love. The film avoids that trap by giving Jenny repeated chances to walk out and having her choose not to. It's also a plus that he doesn't force the baby on her. It's her choice too, in contrast to the alien pregnancies in Chapter Eight.

Karen Allen as the grieving widow who goes from panic to sympathy to friendship to love also turns in an amazing performance. As Bridges says, the film only works if Allen makes us believe that she believes in what's happening. She does, beautifully.

Charles Martin Smith also turns in excellent work as the troubled Smith. Richard Jaeckel gives a solid performance as Fox but his motivation in the script is inadequate. He's hardly the only official in an alien visitor film to see an alien presence as a threat but it isn't convincing. Nor is the military reaction, attacking the Starman's ship despite zero signs of hostility. Dissecting the alien doesn't make any scientific sense: it's a clone body so it won't tell us much about extraterrestrials. All in all, Fox comes off like a complete cipher.

Carpenter says he faced a lot of negative feedback from people who assumed stepping away from horror meant he was selling out for a paycheck. Nevertheless, the film was a hit, which led to a one-season TV spinoff from ABC in 1986. It's supposedly 14 years since the Starman's first visit, which means the original film happened in 1972, five years before Voyager 2 launched.

It turns out that Fox (Michael Cavanaugh) didn't give up. Jenny went on the run and gave up her baby, Scott, to keep him out of Fox's grasp. Years later Scott's (C.D. Barnes) foster parents die; his grief brings the Starman back to Earth, cloning the body of recently deceased photojournalist Paul Forrester (Robert Hayes). Together the father and son go on the run from Fox while hunting for Jenny, finding her near the end of the season, then losing her.

It's another example of how TV romance often differs from films. Keeping Jenny out of reach prolongs the romance, denying the Starman consummation. It also justifies keeping Paul and Scott on the road. This fits not only the movie but the *Fugitive* template many science-fiction shows have used. The 1963–67 series was a smash hit with David Janssen as Dr. Kimball, the the convicted wife killer trying to clear his name by hunting down the real killer, staying one step ahead of the cops at the same time. The set-up allowed the show to shift in tone and story depending on who Kimball encountered in a given week. Science-fiction shows such as *The Immortal, The Visitor, The Incredible Hulk* and *Starman* adopted the same approach.

Hayes didn't give as alien a performance as Bridges, but he was fun in the role. It helped that rather than the lovable Scott Hayden, Forrester was a womanizer and troublemaker whose past scandals kept bedeviling the alien in the present.

Possibly *Starman* also inspired the 1987–91 sitcom *Out of This World*. Protagonist Donna Garland (Donna Pescow) married an alien who was then called back to his homeworld. That left Donna raising her daughter, Evie (Maureen Flannigan) alone and coping with Evie's amazing powers. Evie could, however, communicate with her father (Burt Reynolds, voice only) by using a magic cube.

OTHER FILMS AND TELEVISION

Aliens in the Family (1996) Short-lived sitcom about a happily married alien/human couple. Cookie (Margaret Trigg) abducted Doug (John Belford Lloyd) but they fell in love. Can their blended family make a go of life on Earth?

Beach Babes from Beyond Infinity (1993) Three sexy aliens crash-land on Earth and have fun. Described by one reviewer as a *Beach Party* movie with breasts.

Dead Weekend (1995) A soldier hooks up with a female alien shapeshifter who draws power from sex. A TV movie that amounts to a badly written erotic fantasy.

The Love War (1970) The first made-for-TV alien visitor film. Lloyd Bridges is a burned-out alien warrior fighting a secret war on Earth against his planet's great enemies. He falls in love with a human woman (Angie Dickinson) who turns out to be one of the enemy.

TWELVE

Little Aliens Everywhere

Children, Teenagers and Spacemen

"I've been wishing for this since I was 10 years old."
—*E.T.*

Movies and TV have been making stories about children or marketed to children for decades. It's no surprise some of them are alien visitor movies. They're a natural fit.

Invaders from Mars from 1953 is an alien-infiltration story told from a child's point of view. Bobby (Bobby Driscoll) discovers Martians are trapping and mind-controlling everyone around him: the neighborhood cop, his best friend, his parents. The Martians want to do the same to him.

The difference between this and *Invasion of the Body Snatchers* is that a kid doesn't have the options Miles Bennell does. Even if Bobby could knock out someone with a hypodermic, where would he run? How would he survive? It's a nightmare he can't escape from until he finds a couple of adults who believe him.

In the opening episode of the TV series *The Whispers* (2015) a young girl named Harper (Abby Ryder Fortson) plays a game with her imaginary best friend Drill. She invites her mother to participate, unaware the game is dangerous. An adult would have been less likely to trust Drill, but children don't have the same perspective.

Children are fascinating subjects for fiction because they occupy a liminal space. They're individuals with their own personalities, interests and needs but they're burdened by parental expectations that clash with all of that. They live under rules they have no say in and are encouraged to strive for things they may not care about. Adults are constantly watching and supervising them. They're a source of pride and love for parents but also fear: will they do the right thing? Will they live up to our expectations? Are we doing a good job raising them?

That's a lot for kids to deal with. As Ray Bradbury's short story "Zero Hour" puts it, "Sometimes children loved you, hated you—all in half a second. Strange children, did they ever forget or forgive the whippings and the harsh, strict words of commands? She wondered. How can you ever forget or forgive those over and above you, those tall and silly dictators."

Children also enjoy seeing a hero they can identify with, meaning a kid like them. Movies marketed to kids are often more optimistic than *Invaders from Mars* about their ability to fight against an alien invader. In *Aliens in the Attic* (2009) a group of children discover tiny aliens attacking their summer house to recover a beacon that will summon an invasion fleet. The aliens have mind-control rays that work on adults but not on anyone underage. The adults can't fight so the kids have to overcome the aliens on their own.

Teenagers share some of the liminal condition of younger children, but with a difference. Teenagers have a lot more ability to act: they're stronger, have more independence and they often have driver's licenses with all the freedom that brings. All of which can make the adult rules imposed on them several times more frustrating.

Teens can be busted for all kinds of things adults get away with. They're still answerable to their parents and other authority figures. Like younger children, "parents don't understand" is a common theme in teenage stories. Parents want their teenager kids to do something, or not do something—stay virgin, get into the Ivy League, become star quarterback—and emotionally it can become the biggest thing in the world. Once a child enters puberty, love and sex become serious concerns and "I do not want you dating that boy/girl again" is a time-honored point of conflict, as in *The Coneheads*.

Teens have their own cultures, friends and activities. So do children, but teens get to engage in them with less supervision. *The Blob* (1957) and *Invasion of the Saucer Men* (1957) both have protagonists encountering alien visitors while making out in their car, away from adult eyes.

The Blob emphasizes that the teens in town have their own hobbies, games and peer group, not entirely approved of by adults. When Steve (Steve McQueen) and his girlfriend Jane (Aneta Corseaut) report the existence of an oozing alien lifeform that dissolve human flesh, the cops write it off as another teenage practical joke. Kids these days!

Still, the default assumption is that kids are good as long as they're brought up properly. Conversely, bad kids are the result of bad parenting. *Santa Claus Conquers the Martians* (1964) emphasizes that Martian children are raised as miniature adults, lacking any sense of fun or spontaneity; the *Teenagers from Outer Space* (1959) are ruthless agents of their planet's tyrannical leader because they're not raised by their parents. This resembles a theme media scholar Lynn Spigel says was a recurring belief in the 1950s and 1960s—Americans know how to bring up kids better than any other nation.

Many child and teen alien-visitor films focus on families and the problems that beset them. In *The Space Children* (1958), families are under stress at the start of the film. One kid's stepfather (Russell Johnson) is an abusive drunk. The two lead kids are better off, but the family is still strained by Dad uprooting them to the isolated research station he's working at. The alien brain kills Johnson when he gets violent while the core family are healed by their passage through fire.

E.T., Steven Spielberg says, is about an alien visitor healing a family that's been shattered by divorce. In a much lighter vein, *Aliens in the Attic* has the children learning to put aside their differences and fight the aliens as a family.

Other films emphasize children's alienation and loneliness. Elliott (Henry Thomas) feels some of that before he befriends *E.T.* The high-school protagonists of *The Faculty* (1998) are mostly outcasts—nerdy wimp, new girl, alleged lesbian—whose fight against alien infiltrators changes their lives for the better. A running plot element in the teen soap opera *Roswell* was the alien teenagers reconnecting with people from their own planet. This helps them figure out who they are and what their role in the universe was.

Loneliness frequently leads young protagonists to make friends with an extraterrestrial, as Elliott does. In the animated *The Iron Giant* (1999), Hogarth (Eli Marienthal) is a child of divorce with a working mother (Jennifer Aniston) and nobody around to play with. The solution arrives in the form of a metal titan who crashes to Earth outside town. In *Lilo and Stitch* (2002), young Lilo (Daveigh Chase) similarly bonds with the troublemaking alien she calls Stitch (Christopher Michael Sanders). In both cases the alien helps fix the fraying bonds between the child and their parental figure—Hogarth and his mom, Lilo and her big-sister caregiver Nani (Tia Carrere).

In real life, parents worry that their kids' friends will turn out to be a bad influence. And some alien visitors are. Like a Pied Piper, aliens can lead their young friends away from their parents and down a sinister path, as Drill does in *The Whispers*. In the same vein the *Outer Limits* episode "The Special One," has sinister alien Mr. Zeno (Richard Ney) recruiting super-intelligent mutant children around the world. Zeno flatters his best protege (Flip Mark)—you'll be in charge, not your parents!—to make him a tool for conquest. Unlike the children in *The Whispers*, the boy sees through the lies and saves the world.

Things didn't work out so well in "Alien Lover," an episode of ABC's *Wide World of Mystery* anthology series. Orphaned Susan (Kate Mulgrew), whose caregiver relatives are mostly interested in her money, makes friends across the dimensions with an alien her own age. In his world, he tells her, teens rose up and overthrew the adults, establishing a teen-ruled dictatorship. Now that they're so close, won't Susan help him come to Earth and do the same thing there? She does.

Not every Pied Piper is evil, though. *The Space Children*'s alien-brain mentor has them doing things their parents wouldn't approve of, but it's for the greater good of preventing nuclear war. In the BBC series *Chocky* (1984), based on John Wyndham's novel, young Matthew's (Andrew Ellams) imaginary friend Chocky (Glynis Brooks) is an alien envoy. She hopes to steer him into science and eventually lead him to discover a limitless source of clean energy. When powerful men take an interest in exploiting Matthew, Chocky leaves, but returns to finish her work in *Chocky's Children* (1984) and *Chocky's Challenge* (1985).

SPOTLIGHT

E.T. The Extra Terrestrial *(1982)*

Universal. 105 minutes. Release date June 11, 1982

CAST: Dee Wallace (Mary), Henry Thomas (Elliott), Peter Coyote (Keys) Robert Macnaughton (Michael), Drew Barrymore (Gertie), K.C. Martel (Greg), Sean Frye (Steve), Tom Howell (Tyler), Erika Eleniak (Pretty Girl), David O'Dell (Schoolboy), Richard Swingler (Science Teacher), Frank Toth (Policeman), Robert Barton (Ultra Sound Man), Michael Darrell (Van Man)

CREDITS: Director: Steven Spielberg; Screenplay: Melissa Mathison; Producers: Steven Spielberg, Kathleen Kennedy; Associate Producer: Melissa Mathison; Production Manager: Wallace Worsley; Photography: Allen Daviau; Production Designer: James D. Bissell; Music: John Williams; Editor: Carol Littleton; Visual Effects Supervisor: Dennis Muren; ET created by Carlo Rambaldi Special Effects

Open on a visual of a night sky over a pine forest, while John Williams' score plays. The camera comes to rest on a parked spaceship, ramp extended to the ground with the interior light streaming over the forest. A barely seen alien walks through the woods, then goes inside the ship to add to the vast botanical collection of Earth plants. Outside,

E.T. The Extra Terrestrial (1982). E.T. levitating Elliott to bicycle across the night sky was such an iconic moment, it became part of Spielberg's Amblin Entertainment logo.

another alien uproots a small plant carefully while a rabbit watches, unfazed. The alien then ambles over to the top of a hill, staring down at the suburb below.

Trucks pull up, lights knifing through the fog, and the second alien hides, his chest glowing a bright red. The people from the trucks spot him, so he bolts like a jack rabbit while the spaceship captain, her own chest glowing red, takes the ship up into the atmosphere. As the humans keep up their search, the camera focuses in on one man—not his face but the key ring on his belt. The credits identify him only as Keys (Peter Coyote).

Cut to a family home in that suburb, where tween Michael (Robert Macnaughton) is playing D&D with his friends. Michael's younger brother Elliott (Henry Thomas) wants to play, but they won't let him join mid-adventure. Instead, they hand him some money and send him outside to pay for the pizza they ordered. After collecting the pizza, he hears a noise in an open garden shed. Elliott tosses a baseball inside, presumably expecting to startle a cat or some wildlife. Instead, someone throws it back. Elliott drops the pizza and rushes indoors, but none of the older kids, nor Elliott's mother Mary (Dee Wallace), believe he saw anything.

Later that night, Elliott goes out again, hunting the intruder with a flashlight. He finds E.T.—the first time we see the alien clearly—but the small creature panics and flees. Next morning Elliott searches the nearby woods, leaving candy as bait. At family dinner that evening, he still can't convince anyone and ends up sitting sulking on the opposite side of the table from Michael, Mary and little sister Gertie (Drew Barrymore). Mary suggests he imagined it; Michael suggests he saw some sort of deformed kid. An outraged Elliott retorts, "It was nothing like that, penis breath!"

Mary suggests Elliott talk it over with his dad, but Elliott replies that his father's in Mexico with Sally. Mom falls silent and goes to do the dishes. Michael, who's old enough to realize the divorce is still raw for Mary, reads Elliott the riot act for bringing it up

That night Elliott sneaks out again, falls asleep in a deck chair, but wakes up when the alien approaches, lurching awkwardly on its stubby legs. Elliott lures it indoors and up to his room with Reese's Pieces, then closes the door. Unperturbed, the alien explores Elliott's possessions and mimics his gestures until Elliott, exhausted but triumphant, falls asleep. Then we cut away to the hunters, one of whom finds the candy in the woods.

The next morning Elliott fakes being sick so he can stay home. Once Mary leaves for work, Elliott introduces himself: "Me human. Boy. Elliott. Do you talk?" He also introduces E.T. to Coca-Cola, *Star Wars* toys (while Reese's Pieces was the product placement everyone remembered, it's far from the only one), Elliott's fish tank and Pez. After E.T. bites one of Elliott's toy cars, the boy heads into the kitchen to make his new friend some food. Harvey, the family dog, encounters E.T. in the bedroom and both dog and alien freak out. E.T. then freaks out again when he opens an umbrella. In that same moment, Elliott screams and drops a carton of milk on the floor. It's only clear later that Elliott has become linked to his guest: when E.T. feels panic, so does Elliott.

When Michael returns from football practice, Elliott demands his brother give him "absolute power" over what he's about to see. Confident Elliott's making a fuss over nothing, Michael promises with a laugh, turns around and his jaw drops. Gertie comes in, shrieks and everything dissolves into chaos, which almost leads to Mom discovering E.T. After Mary goes to take a shower, Elliott tells Gertie that even if she told Mom about E.T., adults can't see him—to which his sister snorts, "Give me a break!" After the brothers threaten her favorite doll, she agrees to stay quiet.

Later that night, the siblings try feeding their guest various foods and debate his origin—could he be a bald orangutan? Elliott shows E.T. on his world globe where the house is. E.T. responds by pointing at the sky, then levitating some balls to (presumably) recreate his solar system. Later, while Elliott's in bed, E.T. studies an ABC coloring book, absently causing a pot of dead flowers to bloom again.

Elliott and Michael have no choice but to go to school the next day. Elliott wonders how to explain school to an advanced alien; Michael suggests E.T. might not be advanced—perhaps he's just a tech drone who pushes buttons? They snark with Michael's friends at the bus stop, Elliott calling one "zero charisma," a Dungeons and Dragons term for being highly unappealing. While they're gone, E.T. explores the house under the dog's uneasy gaze. The empathic link with Elliott begins to cause problems. E.T. downs several cans of beer and Elliott gets drunk; E.T. yearns to escape to freedom, Elliott liberates the frogs from his science class; E.T. sees John Wayne kissing Maureen O'Hara on TV in *The Quiet Man*, Elliott smooches a cute classmate (Erika Eleniak).

A *Buck Rogers* strip showing the space adventurer building an interplanetary communicator inspires E.T. to MacGyver one together from household tools and electronics. Mary comes home with Gertie and in a sitcomish bit, keeps missing E.T. as he walks past, despite Gertie's best efforts to introduce them. While Mary listens incredulously to a phone call from school about Elliott's drunkenness, Gertie discovers E.T. has learned English. When Elliott returns home, he's horrified Gertie has dressed E.T. up in her clothes. When she demonstrates he speaks English—she takes credit for teaching him— Elliott's amazed. E.T. sums up his new plan in what became a catchphrase—"E.T. phone home."

By late evening, Keys' people are eavesdropping on the house (presumably all the houses in the area as they don't yet know E.T.'s there) but all they hear is Elliott and Michael reminiscing about their father. Later, E.T. heals Elliott's cut finger; Michael notices Elliott keeps referring to E.T. as "we." Mary reads Gertie part of *Peter Pan* in which Peter says the only way to save a dying Tinkerbelle is for everyone to believe in fairies.

Halloween arrives, giving the kids an opportunity to get out of the house with E.T. hidden under a ghost sheet. Elliott and E.T. bicycle out into the woods to set up his phone. When the road gets too bumpy, E.T. simply levitates the bicycle, bringinng Elliott's face alive with delight and a hoot of joy. The shot of the bicycle passing in front of the full moon was another iconic moment in the film. The makeshift transmitter begins to work and E.T. croons "Hoooome." Elliott, speaking despite a sudden cough, suggests E.T. stay on Earth: "I wouldn't let anyone hurt you. We could grow up together." E.T. repeats "home."

Elliott goes to sleep in the woods and wakes up to find his friend gone. He returns home to his mother's relief, then sends Michael out to look for the alien. Michael finds E.T. passed out and weak, takes him home and shows him to Mary. As she grasps that the creature is not a toy, Elliott tells her, "We're sick. I think we're dying." This is never explicitly explained but it's clear E.T. and the other aliens are symbiotically linked; without his people E.T. can't keep going.

As if all this wasn't enough of a shock for Mary, men in space suits enter the house. More men approach outside, seen as shadows against the setting sun. In a few minutes there's a military/police cordon around the family home which is also covered by a plastic quarantine tent. Doctors begin interrogating the family while hooking up Elliott and E.T. to life-support. Elliott refuses to tell Keys what the transmitter does, though Keys makes it clear he's not the enemy: "I've been wishing for this since I was ten years old. I don't want him to die … his being here was a miracle.… You did the best anybody could do. I'm glad he met you first."

With E.T.'s condition worsening, he frees Elliott from their link. Elliott's now fine but the alien flatlines; the flowers he regenerated suddenly wither and Elliott breaks down in tears. After the doctors place E.T. in a container for future examination, Elliott tearfully tells his friend how much he means to Elliott. The flowers bloom again and Elliott discovers E.T. has revived, due to the spaceship returning to pick him up.

Despite Keys' declaration, Elliott's not going to trust his friend's life to the feds. With Michael's help he sneaks E.T. onto one of the government's vans, then Michael drives it off but not well—this is waaay beyond his limited driving experience. Keys' people, Mary and Gertie all follow, but the brothers lose them and meet up with Michael's buddies. The guys laugh at the brothers' crazy story until E.T. emerges. One of the guys asks why E.T. can't just beam up to his ship, only to be told, "This is reality."

The kids and E.T. take to bicycles, outmaneuvering Keys' people but eventually coming smack up against a roadblock crewed by cops with shotguns. No problem: E.T.'s at peak strength and simply levitates everyone over the police. They don't come down until they reach the pickup site in the woods. With Keys and Mary watching, Elliott and E.T. say goodbye, though not without inviting each other to stay or go, as appropriate. The alien taps Elliott with a glowing fingertip, telling him, "I'll be right here" and then departs.

Like several other movies in this book, the polished, enchanting story on screen gives no hint of how complicated its origins were. On the various DVD special features, Spielberg says he had one of the key ideas while working on *Close Encounters of the Third Kind*: what if one of the aliens had stayed behind? But he had other projects to work on, one of which was *Watch the Skies*, later renamed *Night Skies*.

Night Skies got on Spielberg's to-do list because Columbia wanted him to make a sequel to *Close Encounters*. He demurred, saying that just dealing with the government cover-up would take a movie in itself. Spielberg proposed a darker film, inspired by a 1955 close encounter near Hopkinsville, Kentucky. The Sutton family reported being besieged and harassed by three-foot-tall silvery green aliens, giving rise to the "little green men" concept of aliens. No evidence turned up when the Air Force investigated and locals credited it to either a publicity stunt or too much moonshine.[1]

The family didn't want their name or personal histories used so *Night Skies'* script put distance between the original encounter and the fiction. In the script, alien scientists arrive on the farm to study, and possibly dissect livestock and humans. In the middle of the nightmarish encounter, one alien, less cold-blooded than the others, develops a friendship with the family's autistic son.[2]

Spielberg said he began having second thoughts when he was in the middle of directing *Raiders of the Lost Ark*. Amidst the chaos, stunts and non-stop action, he found himself longing for a tranquil, upbeat story like *CE3K*. After he shared parts of the script with scriptwriter Melissa Mathison, she told him the interaction between the boy and the alien had been sweet enough to bring her to tears. That made Spielberg see the movie could be something other than horror.[3]

In *E.T.* he went back to the idea of an alien stranded on Earth. He combined it with a project he'd wanted to make for years, a personal, autobiographical film about being a child of divorce. How his parents' divorce had affected him, how he'd longed for someone magical to enter his life and make things better. Elliott's nice, suburban family, he said, did a better job than his own at keeping the pain and anger bottled up: "It was polite … suburban … it was my dream of suburbia."

Columbia opted out, dismissing the film as a "wimpy Walt Disney movie." Spielberg thought they weren't entirely wrong, and that the core audience would be kids who caught Disney's live-action movies of the era. It's a good comparison. Disney films such as *Candleshoe* (1977), *The Apple Dumpling Gang* (1975), *Escape to Witch Mountain* and *No Deposit No Return* (1976) had cute moppets outwitting crooks, thwarting unreasonable authority figures and thawing the hearts of gruff, cantankerous oldsters. The climactic chase, with the kids running rings around the authorities, is very much in that spirit, though it's also forced—why would the cops be using shotguns?

That era of Disney was a low point in the company's history; *E.T.* played in an entirely different league. Peter Coyote say she didn't realize what a blockbuster it was until some of the crew on his next film saw it in the theater, came back and suddenly started treating him as a good luck charm—if he could be in one success, maybe it would carry over?

Part of what makes it work is that the kids aren't simply adorable angels. They're good kids but fully capable of ignoring each other, snapping out insults or acting selfishly. Gertie promises to keep E.T. secret but she can't resist trying to show him to her mother. The children feel real. The film sticks to their point of view. Except for Mary and Keys, we almost never see adult faces clearly and Keys doesn't get a name. Adults aren't part of the story, they're just a subplot.

E.T. is another example of how alien visitors can echo older folklore. Although he arrives in a spaceship and builds an interplanetary phone, his abilities, like Starman and others, seem more magic than science. Like Peter Pan, and like Spielberg's childhood daydreams, he enters the lives of some unhappy kids and turns everything around. Like *E.T.*, *Peter Pan* features flying, a neglectful or absent father, and an adult adversary named for a metal implement (Keys and Hooks). Keys of course, turns out to be a good guy, a marked twist on most alien hunters in films. Coyote said he loved playing Keys as an essentially decent man.

That said, the idea of the broken family doesn't entirely come off. Elliott's life at the start of the film isn't idyllic but it doesn't seem terribly broken either. His brother and friends refusing to include him in the D&D game is a common enough reaction by older kids to younger siblings. Mary's hurting but there's no sign she's neglecting the kids or suffering financially.

When it came out in 1982, critics and news articles held up *E.T.* as proof of how far we'd come since the days of *War of the Worlds* and *Invasion of the Body Snatchers*. *CE3K* showed us invaders could be friendly; *E.T.* proved they could be adorable. We were no longer afraid. That John Carpenter's very uncuddly Thing hit the screen the same year didn't change the narrative.

Spielberg's *E.T.* was repeatedly parodied, referenced and joked about for years. It was, of course, also imitated. One of the most blatant knockoffs was *Mac and Me* (1988) in which the ET-like MAC ("Mysterious Alien Creature") arrives on Earth from his dried-out planet. He befriends a young girl who works at McDonald's and wears her uniform even when she's off-work—no subtlety to the product placement here! Eventually MAC and his family regain their strength from drinking Coca-Cola (phew!).

E.T. would break the *Star Wars* (or as it's now known *A New Hope*) box office record and remain the top grossing film for a decade. It deserves the success. *E.T.* remains a remarkably warm, funny, endearing movie 40 years later.

The Whispers *(2015)*

ABC.

CAST: Lily Rabe (Claire Bennigan), Barry Sloane (Wes Lawrence), Milo Ventimiglia (Drew Bennigan), Derek Webster (Jessup Rollins), Kristen Connolly (Lena Lawrence), Kylie Rogers (Minx Lawrence), Kyle Harrison Breitkopf (Henry Bennigan)

The protagonist of this 2015 ABC series is FBI Agent Claire Bennigan (Lily Rabe), an FBI agent who specializes in investigations involving young kids. She's been out of action since the death of her military husband, Drew (Milo Ventimiglia) in a crash at the North Pole. In the first episode of *The Whispers,* Harper lures her mother up to her treehouse as part of a game the girl is playing with her imaginary friend Drill. The "game" culminates with Mom falling through a loose patch on the floor—something Drill arranged. The girl doesn't realize it and continues thinking of Drill as a friend.

The FBI brings Claire in to interrogate Harper. The girl mentions her imaginary friend, but Claire doesn't attach any significance to it. Drill, however, is busy making more friends. Claire's deaf son Henry (Kyle Harrison Breitkopf) gets his hearing back thanks to Drill. Minx (Kylie Rogers), the daughter of federal agent Wes Lawrence (Barry Sloane), hacks her father's computer for drill and accesses plans to a nuclear power plant. Meanwhile a heavily tattooed, amnesiac John Doe begins lurking around the fringes of Claire's investigation, with tattoos that seem to direct him to Drill's next "game." This may be a shout out to the precognitive tattooed man of *The Illustrated Man*, the Ray Bradbury collection that includes "Zero Hour," the basis for *The Whispers.*

Claire and her partner Rollins (Derek Webster) end up at a DC area power plant. Drill's game also brings Henry and the John Doe—who's really the not-so-dead Sean—to the plant. The plans Minx provided Drill let him overload the system and start a meltdown. As he anticipated, Claire's efforts to save Henry and Sean by delaying flushing the core with water make it impossible to prevent the meltdown. When the plant goes critical, though, the radiation mysteriously vanishes.

Over the next few episodes, Claire & Co. continue hunting down Drill. They learn that another Drill came to Earth years earlier and took over a child's body; the boy's brother electrocuted him, the one way to destroy Drill. An attempt to trap Drill the same way fails, and Drill soon takes refuge in a human host. The government has by now identified Drill's friends and interns them all. The alien is hiding in the president's daughter (Kayden Magnuson) but she frames Minx as the host body. This almost gets Minx killed but it buys Drill time to summon his people to Earth.

In the final episode, mind-controlled sleeper agents from Drill's previous visit capture Claire and some of her allies. Drill's current friends, also apparently mind-controlled, escape from their adult supervisors as ships from Drill's world arrive overhead. At the episode's climax, Drill's friends are all teleported away, but not Henry—Claire knocks him out of the transporter beam at the price of being abducted herself. We'll never know what was behind it all, as the ratings didn't merit a second season.

This is creepy example of the alien friend as Pied Piper. Drill plays his "friends" like pawns, helping them or threatening them as need be. Through them, he can manipulate adults. In one scene a girl climbs up on the roof of her house putting her in serious jeopardy, then tells her mother what Drill wants Mom to do. An adult might find a way out of dealing with Drill but the kids are trapped.

That said, the ending episode made him a lot less interesting. The implication he has some sort of control over his former friends now that they're adults isn't as intimidating as the manipulative mind games he played early in the season. There are also several loose ends such as what, exactly happened to the radiation Drill soaked up. Perhaps it would all have made sense in the second season. Perhaps not.

The Faculty *(1998)*

Dimension Films. 104 minutes. Release date November 12, 1998.

CAST: Bebe Neuwirth (Principal Drake) Salma Hayek (Nurse Harper), Robert Patrick (Coach Willis), Famke Janssen (Miss Burke), Clea DuVall (Stokely), Laura Harris (Marybeth), Jordana Brewster (Delilah), Josh Hartnett (Zeke), Shawn Hatosy (Stan), Piper Laurie (Mrs. Olsen), Chris McDonald (Casey's Dad), Usher Raymond (Gabe), Jon Stewart (Furlong), Daniel Von Bargen (Tate), Elijah Wood (Casey), Summer Phoenix (Angry Girl), Jon Abrahams (Angry Boy), Susan Willis (Mrs. Brummel), Pete Janssen (Meat), Christina Rodriguez (Tattoo Girl), Danny Masterson (F UP #1), Wiley Wiggins (F Up #2), Harry Knowles (Knowles), Donna Casey (Ina), Louis Black (Lewis), Eric Jungmann (Freshman #1), Chris Viteychuk (Freshman #2), Jim Johnston (PE Teacher), Libby Villari (Casey's Mom), Duane Martin (Officer #1), Katherine Willis (Officer #2), Mike Lutz (Hornet Mascot), Doug Aarniokoski (Brun Coach)

CREDITS: Director: Robert Rodriguez; Screenplay: Kevin Williamson: Story: David Wechter, Bruce Kimmel; Producer: Elizabeth Avellan; Executive Producers: Bob Weinstein, Harvey Weinstein; Line Producer: Bill Scott; Photography: Enrique Chediak; Music Marco Beltrami; Editor: Robert Rodriguez; Production Designer: Cary White; Visual Effects Supervisor: Brian M. Jennings. Special Make up and Creature Effects: Robert Kurtzman, Gregory Nicotero, Howard Berger

The film opens at Harrington High in Ohio, during football practice. The big game against the school's arch-rival, Brun, is this coming Friday and Coach Willis (Robert Patrick) wants to win. He tears into his players' performance, hurling the F-bomb at them, including at quarterback Stan (Shawn Hatosy). After the players head to the locker room someone approaches Willis off camera. He turns to meet them with a pissed-off scowl.

Cut to an evening faculty budget meeting where Principal Drake (Bebe Neuwirth) is telling drama teacher Mrs. Olsen (Piper Laurie) and history teacher Mr. Tate (Daniel Van Bergen) there's no money for their projects—everything, as always, goes to the football team. The school board and the parents like it that way. After the meeting Drake walks down the dark hall and enters her office, then discovers Willis watching her. He tells her how pretty she is and asks for a pencil. She hands him one but being thoroughly creeped out, orders him to go. Instead he stabs a pencil through her hand, declaring "I always wanted to do that."

Drake slashes the coach's face with her keys, then runs to the exit. The doors are padlocked, though, and she dropped her keys when she struck Willis. Skulking through the dark hall she finds Olsen outside another exit, but she doesn't have her keys either. Drake makes a run back to her office, gets her keys, gets out of the building and locks the door in Willis' angry face. Olsen then stabs Drake in the back, saying "I always wanted to do that."

Next morning, we meet our heroes. Zeke (Josh Hartnett) pulls up unsubtly in a cool car, parking to take up two spaces. He's an outcast and bad boy we later see peddling his own designer drug, "scat," to some classmates along with fake IDs. Casey (Elijah Wood) is the school newspaper photographer, small, nervous and constantly bullied. Delilah later describes him as "the Stephen King kid." Black-garbed Stokely (Clea DuVall) is a surly loner, a science fiction nerd and allegedly a lesbian.

Delilah (Jordana Brewster) is the cool one, a cheerleader and the newspaper editor. She's dating Stan (Shawn Hatosy), the quarterback, but she blows him off when he tries to kiss her—"Estee Lauder lips. They take 72 minutes to apply." In the background as they talk, a couple of girls are fighting.

Finally MaryBeth (Laura Harris) shows up. A Southern girl newly arrived at school, she uneasily asks a sullen, tattooed girl where the administration office is ("I love what you've done with your nose ring. It really brings out the color in your eyes"). As Mary-Beth goes through the halls, we see more fights break out. In the office, Nurse Harper (Salma Hayek) is sick but refusing to take sick leave until she's well enough to enjoy it. Tate is lacing his drink with something from his hip flask. Willis is guzzling water from the water cooler and Olsen has given herself a makeover.

Cut to English class where we meet the last of the core cast, bespectacled teacher Burke (Famke Janssen). She's acutely anxious and shy as she debates the interpretation of *Robinson Crusoe* with Zeke. Although he's a complete smartass who enjoys making her uncomfortable, he's also more engaged on the topic than anyone in class.

Later that day, Stan tells Delilah he's quitting football, which doesn't go over well: given her status in the school, she expects her boyfriend to be correspondingly A-list. Stan says while this will cost him his shot at a football scholarship, he intends to study more. Delilah scoffs that he's a lousy student but Stan says, "it's time I tried something I'm not good at."

Later that day, MaryBeth strikes up a conversation with Stokely, intrigued she's reading Heinlein's *Double Star*. Stokely asks why they're talking; MaryBeth says she doesn't have any friends and "it seems to me you have one less than that." Delilah walks over and warns MaryBeth against hanging with a dangerously violent lesbian, at which point Stokely storms off. Stokely later tells MaryBeth she's not a lesbian, but claiming she is keeps everyone else at arm's length.

Casey discovers a strange dead invertebrate on the football field and takes it to Furlong (Jon Stewart), the science teacher. Furlong says some of its features resemble squid, which is not something you find in Ohio, and possibly it's a new species. Zeke, watching, demonstrates solid science knowledge. The "dead" creature revives when it touches water, so Furlong dumps it into the fish tank. It grows into something alien, buds off a second self and bites Furlong when he puts his hand in the tank.

After practice, Stan tells Willis he's dropping out right before the big game but the coach is quite mellow about it. As Stan showers in the locker room, Brummel (Susan Willis), an elderly teacher, stumbles in gasping that "they want everyone" before collapsing against him. When he tries to support her, her scalp comes off. After he calls for help, Olsen assures him that it's nothing strange, nope—Brummel's just hallucinating and losing hair from cancer treatments.

Burke finds Zeke selling racy videos out of his car in the parking lot and tries to discourage him. It's clear she finds him attractive and he seems to reciprocate but nevertheless he torments her with an offer of free condoms or free laxatives—which will help her loosen up?

Casey pitches Delilah on a story about the new species but she only mocks the idea. They sneak into the faculty lounge to snoop for something scandalous and Casey finds Tate's flasks. Delilah reminds Casey they covered that last year and nobody cared. It's clear Casey crushes on Delilah but she doesn't reciprocate.

When Olsen and Willis enter, the teens duck into the closet and overhear them saying Brummel died because she couldn't take the heat. Then they discuss how the takeover of the school is going. When Harper enters, Willis pins her to the couch and—though the kids can't see it—spits one of the new species into her mouth. The kids back up inside the closet, bumping into Brummel's desiccated corpse. That freaks them out enough to burst loose, race past the teachers and call the police.

As usual in alien infiltration films, it doesn't help. Drake, looking much sexier than the night she died, shows the police the kids just overreacted to a mannikin used in CPR training. Harper fell because she was sick. And what were the kids doing in the faculty lounge anyway? Burke takes one cop into her office for further discussion; when they emerge, he's obviously been taken over.

Casey's parents (Chris McDonald, Libby Villari) arrive, horrified their son is misbehaving. Casey tries to argue his case but caves and agrees to therapy to stop Drake getting his mother alone for a talk. Back home his folks search his room for drugs without success and tell him he's grounded indefinitely. Except, of course, he has to go back to school.

Dad drives Casey to school the next day, then worries his son by going to talk to Willis. Delilah shows up in disguise, meaning no makeup, and glasses instead of contacts. Her mom didn't believe her either so Delilah suggests calling the police. Casey points out they already tried that. Meanwhile the faculty lounge is ordering in gallons of bottled water and keeping the malfunctioning window air-conditioner going full blast.

MaryBeth has figured out that Stokely, despite apparently relishing her loner status, has a thing for Stan, so she "accidentally" shoves Stokely into his lap. It turns out Stokely follows football just like the rest of the school. Unlike Delilah, she listens sympathetically when Stan explains he quit because Furlong turned his D on a biology test into an A. He's tired of getting a free pass just because he's good at throwing the pigskin.

MaryBeth has a conversation with Zeke, establishing her parents are dead while his are "still breathing but for all intents and purposes they're very much dead." As another angry argument erupts near them, Zeke asks MaryBeth if some of the students doesn't seem "off" to her. She replies that to a Southerner, everyone in Ohio seems off. A couple of Zeke's clients show up for more scat but Burke shows up too. She's dressing sexy and comes off both confident and cruel, sneering that Zeke's mother won't even live in town because she can't stand her "bastard mistake." Burke warns Zeke that if he ever crosses her again, she'll ram her foot so far up his ass "you'll be nibbling my toes until graduation."

Later Stokely grumbles to Casey that the school is being taken over by "pod people." When she explains the reference, he suggests maybe Finney was writing a true story. Stokely replies that *Invasion of the Body Snatchers* is in the fiction section. Casey: "So is *Schindler's List*." Stokely says the book was a rip-off of Heinlein's *Puppet Masters* so it can't be true. Meanwhile Burke is ordering the student body, one after another, to come to her office.

Casey and Stokely collect Delilah and Stan and take them to Furlong's classroom to show them the creature. It's gone. MaryBeth and Zeke, raiding the science lab next door for equipment, overhear Casey arguing that "if you're going to take over the world, would you blow up the White House *Independence Day*–style … or sneak in the back door?" Zeke goes in and laughs that if there's any alien in school, Casey is it.

When Furlong arrives, Zeke tells him Casey's suspicions. The teacher attacks them with superhuman strength, his body reassembling even when they cut a piece off. When Zeke stabs Furlong in the eye with scat vial, the teacher collapses and dies. The kids can't deny something's horribly wrong, so they pile into Zeke's car—and find the cops blocking the road out of town. They hole up in Zeke's basement lab instead. Casey recovered a specimen of the creature, which Zeke figures out is a parasite. They thrive in water, the main component of our bodies, but caffeine—scat's primary component is crushed caffeine pills—dries the host body out and kills them.

As the SF expert, Stokely tells them they must kill the queen of the alien swarm; in theory that will kill the entire hive and free their victims. Then Delilah begins pointing out how odd the others are acting: why did Stan quit the football team? Since when did Stokely like boys? Is it a coincidence this all started after MaryBeth arrived? Stan replies that Delilah going around without makeup is equally abnormal.

Zeke decides to settle things by forcing everyone to take scat. Everyone passes the test but Delilah refuses, then smashes Zeke's scat-making lab with superhuman strength. Casey grabs Zeke's gun but he can't bring himself to shoot her. Stokely has no qualms, but Delilah gets away first.

The teenagers realize they have one option left, killing the queen—probably Principal Drake—with their remaining scat. Figuring even aliens will turn out for tonight's big game, they head back to school. As they arrive, they see the football team infecting their opponents; looking around, they realize how many potential victims are in the stands.

The kids retreat to the gym to plan their next move. Drake catches them, they trap her in a volleyball net, then Zeke shoots her. It doesn't kill Drake but MaryBeth emptying the last of the scat onto her does the job. Stan heads out to see if the other faculty are free now; Stokely kisses him before he leaves.

Stan returns a few minutes later, begging them to let him in before Willis catches him. Zeke hands him one final tube of stat through the door, telling Stan to prove he's human. Instead, Stan empties it on the ground and assures his friends they're going to like what's about to happen to them. No fear, no pain, Stokely can be beautiful—and in any case, the aliens have already won.

Instead of giving up, Casey and Zeke sneak out to the latter's car to see if they can find more scat, after which they'll gamble Willis is the hive queen. When the football team comes hunting, Casey lures them away from Zeke, then hides on a school bus. Delilah finds him there and mocks him: "Class wuss. Eternal little loser, comes to school every day knowing this will be it. You've been pathetic since first grade." But if he gives in, that can all change: they can even be together. Casey escapes her instead and resumes running.

As Zeke searches his car, Burke arrives, her manner both flirting and threatening. Zeke drives away but she clambers onto the car, sprouting tentacles. He crashes the car which sends her flying off. The impact tears her head off but doesn't kill her, and the head grows legs to walk back to her blindly groping torso. It's reminiscent—intentionally, I'm sure—of a similar moment in *The Thing*.

Waiting in the gym, a pessimistic Stokely tells MaryBeth that in *Body Snatchers*, the humans lose. Her friend replies that maybe humans win—isn't it tiring being someone you're not? Being confused about what you want and what you should do? She sprouts a tentacle and slaps Stokely to the floor. Casey comes running back in as MaryBeth takes her full alien shape. The two humans run but as they pass the swimming pool, Mary-Beth drags Stokely in. Casey pulls her out and they resume running.

When Zeke returns, Stokely and MaryBeth tell him the other's the alien. Zeke realizes it's MaryBeth: a flashback reveals she beat the scat test by sealing her nostrils so she didn't inhale. Zeke tries to stab her with his last scat pen but Stokely's been turned and attacks him. Casey flings Stokely into the equipment cage and locks it but MaryBeth clobbers Zeke, then pursues Casey through the locker room.

As she stalks Casey, MaryBeth tells him how she fled her drought-ridden world for Earth. Arriving in school, she thought he and the others were kindred spirits, as lost and alone as she felt. She's offering them a world "where the under-achiever goes home at night to parents who care. Where the jock can be smart, the ugly duckling beautiful." They can't see it because they're "a bunch of lonely little outcasts who truly believe their disaffected life is the only way they can survive." Casey tells her he'd sooner live in fear and stay himself. He flees behind the bleachers, she follows, he flips on the switch that causes them to close. This pins her in place long enough for him to stab her with that last dose of scat.

A month later, life is back to normal, sort of. Casey's claims about an alien invasion have made him a media sensation, even if the authorities refuse to confirm them. He and Delilah are now dating. Burke is her shy self again, but she and Zeke, who's now on the football team, are a covert couple. Stokely and Stan are openly together.

While I've seen this film described as a spoof, it isn't. There's a lot of humor but the stakes are serious; unlike *Mars Attacks!* there's no suggestion this is all very silly. *The Faculty* takes its genre seriously but much like screenwriter Kevin Williamson's 1996 film *Scream*, the film is very aware of the genre it's working in, as are some of the characters.

At least that's the idea, but much as Stokely name-drops *Body Snatchers* and *Puppet Masters*, Williamson doesn't seem to have read them. There's no hive queen in either novel and *Body Snatchers* is not a *Puppet Master* knockoff. As detailed in Chapter Four, the stories are significantly different and Finney's book is better. The aliens are physically more like Heinlein's mind-controlling slugs, but like Finney they claim the transformation improves people. Though I do wonder if MaryBeth is lying, ditto Delilah and Stan when they endorse their transformation.

It's hard to tell because the effects of possession are murky. In the opening scene, Olsen and Willis act out their inner urges in attacking Drake; Burke is obviously acting on hers when she bullies/flirts with Zeke. Nobody else seems to react that way. "I always wanted to do that" does not become the catchphrase I expected. Nor does Tate quoting to his class that "only through conformity among the masses can the unified state offer the benefits of power, order and security" feel like foreshadowing. Perhaps Willis turning mellow is a sign he didn't like being a hardcase, but there's no way to tell. There's no other indication the possessed are nicer than their old selves.

The most notable change is Olsen, Burke and Drake suddenly glamming up when nobody else does. MaryBeth doesn't look like a sex bomb, Willis and Furlong don't show off their bodies and the female students dress as usual. The change seems to be pure Hollywood logic—why waste Neuwirth and Janssen's good looks? Though Janssen sells

The Faculty (1998). In high school, Robert Rodriguez says on his website, everyone changes. So how can you differentiate the alien-controlled kids from the ones who are merely trying something new?

the transformation more with acting than with fashion, replacing her socially awkward mannerisms with an aggressive swagger.

Like *E.T.*, this is told almost entirely from the teen perspective. Outside of the possessed faculty, the only adults we meet are Casey's clueless parents and a few cops. Zeke's mother is away. Delilah's father is dead.

It's much more about the kids, their discomfort in high school and their inability to show or be accepted for who they are. Casey, as Delilah points out, has been "the Stephen King kid" since first grade. Stokely claims to be happy as a loner but she clearly isn't. Marybeth has fled a dying world and possibly does feel lonely. Stan's tired of being just a jock. Delilah, though, doesn't fit. She's beautiful, sits securely atop the school's social hierarchy and doesn't seem to be leading a life of quiet desperation underneath. She says at one point that she hasn't been happy since her father died but that never comes across otherwise.

Films from the 1950s about teens often showed them maladjusted but it was a generation gap. In the small town of *The Blob* the kids get along great with each other; it's conflict with the adults that's the problem. The *Teenagers from Outer Space* have been ruined by their bad upbringing. In *The Faculty*, the real injuries are those teenagers inflict on each other. On his website, director Robert Rodriguez says that's what intrigued him about the project. High school is a place where everyone struggles with alienation, individuality and conformity, making it perfect for a "are you you?" movie.

The film has a strong resemblance with TV's *Buffy the Vampire Slayer* (1997–2003) which similarly showed a group of outcast kids joining together to battle monsters. Where Buffy showrunner Joss Whedon's approach was that high school is hell, *The Faculty* assumes it can be wonderful. The kids end up the movie free of their outcast status, in new and happier roles and they've found love—though Delilah seems interested in Casey purely because he's a celebrity.

Still the strength of the cast and the solid bodysnatching plot does make this a good finish for this chapter.

OTHER FILMS AND TELEVISION

Alien Arsenal (1999) Two teenagers acquire alien superweapons and take revenge on bullies. Then the owner of the weapons comes looking for them.

Aliens Ate My Homework (2018) A tween boy helps action-figure sized alien cops help track down an alien supervillain plotting to conquer Earth.

Explorers (1985) Three boys receive dream directions for building a spacecraft. Flying up into space, they meet a trio of pop-culture obsessed alien kids.

Invaders from Mars (1986) Remake of the 1953 version. Better special effects but much less imagination.

Laserblast (1978) Pointless film in which a lonely teenage boy acquires an alien ray weapon and goes on a shooting spree.

Ocean Girl (1994–97) Kids at an oceanic research station meet an alien orphan, Neri, who swims like a fish and can communicate telepathically with whales.

Roswell, New Mexico (2019–) A woman returns to her home town of Roswell for her 10-year high school reunion. She discovers her teenage crush, now working as a county deputy, is an alien who survived the Roswell crash.

Super 8 (2011) Teenage boys making an amateur film become caught up in the military hunt for an alien that's escaped from custody. Director J.J. Abrams pays tribute to Steven Spielberg with this one.

Supersonic Saucer (1956) British kids' film in which schoolchildren help an alien from Venus escape the gang of crooks hunting him.

Timeslingers (1999) Two kids travel back through time to the Old West where they help an alien child reunite with its family. Also known as *Aliens in the Wild, Wild West*.

THIRTEEN

Laugh, Spaceman, Laugh

Alien Visitor Comedies

"I'll send you a copy of our book, *Simple Science for Senators*."
—*Moon Pilot*

Alien visitors can kill us, blow up our national monuments, abduct and torture us—but they can also make us laugh. Sometimes simultaneously.

The first comical alien visitor on screen was Looney Tunes' Marvin the Martian. In his first appearance, *Haredevil Hare* (1948), he battles Bugs Bunny on the moon. He's unnamed there and in the follow-up, 1952's *Hasty Hare,* which brings Marvin to Earth. Where Bugs' earlier recurring antagonist, Yosemite Sam, is loud, blustery and hair-trigger, Marvin is normally quiet, soft-spoken and patient. It's unfortunate that facing Bugs Bunny or Daffy Duck, those qualities don't get you anywhere.

The 1950s produced several dreadful films such as *Robot Monster* (1953) and *Plan Nine from Outer Space* (1958) that have made audiences laugh ever since. The only intentional alien-visitor comedy was 1957's *Invasion of the Saucer Men.* This shaggy-dog story has literal "little green men" show up in Hicksburg ("I'm not kidding, that's the name!"), where the local teens wind up trying to stop them from doing—well, we never learn what they want, not even whether they're invading or just crashed. Mostly they seem intent on covering up their presence, for example, by framing a local teen for the death of a man they killed.

The 1960s found more humor in its spacemen. Jerry Lewis starred as an infantile, supposedly amusing alien in *Visit to a Small Planet*, an adaptation of a Gore Vidal play. *Pajama Party* (1964) fit alien invaders into AIP's successful Beach Party series. *Invasion of the Star Creatures* (1962) was a very unfunny comedy showcasing a talentless comical team. Disney's *Moon Pilot* (1962) satirized the space race and politics. On TV, we had *My Favorite Martian*, plus the cartoon extraterrestrial *The Astronut* causing chaos for his long-suffering human friend Oscar.

Alien visitor comedy would continue with varying results over the subsequent decades. There have been impressive hits such as *Men in Black, 3rd Rock from the Sun* and the cult classic *Rocky Horror Picture Show* (1975). There have been plenty of flops too, including *The Cat from Outer Space* (1978), *National Lampoon's Men in White* (1998) and *Howard the Duck* (1986).

Comedy is a tough genre to succeed in. A serious story of alien invasion can entertain viewers even if it's not the thrilling epic the trailers promised. A comedy that's not funny rarely provides anything worth sitting through. The movie remake of *My Favorite Martian* (1999) has a good cast—Jeff Daniels as Tom and Christopher Lloyd as Martin—but it's a flat, unfunny film that relies too much on wacky special effects.

Another problem is that comedy can go stale fast. *Predator* provides thrills 30 years after it came out; George Pal's 70-year-old *War of the Worlds* is still impressive. Comedies mocking dumb blondes, gays or Asians with funny accents and silly names—stock tropes when I was a kid—haven't aged well. *Mork and Mindy* at its peak was immensely funny; the jokes about Mork's massively overweight boss Orson (Ralph James, voice only) don't sound so amusing now.

Satire that mocks the issues or interests of one era may be incomprehensible a generation later. Parody may not work if the viewer doesn't know what's being mocked. In *Looney Tunes: Back in Action* (2003), Bugs Bunny and his companions visit Area 52, the government's secret UFO research center (Area 51 is a just a red herring to fool the public!). The lab, run by mad scientist Joan Cusack, includes Marvin the Martian, a Dalek and aliens from *This Island Earth* and *Robot Monster* as prisoners. Would someone who can't identify any of the aliens find it funny?

There are several ways to make alien visitors comical. They can be buffoons in themselves like the clownish Solomon family of *3rd Rock from the Sun* (1996–2001). They can satirize human conventions or the clichés of alien-visitor movies. Some films slip aliens into what would otherwise be a generic comedy. Some are so dreadful that they're laughably bad.

Robot Monster (1953) is a classic example of the latter group. During a family picnic little Johnny (Gregory Moffett) falls asleep. When he wakes up, he hears the robot Ro-Man (George Barrows) declare the human race has been wiped out except for Johnny and his family, due to the calcinator, a death-ray device that gives off bubbles. Ro-Man must now kill the remaining humans but he can't bring himself to destroy Johnny's sister Alice (Claudia Barrett). When his superior on Ro-Man—it's the planet as well as the individual—tells him he has to finish the genocide, Ro-Man laments, "I cannot—yet I must. How do you calculate that? At what point on the graph do 'must' and 'cannot' meet?"

Did I mention that as a robot suit was out of producer-director Phil Tucker's price range, he settled for a gorilla suit topped by a diving helmet? The entire film turns out to be Johnny's dream, except after he wakes up, we see Ro-Man again…. Tucker didn't set out to shoot a comedy but that's the result

The Watch (2012) is a case of including aliens in a comedy that isn't primarily about them. The story of Ben Stiller and his buddies forming a neighborhood watch, overcoming their personal problems and going from zero to hero is a standard male-bonding comedy in most respects. But it's also a story about the neighborhood watch saving us from an alien invasion.

Monsters vs. Aliens (2009) is an animated comedy with an alien invasion but it's more a parody of 1950s monster films than of *War of the Worlds*. After a radioactive meteor turns Susan (Reese Witherspoon) into a giant, the military locks her up with monsters based on *The Fly, Creature from the Black Lagoon* and *The Blob*, just as Susan, AKA Ginormica, is a takeoff on *Attack of the 50 Foot Woman*. The alien invaders in the film aren't anywhere near as parodic.

Film comedy and TV series have one key difference, which is length. A film only requires a premise that can sustain 90 minutes or two hours of laughter. Consider *Martians Go Home* (1990), based on the same-name Fredric Brown short story.

Unsuccessful songwriter Mark (Randy Quaid) accidentally hits on a tune that functions as a universal greeting. When his girlfriend (Margaret Colin) accidentally

Robot Monster (1953) is a terrible, ridiculous film. Even so, the eponymous invader is so distinctive it pops up as an Easter egg in unrelated films such as 1976's *Hollywood Boulevard*.

broadcasts it into space, Martians take it as an invitation to drop in (maybe communicating with other worlds really is a mistake). Rather than conquer us, they mock us, interfere with sporting events and drop in on couples in the middle of sex. As the Martians are invulnerable to anything we throw at them, we're stuck until Mark finds a way to reverse his song and send them home. It's a fun film, but it would have been hard stretching out the premise to a full season of half hour episodes, let alone several years.

Perhaps that's why TV series rely so heavily on the trope of an alien living on Earth and struggling to fit in. Whether it's an immigration metaphor or not (see Chapter Seven), it's been the go-to for alien humor from *My Favorite Martian* through *ALF* and *3rd Rock* to 2021's *Resident Alien*. It's a premise that never goes out of style: you have fish-out-of-water comedy such as Mork going on a date. You can also engage in satire on our human attitudes and ideas. Which is not to say it guarantees a hit every time. Despite the talents of Bronson Pinchot as the alien *Meego* (1997), the series about the stranded alien working as a nanny couldn't make it past six episodes.

SPOTLIGHT

Tribulation 99: Alien Anomalies Under America *(1992)*

Other Cinema; 47 minutes; Release date Nov. 27, 1992
NARRATOR: Sean Kilcoyne
CREDITS: Director/Screenwriter/Editor: Craig Baldwin; Photography: Bill Daniel; Music: Dana Hoover

The opening of Craig Baldwin's mockumentary assures us "this film is not fiction—it is the shocking truth about the coming apocalypse and the events that have led up to it." Then follows a quote from *Revelation* 20, verse 7: "And when the thousand years are ended, Satan will be loosed from his prison and will come out to deceive the nations which are at the four corners of the earth, to gather them for battle."

The story opens a millennium ago on Quetzalcoatl, Earth's twin on the far side of the sun. Around 1000 CE, a thermonuclear war destroyed the planet, creating the asteroid belt, as demonstrated by the image of tall, alien buildings being suddenly replaced by storm clouds, then fireballs. The Quetzal elite escaped in their flying saucers to Earth—we also see shots of other types of spacecraft—but the radiation inflicted massive genetic damage to the birdlike aliens. Their reproductive organs are, in fact, so mutated they can only maintain their population by mating with reptiles.

The aliens entered inside the Earth through a hole at the South Pole, then drilled into the rocks with their sophisticated lasers. The same ray weapons could also project thoughts into human minds to control them. The Quetzals tunneled between caverns, constructing huge cities out of their own excrement and practicing saucer maneuvers inside the Earth. All this narration is illustrated with a constant montage of movie clips and other images, too rapid-fire to describe effectively here. It also includes multiple text blurbs, not necessarily related to what's happening on screen:

CLIMAX OF THE SUNSPOT CYCLE
SOMETIMES THEY SHRINK THE WHOLE HEAD
THESE ARE THE END TIMES
HARMONIC CONVERGENCE

Over the following thousand years the Quetzals continued to mutate and continued to dig: they've infiltrated our bomb shelters, our sewers and even Ft. Knox. Their presence has disrupted the subterranean ecological balance, causing killer bees and army ants to swarm north. Still, the aliens weren't actively hostile until the U.S. began underground nuclear testing. The Quetzals couldn't tolerate the radiation and vowed the destruction of the United States.

President Truman learns of the threat and creates the CIA to fight against it. The Quetzals strike first, using their mind-control rays to make Secretary of State James Forrestal leap to his death from a hospital window. They begin flying their saucers more openly and mastering the science of creating human duplicates. President Eisenhower meets with Quetzals and takes a flying saucer ride but decides to hide the truth rather than risk a panic. The official story is that he disappeared to get treatment for a dental emergency.

The aliens begin their war on America by replacing our trusted ally, President Jacobo Arbenz of Guatemala, with a duplicate. The alien-controlled "dupe" establishes a cult offering human sacrifices to the saucers. The blood-drinking aliens also begin draining cattle blood through mutilation while propagandist dupes claim the attacks are an attempt to stop cattle ranching despoiling the Amazon rain forest. Arbenz eventually seizes land owned by America's United Fruit Company, supposedly to share it with peasants, but in reality to set up more Mayan temples for more sacrifices. The Quetzals' bloodlust is insatiable.

Washington cannot let this abomination go unchallenged, so the CIA organizes a coup. Backed by the U.S., Carlos Armas overthrows the Arbenz government and drives the Quetzals back underground. He's murdered by his own troops and 100,000 lives are lost in a scorched-earth fight against the aliens. The Quetzals then seize power in Cuba, where a U.S. backed attempt to drive them out becomes the Bay of Pigs debacle. In retaliation Lee Harvey Oswald, a Quetzal creation, assassinates JFK; we know he wasn't human because "no human being could hit a moving target two times within 1.8 seconds." The Warren Commission on the assassination covers this up.

The CIA then tries to destroy the Fidel Castro dupe, even recruiting spy novelist Ian Fleming to find a method. Nothing works: "After 33 assassination attempts entailing two thousand people and 50 million dollars, they were horrified to realize you cannot kill something which was never alive." However, a variety of plagues strike Cuba, raising the question of whether God himself is enraged at the Quetzals.

The battle continues. Watergate was Nixon's attempt to see if the Quetzals had infiltrated the Democratic Party leadership. The hole in the ozone layer that developed over the South Pole not only made it easier for flying saucers to operate but it hurts white people by increasing their rate of skin cancer. Alien dupes take over Chile, with President Salvador Allende altering Earth's rotation to cause global warming and drought. Fortunately the CIA, Howard Hughes and corporate America join forces to restore the Earth's rotation before Allende completes his plan to "stand America on its head."

In the 1980s, after the prime minister of Grenada calls for an international effort to investigate UFOs, he's overthrown by Maurice Bishop, alien leader of a gang of psychic

vampires. Bishop constructs a base for the flying saucers from which the aliens' parti-
cle beams blow up the Challenger space shuttle. After Bishop's voodoo priests resurrect
cult leader Jim Jones and attack the minds of American medical students studying in
Grenada, Reagan sends in the Marines. The controversial shelling of a Grenadan mental
hospital was because it practiced supernatural, pseudoscientific treatments.

Under Reagan, the U.S. actively supports freedom fighters working against the
aliens' Illuminati agents in Panama and Nicaragua. The CIA obtains added funding
by helping the Medellin coffee cartel import coffee to the U.S., leading to a price cut
for consumers. The Quetzals fight back, for example replacing Panama's Noriega with
a "voodoo spouting freak" of a dupe, forcing President Bush to invade and retake the
country (our thirteenth invasion of Panama!).

Knowing the Quetzals can't stand radiation, the U.S. builds a massive dam that
releases radioactive waters into the Panama Canal. In 1999, the dam melts and collapses,
flooding the Isthmus of Panama. The Atlantic and Pacific Oceans merge, transforming
the oceanic currents. This allows radioactive water to reach the poles and melt the ice
caps. The apocalypse is finally here, but a handful of stealth mother ships take human
survivors to Mars, where they'll rule a millennial kingdom.

This synopsis doesn't capture the weird mix of film clips that provide the visuals,
nor the off-kilter black humor of this film. As so often said, nothing kills comedy like
explaining it. Auteur Craig Baldwin says on the commentary track that one of his influ-
ences was pseudoscience documentaries such as *Chariots of the Gods* and their ability to
spin elaborate theories out of coincidences. Despite the lack of science in *Chariots*, Baldwin says, he's impressed by its grasp of the language of film.

Eisenhower's UFO trip while he's supposedly at the dentist is a good example of
Baldwin's technique. In 1959, Eisenhower did disappear for what the White House
claimed was a dental emergency involving one of his crowns. Historians have speculated
it was the cover for something secret, such as planning for the Bikini nuclear test. Baldwin simply takes the incident and fits it into his imaginary mythology.

There's a whole boatload of pop pseudoscience and legend worked into the film.
Although science has ruled out an Earth counterpart on the far side of the sun, the idea
has been popular in science fiction, for example, in the film *Journey to the Far Side of the
Sun* (1969). The idea the Earth might be hollow and the insides might be occupied goes
back centuries. The Quetzals manipulating humans on the surface resembles Raymond
Shaver's 1930s stories of the subterranean Derro doing the same, stories Shaver claimed
were true.

Baldwin said *Tribulation 99* is also the "product of many years living under Ronald Reagan." The film presents a bizarro version of the United States' unpleasant history
of overthrowing democratically elected governments in Latin America in favor of military dictators more supportive of our political agendas or the needs of American cor-
porations. In Reagan's worldview, rightwing dictatorships were upstanding democratic
governments: El Salvador's death squads, who targeted anyone who pissed off the government, were heroic freedom fighters. Reagan used fearmongering about the communist threat to the U.S.; *Tribulation 99* likewise whips up paranoia and fear.

It's a remarkable achievement and if you know the politics it's insanely and utterly
funny in a black-humored way. But what if you don't know the politics? The CIA helping the Medellin drug cartel ship coffee, for instance, refers to the CIA allegedly col-
laborating with the cartel's drug sales to raise funds for anticommunist guerrillas in

Nicaragua. Does the irony come through if someone has to look up the meaning online? Is *Tribulation 99* funny at all to someone too young to remember the history?

Maybe. The U.S. hasn't stopped overthrowing governments in the 21st century or meddling in other nations' affairs. Even if the specific topical references don't work in a parody, perhaps the lampooning of U.S. interference and of elaborate, tortured conspiracy theories will still resonate.

The Coneheads (1993)

Paramount. 88 minutes. Release date July 23, 1993.

CAST: Dan Aykroyd (Beldar), Jane Curtin (Prymaat), Michael McKean (Seedling), Jason Alexander (Larry Farber), Chris Farley (Ronnie), David Spade (Turnbull), Sinbad (Otto), Phil Hartman (Marlax), Jan Hooks (Gladys Johnson), Michelle Burke (Connie), Robert Knott (Air Traffic Controller), Jonathan Penner (Captain Air Traffic), Whip Hubley (F-16 Pilot), Howard Napper (ANG Pilot), Michael Richards (Hotel Clerk), Eddie Griffin (Customer), Adam Sadler (Carmine), Hispanic Men (Art Bonilla, Grant Martell), Rosa Briz (Hispanic Woman), Cooper Layne (Engineer), Sarah Levy (Hygienist), Drew Carey (Taxi Passenger), Shishir Kurup (Khoudri), Sydney Coberly (Nurse), Barry Kivel (Doctor), Terry Turner (Sketch Artist), McNally Sagal (Female Agent), Richard M. Comar (Agent), Danielle Aykroyd (3-year-old Connie). Nicolette Harnish (Connie at 10), Lisa Jane Persky (Lisa Farmer), Joey Adams (Christina), Kevin Nealon (Senator), Walt Robles (Fire Marshall), Todd Susman (Ron), James Keane (Harv), Sam Freed (MC), Garrett Morris (Captain Orecrusher), Tom Davis (Supplicant), Dave Thomas (High Master), Peter Aykroyd (Highmaster Mentot), Laraine Newman (Laarta), Nils Allen Stewart (Guard), Tim Meadows (Athletic Cone), Mitchell Bobrow (Garthok Combatant), Laurence Bilzerian (Cone Battle Commander), Parker Posey (Stephanie), Topper Lilien (Cone Pilot), Julia Sweeney (Principal), Ellen DeGeneres (Coach)

CREDITS: Director: Steve Barron; Screenplay: Tom Davis, Dan Aykroyd, Bonnie Turner, Terry Turner; Producer: Lorne Michaels; Co-Producers: Dinah Minot, Barnaby Thompson, Bonnie Turner; Executive Producer: Michael Rachmil; Production Design: Gregg Fonseca; Photography: Francis Kenny; Costume Design: Marie France; Original Score: David Newman; Editor: Paul Trejo

Open on yet another spaceship approaching Earth. It's picked up on radar but the radar operator (Robert Knott) is glued to the *Star Trek* episode "Arena" and doesn't notice at first. When he does, he sends military jets scrambling, demanding the ship land or else. The ship doesn't obey; the jets jump to "or else" and launch missiles. The pilot, Beldar (Dan Aykroyd), turns his ship invisible but damage from the missiles sends the ship crashing into New York Harbor. Beldar and his mate Prymaat (Jane Curtin) wade to shore and stride through the rain to a motel. They're quite obviously not human, having missile-shaped Heads and razor-sharp teeth.

None of this fazes the night clerk at the motel (Michael Richardson) when they ask for a room. Neither does Beldar's disregard of personal space—he asks questions standing a couple of inches from the clerk—or the way he has to use both hands to awkwardly work the pen and sign the register. Beldar is flummoxed when the clerk asks for cash, but Prymaat electrifies a vending machine outside to cough up enough "metallic tender disks" to cover the cost. In their room Prymaat laughs hysterically as she reads a Gideon Bible, while Beldar tastes some soap and toilet paper.

Although the couple came to Earth as advance scouts for an invasion from their planet, Remulac, they have no choice but to blend in with the "bluntskulls" until they can phone home. A short while later, "Beldar Conehead" is working electronics repair for Otto (Sinbad), who's blown away by Beldar's skills and work ethic ("White boys and the brothers show up late, loaf around—all they want is a check") if bemused by his inability to speak normal English. The job also gives Beldar access to electronics parts. He tells Prymaat over reheated pizza in their trailer that he's acquired the final component for a communicator.

The call does not go well. Their contact Marlax (Phil Hartman) expected them to have conquered Earth by now, not be living in hiding. The Coneheads are equally dismayed the rescue ship won't arrive for seven zerls (apparently a zerl is around two and a half years). After they break contact, Prymaat tells her husband something even more startling: she's pregnant. Her belly's bulging and a small cone is pushing the bulge outward.

Later that day, when Otto asks for Beldar's Social Security number, Beldar confesses he's an illegal alien. Reluctant to lose his best worker, Otto puts him in touch with Carmine, a fake ID expert (Adam Sandler) who fabricates Beldar an identity as "Donny DiCicco." Driving home, Otto tells Beldar that to avoid immigration problems he needs to hide his cone, cap his teeth and own his own business. Otto asks to borrow some chewing gum but reconsiders when he sees Beldar's gum is a condom.

Cut to Turnbull (David Spade), an immigration officer informing the Spanish men at his desk that when they talk "all I'm getting is clicking noises." A skilled brown-noser, Turnbull is chief toady to Seedling (Michael McKean). It turns out that Carmine has given DiCicco's identity to several people before, so when Otto entered the name and Social Security number, it sent up red flags. Seedling's ready to bust whoever's using it this time.

After a teeth-capping appointment with a somewhat uneasy dentist (Jon Lovitz), Beldar returns home and goes to sleep with Prymaat. When she spots the Immigration agents outside, the Coneheads escape in the nick of time. Turnbull can't find anything showing where they're from, but he thinks their strange writing is Korean.

Skip ahead a few weeks and we see Beldar working as a taxi driver, his cone concealed by a turban. He and Prymaat live in a small two-story house in a blue-collar neighborhood rented to them by Beldar's employer Khoudry (Shishir Kurup). Beldar has been working triple shifts to ensure they have money ready when the baby comes but Prymaat tells him to stop. She's been saving enough that if he works a normal schedule they can still move into a better neighborhood. Then her water breaks, flooding the floor. A short while later, Prymaat gives birth to Connie (played as a teenager by Michelle Burke). Beldar looks shell-shocked; Otto and Khoudry, attending the birth with him, are thrilled.

Seedling, meanwhile, has grasped the DiCicco family aren't human. Seedling tracks the Coneheads to Khoudry's rental house but the family have already moved out. As Seedling contemplates his next move, he learns he's been promoted to enforcement chief for the Southwest U.S. He loses all interest in hunting down a couple of NYC illegal aliens, even space aliens.

Home movies carry us forward through time, ending with the family living in the suburbs, Beldar running a driving school and Connie in her teens. Everyone around blithely accepts that the Coneheads are from France. Connie, however, is completely American except for her cone and has conventional arguments with her parents about how much makeup she uses and whether she can get her cone tattooed. Beldar plays golf at the local country club, Prymaat goes shopping with friends, Connie hangs out with

The Coneheads (1993). Dan Aykroyd told *Entertainment Weekly* that in his original concept, the Coneheads really were from France. *Saturday Night Live*'s Lorne Michaels suggested making them extraterrestrials instead.

her schoolmates. When she sees a local mechanic, Ronnie (Chris Farley), mouth off to Beldar about his car repairs, she's amused and interested; Ronnie's interested back.

Seedling meanwhile discovers his past has caught up with him: his appointment as head of INS has been blocked because of spending $250,000 trying to apprehend an extraterrestrial. Unless he catches the Coneheads and proves he was right, he can't get the promotion. He orders Turnbull to start the hunt again.

Connie and Ronnie start dating. Ronnie assures her that he gets her parents are from the old country and therefore weird, just like his grandfather, though he's not sure which old country his grandfather is from. While Coneheads don't normally kiss, Connie turns out to be a natural. Ronnie pushes her to go all the way, which leads to her storming off and venting to her parents.

Outraged, Beldar informs Ronnie that "if I did not fear incarceration by human authority figures I would terminate your life functions by applying sufficient pressure to your blunt skull so as to cause its collapse." Connie, however, is still in love with Ronnie so she's horrified. Beldar assures her she'll forget Ronnie once they return to Remulac, but that horrifies her worse. She still doesn't want to leave Earth.

Turnbull and Seedling show up at the Coneheads' home, posing as Jehovah's Witnesses. Beldar and Prymaat, preparing for a costume party at the country club, hear the two men claim 144,000 people will be saved in the End Times and laugh; they can't imagine the invasion leaving that many alive. Seedling tries to trip up the Coneheads by questioning them in French but Beldar and Prymaat are fluent in it. Then the call from Remulac finally comes. Beldar throws the humans out, then he and Prymaat catch up with Connie at the dance and reveal the ship home is on its way. She's finally going to see the beauties of Remulac!

While the parents tell their friends they've been suddenly called back to France, Connie drags Ronnie home to use the sensor rings Remulackians employ in sex. When the parental units catch them, they're shocked. A defiant Connie says she's not leaving Earth or Ronnie; Ronnie vows that wherever she goes, they'll follow. As proof of his love, when the INS show up in force, Ronnie buys the family time to escape. Seedling and Turnbull corner the fleeing Conehead car but then a spaceship levitates it. With a commendable sense of duty, the INS agents jump and hang on as it rises.

When the ship arrives on Remulac, Beldar offers Turnbull and Seedling as slaves to the Highmaster (Peter Aykroyd), part of the gifts Beldar is expected to shower on his leader. The Highmaster is unimpressed, particularly as Seedling refuses to back off his anti-immigration stance ("The United States can no longer solve the employment problems of the rest of the universe"). The ruler is also displeased that Beldar has capped his teeth so he sends him to the arena to battle the monstrous Garlak.

After several other unfortunates die fighting the Garlak, Beldar uses his golf skills to drive a small rock down its throat, choking it. This entitles him to ask any request of Highmaster; he asks that he and Prymaat be allowed to return to Earth at the head of an invasion fleet, taking the humans along. The Highmaster allows him to take Seedling. Turnbull immediately starts sucking up to the planetary ruler, who's quite receptive.

Beldar, however, is playing an angle. Reaching Earth ahead of the armada, he destroys his own ship, claiming Earth has activated an invincible laser-armed satellite network. The armada retreats to Remulac, leaving Earth safe. Beldar tells Connie he loves her too much to do otherwise, then offers Seedling his life in return for legal status. A bureaucrat to the end, Seedling declares it's acceptable "if you have a special job skill no U.S. citizen possesses." Beldar assures him that's no problem. We close on prom night as Connie and Ronnie head out, though Dad insists on them using his reinforced car rather than Ronnie's jalopy.

Beldar and his family debuted in a handful of skits on *Saturday Night Live* in the late 1970s. They might have ended there except that another *SNL* skit-series, "Wayne's World," became a successful movie in 1992. That inspired *SNL* producer Lorne Michaels to try and try again—*It's Pat, Superstar, Stuart Saves His Family*—but *Wayne's World*'s success proved an outlier.

The Coneheads didn't break the losing streak. At its heart it's a one-joke movie, the joke being that they're quite obviously nonhuman yet nobody notices. Despite their weird habits, such as eating five times what a human being would and smoking an entire pack of cigarettes at once, their neighbors, landlords and employers blithely accept they're French. The film is an idealized version of the immigrant experience: work hard, assimilate and America will accept you. The alien square pegs confidently act as if they could fit perfectly into a round hole, and they do. It's a one-joke movie, but I find the joke funny enough.

It doesn't hurt that we have huge number of funny actors in the cast, even filling minor roles.

On the downside, the humor fades away when we leave Earth for Remulac. Life there is a lot less funny and the implied parody of "The Arena" isn't that clever. Seedling's attitude shifts according to the plot needs. When we first meet him, he's advocating deported illegal immigrants should be forced to wear booby-trapped collars that will blow up if they return. Having him stop hunting the Coneheads when he gets a promotion is funny—it's such a contrast from fanatics like Fox in *Starman*—but it doesn't seem to fit. The movie also ignores that he needs to bust DiCicco to get the INS head slot—is he just going to give up on that?

Resident Alien *(2021)*

Syfy, 2021–

CAST: Alan Tudyk (Harry Vanderspeigle), Sara Tomko (Asta Twelvetrees), Corey Reynolds (Sheriff Mike Thompson), Alice Wetterlund (D'Arcy Morin), Levi Fiehler (Mayor Ben Hawthorne), Mandell Maughan (Lisa Casper), Alex Barima (David Logan), Elizabeth Bowen (Deputy Liv Baker), Linda Hamilton (General McCallister), Gracelyn Awad Rinke (Sahar), Judah Prehn (Max Hawthorne), Michael Cassidy (Dr. Ethan Stone)

Resident Alien is a TV series about an alien immigrant that doesn't seem to be an immigration metaphor. It had a profoundly odd and often messy first season, anchored by Alan Tudyk as Dr. Harry Vanderspeigle, an alien hiding in a Colorado town while preparing to wipe out humanity. It's a rather black comedy.

The series is based on the same-name comic book by Peter Hogan and Steve Parkhouse. The premise there is simple: it's the TV series *Diagnosis Murder* if Dick Van Dyke's doctor had been a spaceman. Harry Vanderspeigle, a recluse living in the Pacific Northwest, is actually an alien who crashed to Earth three years ago. While Harry can disguise himself as a human, imitating human behavior is difficult enough that he finds it safer to isolate himself.

Then someone murders the town doctor in nearby Patience. The local sheriff asks Harry to help provide coroner duty as they have nobody else for the job. The mayor then talks Harry into working as town doctor, temporarily. And much to Harry's surprise, connecting with people such as local nurse Asta Twelvetrees feels … good. And wouldn't you know, there's soon another murder to solve?

The TV series radically reworks the core concept, not to mention moving the setting to Colorado. As we eventually learn, Harry's people once played the gods-from-outer-space gambit, coming from the heaven to shape and guide humanity (no genetic engineering that we know of). Eventually they left us on our own; checking in on us more recently, they decided we've lost our way. The primary issue seems to be our poisoning the environment. In a telepathic conversation with an octopus—Harry's people are related to cephalopods—Harry listens sympathetically to its account of a friend getting tangled in plastic rings from a six pack of beer. Harry assures the octopus that will soon be a thing of the past.

As the first episode shows, the alien arrived here on Earth with a suitable doomsday device, only to crash his ship and lose the device in the Colorado mountain snow. Desperate to hide out, he eventually kills the real Harry Vanderspeigle, who's vacationing in a mountain cabin, and takes his place with an illusion-generating ability. He stays a recluse, watching *Law and Order* on the TV to learn about our culture before the murder of the town doctor forces him to interact with the people of Patience.

When comic books jump to TV, the supporting cast often gets more fleshed out. Once you cast good actors, it's natural to want to give them something they can sink their teeth into. Thus the Patience that Harry stumbles into is packed with far more subplots than the comics. His nurse Asta (Sara Tomko) is secretly spying on the teenager she gave up for adoption years earlier; Sheriff Thompson (Corey Reynolds) is a jovial guy who invites everyone to call him Big Black; the mayor's son Max (Judah Prehn) is one of the rare people who can see behind Harry's illusory face. Harry makes several attempts to kill him before finally accepting they'll have to find some way to tolerate each other. And sinister General McCalister (Linda Hamilton) is determined to track the alien down.

Much of this isn't meant to be funny. It's the star turn of Alan Tudyk as Harry that adds most of the comedy and Tudyk is more than up for it; even reviewers who hate the show seem to enjoy his work. In the tradition of Jeff Bridges' Starman he's really, really bad at playing human. At his best he comes off as extremely socially awkward and unsure. At his worst—well, when he laughs it's quite obvious he's seen people laugh and knows the mechanics but can't make it sound like anything normal.

Harry frequently plays the baffled commenter on human society. When he winds up drinking with Asta at D'Arcy's (Alice Wetterlund) bar, he wakes up with a horrendous hangover. Clearly alcohol doesn't affect humans the same way, he decides, otherwise they'd never drink it. When he offends D'Arcy in a later episode—they try dating briefly—he realizes he has to apologize even though he's in the right. After all, a man who doesn't apologize to a woman would have to be an alien, right?

In other scenes, the humor comes from Harry's considerable vanity. When Patience gets Ethan Stone (Michael Cassidy) as the new town doctor, he turns out to be nice, humanitarian ("I keep speaking French because of all the relief work I did in Haiti") and handsome. This leaves Harry thinking to himself that if the locals saw how cool he'd look when he flies his ship, they'd *know* he's just as sexy. There are also running gags about Harry's distaste for the Greys (anal-obsessed perverts) and the insidious Reptilians.

There are also Harry's frantic efforts to cover up the murder of the real Harry, in a long tradition of dark comedies about murderers trying to get away with it. How this will be affected by the reveal that Harry—the real one—poisoned the previous town doctor, viewers don't know yet.

For some viewers the oddball show is overloaded with subplots but it won enough fans to come back for a second season in 2022.

OTHER FILMS AND TELEVISION

Alien Avengers (1996) A comedy about two alien tourists on Earth who like to kill and eat human criminals. Followed by a sequel cleverly titled *Alien Avengers II.*

American Dad (2005–) Satirical cartoon about CIA agent Stan Smith and his family. The Smith household includes Roger, a conniving, duplicitous Grey living on Earth since the Roswell crash.

The Cape Canaveral Monsters (1960) Aliens arrive on Earth to destroy the U.S. space program. Another laughably bad film from the creator of *Robot Monster.*

Dr. Alien (1989) As part of an experiment, a teacher turns a nerd into an irresistible stud with a phallic growth on his head.

Dude, Where's My Car? (2000) Two hungover guys try to reconstruct what happened to them the night before. The answer involves gorgeous women, UFO cultists and aliens.

Howard the Duck (1986) Bad, unfunny adaptation of Marvel Comics' extremely funny satirical comic-book. A duck on a world of intelligent avian humanoids gets transported to Earth and thwarts an alien invasion.

Mars Attacks! (1996) Alien invaders blow up monuments and kill people despite a pipe-smoking scientist's (Pierce Brosnan) predictions they come in peace. Based on an infamous line of bubble-gum cards.

Marvin Marvin (2012–13) Yet another TV sitcom about an alien trying to adjust to life on Earth.

Meatballs Part II (1984) In-name only sequel to 1979's *Meatballs.* Hijinx at a summer camp including the kids trying to hide an alien

Meet Dave (2008) Eddie Murphy leads the tiny crew of a humanoid spaceship that looks like Eddie Murphy. Love gets in the way of their plan to steal Earth's oceans.

Men in Black (1997) Brilliantly funny film starring Tommy Lee Jones and Will Smith as agents for the organization that watches over the alien immigrants living on Earth. Followed by multiple sequels and a TV cartoon spinoff.

Muppets from Space (1999) Gonzo's search for his roots leads him to discover his family are literally from another world.

My Stepmother Is an Alien (1988) Trying to save her endangered planet, Kim Basinger comes to Earth. She doesn't anticipate falling in love with Dan Aykroyd.

National Lampoon's Men in White (1998) A bad TV-movie comedy in which two garbagemen battle an alien invasion.

Paul (2014) A couple of nerds meet an alien escapee from Area 51 and try to help him get home before the Men in Black catch up.

Plan Nine from Outer Space (1958) Incredibly bad film in which aliens plot to raise an army of the dead to force the government to pay attention to them.

Plan 10 from Outer Space (1994) Indie film satirizing Mormon theology. A woman discovers the writings of a mad Mormon prophet warn of an extraterrestrial invasion.

Repo Man (1984) Repo man Emilio Estevez takes possession of a car that may have a radioactive alien in the trunk.

Scooby Doo and the Alien Invaders (2000) Scooby Doo and his human friends help a pair of aliens escape sinister humans trying to trap them.

Spaced Invaders (1990) Catching Orson Welles' *War of the Worlds* broadcast convinces some dimwitted Martians to invade Earth.

TerrorVision (1986) An alien monster enters people's homes via television and eats them.

The Three Stooges in Orbit (1962) The Stooges help a scientist battle Martian spies and thwart an invasion.

World's End (2013) Simon Pegg decides to relive his glory days by nagging his former school chums into re-enacting a pub crawl they never finished. An alien invasion gets in the way.

FOURTEEN

Government Denies Knowledge

UFO Cover-Ups and the Men in Black

"The laws of physics don't have much relevance to my line of work."
—Fox Mulder, *The X-Files*

Aliens are real and the government knows it.

The military keep UFOs and alien corpses in Area 51. Including the ship from Roswell, which was definitely not a weather balloon. The government doesn't want a panic so it covers up the truth about aliens, about abductions. If you have a close encounter, the evidence will disappear and the men in black will convince the witnesses to walk every statement back. The truth is out there, but we'll never learn about it.

Perhaps even the movies I'm writing about in this book are part of the cover-up. If people see Reptilians hey, maybe they've just watched *V* too many times. Maybe the guy who claims he was abducted spent last night watching *Fire in the Sky*. Nothing to see here, just overactive imaginations. Maybe I'm part of the cover-up too.

UFO cover-up beliefs are a subset of conspiracy-theory thinking. We all know the government lies and covers stuff up. It's a small step to assuming any information we don't like is a cover-up. Can't reconcile a support for unlimited gun access with the horror of school shootings? Tell yourself it's a false flag that never happened. Want to believe in UFOs? Assume the absence of evidence is proof positive.

"Do I believe the government lies to us?" *The X-Files'* Chris Carter asks in a *New York Times* opinion piece. "Absolutely. I'm a child of Watergate. Do I believe in conspiracies? Certainly. I believe, for example, that someone is targeting C.I.A. agents and White House officials with microwave radiation, the so-called Havana syndrome, and your government denied it."

Like so many real-world beliefs, this one carries over into alien visitor films and television. The secret conspiracy hiding the truth about aliens—maybe for our own good, maybe for sinister purposes—has been an element in movies going back to the 1950s. Depending how monstrous the conspiracy is, the "men in black" may be willing to kill anyone who knows too much. In a TV series with an ET protagonist, the government may be equally determined to cage or kill them, even though they pose no threat to the world.

UFO Investigations and Men in Black

As discussed in Chapter One, Lt. General Nathan Twining's response to the first flying saucer reports was a memo stating the phenomena were real and they demonstrated extreme rates of climbing and maneuverability. That memo led to the creation of Project Blue Book. When the project shut down in 1969, the final report was negative: all but 701 sightings could be explained away. None of the sightings indicated craft possessing superior technology. None of them suggested a threat to national security. None of them suggested extraterrestrials. For some UFO believers, these statements are just part of the cover-up.

Who enforces the cover up? The men in black, of course. In 1947, Harold Dahl reported seeing a UFO in Puget Sound, then receiving a visit from a man in a black suit. The man claimed great knowledge of UFOs and warned Dahl not to say anything about what he'd seen. Dahl later admitted his story was a hoax, though to some believers, that later statement is the real hoax.[1]

The story that really established the Men in Black in popular culture came a few years later. Albert Bender, founder of an amateur research group, the International Flying Saucer Bureau, claimed that he'd been visited by a trio of dark-clad men, described as looking like clergymen in Homburgs. They warned him against continuing his UFO research; he took the hint and backed off. In various retellings of the encounter, Bender identified them as government officials, or as extraterrestrials. In a later book about the incident, *Flying Saucers and the Three Men*, he said they'd been accompanied by three beautiful women in tight white uniforms.[2]

UFO magazine publisher Gray Barker incorporated this account into his allegedly nonfiction 1956 book, *They Knew Too Much About Flying Saucers*, coining the phrase "men in black" to describe the trio. Barker considered himself an entertainer more than a reporter and was tied to other hoaxes, such as sending a UFO believer a letter confirming the government had proof of UFOs. Regardless of which, the name stuck.[3]

Even believers in a cover-up don't necessarily agree on what the secrets are. In films, it's typically that the government wants to prevent panic by hiding the existence of UFOs or the truth about alien abductions. Author Robbie Graham says, however, the government has been hand in glove with Hollywood for decades, using films such as *Close Encounters of the Third Kind* to prepare us for the big reveal.

The Government in Alien Visitation Films

The science fiction films of the 1950s were generally supportive of government. If an official tells the press not to report the film's breaking news, there's a good reason. The press may grumble but it accepts that. The Air Force in *The Thing from Another World* has declared flying saucers do not exist; the film proves they do. It's a bonehead mistake by the military brass, but it's not a conspiracy to hide the truth.

In *Invasion of the Saucer Men* (1957), however, the Air Force are not on the up-and-up. After the aliens show up in Hicksburg, Col. Armrose (Sam Buffington) and his team rush to the landing site, remembering the last crash where "Army intelligence scooped us." Armrose reminds Lt. Wilkins (Douglas Henderson) "our job is to prevent a possible nationwide panic" by covering up the truth about flying saucers.

Armrose is astonished when it turns out the saucer is intact, rather than a crashed wreck. After attempting first contact without luck—the aliens are all skulking around town—Armrose has an engineering crew cut into the saucer with an acetylene torch. Like the saucer in *The Thing from Another World*, the metal catches fire and burns up.

Wilkins lies to the cops that the fire was a crashed jet, then Armrose's unit hides all the evidence the landing ever happened.

Armrose tells the lieutenant it's a proud thing, that only they and the president know what's really going on. He's unsettled when Wilkins wonders if they know themselves—what if other teams are covering up other landings they never hear about? *The X-Files* couldn't have been more suspicious.

Ed Wood's infamously dreadful *Plan Nine from Outer Space* (1959) proposes the government's even covering up acts of interplanetary war. When flying saucers appear overhead, Army Colonel Tom Edwards (Tom Keene) orders his artillery unit to fire on them. It has no effect on the saucers but leaves Edwards wondering about the reasons for their visit. A puzzled Lt. Harper (Duke Moore) asks, "Are big guns the usual way of welcoming visitors?"

Edwards replies that when they contacted the saucers by radio, they didn't reply. Instead "they attacked a town—a small town, I'll admit, but nevertheless a town of people, people who died" (Wood's dialog is bad, but it's memorable). The military blamed the deaths on a natural disaster; now, Edwards says, every time he reads about a flood or an earthquake wiping out a town, he wonders what the truth is. Harper, seeing the big picture, realize the recent close encounter will be written off as "a little practice firing at the clouds." There's a theory Wood deliberately made the film bad so that he could get away with attacking the military-industrial complex. This ignores that all of Wood's films are terrible.

Those films aside, the default assumption for the 1950s and for a while afterwards was that government was on our side. In the 1970s British series *U.F.O.*, SHADO—the Supreme Headquarters Alien Defense Organization—relentlessly covers up the truth that aliens use human bodies as a source of organ transplants. Nevertheless there was no question SHADO's goals and intentions were honorable. In 1978's *Project UFO*, a fictionalized version of Blue Book, two Air Force officers investigate UFO sightings every week, finding logical, non-alien explanations for almost all the sightings. The show was dully and talky but there was never any doubt the investigators were sincere. If they rejected a sighting, it was based on the evidence, not orders from higher ups.

The 1970s, however, was the decade that ripped the lid off government corruption. The Watergate scandal showed President Nixon breaking the law to achieve re-election. Stolen FBI documents revealed the bureau had harassed left-wing protesters and spied on people without authorization. The CIA had overthrown democratically elected governments and carried out assassination attempts without authorization. The Pentagon Papers showed America's top military and civilian leaders knew the Vietnam War was unwinnable years before we finally gave up. Cynicism and skepticism about the government became the order of the day.

As the 20th century progressed, that cynicism affected alien visitor films. *The Andromeda Strain* (1971) shows the government probably wants the Andromeda organism as a bioweapon. In the 2008 *Andromeda Strain* TV miniseries the government definitely wants it as a weapon, and murders people to cover this up. In contrast to *Project UFO*, *Project Blue Book* (2019–20) assumes the Air Force investigation of UFOs is a sham. General Harding (Neal McDonough) knows UFOs exist, as he has one in custody. Captain Quinn's (Michael Malarkey) real mission is to discredit genuine sightings. Astronomer J. Allen Hynek (Aidan Gillen) is a stooge, a front man to make the investigations look legitimate.

It wasn't just real-world political distrust that wrought such a sea change. I suspect a lot of the credit goes to the way "child of Watergate" Chris Carter channeled that distrust into *The X-Files*. It wasn't just that the series told us to "trust no one"—it did so while running nine seasons, getting great ratings and enjoying critical acclaim.

Many other post–1970s cover-up stories went with the One Bad Apple approach. In *Hangar 18*, the cover-up is the fault of one man, presidential adviser Robert Vaughn. In the world of *The X-Files*, the corruption is systemic and widespread; knock off one puppet master and another picks up the strings. As Mulder (David Duchovny) says in the final episode, "I thought my victories counted—I didn't realize no one was keeping score."

That said, the success of *The X-Files* didn't eliminate the idea that cover-ups are necessary. The protagonists in 1997's *Men in Black* and all its sequels routinely wipe people's minds to hide the truth about aliens on Earth, as does the British agency *Torchwood* (2006–11). The agents in TV's *Threshold* (2005) pose as agents of multiple different federal agencies; in *Roswell Conspiracies; Aliens, Myths and Legends* (1999–2000) Agent Fitz takes positive glee in coming up with absurd cover stories. Despite lying, they're the good guys.

Spotlight

The X-Files *(1993–2002, 2016–18)*

FOX

CAST: David Duchovny (Fox Mulder), Gillian Anderson (Dana Scully), The Cigarette-Smoking Man (William B. Davis), Mitch Pileggi (Deputy Director Skinner), Robert Patrick (Agent John Daggett), Annabeth Gish (Monica Reyes), Nicholas Lea (Krycek), Brian Thompson (Alien Bounty Hunter), Laurie Holden (Marita Covarrubias), Jerry Hardin (Deep Throat), Steven Williams (Mr. X), Chris Owens (Jeffrey Spender), Mimi Rogers (Diana Fowley), Tom Braidwood (Frohike), Dean Haglund (Langly), Bruce Harwood (John Byers), John Neville (Well-Manicured Man)

The first episode of *The X-Files* opens with a terrified woman stumbling through the woods. A man appears and the scene fills with light. The next morning, she's found dead, with two strange marks on her back.

Cut to the opening credits, a montage that includes a flying saucer, shadowy figures, jarring images (a white, ghostly figure falling into a palm print) and computer patterns, with text such as PARANORMAL ACTIVITY, GOVERNMENT DENIES KNOWLEDGE and THE TRUTH IS OUT THERE. To this, add clips of FBI badges belonging to our protagonists, Fox Mulder (David Duchovny) and Dana Scully (Gillian Andersen). The credits stayed largely the same for the original run of the series, though the text messages would change for individual episodes to make a point—e.g., APOLOGY IS POLICY.

When the credits are done, Scully—a physics student turned MD, recruited by the FBI while in medical school—meets with her superior Blevins (Charles Cioffi), sitting in his office with a cigarette-smoking man (William B. Davis). Blevins asks if she's ever heard of Agent Fox Mulder. Dana replies he's an expert at psychological profiling and analysis, but his odd worldview has gotten him the nickname "Spooky" at Quantico. Blevins tells Scully she's been assigned to work with Mulder in the X-Files, which handles unexplained and unexplainable FBI cases. It's implied Scully's job is to discredit Mulder's findings.

When Scully meets Mulder in his basement office, decorated with UFO images, he's fully aware why Blevins assigned her, and that she thinks it's a demotion. He also knows she's a skeptic about the paranormal where he's a believer. Nevertheless they set out together for his newest case, a series of deaths in Oregon involving the 1989 graduating class of a small-town high school.

The case has plenty of strange features. A wheelchair-bound paraplegic dies running in front of a truck. Some of his classmates have wound up in the woods with no memory how they got there. Scully and Mulder experience a nine-minute memory gap themselves, something Scully realizes Mulder anticipated. When they exhume the body of one victim, the coffin contains what Scully thinks is an ape. Mulders scoffs that nobody would swap out a corpse for an ape; he thinks it's an EBE, an extraterrestrial biological entity. Scully discovers that during the nine-minute gap someone put a small implant in her nose. A fire burns down the motel where the agents are staying, destroying most of the evidence, including the corpse.

During the investigation, Scully learns Mulder's backstory. When he was 12 and his sister Samantha was eight, she vanished, shattering the Mulder family. Repressed memory treatments showed Mulder his sister was abducted by aliens: "This thing exists. The government knows about it and I've got to know what they're protecting. Nothing else matters to me."

Later, after Mulder behavioral expertise cracked some major cases, he got the clout to pick his assignments. He chose the X-Files in the belief somewhere buried in them he'd find the truth about his sister, and about the cover-up. The conspirators behind it have done their best to stop him, but Mulder has made influential contacts who have the power to protect him.

Based on the accumulated weirdness, Mulder develops his theory: aliens are controlling Billy Miles (Zachary Ansley), a comatose '89 graduate, using him to collect his classmates for abduction and experimentation. Scully's skeptical; the local sheriff does his best to obstruct the agents. Despite the sheriff, the agents catch up with Billy after he abducts another member of his class. Mulder and Scully see Billy offer up his classmate to something in the sky, then he wakes up from his coma. His testimony under hypnosis confirms Mulder's theory.

When Scully reports back to Blevins, he tells her this amounts to a big pile of nothing without physical evidence. Scully hands him the implant, which is made of an unknown material, but it doesn't convince Blevins. Later, the Cigarette Smoking Man, AKA the CSM (also known as Cancerman and "the black-lunged son of a bitch!") locks the implant away in a vast Pentagon storeroom. Mulder discovers the case files back in Oregon have all vanished. The Billy Miles mystery will remain an unexplained, unconfirmed X-file.

So began the insanely successful mix of ufology, conspiracy theories, paranormal weirdness and general weirdness. While it would take several episodes before the show really took off, the basic template was there. Mulder drags Scully into investigating something peculiar. "Spooky" forms a theory involving aliens, psionics, aliens, ghosts, aliens, the Jersey Devil, aliens, time travel or, of course, aliens. Scully offers a rational alternative involving hallucination-inducing chemicals, fraud or physics. Mulder turns out to be right, but never with enough hard evidence in his hands to prove it to anyone else. Despite their different perspectives, the agents were an effective team and did bust a variety of perps over the years. Although Mulder's mantra was "trust no one," he and Scully could always count on each other.

The series drew on many strands of pop culture and paranoia but one of the strongest roots was the 1974 TV series *The Night Stalker* starring Darren McGavin as reporter Karl Kolchak. First appearing in the 1972 TV movie *The Night Stalker,* Kolchak is a reporter with an unwanted flair for stumbling into supernatural situations. Jack the Ripper, still alive. Vampires. A werewolf. A witch. A woman who drains youth to restore her own. A murderous, headless biker. Invariably he finds some way to destroy or banish the evil but there's never enough evidence left afterwards for him to get the front-page story he wanted.

As detailed in *The X-Files FAQ* and elsewhere, *X-Files* creator Chris Carter was an immense fan of *Night Stalker.* He's said that part of the inspiration for *The X-Files* was that law enforcement routinely ignored Kolchak's theories or shut him out of their investigations. What if the reporter had legal authority so people had to pay attention? Hence Mulder and Scully, occult investigators with a badge. McGavin guest-starred in the fifth season as the agent who founded the X-Files.

The Watergate scandal was another influence. It's not coincidental that Mulder's first government contact (Jerry Hardin) uses the pseudonym Deep Throat, given by Watergate reporters Bob Woodward and Carl Bernstein to informant Mark Felt. The second season opening episode, "Little Green Men," takes place partly at the Watergate Hotel. In a flashback to Samantha Mulder's abduction we see scenes from the Watergate investigation on TV in the background.

Carter's protagonists were worthy successors to Kolchak, smart and capable. Unlike Kolchak, whose personal life played little role in the series, Scully and Mulder got fully fleshed-out backstories, with friends, family and former partners. Despite her skepticism about the paranormal, Scully is also a lifelong Catholic where Mulder is a religious skeptic.

As a doctor, a scientist and a rationalist, Scully was an outlier among female TV characters at the time. She was also an outlier in rarely looking glamorous. A blazer and standard, sensible FBI agent outfits were good enough—unusual in a medium where looking hot is valued and FOX suits thought Anderson wasn't attractive enough.

The leads flip some traditional gender stereotypes. The standard convention is that women run on intuition and emotion, men operate by logical analysis and science. In *The X-Files,* Scully is the rationalist, trusting in science and demanding evidence. Mulder makes intuitive, speculative leaps that invariably turn out to be right; as a skeptic in *The X-Files* universe, Scully's usually wrong. She's a rationalist in a world where, as Mulder put it in the pilot, "the laws of physics don't have much relevance." In *The X-Files* universe, the truly rational approach is to embrace the irrational

Once in a while, Scully gets to be right. In "Colony" Mulder is thrilled to meet a CIA agent who believes in the X-Files but Scully smells a rat. She's right: the agent is an alien shapeshifter (Brian Thompson) using them to track down some clones he intends to kill. Generally, though, Scully's sensible, logical conclusions only make her look like a plodding Watson to Mulder's brilliant Holmes.

In the first *X-Files* film, *Fight the Future* (1998), Scully worries she's holding Mulder

JULY 25, 2008

The X-Files (1993–2002, 2016–18). WWEST, a group for women in tech, says many young women who watched Dana Scully (Gillian Anderson) on *The X-Files* developed more interest in STEM careers.

back in his investigations. He tells her that by pushing him to rationalize his beliefs, she's helping him. She's wrong, but she's *helpfully* wrong. The partnership is unbalanced in other ways. As Scully points out in the fourth-season episode "Never Again," Mulder always picks their assignments. He has a desk in their basement office with a nameplate. She doesn't. The episode lampshades the imbalance but doesn't alter it much.

That said, the partnership was an intensely close and eventually a sexual one. In the second season episode "One Breath," Scully returns comatose from an apparent alien abduction. Mulder, knowing the CSM had a hand in this, is willing to kill him in revenge. Later that season, in "End Game," Samantha Mulder (Megan Leitch) apparently returns. When that shapeshifting alien (Brian Thompson) offers to trade Scully for Samantha, Mulder puts Scully's life ahead of his sister's—though, as it turns out, she's a clone with Sam's DNA.

The portion of the show's fandom that rooted for Scully/Mulder as romantic partners, not just professional ones, coined the word "shipping" which is now ubiquitous in discussing on-screen romances. Other fans, however, preferred they stay platonic; some found Mulder simply too big a jerk towards Scully at times. Some fans criticize the way Scully seems to get jealous whenever it appears she's not the most important woman in Mulder's life, for example, when his former partner Fowley (Mimi Rogers) shows up. Even so, they were a remarkable team and they've had a continuing influence on TV since, as I'll cover later.

The leads weren't the only groundbreaking part of the show. In between done-in-one episodes dealing with the Jersey Devil, the Fluke Man or a modern-day Frankenstein, several episodes each season contributed to a single long story, the "mytharc," stretching across the seasons. The mytharc gave the series a big epic to tell, while the one-shot menaces kept the show from bogging down in an endless fight against the CSM and the Syndicate he belonged to.

The mytharc involving Extraterrestrial Biological Entities was a grab bag of UFO beliefs: abductions, recovered memories, alien/human hybrids, Roswell, government coverups and alien autopsies. Plus conspiracies. Lots of conspiracies. Trusting the government is always a mistake; the Syndicate is everywhere, pulling too many strings. Mulder's most reliable informants are conspiracy theorists Frohike (Tom Braidwood), Langly (Dean Haglund) and Byers (Bruce Harwood), AKA the Lone Gunmen. In another show, they'd be nothing but politically paranoid kooks, probably comic relief. In *The X-Files*, they're reliable sources of intel, more so than official channels. Official people are dangerous. Official stories are lies.

The CSM in various episodes is credited with shooting JFK, faking the moon landing and ensuring the Buffalo Bills never win the Super Bowl, though even these truths may not be true. The series did tie the Syndicate into real-world conspiracies: the government recruiting Nazi war criminals to work on various projects after World War II, post-war radiation experiments on humans without the test subject's consent. The link to real history helps give ballast to the more outrageous claims, such as Scully discovering aliens can track us through genetic markers in smallpox vaccines.

The nature of the conspiracy and its goals was revealed slowly. In the final first-season episode, "The Erlenmeyer Flask," Deep Throat tells Mulder about experiments creating human/alien hybrids. Later it turns out the Syndicate is working on the experiments in alliance with the aliens. The EBEs believe that humanity has had its day in the sun and hybridization will position them to step in and inherit the Earth. It later turned out that the real purpose of the hybrids was to serve as a slave species for after the conquest. The alien shapeshifter turned out to be working for another alien faction that regards mingling the races with revulsion.

Another part of the puzzle, the "Oileans," were entities composed of living black ooze. They take over the body of whoever touches them, shown visually by their eyes turning black. After infecting a human being they can eventually transform their host into a Grey.

The hybridization project is part of the Syndicate's Hail Mary play to stop immediate colonization. In 1973, its members, including Fox Mulder's father, William, handed an American flag to a party of aliens, acknowledging their superiority. They proposed a deal to buy time, working with the aliens to on hybridization while developing a defense against the Oileans. As proof their good faith, the humans were required to give up family members for alien experiments; Mulder Sr., resisted but eventually let the aliens abduct Samantha. This may mean some of the Syndicate genuinely thought they were doing the best thing for the world; others appear to be intent on using the situation to their personal advantage.

The CSM gave up his wife, Cassandra (Veronica Cartwright), who underwent hybridization experiments. In the sixth season it turned out she was the perfect human/alien hybrid. That was bad news for the Syndicate as it gave the aliens a green light for colonization. When the Syndicate met with the aliens, however, the anti-hybrid faction struck, killing Cassandra and several Syndicate leaders. While a satisfactory moment of triumph, that didn't stop the colonization agenda. The aliens began recruiting human allies and turning them into super-soldiers, strong and almost unkillable unless exposed to magnetite.

During Mulder's long struggle with the Syndicate, many of the leaders advocated killing him. The CSM consistently argued them down. Making Agent Mulder a martyr would make his outrageous claims look plausible. Direct him toward the cases we want investigated and he can help our cause. None of the CSM's allies, nor Mulder himself, knew the CSM had had an affair with William Mulder's wife and was Mulder's biological father. That wouldn't stop him sacrificing his son if need be, but he'd rather keep him alive.

Though in the final episode of the original run, after revealing colonization will begin in 2012, and is inevitable, the CSM says he spared Mulder solely to gloat. All his son's efforts to save the world were just dust in the wind. Although perhaps that was another lie. It's hard to tell.

Syndicate member Deep Throat played similar ambiguous games. He assured his allies that the help he gave Mulder was a way to pull the agent's strings, keeping him pointed in directions that would benefit the Syndicate. Leaving Mulder to chart his own course was more likely to cause trouble. In Deep Throat's case, though, he sacrificed his life at the end of the first season to save the agent. Mulder's next contact, X (Steven Williams) told the agent bluntly he'd only get information when it suited X's agenda. In one episode FBI Deputy Director Skinner (Mitch Pileggi) had to beat the necessary information out of X.

Skinner was an ally to the heroes but he was also an organization man; when orders came through the FBI hierarchy, his preference was to follow them. The agents weren't above lying to their boss, as when they let him think Mulder had committed suicide in "Gethsemane." Usually, though, Skinner would come through in a pinch. After Deep

Throat's death, the Syndicate shut down the X-Files and split up the partners. Later, after the abduction that left Scully in a coma, Skinner reopened the X-Files, the one thing the Syndicate seemed to fear. The X-Files would be shut down or destroyed a couple more times before the series ended.

The mytharc was what distinguished *The X-Files* from earlier series about humans thwarting alien invaders. In *The Invaders*, David Vincent's (Roy Thinnes) struggle against the aliens changed little on a weekly basis. He discovers an alien plot and thwarts it but fails to prove their existence to the authorities; next week he thwarts another plot with similar results. Prime-time TV in the 1960s was static, trying to deliver the same thing week after week; while David did get a group of allies, the Believers, late in the second season, it didn't shake up the status quo too much.

The same can be said of *U.F.O.* The episodes are presented out of order on some DVD sets but it doesn't matter: there's no continuity between one episode and the next. In *The X-Files*, one mytharc episode builds on earlier ones. In the pilot Mulder suspects the bizarre corpse they exhumed could be the result of genetic experiments. At the end of the season, Deep Throat confirms such experiments are ongoing. In the opening arc of season three, Mulder discovers dozens of apparent hybrid corpses, the result of experiments modeled on Josef Mengele's work.

The scope of the plot was offered up dribs and drabs, something Mulder complains about in "The Erlenmeyer Flask"—why can't Deep Throat just explain things flat out? It comes off like a meta-commentary on the way the series slowly reveals its cards, and often took them back right afterwards. Even when the agents uncovered the truth, was it really the truth? Or was the man behind the curtain just standing in front of another curtain?

The second-season two-parter "Duane Barry/Ascension" is an excellent example. In the first episode, a psychiatric hospital calls Mulder in to deal with Barry (Steve Railsback), a psychiatric patient who's snapped and taken hostages. Why Mulder? Barry has delusions he's been abducted by aliens multiple times, anticipates another abduction and wants to avoid it. Mulder naturally identifies with Barry's trauma and tries to talk him off the ledge. Scully digs into Barry's medical history and discovers he's suffered physical brain damage that may have destroyed his moral center. Barry's become a sociopath who'll say anything and make up any story to get what he wants, which is out of the hospital.

An FBI sniper takes Barry down. After he's taken to a hospital, an examination turns up an implant with a bar code in his chest. Scully tries using the bar code in a supermarket scanner and drives the scanner wild. Meanwhile Barry wakes up in hospital, haunted by visions of the Greys. He clubs a guard, escapes and goes after Scully.

In "Ascension" it becomes clear Barry sincerely believes he's been abducted. He figures the only way to avoid another round of anal probes is to offer the aliens Scully as a substitute guinea pig. Mulder pursues them but thanks to the CSM and Mulder's treacherous partner Kryceck (Nicholas Lea), he's too late. Scully's gone. Mulder drags Barry back to FBI headquarters for interrogation but Krycek murders Barry before he can talk. So was Barry an agent for the Syndicate? A pawn? If he's a true believer, how did the CSM know what he was going to do? And what happened to Scully? Where do the lies stop and the truth begin?

The answer slowly came out: the Syndicate faked the alien abduction, then took Scully for their hybrid experiments. She returns in "One Breath," comatose but revives after an intervention by some sort of guardian angel. Mystical events like that happened on *The X-Files*; Mulder dies at the end of the third season, for instance, but returns to life through a Navajo mystic ritual.

Later Scully discovers the experiments gave her terminal cancer, though it conveniently goes into remission. One thing we never learn is why the Syndicate was dumb enough to select her. Not only did it reactivate the X-Files but if you're worried about Mulder going rogue, hurting Scully's the last thing you should do.

Then again, some episodes propose that the CSM is right: Mulder serves the Syndicate's purpose by promoting belief in UFOs. In "Jose Chung's 'From Outer Space'" a military man tells Mulder all evidence of UFOs has been created by the government to distract from tests of our most advanced aircraft. Alien abductees have been hypnotized to believe what they're saying. However, the officer says, he's had an abduction experience himself—so who took him?

That account was filtered through an unreliable narrator but the story arc of "Gethsemane," and the two-part "Redux" make the same claim. After Mulder investigates an alien corpse found preserved in mountain ice, an official tells the agent that the body is a fake. All UFO evidence is fake, a propaganda campaign started by the government after the USSR acquired nuclear weapon technology. The government worried the public would push back against the military-industrial complex out of fears of nuclear war ("The faces of Hiroshima wasn't anything Americans wanted to see when they looked in a mirror") so they created the UFO legend to distract them. Like other government dupes, Mulder's memory of Samantha's abduction was implanted by his hypnotherapist.

Mulder surprisingly buys into this, setting up his apparent suicide. It's a number of episodes before he realizes the story is just more propaganda and mind-gaming.

After the defeat of the Syndicate, the mytharc headed in new directions. It had to, given that first Duchovny, then Anderson, stepped away from the show in favor of new agents played by Annabeth Gish and Robert Patrick. Mulder discovered Samantha had died several years after her abduction; he and Scully spent a night making love and Scully became pregnant. She gave the baby, William, away when it became clear he was of great interest to the alien colonizers.

All of which was still open-ended when the series ended, with the CSM's ominous threat hanging over the world. That's the drawback to attempting a mytharc. If the series dies too soon, the arc remains unfinished. It's amazing *The X-Files* was able to develop it as long as they did.

Then came the tenth and eleventh seasons, in 2016 and 2018, respectively. Having cheated death yet again, the CSM had a plan to trigger a pandemic eliminating most of the world's population. Mulder and Scully returned to the fray. Over the course of the two seasons, they learned Mulder wasn't William's father: the CSM had roofied her, then implanted alien DNA in her eggs. In the final episode, William, who wielded amazing mental powers, kills his biological father and fakes his own death in the hopes he can go back to a normal life. In the aftermath Scully reveals she's pregnant and this time Mulder really is the father.

My apologies if that was confusing; synopsizing a nine-season long mytharc is a lot harder than giving a feel for *Invaders*. For casual viewers or non-fans, the mytharc was frustrating even as it unfolded: nothing was what it seemed to be and even figuring out to be was hard. For fans, though, it was immensely intriguing, building a story bigger than one episode or even a single season could possibly do.

To the Carter team's credit, they were also capable of turning in off-the-wall one-shots with a sharp change from the usual tone or style. "Jose Chung's 'From Outer Space'" for example, has bestselling author Chung (Charles Nelson Reilly) riding along on the agents' current case as research for his book on alien abductions. Not that he's a believer, but his publisher thinks it'll be lucrative and Chung's cool with that. The results are not at all a typical X-file case and include one of the civilians involved identifying Scully and Mulder as alien Men in Black—seriously, no human woman has hair that shade of red! In other one-shot episodes the agents encountered a modern-day Dr. Frankenstein ("The Post-Modern Prometheus") and got caught up in an episode of FOX's reality TV series Cops ("X-Cops.").

While the ratings had dropped from their fifth-season peak when the axe came, the show's influence on TV remained strong. For a start, there were the leads: matching up a rationalist woman with a guy who operates on gut instinct has become quite common since *The X-Files* launched. On the TV series *Bones* (2005–17), we have the brilliant, hyper-rational Temperance Brennan (Emily Deschanel) and impulsive FBI field agent Seely Booth (David Boreanaz). On *Castle* (2009–16) a seasoned cop, Beckett (Stana Katic) is stuck working with Richard Castle (Nathan Filion), a mystery novelist whose crazy theories about their cases are usually right. On *The 4400* (2004–07) it's Tom Baldwin (Joel Gretsch) and Diana Skouris (Jacqueline McKenzie). On both *Castle* and *Bones* the professional partnership eventually becomes personal. There are other examples.

The show's emphasis on science? Working on autopsies, analyzing toxicology and studying the data, Dana Scully foreshadows the CSI elements in lots of police shows, including *Bones*.

The idea of a mytharc with constant new reveals is now normal—someone watching *The X-Files* after *Lost* (2004–10) and *Manifest* (2018–21) might not realize it was a groundbreaker. In the smash hit *Lost*, a jet plane crashes on an island where nothing is what it seems including the passengers; our initial impressions of most of them turn out wrong. There was a vast overarching mythology, endless questions and murky answers that make Deep Throat's cryptic hints look like infodumps.

In *Manifest*, a plane touches down in NYC to discover that their brief flight from the Caribbean is five years late. What happened to them? What was the reason behind it? There's a government conspiracy, a secret that somehow ties them to Noah's ark—but as NBC pulled the plug after three seasons, it looked like fans would never get the answers. Netflix, however, has announced a fourth and final season.

I'm also inclined to think TV shows that involve covert government agencies investigating superhumans, aliens or other supposed threats owe a lot to *The X-Files*. That would include *Heroes, Painkiller Jane, Tomorrow People* and a couple of others. Though I might be wrong—I was surprised to learn *Men in Black* was based on a comic that came out three years before *The X-Files* began.

Two series deserve particular attention for hewing very closely to *The X-Files* template while putting their own spin on it—and both deal with alien visitors.

The spin in *Dark Skies* (1996–97) was history. Loengard (Eric Close), a young idealist working in the Kennedy administration, discover the existence of a covert agency, Majestic 12, headed by the ruthless, pragmatic Bach (J.T. Walsh). Majestic fights the Hive, an alien race whose spidery members can creep into a human body and take it over. Now that Loengard and his fiancée Kim (Megan Ward) know the truth, Walsh gives them no choice but to sign up with the agency.

This was another mytharc that fell short of its goal, a five-season story arc that only made it to the end of the first season. In that time, however, we got the "truth" behind JFK's assassination, the murder of Lee Harvey Oswald, the Gulf of Tonkin incident and Charles Manson.

The animated series *Roswell Conspiracies: Aliens, Myths and Legends* (1999) gave us a hero with an alien abduction in his past, all sorts of conspiracies and a male/female team of protagonists. In the opening episode, bounty hunter Nick Logan (Alex Zahara) discovers his latest target is a monster disguised as a human. It turns out that Nick, like his long-vanished father, can see aliens passing for human and there are a lot of aliens out there. Voodoo spirits, banshee, Yeti, vampires and werewolves are among the myths and legends spawned by the presence of multiple alien species on Earth.

By the end of the two-part opening episode, Nick is working for the Alliance, the very black ops agency that covers up the existence of aliens and does its best to lock them away. According to the Alliance leader General Rinaker (L. Harvey Gold), Earth belongs to humanity, not the Other. Nick, whose father helped found the Alliance, reluctantly becomes an agent alongside banshee partner Sh'lain (Janyse Jaud). The agency's increasing ruthlessness makes Nick suspect something is very wrong—like perhaps a conspiracy?

The show includes occasional appearances by legendary reporter "Carl McGavin." It also has a twist on the Lone Gunmen conspiracy theorist, a crackpot neighbor of Logan's who turns out to be the host body for a malevolent spidery alien.

OTHER FILMS AND TELEVISION

Eyes Behind the Stars (1978) Italian film in which a newspaper photographer gets photographs of a flying saucer, bringing unwelcome attention from the men in black.

Night Visitors (1996) Faith Ford struggles to expose a government UFO cover-up.

Shadow Men (1997) After an alien abduction, a family finds themselves harassed by the men in black.

The Signal (2014) After an alien encounter, three teenagers end up in detention at a government facility. It turns out they're really on an alien spaceship.

FIFTEEN

Another Kind of Alien Hybrid

The Genre Mashup

"We're looking for a satellite and a 30-foot giant out on 66."
—*Attack of the 50-Foot Woman*

As I've mentioned before, you can put an alien into almost any setting or genre and make an alien visitor film out of it. *Alien Nation* (1988) reworks clichés from movies about buddy cops. *Dark Skies* (2013) converts *Poltergeist* tropes into an alien abduction story. The *Resident Alien* comic book has an ET playing amateur detective.

In some genre mashups, the aliens are integral to the story. The plot of *Alien Nation* might be stock, but if you remove the Newcomers, there is no plot. The whole point of *Cowboys and Aliens* (2011) is to mash-up aliens and cowboys in a single movie.

In other movies, the alien elements could be replaced without changing much. *Zone Troopers* (1985) has a trio of World War II GIs trying to protect a stranded alien and its spaceship from falling into Nazi hands. Replace the alien with a human scientist and his amazing invention ("If the Axis acquires my radium transmitter it could alter the course of this war.") and nothing would change.

That doesn't mean the alien elements are extraneous. A World War II or Western movie with spacemen is different, and for some people more interesting than one without. *Zone Troopers* is a war movie, but it exists in a different reality from *Battleground* or *Saving Private Ryan*. *I Come in Peace* (1990) is a bad film with a lot of cop-movie clichés. Even so, making the villain that Dolph Lundgren is hunting an *alien* drug dealer makes the film stand out from countless equally clichéd productions.

That said, some movies mix genre elements together better than others.

SPOTLIGHT

Predator *(1987)*

20th Century Fox. 106 minutes. Release date June 12, 1987

CAST: Arnold Schwarzenegger (Dutch), Carl Weathers (Dillon), Elpidia Carrillo (Anna), Bill Duke (Mac), Jesse Ventura (Blain) Sonny Landham (Billy), Richard Chaves (Poncho), Shane Black (Hawkins), R.G. Armstrong (General Phillips), Predator (Kevin Peter Hall)

CREDITS: Director: John McTiernan; Screenplay: Jim Thomas, John Thomas; Producer: Lawrence Gordon, Joel Silver, John Davis; Executive Producers: Laurence P. Pereira, Jim Thomas; Production Designer: John Vallone; Photography: Donald McAlpine; Special Visual Effects: R. Greenberg; Creature Created by Stan Winston; Music: Alan Silvestri; Editors: John F. Link, Mark Helfrich.

As the credits roll, a spaceship drops a landing capsule into Earth's atmosphere, then we cut to a chopper landing somewhere in Latin America. A crew of tough, muscular men gets off while Dutch (Arnold Schwarzenegger) lights a cigar before joining them. Inside a nearby building, Dutch meets with General Phillips (R.G. Armstrong) and a former comrade, Dillon (Carl Weathers), now with the CIA. They tell him guerrillas recently captured an important politician and key U.S. ally after his helicopter crashed in the jungle. They're holding him in the territory of a neighboring, unfriendly government and the U.S. needs him back within 24 hours. Nobody but Dutch's elite rescue team can pull it off.

The team includes Blain (Jesse Ventura), a tobacco-chewing loudmouth; Hawkins (Shane Black), a nerd who tells dirty jokes badly; Native American tracker Billy (Sonny Landham); Mac (Bill Duke) who's black; and Poncho (Richard Chaves), a Latino. Phillips assigns Dillon to accompany them, despite Dutch's objections he and his men work best without supervision. They soon locate the crashed chopper but Dutch smells something fishy: it was brought down with a heat-seeking missile and the region's guerrillas don't pack that kind of firepower. Dillon shrugs it off and does the same when Billy reports men wearing U.S. Army boots are following the guerrillas' trail.

They didn't follow it for long: Billy soon discovers the three trackers hanging by their heels and skinned. Their dog tags prove they're Green Berets, but Dillon denies any knowledge of their activities. Billy says the Americans died after a firefight but whoever killed them left no footprints. The team resume tracking the guerrillas, unaware they're being tracked in turn. We see the tracker's viewpoint as a heat map of the scene.

Dutch and his crew reach the guerrilla camp in time to see them shoot one of their captives. The good guys kill the sentries, then go in with guns blazing. It's now 25 minutes into the film and it still looks like a typical Schwarzenegger action movie. We even get the kind of tough-guy quip associated with Schwarzenegger back then: when he impales one man with a thrown knife, he tells him to "stick around."

When the battle ends, a woman, Anna (Elpidia Carrillo) attacks Dutch, who knocks her cold. It's clear Dillon and Phillips have been lying: the captors are Russian special forces while the prisoner is CIA. Dillon explains taking out the Soviet soldiers has prevented a Russian-backed invasion of a U.S. ally in the region. Dutch is the only one who could have pulled it off; as he no longer accepts killing missions, Dillon lied. When Dillon coldly adds that his former friend is an "expendable asset," but Dutch replies that his men are *not* expendable.

The crew flee back over the border with Anna, ahead of the local military. They're still under infra-red scrutiny and the watcher is also recording their voices. Billy senses their shadow's presence, apparently for no other reason than Native American super-senses. The other men eventually notice it too, but they can't locate it. Anna attempts to escape but Hawkins chases and recaptures her. An invisible figure (Kevin Peter Hall) kills Hawkins, then removes his boot. Contrary to action-movie clichés about the black guy dying first, this time it's one of the white men.

The invisibility is a great effect. It's less true invisibility than a chameleon ability to blend into the background, constantly adjusting as the Predator (never named that in the film itself) moves. Anna sums up what she saw by saying the jungle came alive. At this point everyone realizes they're in something other than a pure action film. They're too seasoned to panic, but they're plenty scared. As they scout the area, Blain confronts what turns out to be a harmless ground animal, then the Predator ray-blasts him from behind. Mac spots the alien, but it escapes, so the team spray the surrounding jungle with gunfire. Anna spots some green blood on the nearby leaves, showing they hit it. Dillon discovers Blain's fatal wound came from something so hot it cauterized the wound site.

The injured alien retreats to pull out its medical kit, giving us our first look at it without camouflage: a big, armored humanoid with hair in dreadlocks. While it patches itself up, Mac booby-traps the camp perimeter and Dillon arranges for a helicopter pickup, though they'll have to cross quite a distance to reach it. Billy isn't optimistic about the odds. When one of the team says he's never seen Billy scared of any man, Billy replies that "it ain't no man—we're all going to die."

That night the Predator uses a wild pig to trigger the boobytraps, distracting everyone while he takes Blain's body. Anna describes the attack, showing she can speak English. Dillon refuses to believe they're up against a single fighter this formidable but Dutch believes Anna. He realizes they'll have to kill their enemy to reach the helicopter alive—but if Anna's right and they bloodied it, they can kill it. After he cuts Anna's bonds, she tells them the Predator has hunted in the region for years, mostly when the weather is at its hottest.

The men catch the Predator in another trap. It breaks out and retreats, but its camouflage tech is temporarily offline. Mac sets out in pursuit, then Dillon goes after Mac while telling Dutch to get everyone else to the pickup site. It's Dillon's way of atoning for getting them into this mess. Mac and Dillon spot the alien but it blows Mac's head off. Dillon has slightly more success, then the alien delivers a killing stroke with a vicious-looking knife.

The alien resumes its pursuit of the others. Billy dies fighting a rearguard action, then Poncho goes down. Dutch sends Anna on ahead while he leads the Predator away. Dutch falls down a waterfall into a lake, then sees the Predator dive in after him. Dutch is weaponless but as he reaches the shore, he smears himself with mud. With its heat-sensing ability blocked, the Predator returns to the ship to admire its trophies from the hunt.

Dutch uses the brief respite to create an arsenal of makeshift, low-tech weapons and set a couple more traps. When the Predator returns Dutch greets it with a gunpowder-laden arrowhead that destroys its chameleon tech. The Predator's counterattack injures Dutch, then it begins tracking him by sound and the movement of the foliage.

The final showdown has the two adversaries using trick and counter-trick, attack and counterattack. After Dutch's mud washes off him in the water, the alien confronts him, but instead of delivering the killing stroke it backs off and removes its helmet. In an apparent act of sportsmanship, it meets Dutch face to face, hand to hand. The fight goes against Dutch until he triggers one of the booby traps and crushes the Predator under a heavy log. Fatally injured, the creature uses one of its recordings to mimic Dutch's earlier question, "What the hell are you?" Then it activates a bomb on its wrist, laughing as it shows Dutch the countdown. So much for sportsmanship.

Dutch races away and by the time the wrist-bomb explodes in a mushroom cloud he's outside the blast range. That's right, he outruns a nuclear explosion. Dutch reaches Phillips and Anna in the helicopter and lies there, battered and shaken, as it flies away.

Scriptwriters Jim and John Thomas originally conceived a story as involving a pack of alien hunters, then realized a single hunter, going up against some of Earth's toughest humans, would work better. It's reminiscent of Richard Connell's 1924 short story "The Most Dangerous Game," in which Count Zarov, a Russian hunter, traps men on his isolated island so that he can hunt a prey animal as intelligent as he is. When a big-game hunter washes up on the island, it's master hunter vs. master hunter. The idea has been filmed, adapted and knocked off many times.

The movie also looks like *Rambo: First Blood II* (1985) was an influence. In *Rambo*, Sylvester Stallone's Rambo goes into Vietnam and discovers proof that the Vietnamese are still holding American POWs. After his high-tech, top-of-the-line weapons are destroyed or lost, Rambo fashions himself a bow-and-arrow—and at one point hides in a patch of mud—which is all he needs to butcher the Vietnamese and Russian forces fighting against him.

Other than the opening spaceship shot, *Predator* is pure action-film for the first twenty minutes. Even after the infra-red point-of-view begins—special features on the DVD say they didn't use real infra-red scanning because it didn't look right visually—it's forty minutes into the movie before we see the camouflaged alien, and much later before we get a clear look at it.

Director John McTiernan says the initial design for the creature was smaller, less visually impressive and with a single eye; he shot several scenes using it, then sent the footage to Fox, which quickly agreed to a redesign. Veteran F/X man Stan Winston developed the final concept based on a Rastafarian warrior. It's visually striking, though the creature's dreadlocks have generated criticism—from Roger Ebert, for example—that it invokes stereotypical images of hulking black thugs. The Predator's strange, pinched face behind the helmet is memorable too, though some viewers have joked it resembles female genitalia.

The casting is solid. The DVD commentary track says Weathers was chosen as the main human antagonist because he had more acting experience than Schwarzenegger. Black was picked because he's a screenwriter and McTiernan worried there might need to be rewrites on set. As the Predator, Kevin Peter Hall was big enough to look believable going mano a mano with Schwarzenegger, but he also infuses the alien with personality, despite not speaking. It's possible to imagine it swapping stories with its fellows back on the homeworld—"They call it a 'Dutch'—let me tell you what a fight it gave me!"

The script gives the characters individual characterization such as Hawkins' complete inability to tell a dirty joke straight. Being a 1980s action film, they also have guns. Big guns. Each man has his own individual weapon; Blain carries a massive Gatling gun. Although Ventura was strong enough to handle it, it's an absurdly clumsy weapon to carry into the jungle. Still, it does make for an impressive visual. Schwarzenegger has compared his team to *The Magnificent Seven* in which each of the cowboys defending a small village has a distinctive personality and skill set.

Politically the movie is laden with post–Watergate skepticism about government. The generals in *The Thing from Another World* make a lot of bad decisions but nobody suggests they're hiding the truth about the Thing from Hendry and his crew. In *Predator*, the operation is a lie from the start. Neither Dillon nor Phillips have any qualms about using Dutch's team as expendable assets—okay, Dillon may have qualms, but he crushes them. Hendry in *The Thing* shows better judgment than the people giving him orders; Dutch shows better ethics.

Like *Thing from Another World*, the characters are tough, but the film emphasizes it more. Typical for action films of the era there's much displaying of hard masculine bodies. When Dutch and Dillon first shake hands, it becomes an impromptu arm-wrestling match that shows off their bulging biceps. When Dutch wins, he tells Dillon, "they got you pushing too many pencils." References to past heroic missions ("Remember Afghanistan?" "I wish I didn't") establish these guys aren't easy prey—if the Predator can take them down, it has to be good.

Anna provides the only female presence in the film, but she feels oddly pointless. We never learn why a camp of Russian special forces had her around or whether she was a real guerrilla working with them. She gets none of the character quirks the guys do, doesn't play a role in the fighting and isn't there to be a love interest. It feels like her purpose is to keep the film from being entirely male and to provide some exposition.

That said, *Predator* works very well as an action film, a science fiction film and a combination of both.

Predator 2 *(1990)*

20th Century–Fox, 108 minutes, Released November 21, 1990

CAST: Danny Glover (Lt. Harrigan), Kevin Peter Hall (Predator), Ruben Blades (Archuleta) Maria Conchita Alonso (Cantrell), Robert Davi (Heineman), Kent McCord (Pilgrim), Morton Downey, Jr. (Pope), Gary Busey (Keyes), Bill Paxton (Jerry Lambert), Adam Baldwin (Garber), Calvin Lockhart (King Willie), Steve Kahan (Sergeant), Henry Kingi (El Scorpio), Corey Rand (Ramon Vega), Elpidia Carrillo (Anna), Lilyan Chauvin (Irene Edwards), Michael Mark Edmondson (Gold Tooth), Teri Weigel (Colombian Girl), William R. Perry (Subway Gang Leader), Subway Gang (Alex Chapman, Gerard G. Williams, John Cann, Michael Papajohn), Louis Eppolito (Patrolman), Charles Haugk (Charlie) Sylvia Kauders (ruth) Charles David Richards (Commuter), Julian Reyes (Juan Beltran), Casey Sander (Fed), Pat Skipper (Fed), Carmine Zozzora (Fed)

CREDITS: Director: Stephen Hopkins; Writers: Jim Thomas, John Thomas; Producer: John Davis, Lawrence Gordon, Joel Silver; Co-Producer: Terry Carr, Tom Joyner; Executive producer: Lloyd Levin, Michael Levy; Production Design: Lawrence G. Paull; Special Visual Effects: R. Greenberg; Photography: Peter Levy; Music: Alan Silvestri; Editor: Mark Goldblatt, Bert Lovitt

Predator 2 mixes alien visitors into a cop movie effectively. The results, however, prove a good genre mashup isn't always a good movie.

The film is set in the dystopian, crime-ridden Los Angeles of 1997. Drug cartels rule the streets, packing enough firepower to outgun law enforcement. The opening scene demonstrates this by pitting Lt. Harrigan (Danny Glover) and his team—most importantly Archuleta (Ruben Blades) and Cantrell (Maria Conchita Alonso)—against a gang that can blow up a cop car with their high-powered weaponry. Never mind that the weapons look unconvincing, like something from a cartoon tie-in toy line.

The film soon shows Harrigan gets little support from the LAPD. Harrigan's superior, Pilgrim (Kent McCord, who played an LA cop years earlier on the TV show *Adam 12*), has his hands tied by red tape while rising LAPD star Heineman (Robert Davi) is a careerist and ass-kisser. The media are useless too. They're represented by Pope (TV personality Morton Downey, Jr.), an obnoxious sensationalist constantly ranting about how ineffective the police are at maintaining order.

Everything changes when *something* (Kevin Peter Hall) butchers one of the drug gangs in their luxury penthouse. The cops, unlike the audience, have no idea what they're dealing with. Harrigan starts investigating, but federal agents Keyes and Garber (Gary Busey, Adam Baldwin) shut him down and take over. Heineman, being a weasel, backs the feds up.

Archuleta nevertheless investigates the crime scene and discovers part of a leftover Predator weapon. The alien kills him, making Harrigan's more determined than ever to find the creature despite the feds warning him off. Harrigan shows the piece Archuleta found to a scientist and learns it's not made of any metal known on Earth.

The Predator continues its killing spree and has no qualms about hunting cops. In a battle on the LA subway (which Los Angeles doesn't have—the story was originally set in New York) it does spare Cantrell when her heat signature shows she's pregnant. Eventually Harrigan gets the truth out of Keyes. The government knows about the events of *Predator* and has studied multiple other similar Predator hunts. Keyes' mission is to trap the creature so the government can exploit its alien technology and knowledge. The job is all the tougher because Predators, as in the original film, will commit ritual suicide by nuke if their prey overcomes them.

Harrigan can't turn a blind eye to the rising death count, so he strikes a deal with one of the drug gangs to trap the creature. They blind it with UV, which negates its infra-red vision, but the Predator manages to escape. Harrigan pursues it through apartment buildings and onto rooftops; when Keyes attempts to capture it the alien kills him with a razor-edged throwing disc. The alien ends up hanging helpless from the top of an apartment building so it activates its wrist bomb. Harrigan slices through its wrist with the throwing disc, deactivating the bomb.

The Predator makes it off the roof and into the building via a window. Harrigan pursues it and they end up inside the alien's spaceship, where Harrigan kills it. Other Predators show up and rather than go nuclear they pay tribute to Harrigan by giving him a flintlock pistol from the 1700s.

Rather than an action film, *Predator 2* is a mash-up of alien visitor and "copaganda" movie. Much like 1971's *Dirty Harry*, crime is rampant and the cops on the street are the only defense the city has. Everyone else in authority exists to make the officers' job harder. Harrigan's superiors are self-serving or ineffective, the feds have an agenda that doesn't include protecting civilians and Pope is a cheap scandal-monger.

Applying Peter Biskind's political framework (see Chapter Two), this film would be far right. It trusts the man on the street more than the smart people in charge; it also assumes the system is rotten and incapable of getting the job done. The Predator targeting the gangbangers fits into this worldview. Much like Marvel Comics' Punisher, it gives viewers the vicarious satisfaction of seeing someone butcher criminals without worrying about those stupid legal rights that tie cops' hands.

Watching the Predator hack up a bunch of drug dealers, however, isn't half as memorable as taking on Dutch's formidable crew. The Predator's voice-imitation tech serves mostly to let it toss off curse words and a couple of mocking lines. It's a pale shadow of *Predator*.

Attack of the 50 Foot Woman *(1958)*

Woolner Productions, Allied Artists. B&W. 66 minutes. Release date May 19, 1958

CAST: Allison Hayes (Nancy Archer), William Hudson (Harry Archer), Yvette Vickers (Honey Parker), Ken Terrell (Jess), George Douglas (Sheriff Dubbitt), Roy Gordon

(Dr. Cushing), Frank Chase (Charlie), Otto Waldis (Dr. Von Loeb), Mike Ross (Tony and Space Giant), Eileen Stevens (Nurse), Dale Tate (Himself), Tom Jackson (Prospector)

CREDITS: Director: Nathan Hertz (Juran); Assistant Director: Ken Walters; Screenplay: Mark Hanna: Producer: Bernard Woolner; Executive Producer/Photography: Jacques Marquette; Music: Ronald Stein; Editor: Edward Mann

Mixing aliens into an action movie or a cop film makes a certain sense. Throwing an extraterrestrial into a drama about an alcoholic woman and her cheating husband is, to say the least, counter-intuitive. The results are not good, but they're interesting, and the film did give us a spectacular, iconic poster. Nancy Archer (Allison Hayes) is one of the few explicitly female monsters in alien visitor movies, though Ymir or the Martians of *War of the Worlds* might be female for all we know.

The movie opens with a TV announcer discussing a flying fireball seen traveling around the world, and which will soon pass over the California desert. That's exactly where we find Nancy, driving furiously down Highway 66 and straight into a close encounter of the third kind. A beeping white sphere descends from the sky onto the highway, forcing Nancy to run away, screaming for her husband

Said husband, "Handsome Harry" Archer (William Hudson), is in town cuddling with Honey Parker (Yvette Vickers) at the local night spot, Tony's Bar and Grill. Nancy drove off because she caught them making eyes at each other which, Harry says, "will make up for all the things she hasn't caught us doing." He admits to Honey that going back to Nancy after she threw him out hasn't worked out great, but if they divorce he won't see a penny of her $50 million. Honey points out that if Nancy dies, Harry inherits everything.

Harry protests that murder's not his game, so Honey proposes Plan B: have Nancy, who's been institutionalized before, permanently committed. Harry says a Dr. Cushing (Roy Gordon) is weaning Nancy off the booze. Honey replies that won't matter if Harry gives his wife the right push—"She's on the brink and you know it."

When Nancy reaches town, she tells Sheriff Dubbitt (George Douglas) about the 30-foot-tall giant who emerged from the "satellite." The alien's spaceship is never called anything but a satellite, presumably because Sputnik's 1957 launch made satellites a big deal. Sputnik beeped so the alien's "satellite" beeps too.

Dubbitt sends his deputy Charlie (Frank Chase) to find Harry and offers Nancy some black coffee, meaning she needs to sober up. She gets the implication and resents it. Charlie finds Harry, but accepts a bribe to say Harry's already taken a cab home. When Dubbitt talks to Harry later, Harry suggests that Nancy must have hidden a bottle of booze in her car.

Dubbitt and Charlie head into the desert with Nancy to recover her car but when they reach it, the satellite is gone. Dubbitt notices Nancy's wearing her priceless diamond, the Star of India—in the real world, the name of a sapphire in the Smithsonian Natural History Museum—and warns her against wearing something so valuable when she's out alone. Nancy heads home in a huff; Dubbitt explains to Charlie that no matter how crazy her story sounds, it's important to humor the town's biggest taxpayer.

Returning to her palatial home, Nancy pours herself a stiff drink under the worried eye of her butler Jess (Ken Terrell). Like many servants in fiction, Jess is less an employee than a devoted surrogate parent who's been with Nancy's family since her childhood. He doesn't like Harry, who reciprocates. As soon as Harry walks through the door he tells Jess to get lost.

Nancy tells Harry to run back to Honey, leading to an argument over whether Harry's cheating or Nancy's unreasonably suspicious. Nancy reminds Harry that if they split up again, it's over: "You're going to make too many passes ... my gigolo, that's what you are. You're a parasite." Although she knows Harry's toxic, she's too desperate for his love to throw him out.

Finally, Nancy tells Harry about the satellite and the giant, whom she believes wasn't grabbing for her but for the Star of India. She assures Harry she was stone cold sober; Harry, carrying her upstairs, responds with an expression that's not quite a smirk. As he puts her to bed, she tells him, "I need you—if you only knew how much."

Over Nancy's protests, Harry dopes her with a sleeping pill, then takes the diamond. Harry intends to show it to Honey in her hotel room, which he pays for, and he's not pleased to find her dancing at Tony's with Charlie. Honey says she's bored waiting around the fleabag hotel, but she perks up when he shows her the necklace. Harry's confident now that Nancy's going to crack up, then Honey will be able to wear the necklace openly.

Dr. Cushing is also worried Nancy's losing it. Worse, she's so emotionally dependent on Harry that if she's locked away from him again, it might kill her. He instructs Jess on Nancy's meds and to keep her away from booze. When Harry returns home, Nancy accuses him of trying to get her committed. Harry realizes Jess is reporting to Nancy about what Harry's up to, though it's not explained how Jess could know about a conversation down at Tony's.

Nancy's condition deteriorates when the news about the satellite leaks out. Dale Tate, a real TV announcer of the time, mocks her relentlessly on the air and laughs that not even an alien giant could love Nancy for herself—"A man can ignore one million dollars but 50? That's too much to ask, even for the man in the moon." Furious, Nancy drags Harry out to hunt the satellite, promising him that if they can't find it, she'll sign the commitment papers. Harry's initially delighted by their lack of success, then the satellite appears beside the road on the drive home. Nancy stops the car and touches it, confirming that it's real. Once again, the giant (Mike Ross) emerges and grabs for her. Nancy's had the sense to come armed, but the bullets don't stop the giant. She screams for help but Harry bolts.

Rushing back home, Harry starts packing. Jess demands he explain where Nancy is, leading to a brawl that ends when Harry cracks a bottle of booze over Jess's skull. When Jess recovers, he calls the cops. Harry meanwhiles rushes to Honey, telling her they're leaving town immediately. But they aren't: Charlie shows up and drags them to the sheriff's office, holding them overnight while a posse hunts for the missing Nancy.

To everyone's surprise she turns up the next morning on the roof of her pool house, with strange, possibly radioactive scratches on her throat. The Star of India is gone. Dubbitt assumes Harry took it, but Honey provides an alibi. Dr. Cushing prescribes meds for Nancy, warning his nurse (Eileen Stevens) that even a slight overdose would be fatal.

It turns out that given an easy, hard-to-prove method of murder, Harry's okay with making himself a widower. Encouraged by Honey, he sneaks into Nancy's room with a syringe of the drug, unaware the nurse is following him. She announces herself by turning on the light, then screams in horror. Nancy has transformed into a giant, though all we see is a large, fake hand projecting from her bed.

The next day, a bemused delivery man drops off meat hooks, four lengths of chain, 40 gallons of plasma and an elephant syringe. Cushing talks to Van Loeb (Otto Waldis),

Attack of the 50 Foot Woman (1958). The transparent Allison Hayes of the movie wasn't as convincing or as large as this titan. It's a truly memorable poster.

a specialist who spouts medical technobabble. They agree to secure Harry's consent for an operation on Nancy's pituitary. Honey tells Harry if he just disappears until it's too late to operate, all their troubles will be over. It's unclear if this means the condition is terminal, that it will snap Nancy's fragile sanity or that giantism is valid grounds for divorce in California law.

Dubbitt and Jess discover giant footprints in the garden, the first evidence that Nancy's not crazy—well, if you overlook that she's turned into a giant. Packing grenades and tear gas, the two men follow the footprints to the satellite. They realize the giant must have taken Nancy home after stealing the Star of India. Inside the satellite they discover the diamond is one of several gems held in glass spheres, apparently as the ship's power source. The men see something terrifying and back out into the desert.

What they've seen is the giant, who emerges in what looks like a knightly surcoat decorated with a heraldic coat of arms. He's also transparent, due to bad special effects photography. The men shoot, with no better results than Nancy had. The grenade hurts it enough to throw Dubbitt's car aside in a rage, with the car turning transparent while the giant holds it. The alien climbs back into the satellite and leaves.

Back at the house, Cushing reminisces with Van Loeb about what a wonderful woman Nancy was before she got married. Once Harry got his hooks in her, her health rose and fell in response to her emotions, which Van Loeb says is "a case not infrequent in the supersonic age we live in." Cushing wonders if he should have encouraged Nancy to leave Harry. His colleague replies that when one person can't live without another, there's no way to get them free. As if to prove his point, Nancy, now chained in her bedroom, wakes up and immediately screams for Harry.

Charlie finds Harry and Honey dancing at Tony's, but Harry refuses to end his fun just because Nancy's suffering. Back at the mansion, Nancy decides not to wait, stands up and tears through the roof. Conveniently for the production code, her clothes have grown too, so everything's covered. Guessing where she'll find Harry, Nancy strides into town, as transparent as the alien. Everyone who sees her flees in terror.

When Nancy reaches town she thrusts her hand into Honey's hotel room, finds it empty, then strides over to Tony's. Harry demands Charlie shoot Nancy but the deputy balks at shooting a woman, even a colossus. Harry has no such qualms, so he snatches the gun and shoots.

It doesn't help. Nancy rips off the roof and pulls Harry out, accidentally killing Honey when a beam falls on her. As she walks past a power transformer, Dubbitt shoots it with a rifle, killing Nancy with the power surge. It's too late to save Harry, who lies crushed in Nancy's hand as she falls. Cushing somberly declares that "she finally got Harry all to herself."

Attack of the 50 Foot Woman has all the elements of a marital suspense thriller or what would later be called a jeop—woman in jeopardy—film. Faithless husband. Wealthy, needy wife. Conniving girlfriend. In an ordinary movie Harry would keep pushing Nancy toward a mental collapse until Jess or Cushing expose him and save her. Or possibly Nancy would have finally snapped and killed Harry rather than lose him.

But then, for some reason, they threw in an alien. I've yet to find any interviews where screenwriter Mark Hanna explains his thought processes. As the original title was *Attack of the Colossal Woman*, a variation on *The Amazing Colossal Man*, presumably he started with the idea of a giant woman, then wrote the movie around that.

While good stories have been written that way, this was not one of them. If the alien needs Nancy's diamond, why does he wait out in the desert instead of trying to find it? How does a 30-foot giant walk from the desert to her mansion without anyone seeing— and why walk instead of flying his sphere? Then there's the way giant Nancy fits without any difficult into the same room where she went to sleep at normal size. According to Bill Warren, the production team had money for better special effects but decided not to spend it. That was probably a good call on their part. Even with adequate special effects this would still be a bad movie.

What the movie does have going for it—it's not enough, but it's something—is the cast. The points of the love triangle are better than the film. Hayes does a good job as a hard-drinking, unbalanced woman on a fast-track to a straitjacket. As Harry, Hudson radiates a weasel aura just sitting there smirking. Vickers is excellent at playing a low-class party girl with a complete lack of principles and a fondness for other women's husbands.

The movie was remade in 1993 with Darryl Hannah, Daniel Baldwin and Christi Conway as the three points of the triangle. The movie company presented it as a "feminist" take on the story, but it isn't. Hannah's Nancy, like Hayes, is determined to save her marriage and win her husband back, no matter what. Dumping the cheating sleaze is never on the table. *Attack of the 50-foot Cheerleader* (2012) is another imitation and Ginormica (Reese Witherspoon) in the animated *Monsters vs. Aliens* (2009) is a riff on Hayes' character.

OTHER FILMS

Alien Agenda: Out of the Darkness (1996) Alien invasion/time travel mashup. In this film and its multiple sequels, present-day Earth is a battleground between future humans and the alien Morphs who want to change history so the future Earth is more livable. It turns out the Morphs are distant descendants of human space colonists.

Cowboys and Aliens (2011) Western outlaw Daniel Craig and rancher Harrison Ford find themselves embroiled in a battle with aliens who are kidnapping people from the local town.

Liquid Sky (1982) Aliens arrive in the middle of a drama about feuding and screwing in New York's punk scene. The alien mission: kill us and drain our pleasure hormones for their own use.

Notes

Introduction

1. Michael Stein, *Alien Invasions: The History of Aliens in Pop Culture* (2020), 14–17.
2. Bill Warren, *Keep Watching the Skies!* (2010), 292–93.

Chapter One

1. David Clarke, *How UFOS Conquered the World* (2015), 14, 197, 217–20.
2. Evan Andrews, "World War II's Bizarre 'Battle of Los Angeles.'"
3. Ralph Blumenthal and Leslie Kean, "'Project Blue Book' Is Based on a True UFO Story. Here It Is"; Missy Ryan and Alex Horton, "Report Does Not Confirm, or Rule Out, Extraterrestrial Activity in Unexplained Aerial Events."
4. Clarke, 285.
5. *Ibid.*, 11.
6. Justin Sablich, "The UFO Sightings That Launched 'Men in Black' Mythology."
7. Mark Buchanan, "Contacting Aliens Could End All Life on Earth. Let's Stop Trying."

Chapter Two

1. I.F. Clarke, *Voices Prophesying War* (1992), 26–35, 84–87.
2. *Ibid.*
3. Warren, 876–87.
4. *Ibid.*
5. *Ibid.*
6. Ben Beaumont-Thomas, "How We Made Independence Day."
7. *Ibid.*
8. Corey Robin, "Remembrance of Empires Past: 9/11 and the End of the Cold War."
9. Josh Plainse, "Kevin Spacey Nearly Played the President in 'Independence Day.'"

Chapter Three

1. Warren, 208–15.
2. *Ibid.*
3. *Ibid.*
4. *Ibid.*

Chapter Four

1. Fraser Sherman, *Screen Enemies of the American Way* (2011), 97–103.
2. Emmanuel Levy, *Small Town America on Film* (1991), 109–43.
3. Sherman.
4. Warren, 419–26.
5. *Ibid.*
6. Sherman.

Chapter Five

1. Kurt Busiek, *Astro City: Life in the Big City* (1996), 7–10.
2. Jake Rossen, *Superman vs. Hollywood* (2008). 5–13.
3. *Ibid.*
4. Brian Cronin, "TV Legends: Did Superman Actually Change in a Phone Booth on TV?"
5. Brian Cronin, "Was Superman's Memory-Wiping Super-Kiss from the Comics?"

Chapter Six

1. Marcelo Gleiser, "Probing Alien Abduction."
2. Breeanna Hare, "The 'Fourth Kind' of Fake?"
3. Dewey Webb, "Where's Walton? Is Arizona's Best-Known UFO Abductee Bound for Hollywood Stardom?"
4. Lee Speigel, "UFO-Alien Abduction Still Haunts Travis Walton."
5. Jeff Richardson, "Alaska Newspapers, Movie Studio Reach Settlement Over 'Fourth Kind.'"

Chapter Seven

1. James Daily and Ryan Davidson, *The Law of Superheroes* (2012), 222–27.
2. Alicia Ault, "Did Ellis Island Officials Really Change the Names of Immigrants?"

Chapter Nine

1. Amy H. Sturgis, "Indians and Aliens."
2. Ann Hornaday, "Chloé Zhao Explains How 'Nomadland' and 'Eternals' Are Cinematic Twins."

Chapter Twelve

1. Warped Factor, "Abandoned Sequels: Close Encounters of the Third Kind 2: Night Skies"; Ryan Lambie, "How Steven Spielberg's Night Skies Became E.T."; Katie Mettler, "Tales from the Path of Totality: 62 Years Ago Today, They Say, 'Little Green Men' Invaded This Kentucky Farm Town.'"
2. Lambie.
3. *Ibid.*

Chapter Fourteen

1. Sablich.
2. Benjamin Bradford, "Men In Black: The UFO Buff's Bogeyman."
3. *Ibid.*

Bibliography

Andrews, Evan. "World War II's Bizarre Battle of Los Angeles." *History.com*, May 6, 2020.

Ascher-Walsh, Rebecca. "Meet the 'Coneheads.'" *Entertainment Weekly*, July 30, 1993.

Ault, Alicia. "Did Ellis Island Officials Really Change the Names of Immigrants?" *Smithsonian*, December 26, 2016.

Barson, Michael, and Steven Heller. *Teenage Confidential: An Illustrated History of the American Teen*. New York: Barnes & Noble, 2005.

Basinger, Jeanine. *The World War II Combat Film: Anatomy of a Genre*. Middletown, CT: Wesleyan University Press, 2003.

Beaumont-Thomas, Ben. "How We Made Independence Day." *The Guardian*, November 8, 2016.

Biskind, Peter. *Seeing Is Believing: How Hollywood Taught Us to Stop Worrying and Love the Fifties*. New York: Pantheon Books, 1983.

Bliss, Michael. *Invasions USA: The Essential Science Fiction Films of the 1950s*. London: Rowman & Littlefield, 2014.

Blumenthal, Ralph, and Leslie Kean. "'Project Blue Book' Is Based on a True UFO Story. Here It Is." *New York Times*, January 15, 2019.

Bradford, Benjamin. "Men in Black: The UFO Buff's Bogeyman." *Live Science*, November 15, 2012.

Brooks, Tim, and Earle Marsh. *The Complete Directory to Prime Time Network and Cable TV Shows 1946—Present* (Eighth Edition). New York: Ballantine Books, 2003.

Buchanan, Mark. "Contacting Aliens Could End All Life on Earth. Let's Stop Trying." *New York Times*, June 10, 2021.

Busiek, Kurt. *Astro City: Life in the Big City*. La Jolla, CA: Homage Comics, 1996.

Carter, Chris. "I Created 'The X-Files.' Here's Why I'm Skeptical of the New U.F.O. Report." *New York Times*, June 25, 2021.

Chaw, Walter. "'Alien Nation'—A Sci-Fi Flick Doubling as a Metaphor for the Asian-American Experience—Is Ripe for Reconsideration." *Decider*, October 14, 2019.

Clarke, David. *How UFOs Conquered The World: The History of a Modern Myth*. London: Aurum Press, 2015.

Clarke, I.F. *Voices Prophesying War: Future Wars 1763–3749* (New Edition). New York: Oxford University Press, 1992

Corrigan, Maureen. "The Sad Lesson of 'Body Snatchers': People Change." *NPR*, October 17, 2011.

Cronin, Brian. "TV Legends: Did Superman Actually Change in a Phone Booth on TV?" *CBR*, September 28, 2016.

Cronin, Brian. "Was Superman's Memory-Wiping Movie Super-Kiss From the Comics?" *CBR*, September 19, 2021.

Daily, James, and Ryan Davidson. *The Law of Superheroes*. New York: Gotham Books, 2013.

Ebert, Roger. "Predator 2." *Roger Ebert*, November 21, 1990.

Fingeroth, Danny. *Disguised as Clark Kent: Jews, Comics and the Creation of the Superhero*. New York: Continuum, 2007.

Fulton, Roger. *The Encyclopedia of TV Science Fiction*. London: Boxtree Limited, 1990.

Gillbert, James. *Cycle of Outrage: America's Reaction to the Juvenile Delinquent in the 1950s*. New York: Oxford University Press, 1986.

Gleiser, Marcelo. "Probing Alien Abduction." *NPR*, November 27, 2013.

Graham, Robbie. *Silver Screen Saucers: Sorting Fact From Fantasy In Hollywood's UFO Movies*. Hove, UK: White Crow Books, 2015.

Hantke, Steffen. *Monsters in the Machine: Science Fiction Film and the Miltarization of America After World War II*. Jackson: University Press of Mississippi, 2016.

Hare, Breeanna. "The 'Fourth Kind' of Fake?" *CNN*, November 6, 2009.

Herman, Ellen. *The Romance of American Psychiatry: Political Culture in the Age of Experts*. Berkeley: University of California Press, 1996.

Hollings, Ken. *Welcome to Mars: Politics, Pop Culture and Weird Science in 1950s America*. Berkeley: North Atlantic Books, 2014.

Hornaday, Ann. "Chloé Zhao Explains How 'Nomadland' and 'Eternals' Are Cinematic Twins." *Washington Post*, November 5, 2021.

Lambie, Ryan. "How Steven Spielberg's Night Skies Became E.T." *Den of Geek*, June 12, 2019.

Levy, Emanuel. *Small-Town America in Film: The Decline and Fall of Community*. New York: Continuum, 1991.

Lichtenfeld, Eric. *Action Speaks Louder: Violence, Spectacle, And the American Action Movie,*

Revised and Expanded Edition. Middletown, CT: Wesleyan University Press, 2007.

Lucanio, Patrick. *Them or Us: Archetypal Interpretations of Fifties Alien Invasion Films*. Bloomington: Indiana University Press, 1987.

McCarthy, Kevin, and Ed Gorman. *"They're Here …" Invasion of the Body Snatchers: A Tribute*. New York: Berkeley Boulevard, 1999 .

Mettler, Katie. "Tales from the Path of Totality: 62 Years Ago Today, They Say, 'Little Green Men' Invaded This Kentucky Farm Town." *Washington Post*, August 21, 2017.

Muir, John Kenneth. *The X-Files FAQ: All That's Left to Know About Global Conspiracy, Aliens, Lazarus Species and Monsters of the Week*. Milwaukee: Applause, 2015.

Nesheim, Eric, and Leif Nesheim. *Saucer Attacks*. Los Angeles: Kitchen Sink Press, 1997.

Plainse, Josh. "Kevin Spacey Nearly Played the President in 'Independence Day.'" *Screen Rant*, July 5, 2021.

Ricca, Brad. *Super Boys: The Amazing Adventures of Jerry Siegel and Joe Shuster—Creators of Superman*. New York: St. Martin's Griffin, 2014.

Richardson, Jeff. "Alaska Newspapers, Movie Studio Reach Settlement Over 'Fourth Kind.'" *Fairbanks Daily News-Miner*, November 12, 2009.

Robin, Corey. "Remembrance of Empires Past: 9/11 and the End of the Cold War." *Cold War Triumphalism*, ed. Ellen Schrecker. New York: New Press, 2004.

Rodriguez, Robert. "The Faculty (1998)." *Robert Rodriguez Archives*.

Rossen, Jake. *Superman vs. Hollywood: How Fiendish Producers, Devious Directors, and Warring Writers Grounded an American Icon*. Chicago: Chicago Review Press, 2008.

Ryan, Missy, and Alex Horton. "Report Does Not Confirm, or Rule Out, Extraterrestrial Activity in Unexplained Aerial Events." *New York Times*, June 4, 2021.

Sablich, Justin. "The UFO Sightings That Launched 'Men in Black' Mythology." *History.com*, January 15, 2020.

Schow, David J., and Jeffrey Frentzen. *The Outer Limits: The Official Companion*. New York: Ace Science Fiction, 1986.

Schwartz, A. Brad. *Broadcast Hysteria: Orson Welles's War of the Worlds and the Art of Fake News*. New York: Hill and Wang, 2015.

Sherman, Fraser. *Cyborgs, Santa Claus and Satan: Science Fiction, Fantasy and Horror Films Made for Television*. Jefferson, NC: McFarland, 2000.

Sherman, Fraser. *Now and Then We Time Travel: Visiting Pasts and Futures in Film and Television*. Jefferson, NC: McFarland, 2017.

Sherman, Fraser. *Screen Enemies of the American Way: Political Paranoia About Nazis, Communists, Saboteurs, Terrorists and Body Snatching Aliens in Film and Television*. Jefferson, NC: McFarland. 2011.

Speigel, Lee. "UFO-Alien Abduction Case Still Haunts Travis Walton." *Huffington Post*, April 23, 2015.

Spigel, Lynn. *Welcome to the Dreamhouse: Popular Media and Postwar Suburbs*. Durham: Duke University Press, 2001.

Stein, Michael, ed. *Alien Invasions: The History of Aliens in Pop Culture*. San Diego: IDW, 2020.

Sturgis, Amy. "Indians and Aliens." *Reason*, August 2020.

Thomas, Kevin. "Allegory Fails to Freshen 'Alien Nation.'" *Los Angeles Times*, October 7, 1988.

Vogt, Tiffany. "RIP STAR-CROSSED: Creator Meredith Averill Shares Her Thoughts on Life After Cancellation." *TV Addict*, May 24, 2014.

Warped Factor. "Abandoned Sequels: Close Encounters of the Third Kind 2: Night Skies." August 11, 2020.

Warren, Bill. *Keep Watching the Skies! American Science Fiction Movies of the Fifties—The 21st Century Edition*. Jefferson, NC: McFarland, 2010.

Webb, Dewey. "Where's Walton? Is Arizona's Best-Known UFO Abductee Bound for Hollywood Stardom?" *Phoenix New Times*, March 3, 1993.

Wright, Bruce Lanier. *Yesterday's Tomorrows: The Golden Age of Science Fiction Movie Posters*. Dallas: Taylor, 1993.

WWEST. "The Scully Effect." October 21, 2019.

Zicree, Mark Scott. *The Twilight Zone Companion*. New York: Bantam, 1982.

Index

Numbers in **bold italics** indicate pages with illustrations